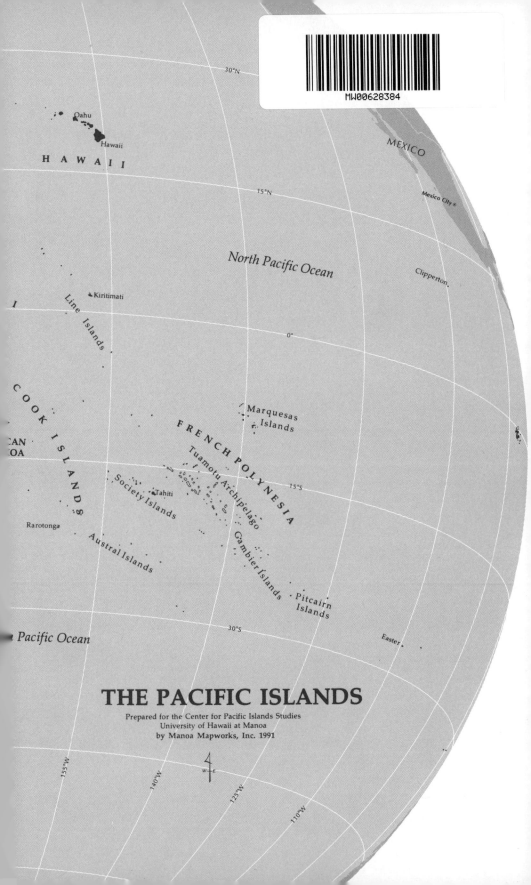

THE PACIFIC ISLANDS

Prepared for the Center for Pacific Islands Studies
University of Hawaii at Manoa
by Manoa Mapworks, Inc. 1991

Broken Waves

Pacific Islands Monograph Series, No. 11

BROKEN WAVES

A HISTORY OF THE FIJI ISLANDS
IN THE TWENTIETH CENTURY

BRIJ V. LAL

Center for Pacific Islands Studies

School of Hawaiian, Asian, and Pacific Studies

University of Hawaii

UNIVERSITY OF HAWAII PRESS • Honolulu

Library of Congress Cataloging-in-Publication Data

Lal, Brij V.
  Broken waves : a history of the Fiji Islands in the twentieth
century / Brij V. Lal.
      p.   cm. — (Pacific Islands monograph series)
  Includes bibliographical references and index.
  ISBN 0-8248-1418-5
  1. Fiji—History.   I. Title.   II. Series.
DU600.L28   1992
996.11—dc20   92-17786
                                                  CIP

4 Cartography by Manoa Mapworks, Inc.
"|' Honolulu, Hawaii

*For Padma
and for
Yogi and Niraj*

Editor's Note

Brij Lal's *Broken Waves: A History of the Fiji Islands in the Twentieth Century* is the eleventh title in the Pacific Islands Monograph Series (PIMS) and is without precedent in the series. Unlike earlier authors, Lal has written a history of his own country, and his perspectives on that history have been shaped by his own life history and experiences as an Indo-Fijian. Early in the twentieth century, Lal's paternal grandfather arrived in Fiji as an indentured laborer from India. Both his grandfather and his father were sugarcane growers in rural Vanua Levu, and Lal spent his formative years in that context in the 1950s and 1960s.

Lal is among the few individuals from Fiji to become historians; like his history, his academic odyssey has been unique. He had the exhilarating experience of being an undergraduate at the University of the South Pacific when it was a new and struggling regional institution. Later, he earned the master's and doctorate degrees at the University of British Columbia and the Australian National University respectively. He then returned to his first alma mater to begin his professional career. In the early 1980s, Lal moved to the University of Hawaii, where he was a cofounder and the first editor of *The Contemporary Pacific: A Journal of Island Affairs*. Most recently, he has returned to the Australian National University, where he holds a position in the Division of Pacific and Asian History, Research School of Pacific Studies.

Broken Waves is a detailed study of Fiji's colonial history and its perhaps inevitable outcome subsequent to independence in 1970. Lal examines the political, economic, and social variables that have shaped Fiji's history since the turn of the century, the military coups of 1987, and the turbulent years that have followed. His analysis of the complexity of Fiji's social fabric is particularly insightful as he outlines the divisive factions internal to each of Fiji's three main ethnic populations: Fijian, Indo-Fijian, and European.

Over the last quarter-century, and particularly within the last half-dozen years, race and ethnicity have become increasingly volatile elements in Fiji society. Lal argues that this turn of events may not be explained by factors inherent to race and ethnicity as such; rather, both have been seized on as emotionally powerful pawns in the struggles for political power that have racked the nation. Lal's narrative captures the drama of recent events in Fiji, and his analysis includes an examination of the motives and roles played by the most prominent actors in that drama.

As Lal himself indicates, the writing of Fiji's history is in part a personal matter, a journey in self-exploration. *Broken Waves* is history with a point of view; it is neither impartial nor ambiguous and may well provoke controversy. Lal's own perspectives and value judgments are explicit, and he does not conceal his disappointment and even anguish over the failure to create a truly democratic multiracial society.

For even the most casual reader, there is an inescapable continuity in Lal's published work. To cite only the major examples, his *Girmitiyas: The Origins of the Fiji Indians* (1983) examines the circumstances that attracted Indians to indentured service in Fiji. *Power and Prejudice: The Making of the Fiji Crisis* (1988) was an initial analysis of the events leading up to the 1987 coups, and several of the themes advanced there are further developed in the work at hand. Lal is currently engaged in the writing of a biography of A. D. Patel, an Indian who played a prominent role in the postwar history of Fiji.

The publication of PIMS is made possible by private funds raised by the University of Hawaii Foundation and the collaborative role of the University of Hawaii Press. The directors and staff of both organizations have shown great interest and support for the series, and their efforts are sincerely appreciated.

ROBERT C. KISTE

Contents

Illustrations

Figures

Maps

Photographs

Tables

Preface

This book continues an exploration of Fijian history I began more than a decade ago. Having written previously on the history of Indian migration and settlement in Fiji and on the dilemmas and problems of contemporary Fijian politics, I have undertaken here a more detailed, synoptic analysis of the major contours of Fijian history in the twentieth century. I have attempted this task partly to fill a yawning gap in modern Fijian historiography, which, in the main, has been dominated by pioneering work on the nineteenth century. The twentieth century has received its share of attention from historians, social anthropologists, geographers, and others; but, with a few exceptions, much of this effort has focused on specific issues and on the histories of particular ethnic groups. This is not a criticism; it is simply the way things are. I hasten to add that these specialized studies have provided valuable building blocks for the structure I have attempted to create here.

I have undertaken this study, however, to do more than simply fill a gap in Fijian historiography. This book is also a journey of self-exploration. My family's Fijian identity goes back to the turn of this century, when my Indian grandfather arrived in the islands to serve his indenture. When his five-year contract expired, he, along with many of his indentured compatriots, decided to settle in Fiji permanently. They leased small parcels of agricultural land from Fijian landlords, raised families, and gradually came to terms with the demands and realities of their new homeland. Their struggles and aspirations in Fiji's plural colonial society and other islanders' responses to them are subjects of more than academic interest to me. They go to the core of how I understand my own identity as an Indo-Fijian.

My journey has been both exhilarating and painful: exhilarating because I was able to peruse a fascinating kaleidoscope of private papers, official dispatches, newspaper accounts, and oral evidence and from them discern the pattern of forces that shaped the history of my country and its peoples; painful because my explorations revealed with stark clarity the opportunities missed and the turning points not taken to provide more just and enduring foundations for a colonial society ridden with conflict and tension. Preoccupied with matters of daily administration, colonial governors of the twentieth century usually lacked the vision necessary to lead Fiji away from its nineteenth-century moorings and through the perils and necessities of the twentieth century. When they did try, they were frustrated by bureaucratic inertia or infighting over the nature and purpose of colonial policy or thwarted by vested interests.

The colony of Fiji was described for much of the twentieth century as a finely balanced, three-legged stool on which each of the principal ethnic groups—Fijians, Indo-Fijians, and Europeans—accepted its designated place and made its separate and unique contribution to the islands' prosperity. Fijians provided the land, Indo-Fijians the cheap labor, and Europeans the capital and technical expertise. This neat division did not always correspond to the reality of life in Fiji. As this study will show, none of these groups was homogeneous; nor did they enjoy equal status, privileges, or access to power. There was no necessary balance between European capital on the one hand and Indo-Fijian labor on the other. On the contrary, many disadvantaged groups of all races struggled to escape their situation at the bottom of the colonial hierarchy. For its part, the colonial government did not brook criticism easily; and those who questioned its foundations or the moral and political values that inspired its policies soon found themselves on the fringes of society. The activities of those men and women who braved the odds and challenged the colonial order receive particular attention in this study.

When Fiji gained its independence from Great Britain in 1970, after ninety-six years of colonial rule, many hoped that its leaders would discard traditional habits of thought and work together to promote nation building on the basis of interracial cooperation and equality. That was not to be. Instead of promoting national consensus and encouraging a common identity, the independence constitution helped entrench communalism, virtually everything in Fijian life coming to be viewed from the perspective of racial needs and interests. The slogan "Race is a way of life" became the foundation of government policy and practice, thus blunting the potentially powerful integrative effects of urbanization, education, and the unprecedented exposure the mass media provided to the outside world, all of which cut across communal boundaries, indeed, rendered them largely irrelevant to the requirements of daily living. In 1987 the clash between old structures and habits of thought and the needs of the new times plunged Fiji into its gravest political crisis this century. As I write, a concerted effort is underway to turn the clock of Fijian culture and politics back to the nineteenth-century. Future generations of Fijians of all races and classes will have to do penance for the myopic vision and failures of the past.

In this account I make no special effort to invoke an impartiality I do not feel. When embarking upon a comprehensive examination of the contemporary history of one's own country, it is impossible to be detached unless, in the words of Professor O. H. K. Spate, one is a "moral and intellectual eunuch." Who would want to be that?

> The impartiality, [says Spate,] which evades responsibility by saying nothing, the partiality which masks its bias by presenting slanted facts with an air of cold objectivity—these are a thousand times more dangerous than an open declaration of where one stands; then at least those who disagree can take one's measure with confidence: "that is why he said thus". . . . The important points are that inference must be based on evidence, as carefully verified as possible; and that the choice shall be made from the evidence, and not from pre-conceived ideas. (1990, 103)

I have tried to act on this advice. Critical attachment rather than cool detachment has guided my scholarly effort here as well as in my other writings.

My research is as complete as I could make it. Still, in any general history, there are unfilled, even unnoticed, gaps as well as subjects that demand more detailed attention in their own right. Among the latter in this study are cultural, religious, and gender issues, some of which have been explored by other scholars. Because of my particular interests, the focus here is social and political. Both intellectual coherence and space limitations demand that I keep firmly to a general perspective, foregoing the pleasure of exploring the local byways where much of the history is actually made—around *yaqona* bowls in Fijian villages, in the cane fields of Indo-Fijian settlements, or, increasingly, in the boardrooms of multinational corporations and lobbies of luxurious hotels. For that reason, too, I have not looked at the important role that Fiji has played in the South Pacific region throughout much of the twentieth century, a subject that requires a book-length treatment of its own.

The tendency in recent historical scholarship on the Pacific Islands has been toward greater specialization. Research is published in monographs and scholarly journals to explain particular theoretical points and edify a small band of scholars already well versed in the finer points of specialized literature. This sort of exercise has an important place in academic discourse, but it also places the discipline of history in the very real danger of editing itself out of the wider public consciousness and debate. To avoid this trend, I have attempted to write this book in the ordinary language of intelligent discourse in the hope of reaching an audience beyond the halls of academia, especially in my own country.

Nor have I engaged in the increasingly common exercise of reflexivity, burdening my readers with a meditation on the philosophical and methodological problems involved in preparing this study. The moral vision that has shaped my interpretation is essentially modernist, democratic, and egalitarian. I will not contest that my approach is necessarily more justified or better than others with different points of departure. Value is a matter of judgment, and there can be no question of finality in scholarly discourse. I will say that I am deeply troubled by some of the conclusions I reached, sometimes much against my will, during the course of preparing this study about such matters as the conditions necessary for the successful functioning of a multiracial society based on the principles of equality and justice and about the place of traditional values and social institutions in the competitive modern political arena. "The world is what it is," V. S. Naipaul has written. "Men who are nothing, who allow themselves to become nothing, have no place in it" (1982, 1). Much as we may desire it, we cannot escape the imperatives and demands of the late twentieth century by retreating to some imaginary, uncomplicated past, or we will do so at our own peril. This does not mean that we have to jettison all those traditional values that give meaning and pleasure to our lives. What it does call for is progressive adjustment and selective adaptation, to change when change is necessary. There does not seem to be any other alternative, for islands today are islands in the physical sense alone.

Acknowledgments

There now remains the pleasant task of thanking those who assisted me in researching and writing this book. The University of Hawaii Foundation honored me with a Fujio Matsuda Fellowship, and Robert C. Kiste, Director of the University's Center for Pacific Islands Studies, provided additional financial assistance. The bulk of the archival research in Fiji was at the National Archives. I thank its Director, Mr. Setareki Tuinaceva, and Margaret Patel, Matai Labaibure, and the late Masud Khan for their valuable assistance. Masud's generosity and efficiency will be sorely missed by all users of the Fiji Archives. The Fiji Broadcasting Commission, the University of the South Pacific Library, and a number of individuals who allowed me access to papers in their possession also have my grateful thanks. At the University of Papua New Guinea, where I spent a semester in 1986 and completed part of the research for this book, Jim Griffin, John Waiko, Clive Moore, and Jean Kennedy offered warm support, and I thank them. At the University of Hawaii, Renée Heyum, former curator of the incomparable Pacific Collection; her equally able successor (and an equally good friend), Karen Peacock; and Karen's assistant, Lynette Furuhashi, know well how much I have depended on them for assistance over the years. *Mahalo nui loa, vinaka vakalevu, dhanyabad.*

The book was written in 1990 when I held a Senior Research Fellowship in the Department of Pacific and Southeast Asian History in the Research School of Pacific Studies at the Australian National University. I could not have found a more congenial surrounding in which to write and reflect. To the School's Director, Professor R. G. Ward, I owe thanks not only for his hospitality but also for his sharing his Fiji material with me. For their many kindnesses in the department, I thank Anthony Reid, Donald Denoon, Niel Gunson, Bill Gammage, Hank Nelson, Deryck Scarr, Dorothy Shineberg, Stephen Henningham, Robert Langdon, and O. H. K. Spate as well as Dorothy McIntosh, Jude Shanahan, and Julie Gordon. Over the years, I have gained valuable insights into the history of Fiji through conversation with friends and former colleagues at the University of the South Pacific too numerous to mention here by name,

though their specific contributions have been acknowledged in the text. At
the University of Hawaii, David Hanlon, Truang Buu Lam, Jagdish
Sharma, Edward Beechert, Doris Ladd, Idus Newby, and Robert Van
Niel of the History Department, Albert Schütz of the Linguistics Department, and Robert Kiste of the Center for Pacific Islands Studies encouraged and supported my scholarly pursuits. From my many graduate students over the years I have learned more about myself and about my
history than they will ever know I learned.

More specifically, I want to thank Jim Sanday, Deryck Scarr, and
Nicholas Thomas for reading the manuscript and making suggestions for
revision. Roderic Alley of the Victoria University of Wellington and John
Kelly of Princeton University, both fellow Fiji researchers, went painstak-
ingly through the text and saved me from many errors of fact and interpretation; needless to say, those that still remain are my own responsibility.
Linley Chapman, Idus Newby, Alan Robson, Philip Herbst, and Roberta
Sprague also have my grateful thanks for removing many stylistic gauche-
ries from the text and improving its readability.

The research for this book began in a Fiji dramatically different from the
one that existed when the book was completed. Throughout the traumatic
period since 1987, the year of the fateful coups, I was sustained by the love
and unstinting support of my peripatetic family. Without their assistance,
neither this study nor anything else I have done in these years would have
been possible. For Padma and me, Fiji, with all its problems and frustrations, will always remain home, the place that formed and deformed our
lives; for Yogi and Niraj, it is a sad, evanescent memory, a flame in a wind-
less spot that does not flicker. As a small token of my love and appreciation, I dedicate this book to my family, with the words of T. S. Eliot:

> A man's destination is not his destiny,
> Every country is home to one man
> And exile to another. Where a man dies bravely
> At one with his destiny, that soil is his.
> "To the Indians Who Died in Africa"

Conventions

Abbreviations

ALTO	Agricultural Landlords and Tenants Ordinance
CO	British Colonial Office, London
CP	Paper of the Fiji Legislative Council
CSO	Colonial Secretary's Office, Suva, Fiji
CSR	Colonial Sugar Refining Company
DC	District Commissioner in Fiji
DO	District Officer in Fiji
FAB	Fijian Affairs Board
FLP	Fiji Labour Party
FNP	Fijian Nationalist Party
NFP	National Federation Party
NLTB	Native Land Trust Board
SIA	Secretary of Indian Affairs
SNA	Secretary of Fijian Affairs
WUF	Western United Front

Fijian Orthography

b is pronounced mb, as in member
c is pronounced th, as in they
d is pronounced nd, as in dandy
g is pronounced ng, as in sing
q is pronounced ng, as in finger

Money

Unless otherwise stated, all sums of money are in Fijian units. Fiji has had its own currency since 1914, when the imperial system of pounds, shillings, and pence was in use. To facilitate rough comparisons, in 1963

F£111 was equal to Stg£100 or NZ£100; F£100 equaled A£111; and F£1 equaled US$2.50. In 1969, Fiji converted to decimal currency, when F£1 became equal to F$2.00. The Fiji dollar has been floating since 1975. In 1986 F$1.00 was equal to US$1.13. In 1987 the currency was devalued twice, for a total of 34 percent. In late 1991 F$1.00 was equal to US$1.47.

Broken Waves

Introduction

Fiji entered the twentieth century firmly tethered to colonial policies put in place in the late nineteenth century. The structures of Fiji's economy, polity, and society were fixed by decisions made soon after the reluctant but unconditional cession of the islands to Great Britain on 10 October 1874. The task, and the tragedy, of modern Fiji has been to confront the twentieth century and the forces of change it has brought while hobbled by political and social structures and habits of thought that outlived their usefulness long ago. The inevitable tensions between the constraints of old and exhausted orthodoxies and the demands of new and challenging times underpin the central theme of this study.

Much has been written of Fiji in the nineteenth century. Indeed, much of the best historical literature on the islands deals with that century and its overarching concerns of cultural contact with the outside world, the great struggles for power between rival confederacies of indigenous Fijians, and the tortuous advent of colonial rule.[1] It is therefore unnecessary to cover that ground here in detail. A brief outline of the major issues and developments will suffice to introduce significant themes.

Land and People

The Fiji Islands lie in the southwest Pacific between 15 and 22 degrees south latitude and between 175 degrees east and 177 degrees west longitude, astride the 180th meridian. Their total land area of 7,055 square miles is scattered across some 250,000 square miles of water. Of the three hundred or so islands that make up the Fijian archipelago, only about a third are inhabited or capable of sustaining prolonged human habitation. These range in size from Viti Levu (4,010 square miles), Vanua Levu (2,137 square miles), Taveuni (168 square miles), and Ovalau (40 square miles) to much smaller, reef-encircled islets of a few square miles dotting the eastern Koro Sea.[2] Most of the larger land masses are high islands of ancient volcanic and andesite rocks and cretaceous and tertiary sedimentation. They are mostly rugged, with sharp mountain peaks, deep, winding valleys, and sudden crags.

The larger land masses also have large areas of fertile flatland and deltas nourished by extensive networks of rivers. The Rewa, which drains about one-third of Viti Levu (Map 1), has created a delta of nearly one hundred square miles; and the Navua, Sigatoka, and Ba rivers on the western side of the island and the Qawa, Wainikoro, and Dreketi rivers in Vanua Levu (Map 2) have formed extensive lowlands of alluvial deposits, where the primary agricultural crops of Fiji—sugar cane, bananas, rice, taro—are cultivated. Here, also, towns, villages, and concentrated farming settlements are situated. The political struggles and economic conflict discussed in this study center on these areas.

Size and natural resources were not, however, the sole determinants of the political significance of individual islands. Throughout the nineteenth century, for example, the fortunes and misfortunes of Bau, a tiny island just off the coast of Viti Levu, dominated the political scene. In the twentieth century, maritime chiefs of the eastern islands in the Koro Sea played a major role in the making of the islands' history while their "mainland" counterparts often played second fiddle. Yet the land the latter controlled produced the bulk of the country's wealth, in the form of sugar cane, pine, and gold. Tensions between the aspirations of the islanders and those of the mainlanders, especially mainlanders in western Viti Levu, constituted one of the important but less obvious themes of Fijian history in the twentieth century.

The islands of Fiji were first inhabited about thirty-five hundred years ago. Archaeological evidence indicates that the original inhabitants came from the area around Vanuatu and New Caledonia, which had been settled earlier by Austronesian speakers from the New Guinea region. From Fiji seafaring migrants moved eastward to Tonga and Samoa, both of which were settled around three thousand years ago. While Tonga and Samoa remained in relative isolation and developed the distinctive social, political, and cultural patterns known today as Polynesian, Fiji continued to receive successive waves of migrants from western Melanesia. Consequently the physical characteristics and social organization of the indigenous Fijians exhibit Melanesian traits. Polynesian traits are particularly pronounced in the maritime provinces, which maintained regular trading and social contact with Tonga and Samoa, while Melanesian traits predominate in the hinterlands of the major islands.

The social and political organization of the early Fijians was diverse, though it cannot be described with certainty because of limited evidence. At the risk of some distortion and oversimplification, it can be said that early Fijian society was hierarchical and based on the principle of patrilineal agnatic descent. Every Fijian belonged to a *yavusa* 'clan' that claimed descent from a legendary founding ancestor.[3] The clan consisted of several *mataqali* 'family groups', whose rank and power were carefully determined by lineal proximity to the founding ancestor. At the top of the apex were the *tūraga* 'chiefs of the leading *mataqali*', claiming direct descent through the male line from the founding ancestor. They provided the ruling chiefs for the *yavusa*. Below them in rank were the *sautūraga* 'executive *mataqali*', who carried out the commands of chiefs and otherwise supported their authority. Lower still were the *matanivanua*, speakers and masters of ceremony for the *yavusa*, the *bete*, priests, and the *bati*, warriors. The smallest units of Fijian society were the *i tokatoka* 'subdivisions of the *mataqali*', which comprised the closely related households living in a defined area of a village and cooperating to perform such communal undertakings as the building and maintenance of houses and the preparation of feasts. In some parts of Fiji, the *i tokatoka* were the landholding units of the tribe, although elsewhere that function was the responsibility of the *mataqali*.

This somewhat schematic pattern of traditional Fijian society was vulnerable to pressures generated by voluntary or enforced migration within the islands and by internal conflicts and the vagaries of war. *Yavusa* broke up, dispersed, or merged with others as circumstances demanded. For social and economic reasons as well as for protection from the predatory designs of hostile chiefs, several *yavusa* might combine to form a confederation called the *vanua* 'state'. Comprising several villages, each *vanua* had a paramount chief whose position eventually became hereditary. Within each *vanua*, the line of *yavusa* succession was clearly defined and rigidly maintained. Toward the end of the eighteenth century, many *vanua* united, voluntarily or otherwise, into a larger state called the *matanitū* 'confederation'.

The power and prestige of these confederations varied greatly across Fiji; in parts of central and western Viti Levu, they were unknown. At the beginning of the nineteenth century, there were about a dozen *matanitū*, of which the most important were Bau, Rewa, and Verata in southeastern Viti Levu; Lakeba in the Lau group; and Cakaudrove, Bua, and Macuata on Vanua Levu. As the nineteenth century opened, these leading *matanitū* were engaged in a byzantine struggle for political supremacy that was soon complicated by outside forces just then beginning to encroach on Fiji.

The Nineteenth Century: Road to Cession

The nineteenth century was a period of fundamental change for most islands of the Pacific Ocean.[4] By the beginning of the nineteenth century, the era of European discovery, exploration, and itinerant trading was over, paving the way for more intensive political and commercial contact between outsiders and the people of the islands. Some Pacific Islands, especially those in Polynesia, soon had small settlements of resident European settlers, traders, adventurers, and beachcombers.[5] New trades in copra, pork, bêche-de-mer, and sandalwood had reached many of the islands, along with new iron tools and novel ways of doing things that

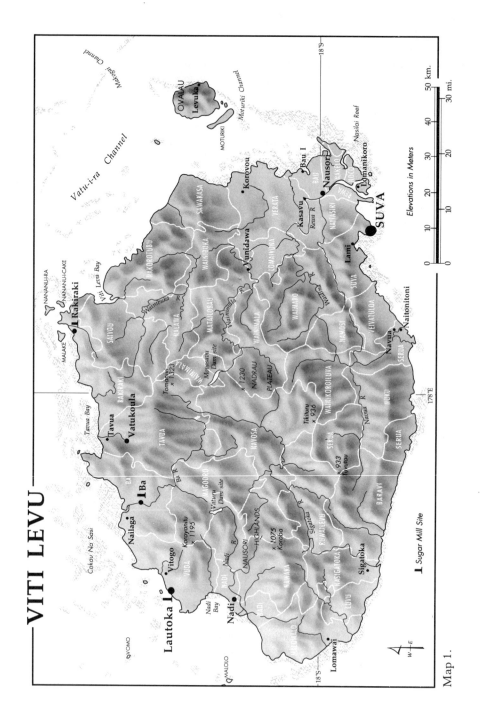

VITI LEVU

Makassau Channel

OVALAU

Levuka

Vatu-i-ra Channel

Moturiki Channel

MOTURIKI

Nasilai Reef

Korovou

Bau I

BAU

Nausori

SAWAKASA

Lomanikoro

NAKOROUBU

Kasavu

Rewa R.

SUVA

WAINIBUKA

Vunidawa

VERATA

NAITASIRI

Lami

NANANU-RA

NANANU-I-CAKE

Viti Levu Bay

SAVOU

WAIMARO

LOMAIVUNA

MALAKE

I Rakiraki

Rewa R.

Waimanu R.

Waidina R.

Naitonitoni

Natuvakula R.

MATAILOBAU

WAINIMALA

NAMOSI

SUVA

RAIWAI

Tavua Bay

RARAWAI

Monasaru Dam site

x 1323

x 1230

NADRAU PLATEAU

Wainimala R.

WAINIKOROILUVA

VEIVATULOA

TAVUA

Tomaniivi

NADRAU PLATEAU

Tikituru x 926

Navua R.

NUKU

Navua R.

Tavua

Vatukoula

Ba R.

HAVOSA

SERUA

SERUA

Cakau Na Sasi

I Ba

MAGODRO

Vaturu Dam site

x 933 Nuvutu

BARAVI

Nailaga

Koroyanitu 1195

SERUA

NAUSORI HIGHLANDS

x 1075 Koroba

NADI

Sigatoka R.

NUWAILEVU

VUDA

Vitogo

Nadi R.

Sigatoka R.

Lautoka I

Nadi Bay

NADI

NAMAWA

Sigatoka

NADROGA

MALOLO

VOMO

Lomawai

18°S

178°E

18°S

W—E
S

Map 1.

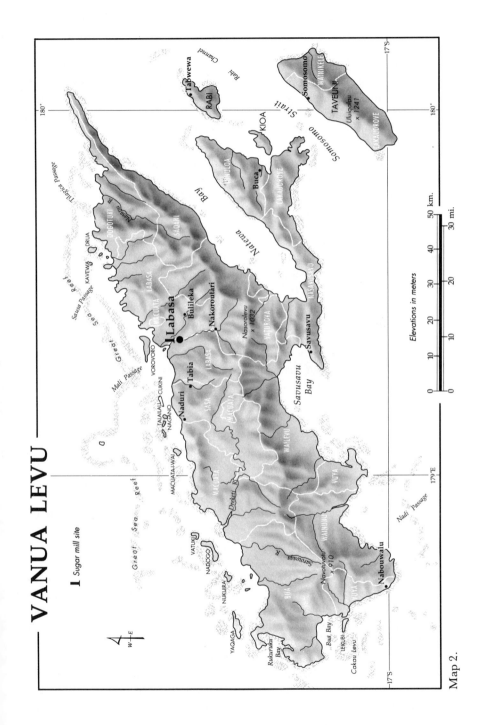

VANUA LEVU

1 Sugar mill site

Elevations in meters

Map 2.

began a restructuring of the islands' internal social and economic relationships.[6] A new Christian faith also spread rapidly after it was introduced by agents of the London Missionary Society in Tahiti in 1797.[7] As a result of these increasing contacts with the outside world, by the middle of the nineteenth century, white people were no longer novelties and no longer perceived as ancestors returning in new color, but permanent fixtures, if at times irritating ones, in most of the major Pacific island groups, except parts of Papua New Guinea that remained untouched by foreigners until the early years of the twentieth century.

Hard on the heels of these early traders, beachcombers, and missionaries came other Europeans with more ominous purposes. The nineteenth century was a time of imperial rivalry among the great powers of Europe and North America. With much of the world already carved up among them, these powers focused their attention on the remote, scattered islands of the Pacific Ocean. One by one they extended the long arm of their imperial reach into the area: Britain, France, Holland, Germany, and the United States. One by one, the islands found themselves objects of imperial claims based ostensibly on "rights" of "discovery" that were enforced for strategic or economic reasons or to placate the demands of European or American nationals in the islands.[8] The impact of this expansive imperial rivalry was such that by the end of the nineteenth century, all the Pacific Islands, except Tonga, which managed to retain a semblance of sovereignty under the arm of British protectionism, had come under the ambit of Euro-American colonialism.

Fiji was no exception to this pattern. The islands were first sighted by foreign explorers in 1643 when the Dutch navigator Abel Janzoon Tasman navigated the reef-infested, hurricane-prone parts of northeastern Fiji. Tasman managed to chart some dozen islands in the group, but made no known landing on any of them. No other Europeans appeared until the English Captain James Cook passed through the southern Lau group in 1774 during his second expedition to the South Seas, without making any significant "discoveries." Lieutenant William Bligh passed through the islands with more significant results in 1789 and again in 1792. More than any other European explorers, Bligh is credited with charting many islands in the group and adding them to the rapidly increasing corpus of knowledge of the Pacific Islands. Other Europeans, such as D'Entrecasteaux and Kermadec, soon followed, and by the late eighteenth century, the rough outlines of Fiji (Feejee) were fairly well known to the outside world. These explorations ended the isolation of the islands, but contributed little to the outside understanding of Fiji's people, who were widely portrayed in the popular literature as ferocious and prone to violence, unlike their eastern Polynesian neighbors in Tonga and Tahiti. Indeed, for a while, Fiji was known somewhat exaggeratedly as the Cannibal Islands, though the practice of consuming human flesh was found in many other places in Oceania.

More intensive and sustained contact between the islands and the outside world began early in 1800, when sailors from the schooner *Argo,* wrecked on the Bukatatanoa Reef east of Lakeba, landed on Oneata. In time, more European ships plied the Fiji waters and brought to the islands "deserters, marooned sailors, [and] derelict scourings of the ports of the Old World, among them some of the worst and lowest of their kind."[9] With them came exotic diseases like measles, whooping cough, influenza, dengue fever, and dysentery, which soon wreaked havoc on a hapless indigenous population that had no immunity to them. Muskets, too, took their toll, though perhaps not to the extent usually portrayed in the conventional literature or contemporary accounts.[10] The advent of the sandalwood trade (1800–1814) at Bua Bay in Vanua Levu and the much longer-lasting bêche-de-mer trade (1820s–1850s) brought a wide variety of European tools and other goods as well as a cash economy and greater contact with the outside world.[11] A new *lotu* 'religion' arrived in 1835 when the Wesleyan missionaries William Cargill and David Cross reached the islands from Tonga. Cargill and Cross wanted to spread the scriptures in the vernacular and with that aim produced the first orthography of the indigenous language. The politics and processes of conversion to Christianity had important ramifications for internal political struggles within Fijian society.

By the middle of the nineteenth century, that society was deeply mired in political convulsions caused in part by the new forces of change from the outside. A great contest for power was under way between the leading rival *matanitū*.[12] Bau was asserting its hegemony over the islands of the Koro Sea, while Rewa was ascendant over eastern parts of Viti Levu; on Vanua Levu, the other main island, Bua and Macuata were asserting their independence. Into this confused picture of byzantine chiefly struggles entered another formidable figure, the Tongan chief Ma'afu, in 1847. Appointed in 1853 by King George Tupou to oversee the affairs of the Tongans long settled in the Lau group, Ma'afu intrigued to secure political paramountcy in the eastern islands and in Vanua Levu. His presence and shrewd diplomacy caused problems especially for Ratu Seru Cakobau, *vūnivalu* 'war lord' of Bau and self-styled king of all Fiji, or Tui Viti.

Ma'afu's growing influence came at a particularly inopportune time for Cakobau. As Tui Viti, Cakobau was held accountable by American Consul John Williams for the looting that occurred after Williams' house had burned down during the Fourth of July celebration in 1849. The initial claim for US$5000 compensation grew to US$43,000 by the mid-1850s, when claims of other American citizens were added. Cakobau was unable to pay this sum, nor, for obvious reasons, would he accept Ma'afu's offer of help in this confrontation. William Pritchard, who arrived from Samoa in September 1858, suggested a way out of the impasse for Cakobau. Cakobau agreed to cede 200,000 acres of Fiji to Britain in return for Britain paying the American debt and guaranteeing Cakobau's title of Tui

Viti. Pritchard approached Britain with the offer, which was formally rejected in 1862. The troubles of New Zealand were fresh in the minds of British officials. Moreover, Fiji offered few encouraging prospects for commercial development, a commission of inquiry under Colonel Smythe concluded. Annexation would be fraught with problems, not the least of which was that Cakobau did not have the authority to make the offer of cession on behalf of the whole of Fiji. The best course of action would be to establish a "native government aided by the counsels of respectable Europeans."[13]

This path was followed in the 1860s, not under the direction of Pritchard, who was dismissed for exceeding his consular authority and meddling in Fijian politics, but that of a new consul, Captain H. M. Jones. A loose confederation of leading chiefs from the *matanitū* of Bau, Rewa, Bua, Cakaudrove, Lakeba, Macuata, and Nadi was formed in May 1865 to provide a semblance of representative constitutional government. The endeavor fell through in mid-1867, when Jones left Fiji and tensions surfaced again between the two principal players in the makeshift government, Maʻafu and Cakobau. The two protagonists then set up separate governments, Maʻafu with his Lau Confederation and Cakobau with his Kingdom of Bau in the west. Both these governments were elaborate affairs, complete with written constitutions and all the rudiments of administrative apparatus, including ministers, assemblies, and bylaws.

The Lau Confederation, nominally headed by Tui Cakau but with Maʻafu and R. S. Swanston as its real powers, was the more successful of the two governments, creating as it did the semblance of government in eastern Fiji. Cakobau's settler-dominated organization was less effective. The problem of the American debt came back to haunt the Tui Viti when the USS *Tuscarora* arrived at Levuka on 11 July 1867. Captain Stanley demanded that Cakobau pay the principal in installments and mortgage certain islands as security that he would pay in timely fashion. The Melbourne-based Polynesia Company came to Cakobau's rescue, offering to pay the debt in return for 200,000 acres of land and a free hand in developing them "in the manner of the old seventeenth century mercantalist monopolies like the East India Company."[14]

The debt was eventually paid, but the payment created new problems. In particular it fostered an influx of European settlers, whose numbers increased from thirty or forty in 1860 to about two thousand in 1870.[15] The new settlers were attracted to the islands chiefly by the prospect of cashing in on the temporary global shortage of cotton caused by the American Civil War. Their arrival brought new problems. The planters wanted more land and cheap labor, and the fraudulence and violence that attended these transactions showed the need for control and regulation by a properly constituted government. So, too, did the importation of 1,649 Pacific Island laborers to work on European-owned plantations in the mid-1860s.

In 1871 Cakobau made a final attempt to form a Fiji-wide government, this time modeled on the Hawaiian monarchy.[16] He divided the islands into separate districts, each ruled by a Fijian governor. A privy council was created consisting of Fijian provincial governors and one additional chief from each of the districts. In addition, a cabinet advised the king, Cakobau, and served as the upper chamber of the legislature, the lower chamber consisting of a legislative assembly, elected for three years by a vote in which all adult males had a franchise. Judicial functions were exercised by a supreme court, one of whose judges was required to be an indigenous Fijian. During its two-year existence, this government enacted numerous legislations and proposed various reforms in an effort to achieve peace and stability.

The effort was futile. Cakobau's opponents attacked his government for ineptness, corruption, and extravagance. More important in the government's collapse was the active and at times violent opposition of European settlers to the "assumed authority" of a "few British subjects forming the so-called Government of Fiji."[17] Among other things, the settlers organized an armed society to subvert the judicial and political authority of the kingdom; their opposition effectively paralyzed the government. All this coincided with growing pressure from humanitarian groups in Britain to force the British government to act against the widely reported abuses in the Pacific Islands labor trade, in which many British nationals were involved. More active British intervention in Fijian affairs was also urged by Australia and New Zealand, both of which were apprehensive about the expansion of the French and German presence in the Pacific Islands. Cakobau, old and tired, summed up the predicament of the islands as Britain moved to enlarge its presence there. "If matters remain as they are," he said, "Fiji will become like a piece of driftwood in the sea, and be picked up by the first passer-by. . . . Of one thing I am assured, that if we do not cede Fiji [to Britain], the white stalkers on the beach, the cormorants, will open their maws and swallow us."[18] For Cakobau, annexation by the British had become the only way out of the threatening instability and was preferable to annexation by some other European power. He therefore acquiesced in what he could not prevent, and Fiji became a British Crown Colony on 10 October 1874.

Cession and Its Legacy

The Deed of Cession was signed by the leading chiefs of Fiji and by Sir Hercules Robinson, lieutenant governor of New South Wales. The chiefs, the deed noted, had "determined to tender unconditionally" the sovereignty of the islands to Queen Victoria and her successors, "relying upon the justice and generosity" of Her Majesty in dealing with her subject peoples. Cession, the chiefs hoped, would promote "civilization" and "Christianity"—their words—in the islands and secure good and stable government for all its residents, native and white, putting an end to the turbulence of the preceding decades. Toward these ends, Robinson promised on behalf of the Crown that "the rights and interests of the said Tui Viti and other high chiefs the ceding parties hereto shall be recognised so far as is and shall be consistent with British Sovereignty and Colonial form of government." In addition, all questions of financial liabilities and engagements were to be carefully scrutinized and dealt with on principles of justice and sound public policy, and more important, "All claims to title to land by whomsoever preferred and all claims to pensions or allowances whether on the part of the said Tui Viti and other high chiefs or of persons now holding office under them or any of them shall in due course be fully investigated and equitably adjusted."[19]

Robinson departed soon after accepting the Instrument of Cession, though not before creating a rudimentary administrative structure for the nascent colony, consisting of an ad hoc executive council, a general court and courts of petty sessions, and broad outlines for the administration of Fijian affairs. It was left to Robinson's successor, the first resident colonial governor of Fiji, Sir Arthur Hamilton Gordon, to lay a permanent foundation for the future course of the colony. Gordon was outstanding among British colonial governors of the nineteenth century. He had been born in 1831, son of the fourth Earl of Aberdeen, Sir Robert Peel's successor as prime minister.[20] From an early age, he confessed to a great ambition for success and fame and showed a remarkable degree of confidence in his abilities. After briefly contemplating a career in the clergy, Gordon entered the colonial service, becoming lieutenant governor of the province of New Brunswick in Canada at the age of thirty-one. He then served as governor of Trinidad and later of Mauritius, both tropical plantation colonies worked by indentured laborers imported from India. In those colonies, Gordon gained a reputation as champion of the underdog against the settler plantocracy. From Mauritius, Gordon came to Fiji in 1875.

There, Gordon's aristocratic connections served him well. He was given a relatively free hand by Lord Carnarvon, secretary of state for the colonies, who thought Gordon the "fittest man within my knowledge to undertake a very difficult and equally delicate task."[21] Gordon was also a shrewd judge of men. He chose as his closest advisors individuals with long experience of and residence in Fiji. These included David Wilkinson, Walter Carew, and, most important, J. B. Thurston, who was himself subsequently appointed governor of the colony, at which time he played a decisive role in consolidating the system he had helped to found under Gordon.

On his arrival in Fiji, Gordon found the colony in acute distress. Some forty thousand Fijians had recently died from an epidemic of measles introduced into Fiji by an Australian man-of-war. Much of the best land in the colony was being claimed by European settlers, who wanted quick and

generous ratification of their claims. Capital was lacking for rapid economic development because the local planters were in straitened circumstances following the collapse of the cotton boom of the previous decade,
and they were eagerly looking to the new administration to protect and
promote their interests against those of others, including the Fijians. The
financial situation was made worse by the reduction of the initial imperial
capital grant of £150,000 to £100,000 because the indigenous population
had declined by 25 percent. These combined problems of land, labor, and
capital had to be solved quickly if the newly acquired colony was to be self-
sustaining, as the Colonial Office directed.

Gordon tackled the problems with the vigor of a man supremely confident of his abilities and of the fundamental rightness of his decisions. "We
want capital invested in the colony," he said in an early address to the
planters. "We want a cheap, abundant, and certain supply of labor; we
want means of communication; we want justice to be readily and speedily
administered; we want facilities for education; and lastly (though, perhaps, that interests me more nearly and especially than you), we want
revenue."[22]

The governor soon recognized that the settler community was insolvent.
"Harsh as it may seem," he said, "I believe that prosperity will be
unknown until the majority of the present planters have either sold their
holdings to others or have sunk under mortgages and have made way for
men of larger capital and wider views."[23] In this context Thurston, who
entered the new administration as auditor general, revived the effort to
establish a sugar industry in Fiji. Thurston and others had been pursuing
that goal unsuccessfully since the islands had been ceded to Britain in
1874. After the cession, the political environment had become more stable,
and the colonial government was finally able to persuade the Australia-
based Colonial Sugar Refining Company (CSR) to extend its operations
to Fiji, which it did in 1882, remaining there till 1973.[24] For nearly a century until 1973, this company and sugar formed the backbone of the Fijian
economy. One foundation of modern Fiji had been laid.

The success of sugar depended not only on capital but on a reliable
source of cheap labor, which also was unavailable locally. Gordon had
restricted the commercial employment of Fijian labor, fearing that "if the
Fijian population is ever permitted to sink from its present condition into
that of a collection of migratory bands of hired laborers, all hope, not only
of the improvement but the preservation of the race, must inevitably be
abandoned."[25] Fijians were little attracted to the drudgeries of plantation
work. Nor could much store be placed on the morally tainted trade in
Pacific Island labor, for which in any case there was intense competition
from more lucrative destinations like Queensland. Between 1864 and
1911, 27,000 Melanesian and Gilbertese laborers were imported into Fiji,
but with the expansion of the sugar industry, that number was far less than

the need. Because of his experience with Indian labor in Trinidad and Mauritius, Gordon turned to the "super abundant population of India," an alternative he had perhaps considered even before arriving in Fiji. Negotiations for Indian laborers were completed in 1878, and the first group of 479 indentured workers arrived from India in May 1879. By 1916, when the importation ceased, 60,639 Indian men, women, and children had arrived in the islands.[26] Another foundation of twentieth-century Fiji had been laid.

The third and most important policy decision of Gordon and his advisors concerned the indigenous population. Underpinning Gordon's approach to the governance of Fiji was the view that the interests of the Fijian people—as Gordon perceived them—should not be sacrificed to political expediency or to the needs of the settlers, as had been the case in other colonies, notably and most immediately New Zealand. The best policy in the circumstances, Gordon proposed, was one that insulated the Fijian people from what he considered the competitive, dehumanizing pressures of the modern world and that preserved their traditional values, ways of living, and political institutions.

To this end, he instituted a number of well-known policies. He began a system of "indirect rule" designed, in his words, to "seize the spirit in which native institutions had been framed, and develop to the utmost extent the capacities of the people for the management of their own affairs, without exciting their suspicion or destroying their self-respect."[27] A permanent Bose Vakatūraga 'Great Chiefly Council' (or Council of Chiefs as it was popularly known) was specifically created to meet annually to advise the governor on native Fijian affairs and to assist him in formulating native regulations. In 1876 the Native Labour Ordinance, followed by other such enactments in later years, restricted the recruitment and commercial employment of Fijian labor and sought to prevent the kinds of abuses that had earlier attended such employment. The Native Taxation Scheme was devised to enable the Fijians to meet tax obligations in kind and thereby live communally without recourse to employment for wages. Land laws were formulated to make further alienation of land impossible and to vest the control of all non–fee simple and non-Crown land in the colony—83 percent of the total land area—in Fijian hands. The Native Lands Commission was created to assess the validity of settler land claims and to authoritatively determine the structure of indigenous land ownership.

For these and other such policies, Gordon and his advisors, notably Thurston, have been widely praised. It is difficult to name another colony anywhere, during the nineteenth century, even without the intense settler opposition that Gordon encountered, in which the land, institutions, and customs of an indigenous people were so well protected. It is therefore understandable that the Fijian people, or at least those who benefited directly from these policies, were less embittered by their colonial experience than were other colonized peoples, including those elsewhere in the Pacific. Nonetheless, the foundations of the Gordon-Thurston system rested on misleading assumptions and erroneous ideas about the traditional structure of the Fijian society that the colonial government was trying to preserve.

This fact plus the inevitable disparity that soon emerged between official discourse and actual practice has been the object of recent revisionism in Fijian historiography. Peter France has convincingly shown how, influenced by the linear theories of nineteenth-century evolutionary anthropology as well as by his own exaggerated and misplaced sense of intimate acquaintance with Fijian language and society, Gordon imposed a uniform, inflexible set of land laws on a people whose traditional patterns of landownership showed kaleidoscopic variety and fluidity.[28] Land had not been owned communally everywhere, as Gordon decreed that it be; nor had the *mataqali* always been the only appropriate proprietary unit. In other instances, too, Gordon chose eclectically among local ideas and practices and incorporated his choices in law or administrative practice. Everywhere, the title *buli* was assigned to the head of a district, but in Bua that title belonged to a minor chief. Similarly, the title *roko* in Tailevu and Rewa belonged to heads of priestly clans, whereas Gordon used it to designate the administrative head of a province.

There were other problems as well. Nicholas Thomas has recently suggested that in trying to combat disease and promote sanitation in Fijian society, the colonial government imposed an array of minutely defined regulations that "did little more than to bring Fijian practice into a degree of conformity with British values."[29] 'Atu Bain has likewise argued that the official policy of "benevolent protectionism" concerning Fijian labor "masked an array of legislative measures which ably defended the interests of plantation capital."[30] Studies of Indian indentured labor in the late nineteenth century have similarly shown that despite official pronouncements to the contrary, Indian laborers were forced to work on sugar-cane plantations in inhumane conditions.[31]

Not only did the colonial government often say one thing and do something else, it also worked actively to suppress and outlaw those precolonial and pre-Christian indigenous cultural and religious practices it found troublesome or offensive to its sense of order and peace. Thus, both the Luve ni Wai practices and rituals and the Tuka movement in central and northern Viti Levu in the 1870s—the last areas to be subjugated by the British—were branded as heathenish and criminal and their followers convicted and imprisoned or exiled, even though both had deep roots in the ancient religious and cultural practices of large sections of the Fijian people.[32] A similar fate awaited those Fijian people in the twentieth century who questioned a polity that in Martha Kaplan's words "was one ruled from the top down by a single, defining, ruling class that insisted on one government and one god."[33] Colonial officials found convenient allies in the high chiefs of coastal and maritime kingdoms, with whom they developed a mutually advantageous relationship by, among other things, making the chiefs the arbiters of Fijian customs. Their dominant role in Fijian affairs was thus ensured and backed by the full force of colonial law and administrative machinery. All of this is to underline the basic point that the "Fijian way of life" as it was sustained and even romanticized by the colonial government was based on highly selective principles that did little justice to the enormous diversity and fluidity of precolonial Fiji.

Gordon intended his policy to be firm but flexible. If the Fijians "can get some 25 years for their civilization to grow and root itself firmly," he believed, "they will hold their own without need of further adventitious help."[34] But twenty-five years is a long time in modern reckoning and, unaltered, Gordon's policies had by 1900 become the basis of a kind of neotraditional orthodoxy. By then it was already evident that imaginative, well-intentioned solutions to one set of problems had planted the seeds of other problems. The Fijian people had been isolated from outside influences, and their culture and institutions had been protected to a degree, even if in distorted form. They were no longer the only inhabitants of the islands. They had been joined by thousands of Indian immigrants whose service as indentured workers entitled them to permanent residence in Fiji. The government of India had sanctioned their emigration with the broad proviso, articulated by Lord Salisbury, secretary of state for the colonies in 1875, that "Indian settlers who have completed the terms of service to which they agreed, as the return for the expense of bringing them to the Colonies, will be in all respects free men, with privileges no whit inferior to those of any other class of Her Majesty's subjects resident in the Colonies."[35] This statement by Salisbury would be constantly revived and would echo down the years in the Indian community as a charter of rights just as the Deed of Cession was for the Fijians. There were also European settlers in Fiji, whose claims to privilege on account of their race and their preponderant economic position offset the relative insignificance of their numbers. The problem of reconciling these competing, indeed, incompatible, interests—paramountcy for Fijians, parity for Indians, and privilege for Europeans—is a central theme of the history of Fiji in the twentieth century.

1 The Second Coming: 1900–1920

On 27 November 1900, the Royal Colonial Institute in London heard a lecture, "The Islands and Peoples of Fiji," by Morgan I. Finucane, inspector of the provinces of Tailevu and Ra and chief medical officer of the colony.[1] For the most part, it was a sanguine self-reckoning of a quarter century of colonial rule in the islands. The future of the principally sugar- and copra-driven economy appeared sound despite fluctuations in world market prices. The immigrant laboring population was content, Finucane said, protected by legislative enactments and the high-minded ideals of their employers. Selfless, philanthropic-minded Englishmen in the colony were engaged in the "high work of civilization and Imperial expansion amongst the coloured races." However, there was, according to Finucane, one exception to this otherwise happy tale of colonial success: the apparent failure of the Gordon-Thurston system of native administration. That system had become hidebound, Finucane observed, "corrupt, inefficient, unreliable," cramping the development of Fijians and encouraging in them habits of "insouciance, lethargy, improvidence and laziness to a degree as to baffle all attempts in the past to bring about improvement."

Finucane's rhetoric and his vision of things were tainted by self-interest and imperialistic thinking. Even so, he was not alone in casting doubt on the Gordon-Thurston system. In the first decades of the twentieth century, that system was subjected to searching inquiry by a succession of colonial governors who genuinely believed that its basic elements were wrong-headed to begin with or had been rendered counterproductive by changing times. A concerted though ultimately unsuccessful attempt was made to wean Fijians from the strictly regulated, chief-led, village-based communal system to one based more on individual enterprise and initiative. In addition to this concern, which consumed so much time early in the century, the colonial officialdom had to fend off settler demands for political supremacy and annexation to New Zealand and neutralize efforts by other groups for larger roles in the affairs of the colony. The first two decades of the twentieth century were years of political flux in the island colony.

Fijians: Shaking the Tree

An account of that flux begins with Fijian society. At the turn of the century, Fijians were administratively organized into seventeen provinces, many under their own hereditary chiefs *(roko tui)* but some under the headship of European commissioners.[2] The provinces were subdivided into some eighty-four districts *(tikina)* under the leadership of the *buli,* who were responsible to the *roko* for the proper maintenance of the villages and for implementing resolutions and regulations passed by the authorities. The *buli* were assisted by "native stipendiary magistrates," who adjudicated local disputes and breaches of the stringent code of Native Regulations, which was designed to preserve the communal structure of Fijian society. At the bottom of the hierarchical order were the *tūraga ni koro,* village headmen, generally responsible for public order and administration at the local level. Over and above all these officials was the Bose Vakatūraga, the Council of Chiefs, composed of *roko,* chiefs, and other officials, which usually met annually to apprise the governor of matters of concern to the Fijian people.

This structure appeared to perform smoothly. The annually prescribed calendar of economic activity was observed, gardens were properly tended, necessary social and ceremonial obligations were met, and the Native Regulations and the various Provincial Council regulations defining the social norms of village life were adhered to. To official eyes, life in the villages followed an age-old, self-sufficient subsistence rhythm under the benign leadership of hereditary chiefs. In practice, however, things were different. Old problems persisted and new ones arose. Among the former, none was more important than the continuing decline of the population caused in part by high infant mortality rates and poor living conditions in the villages. It was caused too by indifference to the problem itself, which in turn grew out of the widespread belief among many non-Fijian observers that Fijians would "shortly disappear at no very distant date from these beautiful islands."[3] Figures for the Fijian population were depressing enough—114,748 in 1881; 105,800 in 1891; 94,397 in 1901; 87,096 in 1911; 84,475 in 1921—which meant among other things an absolute decline of 2,621 in the second decade of the century.[4] However, the decline registered in 1921 was due entirely to the terrible influenza epidemic of 1919, in which 5,154 Fijians—5.66 percent of their total number —died. Mercifully, the 1921 census was the last to record a decline in the Fijian population, though later censuses showed other trends that prevented the *taukei* 'indigenous Fijians' from becoming the most numerous ethnic group in the land of their forebears until late in the twentieth century.

By 1900 many Fijians were joining the influential critics in faulting the Gordon-Thurston system as inadequate or even retrogressive in the face of new problems and needs. The structure itself began to be viewed as an important part of the problem. The loudest protests among the *taukei* came from the Colo provinces in central Viti Levu, where the burdens of British colonialism had been added to those of traditional structures and practices imposed from the maritime provinces and where a tradition of protest had long existed. The sense of grievance among these *taukei* had been sharpened by the proximity of infringing Indian settlements and by occasional opportunities for employment in the sugar industry. They complained of excessive taxation by the government and of the large exactions demanded by the chiefs as traditional dues. As late as 1921 the district commissioner of Colo East recorded 114 cases of disobedience of communal regulations.[5] Frustrated by their inability to get their grievances redressed, some leaders in the area supported a dissident, European-led movement to have Fiji annexed to New Zealand in the misguided belief that annexation would bring them the political freedom and economic relief denied by their own government. This was the first of many rather incongruous alliances between Fijians seeking local self-determination and settler-capitalists with concerns of their own.

Protests against the Gordon-Thurston system, and particularly the abuses and excesses of the rigidly defined communal way of life, gained a sympathetic ear in the government, where the view was widespread that ordinary Fijians were being exploited by the chiefs and the system itself. This view had gained ground since the death in 1897 of Governor Thurston, an ardent champion of the system and of the views on which it rested. The view was officially aired later in 1897 by Thurston's successor, Sir George O'Brien, who characterized the existing Fijian administrative system as being government "by the Chiefs for the Chiefs."[6] This view was shared, to a greater or lesser degree, by several succeeding governors, including Sir Henry Jackson and Sir Everard im Thurn. Soon after his arrival in the colony in 1902, Jackson noted that

> I have seen enough already to convince me that there is pretty widespread feeling of unrest among the natives, and the desire for greater liberty for individual action, but I am at present inclined to think that this is rather due to the fact that there do exist legitimate grounds for complaints than to any political agitation which has been fostered among them, although this has not been without effect in encouraging the natives to speak out.[7]

In the absence of viable alternatives, Jackson argued that the communal system would have to remain. He made it clear, though, that

> our plain duty is to ensure that it shall not be worked exclusively for the benefit of the ruling class; that the obligations of the members of the commune shall be so settled as to give as much liberty to the individual as is compatible

with their due performance, and to provide for the commoner readier redress
for his grievances, and for the Government a means of supervision which
shall ensure that a continuous policy is carried out.[8]

Im Thurn, who governed the colony from 1904 to 1908, took a similar
stand:

> I have always desired to find a safe way for the complete abolition of the com-
> munal system. But a little experience has shown me the danger of doing this
> at present. I have however always sought to relax the communal restrictions
> in the individual natives of marked individuality where it can be done with-
> out handicap to the remaining commune.[9]

Certain aspects of the neotraditional order attracted special criticism,
among them the custom of *lala,* restrictions on contractual obligations
between Fijians and non-Fijians, limits on the engagement of Fijian labor,
and problems of land tenure. The ensuing discussion of these issues will
illustrate how certain institutions and practices of the system attracted particular attention.

Lala

The custom of *lala* was an important and ancient part of Fijian traditional
system in many but not all parts of the islands. According to the custom,
the tillers of the land owed the first fruits of the harvest to the chiefs. The
practice apparently symbolized a tacit division of labor and responsibility
among the *taukei* and cemented bonds of trust and faith between the *tūraga*
'chiefs' and the *lewenivanua* 'people of the land'. The custom, so its proponents argued, had long ago acquired social legitimacy and was one of those
things that held Fijian society together and gave it direction and purpose.
Certainly the chiefs thought so, for *lala* provided them the "sinews of war"
in times of trouble and "ways and means" in times of peace.[10]

After cession, the custom, like many other aspects of Fijian customs,
was codified and made enforceable by law. Its scope, too, was expanded
and, in the process, distorted. According to a Native Regulation enacted
in 1877, the custom included building houses, planting gardens, construct-
ing roads, feeding strangers, cutting wood and building canoes, fishing for
turtles, and any other works of public good. Neglect of any of these obligations was an offense and punishable by law. In 1892 another regulation
added an item that had little to do with the traditional system: "carrying
official letters, ferrying government officers and messengers across the
water and compliance with the resolution of the Provincial or District
Council which shall have the written sanction of the Governor." Clearly,
the custom was transformed into a means of providing readily available,

unpaid labor for the government. Chiefs' rights and prerogatives were similarly codified. According to an 1877 regulation, for example, "The people of the land shall obey and respect their Chiefs and Magistrates in all things lawful." It was no wonder that the chiefs and colonial officials were united in support of *lala*.

Nor is it surprising that there were complaints against the custom from commoners, especially in areas where it had never existed or existed in a much milder form than that written into law under the Gordon-Thurston system. The *lewenivanua* complained bitterly about having to provide food, money, material, and other personal services to officials, especially to those who came from outside traditional districts or provinces.[11] One commoner, "a native of high standing, who holds a position of trust under the Government, and who from education, intelligence and wide experience is thoroughly well able to judge the real state of affairs," wrote to the government newspaper, *Na Mata:* "It is quite true that the chiefs do not consider us commoners and that they are the cause of our being in difficulties, uncomfortable, poor and miserable. . . . The only thing they consider is what they can obtain for themselves even though we, their people, may be left miserable."[12]

Chiefly exactions apart, other abuses, too, had crept into the system. Missionaries and others, for example, used the custom of *lala* to obtain cheap labor under the guise of fulfilling customary obligation. From the Yasawas came a report in 1897 of the *roko* levying seven men from each of his thirty villages to go to Ba, forty miles away by sea, to build temporary accommodations for the annual meeting of the Wesleyan Missionary Church at Nailaga. The *buli* refused this demand, and instead sent a hundred men who worked for a fortnight. The men were paid neither by the *roko* nor by the missionaries. The same *roko* had also ordered thirty men from the Yasawas to plant food gardens for the same missionary settlement. These men, too, worked for a fortnight without compensation.

Such excesses and abuses strengthened the hand of officials already opposed to the communal system, and in 1905 the government abolished the custom of personal and official *lala*. The response from the *taukei* was mixed. The people of Nabitu and Vanuadina in Viti Levu wrote to the governor thanking him for the action. Now, they told the governor, they will be "free to give our attention to other things for the benefit of our wives and children."[13] In contrast, the people of Lau, where *lala* was well entrenched and widely accepted, refused to give up the custom and continued to offer *lala* to their chiefs, thus highlighting the enormous social and cultural diversity of Fijian society and the unwisdom of imposing a single system for the entire population.

In addition to abolishing *lala,* the government acted to remove other abuses that had crept into Fijian life. The Native Department was reorganized to improve the supervision and control of Fijian affairs. To the

Office of the Native Commissioner were added a deputy and an assistant so that visits to all the provinces could be made regularly. In Vanua Levu a branch office of the department was created to oversee the provinces of Bua, Macuata, and Cakaudrove; and across the colony newly appointed provincial inspectors were sent to enforce regulations relating to social and health services. There were problems here. The inspectors were poorly paid and often did not have "a knowledge of Fijian, sound constitution, active habits, sense, perseverance, and tact." Moreover, they sometimes lacked sufficient standing to deal effectively with the *roko* and other provincial officials.

At the same time, Governor O'Brien instituted a "Programme of Work" that included precise instructions for annual work schedules (Figure 1). The impetus behind this regularized work program, which remained in effect for the next four decades, was the perceived need to bring a certain orderliness to village life as well as to foster, indirectly, a sense of individualism among the *taukei*. The intent was to let the *taukei* know well in advance when and how much time would be at their disposal for private work of their own. These relaxations were in line with the new thinking, intended to

> secure for the individual the maximum liberty compatible with the due performance of his communal duties; to endeavor to re-arrange and limit those duties as far as possible, and to make it clear that, while we desire to support the influence for the good of the Chiefs, we will not allow tyranny and undue exactions, and that we mean to discourage such of the old Customs as tend to impoverish the Commoners, and keep them incessantly at work on forced service. We had better try and make the Native Chiefs do their own work, than insist on doing it for them, so long as we [the government] can ensure that their methods are not oppressive.[14]

Taxation

Taxation was another source of complaint from Fijians, especially in such poorer provinces as Serua and Namosi in southeastern Viti Levu. Because one of the principal reasons for the creation of the taxation system was to enable the *taukei* to raise tax revenue within the framework of their traditional subsistence way of life, the scheme was relatively successful. Between 1876, when it was introduced, and 1902, Fijians delivered to the government goods worth £455,040, an average of £17,500 annually. By and large, the system managed to keep Fijians in the villages close to their subsistence life-style and away from "indolent and improvident habits," above the "level of the animal" to which they would have fallen without such control, or so the official view went. The Fijians' foremost desire, according to that view, was "to be left alone to eat, to sleep, and to follow their own devices."[15]

If the system was working satisfactorily, as the official view suggests, what was the problem? The answer was that Fijians, especially in the impoverished parts of Viti Levu, resented the system as discriminatory and burdensome.[16] Why should Fijians alone be assessed a special tax, they asked, when others, constituting 20 percent of the total population, were exempt? In addition, they insisted that they were overassessed, that the existing system was administered harshly and hindered individual enterprise. Why, they asked, should those who could pay their taxes in cash rather than in kind not be allowed to?[17]

The government justified the special tax on grounds that the costs of administering the special program for Fijians were large. In addition, so this view ran, Fijians should pay for their own administration as the Crown had forfeited all claim to unoccupied lands in Fiji, the use of which would have raised a larger revenue than that paid by the Fijians. Although that was true, it did not refute the other charges Fijians made against the system. Governor Jackson acknowledged that Fijians were overassessed and that the irregularities in the system had grown over the years. In 1881, for example, 114,748 Fijians had paid total in-kind taxes of £20,000, while 91,019 Fijians in 1901 paid £19,240.

This disparity was rooted in the system itself and the way it was administered. The original assessments were allotted by province according to population, soil type and productivity, and degree of economic development. Two decades later, all those things had changed in one way or another. Populations had shifted, and with them crops, productivity, and economic development; yet the assessments were unchanged, shifting tax burdens unevenly. In the maritime copra-producing provinces, the burden was bearable; but in areas of Viti Levu where tax crops—sugar cane, maize, and tobacco—depended on the vagaries of the market and seasons, the burden was oppressive. Convinced that there was "genuine cause for discontent," Governor Jackson rejected the advice of defenders of the system and in 1903 reduced the tax assessment by 15 percent, from £19,240 to £16,260. Fortunately the reduction was allocated on the basis of need. It was lowest (10 percent) in the copra-producing maritime provinces and highest (25 percent) in the provinces of Ra, Colo, and Namosi, which had hardly any marketable products at all and had failed to meet their assessment for some years.

A similar flexibility was adopted regarding the mode of taxation. Once again, complaint about taxes in kind had come from the poorer provinces, where the levies had forced Fijians to travel long distances, sometimes across provinces, to cultivate land leased from the people of another district in order to pay their taxes in kind. Although defenders of the system made light of such instances, in places like Namosi, some Fijians regularly traveled more than fifteen miles a day to cultivate tax crops and, fed up, almost refused to pay any taxes at all. They wanted to pay their taxes in

PROGRAMME OF WORK FOR THE PROVINCE OF COLO WEST.

JANUARY.

Plantations. Every able-bodied man in the districts of Qalimare, Bemana, Magodro, Noikoro and Nasikawa, to plant 50 roots of yaqona each. Every able-bodied man in every district to plant 200 dalo, 200 tapioca, 20 voivoi, 50 bananas.

FEBRUARY.

Plantations and house building. Every able-bodied man in the villages of Nawamagi, Narata, Nadrala to plant one acre of cane. The district of Namataku to repair the walls of the Provincial Commissioner's house at Natuatuacoko. The district of Magodro to repair the walls of the Native Magistrate's house at Natuatuacoko, and the district of Nasikawa to repair the Provincial Constable's house.

MARCH.

Plantations and house building. All paths to be weeded, and all bad sections to be repaired. The district of Komave to weed the village path from Nabukelevu to Nabotini. The districts of Qalimare, Bemana, Noikoro, and Nasikawa each to build a house for their Buli.

APRIL.

Plantations and house building. The districts of Mavua, Qalimare, Bemana, Namataku, Magodro, Noikoro, Nasikawa and Koroinasau each able-bodied man to plant 100 roots of tobacco. The district of Korolevuiwai to build the Provincial Matanivanua's house at Tagaqe. The district of Magodro to build the retired Buli's house at Bukuya.

MAY AND JUNE.

All to obtain their Provincial Rate and to pay it in to the Provincial Commissioner before June 30th. Those who remain in their villages to work as ordered by the Buli or Turaga ni Koro.

JULY.

Plantations and house building. Every able-bodied man in the district of Koroinasau to plant 100 roots of yaqona. All paths to be weeded and cleaned and bad sections to be repaired.

kind only when this would cause less hardship. Colonial Secretary William Allardyce rejected such pleas. To allow them, he believed, would open the door to such problems as vagrancy, desertion of wives and children for long periods, and neglect of food gardens and communal obligations, and

AUGUST.

Plantations. Every man to plant 400 yams, 400 dalo and 30 vudidina.

SEPTEMBER.

Plantations and house building. The district of Mavua to build their Buli's house.

OCTOBER.

Plantations and house building. All paths to be weeded, cleaned and repaired.

NOVEMBER.

Plantations and house building.

DECEMBER.

Free month.

BULI'S LALA.

All able-bodied men to work 8 days each in the Buli's plantations.

TURAGA NI KORO'S PAY.

Every able-bodied man in every village to pay 3/- to his Turaga ni Koro before November 30th, and to work for 3 days in his plantations.

VILLAGE WEEDING.

All villages to be weeded every Wednesday.

PROVINCIAL COMPOUNDS.

It shall be the duty of the Provincial Commissioner or Roko Tui to order a village or district to perform any necessary weeding or house building or other work in the Provincial Compounds at Lawaqa and Natuatuacoko or in the Compound of the Native Medical Practitioner at Korolevu and of the Nurse at Tubairata and at Qalimare.

Figure 1. *(Courtesy National Archives of Fiji)*

would threaten the very structure of Fijian society. Governor Jackson resisted such views as Allardyce's and instead sanctioned the practice, already in existence among Fijians living close to urban centers, that allowed those provinces that could to pay in cash.

Trading

To encourage limited individualism among Fijians, the government revised the laws regulating Fijian commerce. As a first step, the Native Trading Ordinance of 1891 was replaced in 1904.[18] According to the 1891 ordinance, Fijians could sign enforceable contracts with non-Fijians for goods and services valued at no more than £5. Contracts involving larger sums were not legally enforceable unless approved by the appropriate magistrate. Non-Fijians entering into such contracts were required, under threat of heavy penalty, to register the contracts with the district magistrate, who could withhold registration if the contract was not to be performed within a year or if its provisions were unclear, involved any breach of native regulation, or was "contrary to sound policy and equity." A non-Fijian could be fined up to £100 or sentenced to up to six months' imprisonment for contracting with a Fijian contrary to the provisions of this ordinance.

These restrictions were ostensibly intended to safeguard Fijians from exploitation by others, but they also reflected the views of colonial officials regarding the Fijian people. According to Native Commissioner W. S. Sutherland, the Fijian entrepreneur was "usually a rogue and undeserving of encouragement or consideration." Fijians, he said, "have little adaptability for business and in their circumstances this is not to be regretted." Allardyce had an even more depressing view of Fijian capabilities:

> The Fijians as a whole are a loyal, communal, conservative, law abiding, good natured people, thriftless unfortunately with no thought for the morrow, like most people to whom nature has been lavish with her gifts, disinclined to anything like hard work where it is possible to be avoided, ceremonious, impressionable, fickle, and with little or no firmness of character or forethought. . . . There is no getting away from the fact that the Fijian is at heart a savage despite 60 years of christianising influence and 26 years of British rule.[19]

These views, which had once exercised a powerful influence over government policy, were now being challenged. As Jackson had told the Colonial Office in 1903, the "Fijian is by no means the simple unreasoning child he is sometimes declared to be by those who desire to keep him in a state of tutelage."[20] What Fijians needed, thought Jackson and others like him, was help to enter the world of commerce, not protection. They needed encouragement and active support to stand on their own, not protective custody by the colonial government. Those who had ample means should not be shielded by law if they breached the terms of a contract they entered knowingly. Nor should those who were eager and showed a talent for commercial activity be barred by law from participating in the economic development taking place around them.

On the basis of such reasoning, the 1891 law restricting Fijian commercial activity was revised. The harsh penalties against non-Fijians who signed contracts with Fijians were removed and did not come under the revised ordinance. Contracts involving amounts of up to £20 were legalized, though contracts involving larger sums still had to be registered with a magistrate. However, no claim could be brought against a Fijian for an amount exceeding £20 unless the claim was based on a registered contract. The courts could also enforce a judgment against a Fijian who could be shown to have the means to pay it. Food crops and communal property were excluded from all these calculations, and the Fijian remained in a sense a ward of the state. A Fijian "may be allowed to purchase for ready money whatever he chooses without the interference of the law," said an official of the colonial government. The Colonial Office in London agreed, calling the new legislation "a well considered step in the gradual emancipation of the native from the regime of status to the regime of contract."[21] This optimistic assessment was premature, as subsequent Fijian history would show; still, the break from the past was clear.

Fijian Labor Laws

A similar relaxation of the Fijian labor laws followed. The original laws formulated soon after Cession had ostensibly been "framed and designed to fit in with the native policy and to meet the social conditions peculiar to the Fijian people."[22] Recruiters were required to obtain licenses to recruit Fijian workers. No Fijians could engage without the permission of the *buli*. Employers were obliged to pay the return cost of laborers they hired. Women and children under age fifteen were prohibited from entering into contracts, and certain districts could be closed to recruitment if the absence of workers conflicted with the fulfillment of traditional communal obligations in the village. In practice, these conditions could be avoided. *Buli* could be bribed to give their consent, and Fijians could be recruited under the 1890 Masters and Servants Ordinance, which gave the district commissioner the power to authorize recruitment without the consent of the chiefs[23] and did away with provisions requiring close scrutiny from local officials. Indeed, by the end of the first decade of the twentieth century, 500 Fijians were working under the provisions of this ordinance, and 750 under the Fijian Labor Ordinance. In 1905, at the behest of the planters, further changes were made to the labor laws that permitted married Fijian men to engage for service for more than three months if the registering officer, either the assistant native commissioner or the stipendiary magistrate, was satisfied that the families of the men had been provided with adequate planting land.[24]

The planters wanted further changes to enable them to recruit more Fijian workers. The result of their insistence was the passage of the wide-ranging Fijian Labour Ordinance in 1912. Under the terms of this ordinance, unmarried Fijians could enter into a contract of service under either the Masters and Servants Ordinance or the Fijian Labour Ordinance provided they had made arrangements to support their dependents in the village. Fijian men who were absent from their villages for two years or more, or had completed their contracts, could enter new ones without seeking the permission of village authorities or provincial officials. Laws regarding vagrancy were no longer to apply to Fijians in regular employment.

The social impact of the 1912 ordinance on Fijians has been debated by historians. Some have seen this legislation as having a profound, almost revolutionary, impact on Fijian society, by enabling, even encouraging, Fijians to leave their villages to work outside. "Communal work has been very seriously affected," wrote one official in the 1920s, "so seriously indeed as to threaten the continuance of the scheme of native government. . . . Much of the unrest amongst the native race during the past few years," he said, "is traceable to this law and to the belief that the Government considered that a supply of labor for agricultural purposes was of greater importance than the welfare of the natives themselves."[25] A more recent assessment considers this view to be exaggerated and suggests that instead of embarking on a revolutionary policy, the government "merely sought to give legal stature to a practice it had tacitly endorsed for some 15 years."[26]

Even after the passage of the 1912 labor ordinance, most Fijians working on the plantations, and all with the Colonial Sugar Refining Company (CSR) were recruited under the Masters and Servants Ordinance, without the protective provisions of the 1912 ordinance. Many Fijians were apparently unaware of the trap involved here, but the employers knew precisely what they were doing. "Most of them know that the contracts are illegal and that laborers could not be prosecuted in court if they broke the contract," wrote Secretary for Native Affairs G. V. Maxwell in 1919, "but the whole thing is a 'bluff' for they take advantage of the fact that the ignorant Fijian does not know that the contract is illegal, and will continue to submit to the demands of his employer under the impression that he is lawfully policed."[27] Be that as it may, by 1926, 2051 Fijians, or 8.7 percent of the taxable age group, were employed under one or the other of the two ordinances.

Land and Land Reform

None of the reforms of the early twentieth century was potentially more far reaching or more controversial than Governor im Thurn's unsuccessful effort to effect fundamental changes in land policy between 1904 and 1908. The new governor was an unsentimental reformer with previous colonial experience in Guyana and Ceylon, where he had been lieutenant governor before coming to Fiji. During his colonial career, im Thurn acquired the reputation as "a governor whose whole interest wherever he has been has rested in and with the natives and he has been most successful with them."[28] His sympathies lay more with the ordinary Fijians than with the Fijian aristocracy, as was nowhere more evident than in his policy on education. "I strongly urge," he said, "that the boys to be educated should be chosen as much for preeminence of intellect as of birth. Other conditions being equal, preference would naturally be given to sons of chiefs as they are the class from which future Native Civil Servants would be chosen, but promising boys of inferior birth should not be denied the advantage of education to be provided by the school."[29]

Governor im Thurn believed that the main cause of Fijian problems was that Fijians were denied the right to think and act for themselves. He also thought that chiefly exactions and the "irresistible strictness of the laws" by which Fijians were bound to serve their chiefs were important obstacles to Fijian prosperity.[30] He therefore endorsed the reform measures of his predecessors and, in reopening the land question, went further than any other responsible official had gone since cession, when Gordon's policies were first put in place. His motives in reexamining this issue were complex. In part he was simply continuing the wider process of questioning the old colonial orthodoxy begun by O'Brien in the last years of the 1890s. In part he wanted to settle definitively the matter of what had and had not been ceded to the Crown by the Fijian chiefs.[31] And in part he believed that the settlement he sought would serve the interest of the Fijian people. As he told the Bose Vakatūraga in 1905, "It is already clear to me that the natives have a great deal more land than they can use; that they at present derive no benefit whatever from this spare land; that there are many persons ready to use this spare land and pay the natives rent for it; and that the natives would be much better off if they had the money."[32]

In addition, im Thurn's reexamination of the land issue was informed by the suspicion that a fraud had been perpetrated by Gordon and his successors, as a result of which the Crown had been forced to forfeit claims to vast areas of land. To support his suspicion, he cited Clause 4 of the Deed of Cession, which read:

> The absolute proprietorship of all lands not shown to be now alienated so as to have become bona fide property of Europeans or other foreigners or not now in actual occupation of some Chief or tribe or not actually required for the probable future support and maintenance of some chief or tribe shall be and is hereby declared to be vested in Her Majesty, her heirs and successors.

The intent of this clause seems clear. It was not only to define ownership rights and Fijian needs, but also to give to the government title to all unclaimed land. The latter intent had not been implemented for reasons to be examined later. Convinced that he was right, im Thurn secured a series of legislative enactments designed to relax the controls imposed on land use and ownership.[33]

Among the most prominent of these was Ordinance IV of 1905, "The Native Lands Amendment Ordinance," which, while upholding the principle of customary (inalienable) tenure, permitted the sale of native land with the consent of the governor-in-council. Ordinance V of 1905, "The Native Lands Acquisition Ordinance," permitted the compulsory acquisition of native land by the government through the right of eminent domain, even without compensation, for such public purposes as building roads, canals, bridges, and paths; and with mutually agreed compensation for other "public purposes." A year later, still another ordinance, XVI of 1906, "The Acquisition of Land Ordinance," defined the phrase "public purpose" to include any undertaking that would advance the interests of the colony. Although native land came under its purview, this ordinance was actually aimed at European landowners in western Viti Levu who had refused to give up land for the construction of a tram line by the CSR. A final piece of land legislation secured by im Thurn was Ordinance IX of 1907, "The Native Lands Amendment Act," which, in line with his policy to promote individualism among Fijians, removed restrictions on the ownership or lease of land by individual Fijians. It also permitted, between 1905 and 1909, the outright sale of 20,184 acres of native land, bringing the total area of fee simple (freehold) land in the colony to 434,799 acres.[34]

Im Thurn has been severely criticized for these alterations in the colony's land policies.[35] The criticisms give the impression of the governor as an insensitive colonialist bent on destroying the basic institutions of Fijian society. Two things need to be pointed out, however. First, im Thurn's land reform was not an isolated policy but an integral part of the larger colonial endeavor to promote, where the Fijians themselves desired it, the ideology of individualism and personal enterprise. Indeed, in embarking on his land policy, im Thurn was following the general guidelines of the Colonial Office, which mandated "a gradual loosening" of the communal structures of Fijian society "as the only policy which will enable the change to a system of individual life and government to be accomplished, not perhaps without friction but at least without serious disturbance."[36]

Second, governors O'Brien and Jackson, im Thurn's predecessors, had endorsed the main lines of the policy he was now implementing. O'Brien thought that the alleged habits of "indolence and wastefulness" he detected among Fijians were caused by the excess land in their possession, while Jackson talked of selling "native land" under close government supervision.[37] All three men thought that the freeing up of land would be used to promote development of the colony as a whole, though what precisely that would mean, neither of them ever specified. As im Thurn wrote a former governor, Sir William Des Voeux, who was apprehensive about the impact of the changes under way, "I am most anxious for the welfare of these interesting natives, and if I ever do anything which may seem like relaxing the former protection it is only in order to leave greater freedom to them now that they are adolescents—or would be but for the protection of recent years—and entitled to claim their position, in the near future, as full British subjects."[38]

The reaction to im Thurn's land legislation within the colony was varied. Local Europeans, planters and members of the business community alike, hailed the changes, for they saw in them the possibility of profit and prosperity for themselves.[39] Perhaps also they thought that their long-cherished dreams for more fee simple land would at last be realized. They were misguided, however, for under im Thurn's reforms, those large European landlords, too, would be forced to unlock their large fee simple holdings to settlement or development. Certainly, im Thurn was no puppet of the Europeans or an unabashed champion of settler interests as some of his more vocal critics at the time alleged. What of Fijian reactions? As Tony Chappelle has concluded, perhaps a bit optimistically, "Almost without exception, the reaction was favourable. What is more, this favour seemed to embrace all facets of 'individualism' as a policy, including the new land legislation."[40]

The same could not be said of the defenders of the old orthodoxy and holdovers from the Gordon-Thurston years. Now in the twilight of their lives, they were angered and humiliated to see their carefully constructed artifact slowly dismantled by their successors. None of im Thurn's opponents was more piqued than David Wilkinson. He had entered colonial service in 1875 and retired in 1882; he then reentered colonial service as native commissioner in 1894 until being forcibly and permanently retired by im Thurn in 1905 at a pension of £200 a year. Im Thurn had no time for Wilkinson; he told the Colonial Office that he was "regretfully bound to report myself convinced that Mr Wilkinson's age and feeble state of health and perhaps his incapacity to advance beyond the unfortunately stereotyped ideas which prevailed during the early days of the Colony, unfit him for the work of Commissioner."[41] Wilkinson alerted Gordon, in 1907 sitting in the House of Lords as Lord Stanmore, to the imminent undoing of his Fijian legacy. In a speech on 16 July 1907, Stanmore attacked im Thurn's land policy as well as the sale of some swampy native land* in Rewa to the CSR that the governor had sanctioned.

There followed a brilliant series of dispatches between im Thurn and the Colonial Office about land and the formulation of colonial policy gener-

---

*Throughout this study, the term *native land,* a term used by both the colonial and the postcolonial governments, refers to land held in inalienable right by the indigenous Fijians. It is not a term that I have coined.

ally, dispatches that have no parallel in Fijian colonial history. They make interesting reading not the least because they are a potpourri of vanity, ridicule, sarcasm, insult, and righteous self-defense. Gordon conceded that im Thurn was correct in his reading of the letter of Clause 4 noted earlier; but, he said, it was the spirit, not the letter, of the Deed of Cession that had concerned him at the time. In the aftermath of the measles epidemic of 1875, Gordon recalled, Fijians were in a state of distress that heightened their suspicions of the new government and uncertainties regarding their land holdings. If the government had acted according to the letter of Clause 4, Gordon suggested, violence could have erupted.

> Great damage would have been done to the property of settlers, [he told the secretary of state for the colonies in 1908, defending his actions.] Great expense would have been incurred, which the Colony was in no position to bear, the Native population would have been irreparably injured, and a legacy of hatred and suspicion would have placed an unsurmountable barrier between the white settlers and the Native population; a thing always undesirable, and where the latter are as was then the case, fifty times more numerous than the former, not unattended with danger.[42]

Then there was the moral argument to consider, Gordon continued. The high chiefs who had signed the Deed of Cession had neither the right nor the power to do so for all the *mataqali* of Fiji. Why, he asked, should those not party to the Cession be deprived of land that had traditionally been theirs? Gordon himself had given assurances to the Fijians, though there was no record of it, that their lands would not be taken away from them; that they would continue to enjoy their accustomed rights *vaka vanua* as they had done before cession. Moreover, several of his successors had renewed these assurances; and to invoke a literal reading of Clause 4 twenty-five years after the fact was, Gordon warned, extremely dangerous now that Fijians had come to believe that all the unused land was theirs.

Despite this reasoning, Governor im Thurn's arguments were legally unassailable.[43] Everyone conceded that Clause 4 had been misapplied; that Gordon had confused ownership and occupation, and thus ignored the intent to surrender all unoccupied Fijian owned land to the Crown; that there was no record whatsoever of the assurances, if any, that Gordon had given the chiefs at the time; and that there was no precise definition in law of what constituted *vaka vanua,* according to which the unoccupied land had been returned to the Fijians. But all this was moot. As the Colonial Office in London noted, "The course of events during the last 30 years has rendered it impossible for the Government of Fiji to adopt any position other than that the waste lands of Fiji must continue to be regarded as the property of the natives as much as the occupied land."[44] When Sir Henry May, im Thurn's successor, once again attempted to reopen the question of Crown ownership of unused land in 1911, the Colonial Office decided that enough was enough. "In the meantime," wrote L. V. Harcourt, the secretary of state for the colonies to May, "I would ask you to bear in mind that the question whether or not his [Gordon's policy] was in accordance with the instructions of the Secretary of State is entirely a matter for the Secretary of State and not one to be discussed by a successor in public."[45]

In the aftermath, new directions were issued about land policy. All non-Crown and non–fee simple land, whether occupied or not, was declared to be the property of the Fijians; no native land was to be sold or otherwise permanently alienated; and land could be leased only with the consent of the government. Sales would be allowed only in exceptional cases and only after the approval of the secretary of state in London. Here the land issue rested until the 1920s and 1930s, when the concern was with security of tenure and not ownership per se.

When Gordon began his administration of Fiji in 1875, and stated that he did not see his policies as fixed for all time, he thought Fijians needed about twenty-five years of paternalistic protection to adjust to the demands of colonialism. It was clear, although unstated, that Gordon envisaged future adjustment of what he had done. O'Brien, Jackson, and im Thurn had embarked on that project, all of them agreeing on the broad goals of "emancipating" Fijians and providing them with the opportunity and the means to live in the kind of competitive, plural society Fiji was becoming by the turn of the century. They did not have as paternalistic or depressing a view of Fijian capabilities to succeed in the modern world as their predecessors had. They were sympathetic to Fijian needs and aspirations, but thought that these could best be addressed through their gradual integration into the broader economic life of the colony rather than through rigidly adhering to a way of life that, as they saw it, had become ossified and unresponsive to the needs of the new times. Their efforts were only partly successful, but the debate these governors opened up would echo through Fijian history for much of the twentieth century, culminating in a series of reforms in the 1960s.

European Planters and Federation

In 1901 there were 2,447 Europeans in Fiji, 411 more than in 1891; in the next two decades, their number increased to 3,878.[46] This modest growth was overshadowed by the relatively larger increase in Part-Europeans, from 1,516 in 1901 to 2,781 in 1921. The latter would become a "political problem" in the late 1920s and 1930s. At the turn of the century, most of the Europeans in Fiji were either Fiji-born (846) or immigrants from Australia or New Zealand (688) or the United Kingdom (620), with a sprinkling from other colonies and Europe. More than half of them lived in Suva (1073), with other concentrations in Lomaiviti (364), Ba and Nadi (237), and Rewa (221). This concentration in urban areas continued in the first two decades of the century.

These Europeans controlled the sinews of the economy. One measure of their dominance was the amount of direct and indirect taxes the Europeans paid in 1911: £122,550, compared with £39,700 paid by Fijians and £38,232 paid by Indians.[47] The largest enterprise in Fiji, the CSR, had an annual turnover of around £1.4 million around the turn of the century and employed three-quarters of all indentured laborers in the colony.[48] Its political influence was proportionate to its economic size. Other large enterprises included Henry Marks and Company, with a registered capital of £112,500 and dominance in wholesale and retail business; Morris Hedstrom, with an annual turnover of £200,000, paid-up capital of £150,000, and major investments in shipping, motorcars, and agricultural machinery; and other general companies, such as Burns Philp, A. M. Brodziak, and Brown and Joske. The dominance of some of these companies would continue unchallenged well into the second half of the century.

So, too, did the Europeans' insistence on social separation from Fijians and Indians. The two government-aided schools in Suva and Levuka were reserved for children of full European parentage; Part-European children as well as those of non-European descent were kept out.[49] This policy was supported by colonial officials. Governor May, for example, heartily endorsed segregated education, noting in 1911 the undesirability of "contact with coloured children whose precocity in sexual matters and whose less careful upbringing at home is a real danger to white children."[50] In 1907, Queen Victoria School, at Nasinu, opened for sons of Fijian chiefs, but Europeans successfully opposed the extension of Western (English) educational facilities to Indians on grounds that that was contrary to colonial policy and inimical to the colony's economic interest. As the manager of the Vancouver Sugar Company wrote to the colonial secretary in 1914, "We most emphatically do not require an Indian community of highly educated labourers, with the attendant trouble which the 'baboo' class has brought to the Indian Government, teaching and preaching sedition and looking generally for immediate treatment on a parity with educated Europeans accustomed to self government for many centuries."[51] This pattern of educational segregation continued for the next four decades.

It was reinforced by parallel forms of discrimination in other areas of life in the colony. Though Europeans were concentrated in Suva and other towns, they were nowhere numerically dominant. In 1901, for example, Suva's total population of 4,559 included 1,073 Europeans, 1,728 Indians and 701 Fijians, alongside 866 Polynesians and 191 others.[52] Yet, the European minority used legislative and other devices such as municipal building and zoning regulations, to exclude non-Europeans from the management of municipal affairs.[53] The government concurred in this arrangement. As May informed the Colonial Office in 1911, "I hold the view very strongly that Europeans inhabiting the tropics are entitled to have set apart for them in towns inhabited by Asiatics and natives of coloured races an area in which they can reside in surroundings not rendered insanitary and otherwise undesirable by persons of the races mentioned."[54] James Borron, whose legacy to modern Fiji includes the State Guest House in Samabula, where Coalition parliamentarians were incarcerated after the 1987 coups, believed that Fijians should not be allowed to occupy land within three-quarters of a mile of the Grand Post Office in central Suva. Virtually all Europeans, whatever their disagreements on other matters, agreed that only "colored servants" should be allowed in certain restricted areas of Suva. First, Toorak, named after a fashionable suburb of Melbourne, and in turn, Muanikau, Laucala Beach Road, and Princess Road were the most exclusive places of European residence in Suva during the first half of the century. After World War II, however, such exclusive enclaves gave way to the social transformations that have marked the modern era.

In the first two decades of the century, most Europeans in Fiji supported unrestricted land reform enlarging the area of fee simple land or, failing that, expanding the amount of land available for very long leases. They voiced their opinion through petitions to the governor and the Colonial Office, debates in the Legislative Council, and letters and articles in the local newspapers. In 1907 a European member of the council moved that "the native owners should not be allowed to defeat the best interests of the community and themselves owing to mental inability, misled, influenced and blinded by white people, and possibly their own superiors, for reasons best known to themselves, and carried away by tradition, superstition or sentiment."[55] A deputation from the Chamber of Commerce told Sir Charles Lucas of the Colonial Office on a visit to Fiji in 1909 that the chamber was "unanimously of the opinion that free alienation of land should be permitted and that freehold tenure should dominate leasehold, in our judgement, for the proper opening of this Colony." Only fee simple tenure would attract the right class of white people to the colony, they told Lucas, for a good man "likes to have something to hand down to posterity. . . . However long the leasehold may be it is not enough, and settlers prefer freehold."[56]

This clamor for more fee simple land was undermined from the outset. Europeans already controlled some of the best agricultural land in the colony, mostly in fee simple ownership, in the Dreketi delta and the Sigatoka Valley, none of which was being opened up for settlement. Instead, as Native Commissioner William Sutherland noted, "The European owned land is being held for a rise in value and bona fide offers for blocks at good prices have been refused and settlement thereby retarded." In addition, the colonial government had at its disposal some 285,000 acres of land available for leasing, further evidence that there was more than enough land available for development.[57] Yet Europeans of all classes continued to clamor for more fee simple land until the late 1920s. By that time the situation had changed, as Europeans moved out of commercial agriculture and were replaced by Indian farmers, who then became the chief advocates of more security of tenure. Eager for Fijian support against growing Indian demands for social and political equality, Europeans would align themselves with the Fijian chiefs. In the first two decades of the century, however, when the Indians were still either under indenture or in the shadow of servitude, the clash over land policy was between Fijian interests and European demands.

The Europeans were equally assertive in politics, where the foremost issue was the demand for greater representation in the Legislative Council. The organs of government had grown slowly since Cession in 1874. The colony's founding 1875 charter provided for a Legislative Council consisting of the governor and not less than two other members, all nominated by him. This provision remained in place until 1903, when the size of the council was increased to six official members (heads of government departments or senior officials) and four unofficial members (nongovernment members from the community), again all nominated by the governor. The system of a completely nominated Legislative Council was opposed by local political aspirants, especially in the urban areas, who wanted representatives elected by the people to have a direct voice in the public affairs of the colony. "No taxation without representation," went up the cry. Partly in response, the government in 1904 made further alterations providing for a nominated Executive Council and a triennial Legislative Council with ten official members (senior public servants), two Fijians nominated by the Council of Chiefs, and six European elected members (three representatives of the European commercial class—one from Levuka and the other two from Suva—two European cultivators owning not less than 100 acres but not engaged in the production of sugar, and one representative of the sugar companies.)[58] There was no provision for Indian representation in the Legislative Council at this stage.

Encouraged by their increased representation in the Legislative Council, the Europeans began to demand a seat on the Executive Council of the colony. Sir Henry Scott made the plea in 1908, but was rebuffed by im Thurn, who thought there was no suitably detached European in the colony who could provide impartial advice. However, the Europeans would get an additional member in 1916 when the Letters Patent were once again revised.

The increased presence of Europeans in the government that these changes signaled failed to satisfy those Europeans bent on controlling the government or seeking alternatives to Fiji's status within the British Empire. One such alternative was federation with New Zealand, support for which had surfaced soon after 1874 when a group of planters and settlers who were dissatisfied with the government's policies toward land and the Fijians turned to New Zealand for support. The effort came to nought, but it was revived around the turn of the century, with new leaders and with a renewed vigor under the auspices of the Fiji Federal League, led by F. E. Riemenschneider, warden of Suva, and Humphrey Berkeley, brother of the colonial chief justice.[59]

The federationists complained bitterly that they were "deprived of rights and privileges which are their birthright as free born Britons." They paid taxes, they said, but had no real voice in running the colony. They were also deprived of the right of trial by jury and hampered by the cumbersome procedures involved in appealing the decisions of the Fiji Supreme Court, which consisted of a single judge. In addition, they had no valid means of seeking redress for their grievance against the colonial government, which was responsible not to the people of the colony but to the secretary of state, in whose ability "to prevent or punish acts of harshness or maladministration, . . . or to afford them that redress of grievance which, as British subjects they are entitled to demand and receive" they had lost all confidence.

Federation with New Zealand would remove some of these disabilities by bringing more accountability of officials, closer supervision of colonial affairs, and an elected legislature. It would mean more free trade between the two colonies and thus an expanded market for Fijian products. "The profits thus derived will enable each to buy more largely than at present of the other's products," said one of the movement's representatives. "The profits accruing to Fiji will attract to her capital, and extend the settlement of white men and their families throughout the islands of the group."

The federation movement attracted a varied assortment of supporters, who embroiled it in their own local concerns. Berkeley, for example, was a colorful socialite lawyer whose life-style aroused much official as well as unofficial opprobrium. His brother, the chief justice, had already fallen out of favor with the local official establishment. But Berkeley had managed to win the support of a group of chiefs from the Serua and Namosi areas who were unhappy over taxation and other such matters. These chiefs joined or supported the federation movement because they believed that political affiliation with New Zealand might work to their advantage. As Ratu Radomodomo wrote in a memorandum in 1901, he and his people in the Serua-Namosi area supported federation with New Zealand because the colonial government in Fiji "makes us the most wretched people." With federation, they added, "We shall then obtain relief and become rich."[60] Meanwhile, New Zealand Premier Richard Seddon, ever mindful of glory for his dominion, told federationists he "would be favourably inclined to consider any proposal regarding Federation of New Zealand with Fiji."[61]

The opponents of federation far outnumbered its supporters. In London the Aborigines' Protection Society told the Colonial Office that the surrender of direct control over Fiji would not only jeopardize the lives and interests of the Fijians, which the Deed of Cession had promised to uphold. It would also jeopardize the welfare of other Pacific Islanders under the jurisdiction of the governor of Fiji, who was also the high commissioner of the Western Pacific.[62] Within the colony, too, there were powerful opponents of federation. Some planters in Navua opposed it lest it cause the government of India to suspend all indentured emigration to Fiji and thus precipitate their ruin.[63] Fiji, these planters and others believed, would never become a white-settler colony. The colony's biggest commercial concern, the CSR, was also opposed to federation, fearing that the application of New Zealand labor laws to Fiji would interfere with the "proper management of matters like the indenture of Indian laborers." The CSR would become a fairly small fish in a large lake, with all the attendant disadvantages that would bring.[64] O'Brien told a gathering of Fijians at Wainibokasi in 1900 that the proponents of federation among them were being misled. Federation with white-controlled New Zealand, he warned, would threaten Fijians with the plight of the Maori: "White men have always taken the land from the coloured owners," O'Brien said. "It has been so in New Zealand where the land once all belonged to the coloured people. Who owns that land now? The white people have got nearly the whole of it; the coloured people are cooped up in the fragment of land that has been left to them, and many of them have no land at all."[65] To prevent further agitation of the issue by Fijians, O'Brien issued an order in council in 1901 authorizing sentences of up to six months in prison for anyone convicted of causing disaffection or subversion among Fijians or encouraging the alteration of the existing form of government.[66]

The federationist kite would flutter on in the next decade under the banner of such organizations as the Fiji Annexation League, which also agitated for a popularly elected government for the colony and an unfettered free enterprise economy. The movement continued to attract a handful of Fijian and even Indian dissidents, including Badri Maharaj, who in 1916 became the first Indian nominated member of the Legislative Council. By then, however, the prospect of annexation to New Zealand was evanescent.[67]

Indians: *Girmit* and Free

The third leg of the Fijian stool at the turn of the century was the Indian community, numbering 17,105, made up of *girmitiya* (as they called themselves, after the agreement of indenture that bound them to service) and of free people whose indentures had expired and whose time was now their own. By 1900, 21,056 indentured Indians had entered the islands, all of them obligated to five years of labor, the terms of which were prescribed in their indentures.[68] The *girmitiya* were required to do plantation work nine hours each week day and five hours on Saturdays. For time-work, men received a shilling and women ninepence. Housing and medical care were provided by the employers at a specified cost. *Girmitiya* could return to India at the end of the five-year indenture at their own expense or at the expense of the government after a second five-year period of "industrial residence." Altogether, 24,000 laborers returned to India after spending varying periods in the colony.

The majority of the *girmitiya* came from impoverished districts of eastern Uttar Pradesh: Basti, Gonda, Azamgarh, Faizabad, districts that in the latter half of the nineteenth century had sent increasing numbers of migrants to the Assam tea gardens and Calcutta jute mills as well as to Mauritius and the sugar colonies in the West Indies. There was some deception involved in their recruiting, but the bulk of would-be migrants were already on the march in search of employment outside their home districts before they encountered the recruiters. After 1903 the North Indian *girmitiya* were joined by counterparts from the south, fifteen thousand of whom eventually came to Fiji. South Indians were late in joining the Fijian exodus because the established route for southern migrants was to colonies in Southeast Asia, and for the most part, North India had been able to supply the demand for such overseas points as Fiji. The indentured migrants were joined by small trickles of free immigrants from the Punjab and Gujarat, which numbered about a thousand by 1907 but increased to a rate of two hundred fifty a year by 1911. These varied sources contributed to a diversified, socially complex community of Indians in Fiji.

Naturally enough, the bulk of this community was in the sugar-growing areas, in southern and western Viti Levu and the province of Macuata in Vanua Levu, where cane cultivation had been extended in the early 1890s. Once their contracts expired, few of the *girmitiya* were willing to reindenture themselves for any extended length of time. Some of the more adventurous found new occupations. In 1887, for example, 20 of 49 hawkers licenses issued were held by Indians; and in 1900, 229 were licensed to set up shops, 225 to practice hawking, and 46 to work as "watermen," providing water to laborers in the fields.[69] The majority of the ex-*girmitiya*, however, remained in agriculture. In 1911 of the total Indian population of 25,976, 10,357 were classed as agriculturalists (7,731 were children or had independent means). In some areas, Indians had by that time become independent producers of sugar cane. In the Rewa area as early as 1900, Indian farmers had leased 768 acres and produced 14,000 tons of cane. In Navua by 1898, Indian planters had already surpassed Europeans in both the tonnage and the value of the cane they produced, and in Ba, the CSR had set aside a large block of land for Indian farmers. The Indians had taken quickly to cane cultivation. One official described them as "skilled agriculturalists, industrious and shrewd."[70] Another noted on a visit to Navua and Rewa, "I was struck by the signs of the industry of the 'free' Indian settlers. In fact it is not possible to travel up the river without noticing on either bank evidences of the aptitude, push and perseverance of the ubiquitous 'free' Indian, with his stores, farms and smiling plantations."[71] Others took to hawking, small shopkeeping, and jewel trading.

In urban areas, the government assisted Indian settlement on Crown land, in Vatuwaqa, as early as 1887, for example, and later in Samabula. In rural areas, free Indians had to lease land on their own, often from Fijian landlords. The procedure was complicated and lent itself to corruption.[72] A farmer first had to select the land he wanted to lease and then apply to the Immigration Department or the appropriate stipendiary magistrate, who passed the application on to the native commissioner. Often the *buli* had to be humored before he would give permission or his recommendation for the land to be leased. The process was time consuming, for the government had to decide among other things whether Indian settlement in a particular area would adversely affect Fijian interests. This cumbersome procedure was reformed in 1916.

Indians settled wherever they obtained leases to fertile land, without regard to their own social, cultural, or religious considerations.[73] This gave rise to dispersed settlements rather than the clustered villages that were the pattern in India. The social structure in the settlements was thus loose and created its own problems, among them the absence of common values and of established means of group endeavor and conflict resolution. Caste, that Indian system of institutionalized inequality sanctioned by religion, did not survive indenture to any effective degree and for all practical purposes disappeared altogether in the decades ahead. The plantation system was a merciless leveler of social hierarchy in the Indian community, for all workers were units of labor exploited for profit. Indian institutions such as the *panchayat,* the five-person council for resolving conflict, did survive, though with uneven effectiveness, for it generally lacked the authority it had in India.

In time a semblance of settled life began to emerge in cane-growing areas. Religious practices, which had been suspended during indenture, began to reemerge, as did traditional festivals, the Ram Lila, the Tazia, and others. Religion began to acquire a prominent role. Sanatani Hinduism was revived after the arrival of Pandit Totaram Sanadhya, who came to Fiji in 1893 and settled in Rewa. The reformist Arya Samaj was organized in 1902 at Samabula and began a school for its members; since then it has taken the lead in Indian education in Fiji. Muslims built a mosque at Navua around 1900 and another at Nausori soon afterwards. Mirza Khan, a *mullah,* who arrived in Fiji in 1898, played an important role in the religious education of Muslim Indians. By this time, political consciousness was emerging, and in such places as Rewa, which had a long history of Indian settlement, the beginnings of political organization and agitation. From there and elsewhere, petitions were sent to the government concerning a variety of issues, including social problems, land policy, and political representation.[74] The arrival of Indian leaders, such as Mani-lal Maganlal Doctor in 1912, accelerated the demand for more official attention to Indian problems.

By that time, life for Indians still under indenture was not as difficult as it had once been. The 1890s were the darkest days of the indenture experi-ence, a time of heart-rending rates of infant mortality, of excessive disci-pline and repressive legislation, and of a general unwillingness on the gov-ernment's part to guard the rights of the laborers.[75] This unwillingness continued even under Governor im Thurn, who said in 1903, "I was (and am) most reluctant to interfere with the Company's management of their own affairs, my view being that a Governor should not interfere except on urgent public grounds."[76] However, the indifference and callousness of the 1890s was giving way to the feeling that more needed to be done to protect the workers. In 1912 the daily task required of each laborer was redefined. "In the case of a male [the new requirement was for] that extent of task-work which can be performed by an ordinary able-bodied adult male immigrant, having the experience of the immigrant to whom it is assigned in six hours working steadily at such work, and in the case of a female three-fourths of such extent of work."[77] In 1913 another ordinance prohib-ited employers from arresting so-called deserters without first obtaining a warrant and from detaining workers longer than was necessary to com-plete their tasks. Other ordinances empowered the agent general of immi-gration to appear in defense of indentured immigrants charged with violat-ing the law in order to prevent irregular prosecution,[78] authorized the immigration officials to appoint scribes to facilitate communication with India,[79] and provided for resident inspectors at Ba, Lautoka, and Labasa and at the headquarters in Suva.[80]

Despite these improvements, life on remote plantations continued to echo the terrors and violence of the past. In Ba in February 1912, J. Barni-coot, in charge of the Rarawai Central Hospital, deliberately poured cor-rosive acid on the penis of *girmitiya* Polygaru and "thrashed him soundly" in a locked dispensary for some minor act of disobedience. He "only meant to frighten him," he said in explanation.[81] Barnicoot was shielded from the authorities by other overseers until he managed to escape to New Zealand. H. E. Forrest, another Ba overseer, gave Thermadu a black eye and a cut over the left temple because his breakfast curry was not satisfac-tory.[82] In March 1912, another Ba overseer forced Sewagram, an Indian worker, to drink kerosene in order to extract a confession to (allegedly) stealing a few shillings from someone in the lines. When Sewagram refused, he was beaten and tied to a tree the next day.[83] In Savusavu, Siga-toka, *girmitiya* Naraini was put to work breaking stone shortly after giving birth to a dead child, and when she was unable to complete the task was beaten senseless by Overseer Broomfield, who escaped with light punish-ment.[84] In Labasa in 1907, the stipendiary magistrate ordered and obtained a group of Fijians from Savusavu, their faces blackened with war paint, to break up a strike of Punjabi laborers, who were subsequently scattered to different parts of the colony. On the Olosara plantation in Sigatoka, turbulence was a regular feature of life, as fights broke out between the *girmitiya* and their overseers.[85] On coconut plantations, things were little better. One overseer told a visiting journalist: "Well, if we had to run things exactly on Government ordinance lines, we might as well shut up shop. What do I mean by that? I mean the stick. Oh, yes, we lick 'em; they know that if they do their task set down for them by a grand-motherly Government, everything will go smoothly, and if they don't they'll get a licking that isn't grandmotherly."[86]

At least occasionally, there was collaboration between the CSR and the Crown to prevent the leakage of embarrassing information about such incidents. This is well illustrated in the murder trial of Kemp, an overseer on the CSR's Drumasi Estate in Tavua, who had "a mania apparently for sampling the indentured women under his authority."[87] He compulsorily separated wives from their husbands, allocated them work in isolated places, and then molested them sexually. In 1916 he was murdered by some Indian men whose wives he had molested. J. W. Davidson of the Immigration Department was ostensibly retained by the Crown to appear for Ramkishen, Kemp's murderer, but in fact his retainer had been paid by the CSR in order to prevent any other solicitor from taking the case and bringing "out evidence of a nature more damaging to the Company and reflecting on the conduct of one of its officers and perhaps endanger their prospect of obtaining further supplies of indentured labor." Davidson pleaded Kemp's insanity (and made light of his assault on Ramkishen which started the attack), thereby removing the ground for Ramkishen to plead provocation. He produced no medical evidence to prove the insanity, and the district medical officer, who believed that Kemp had died not from the attack but from a heart attack brought on by the attack, was not cross-examined. The CSR was spared a probing investigation of the state of affairs on one of its plantations. Fortunately for Ramkishen, the chief justice thought that he (Ramkishen) had not been given the full opportunity of placing his case, and sentenced him to life imprisonment. Binda-chal, another indentured worker involved in the attack, was sentenced to death.[88]

Nonetheless, it is incorrect to portray the plantation managers and over-seers as entirely homogeneous, all equally corrupt or callous toward the people whose work they supervised. Often, they themselves were placed in difficult, even inhumane, situations, away from their families and familiar surroundings among people whom they despised, whose culture they did not understand, and whose language they did not speak. What they all had in common was power over the laborers to a degree that would distort even the most benign personality. As Colonial Secretary T. E. Fell wrote of them in 1921:

> The kindly man remained kindly, but became a trifle too ready to demand those external signs of respect which few benefactors of their fellow men are willing entirely to disregard. The ordinary man—here as elsewhere in the overwhelming majority—remained ordinary: too ready to see all whiteness in his favourites and all blackness in those who annoyed him, but always with the distinction that, within the little circle of his plantation, his whim could elevate or depress beyond all rhyme or reason. The brutal man became more brutal, once he found he could flog and kick with little fear of punishment or retaliation. The lustful man took his pick of the indentured women, and never realised that their readiness to come at his pimp's call was the most damning indictment of the whole system.[89]

Life in the lines, as the living quarters of the *girmitiya* were called, was generally sorrowful, especially in the early years. Family life was still unstable, living quarters crowded, privacy almost nonexistent. As K. L. Gillion has written, "With three bunks and firewood, field tools, cooking utensils cluttered about, smoke, soot, spilt food, flies, mosquitoes, perhaps fowls, or a dog as a precaution against theft, and until separate kitchens were required in 1908, a fire place as well, living conditions were neither comfortable nor sanitary."[90] South Indians, as late arrivals, were sent to remote, newly opened plantations and experienced anew the trials of the pioneer *girmitiya*. In addition, they suffered the cultural prejudices and social discrimination of their North Indian counterparts. One consequence of these compounded problems was that South Indians committed suicide in proportionately greater numbers than other *girmitiya*.

Perhaps the most vulnerable people in the lines were women. Presumed by outsiders to be of low moral character—"unstable and mercenary," according to the agent general of immigration in 1902;[91] "as joyously amoral as a doe rabbit," according to an Australian overseer;[92] or a "rudderless vessel [without any] controlling hand," according to C. F. Andrews[93]—they were traded even by their own men, abused by overseers and sirdars, and blamed for the ills of Indo-Fijian society. Sexual assaults on them were common and frequently ignored by authorities. But no burden was as serious for them as the widespread belief that they were responsible for the suicide rate among Indian men in Fiji, which was the highest among all the colonies of Indian laborers.[94] As the agent general of immigration wrote in 1909, "The number of cases in which the cause of suicides appears attributable to sexual jealousy is as usual large. It is connected with the disproportion of the sexes at present existing on most plantations and the consequent facility with which women abandon partners to whom they are bound by no legal ties for those who offer better inducement."[95]

Unable to obtain or, worse still, keep their women, who supposedly exploited their sexuality to promote their own material interests, the men, so the argument ran, descended into despondency and melancholia and committed suicide. Alternatively, they murdered their women first and then took their own lives.

The truth was more complex; women were as much the victims of indenture as men, and sometimes more so, victimized "not just by the actions, hostilities, or indifferences of men, but by the institutions of law, invested as they were with the majesty of the state, the formidability of the male jurists and lawyers, and the unbroken faith of the public."[96] No doubt some women were unscrupulous, but the harshness of plantation life and the anxiety attendant on the realization that there was no going back to India were sufficient to account for most suicides. Another factor that casts doubt on the emphasis placed on sexual jealousy as the most important cause of suicide is that 22 percent of the suicides occurred within six months of the deceased's residence in Fiji, 30 percent within the first year, and 75 percent within the first five years. Whatever the truth about the suicides, the publication of reports in India of the ill-treatment of Indian women in Fiji led to the abolition of indentured emigration to Fiji in 1916.

Fiji had been receiving attention from India at the turn of the century. The Sanderson Committee, appointed by the government of India, reported in 1910 that emigration was beneficial to India, to the emigrants, and, above all, to the colonies. The committee noted some problems, especially ill-treatment of migrants by overseers or law enforcement agencies, but concluded, with respect to Fiji: "The system appears to have worked well, to have been productive of excellent results, and the local conditions all seem to point to the expediency of its continuance."[97] Four years later another government of India–sponsored inquiry into Indian indenture, led by J. S. McNeill and Chimman Lal, concluded on a sanguine note about the importance as well as the advantages of the system wherever it was properly administered.[98]

These were minority viewpoints, however, and, in the circumstances, necessarily unpopular—not because indenture had brought no economic amelioration to many of those who had left India, for it obviously had; rather, because the moral argument prevailed. C. F. Andrews made the first of three visits to Fiji in 1916 and wrote scathing reports of moral collapse and social ills on the plantations. "The moral ruin is on the pitiful side," Andrews wrote in a typical passage. "Though there are beautiful and stately rivers in Fiji, no women are seen making their morning offerings: no temples rise on the banks. There is no household shrine. The outward life, which the Hindu women in the 'lines' lead in Fiji appears to be without love and without worship—a sordid round of mean and joyless tasks."[99] Other investigators, including J. W. Burton and Florence Garnham and several government officials, corroborated Andrews' findings.[100]

The public was outraged when Kunti's story of her narrow escape from rape by an overseer in Rewa reached India and by other reports of indentured women sometimes "serving" several men.[101] Mahadeva Shukla's lines, published in the popular Kanpur newspaper *The Pratap*, expressed widespread feelings:

> Behold, full of sorrow
> Surcharged with grief
> From beyond the ocean borne
> On the wings of wind
> Comes the wail of their weeping.

The indenture system was thus doomed, despite pleas from Fiji that the colony faced certain ruin without the continued importation of Indian labor and despite promises of major reforms if the system were allowed to continue. As prominent Indian nationalist leader Pandit Madan Mohan Malviya said, "When India is asking for a rightful place in the Empire, this badge of helotry ought not to remain and ought to be completely swept away."[102] Andrews also urged that the system be abolished immediately:

> There will be other evils, such as our inhuman treatment of our own depressed classes, which must be remedied. We shall not forget these, or become self-righteous. But here is an immediate issue, which the whole of India with one united voice can deal with now, while all our hearts are warm and all our consciences are stirred. Here is an issue which is simple, clear and definite, not complicated or obscure. Here is an issue which appeals to the common heart of our humanity, deeper than all divisions of race and sect and creed. Here is an issue, which if rightly and honourably faced, will raise us as a nation in the eyes of the whole civilized world.[103]

The last ship carrying indentured laborers, *Sutlej V*, arrived in Fiji on 11 November 1916; all remaining indentures of Indian laborers in the colony were canceled effective 1 January 1920.

The 1910s: Protest, War, and Death

During the second decade of the twentieth century, the pace of change in the colony began to quicken. Some old issues were finally resolved, and some new ones emerged to complicate matters even further, including the struggle to end the indenture system, the impact of World War I, and the havoc wrought by the 1919 influenza epidemic. Before the 1910s, criticism of the government and its policies was muted and easily managed, often by deportation or internal exile, as in the case of the Serua chiefs, who refused to pay taxes and supported federation with New Zealand. But the situation changed in the second decade. Before 1910 the government mainly had the agitated European planters to deal with. After that date, popular non-European leaders emerged, among whom Apolosi Nawai and Manilal Maganlal Doctor were especially important. These men were different from each other in temperament, social and educational background, and political goals and strategies. In their own separate ways, however, both challenged the premises and foundations of the colonial order and worked to obtain a better life for their people. Both were also popular and charismatic, and both paid the price for dissidence. Their separate stories shed light on the troubled evolution of Fiji in the early decades of the twentieth century.

Manilal Doctor

Manilal was not a doctor but a lawyer, trained in London. He was born in 1881 into a high-achieving, politically prominent family in the princely state of Baroda, India, where he received his early education before attending the Middle Temple to complete his barristership. He then returned to India and joined the Servants of India Society before settling in Mauritius, where he led efforts to improve the lot of Indian immigrants, much as Mohandas Karamchand Gandhi had gone to Natal to assist in the struggles of the Indians settled there. Manilal was an activist who resented even petty acts of social and political discrimination, and he fought tenaciously for their removal. One story illustrates this well. During an appearance in court, Manilal was told by the presiding magistrate that he could not wear both his turban and his shoes in the courtroom, but must remove one or the other as supposedly was the custom in India. Manilal resisted the directive and won his right to have it set aside. To spread his philosophy, he began a newspaper, the first issue of which appeared in Port Louis on 15 March 1909, its headline proclaiming, "Liberty of Individuals! Fraternity of Men! Equality of Races!" Manilal wrote:

> If the true destiny of man is divine, one man or one race cannot, morally speaking, enslave, dominate, or even exploit another for mere private gain. If the political and economic conditions of today have not yet permitted a fulfillment of this principle in practice, there is no reason to believe . . . that the secret forces of the world are not in fact tending towards the invisible ideal by an unnoticed and unnoticeable march of human development.[104]

From this background, Manilal came to Fiji in December 1912, apparently at the request of a group of Indian workers whose indentures had expired and who wanted an English-speaking Indian lawyer to help them in their various struggles.[105] He set up practice in Rewa, then the primary area of Indian settlement, and began his work, which was at first social and charitable. In 1915 he petitioned the governor to amend an 1892 ordinance to allow Indian girls between the ages of twelve and fifteen to marry without parental consent. His concern in doing so was not to encourage early marriage but to prevent the practice of mercenary parents trafficking in their daughters.[106] He also petitioned for a relaxation of divorce laws to take "account of the prevalent disproportion of the sexes and its attendant evils."[107] He joined Indians in petitioning the governor to commute the death sentences of Indians convicted for murder because "the majority of those found guilty of such crimes are otherwise quiet and law-abiding, and the murders, for which they are condemned to death, are not due to any murderous instinct in them, but really to jealousy which to the Indian mind is a legitimate and honourable thing."[108] He wanted Hindi-speaking interpreters permanently attached to the Supreme Court, as English translators often missed nuances of the Indian languages and thus of cases in which Indians were involved.[109] In 1916 he even urged the government to accept the offer of some thirty Indians to form an Indian platoon to "take part in the responsibilities of the Empire at such a critical time as the present."[110] The offer was refused. A large part of Manilal's time and energy was spent defending indentured laborers against charges of assault, fraud, and other such offenses. His insistence that an overseer had "no right to assault his laborers under any circumstances" brought him into conflict with the powerful planters, who were inclined to view their laborers as their property to deal with as they saw fit.[111]

Inevitably, Manilal's quest for reform in the status and treatment of Indians brought him into conflict with colonial society. He sought membership for Indians on the Suva Municipal Council. To Sir Henry Jackson's argument that enfranchising Indians and Polynesians would introduce corruption into municipal elections, Manilal wrote, with more truth than tact, "Instead of welcoming such [qualified] Indians who have given yeomen service to the island, and associate them with the work of the administration and extend to them higher privileges of participation in the legislature of the Colony, the Saxon element, rather the Australian element of the colonists, is trying to stifle their growth and destroy them as it did the Bushman of Australia."[112] On the exclusion of Indian (and Fijian) children from public schools, he wrote, "Lord Sinha's son who would be free to attend Oxford or Cambridge would not be allowed into the Suva Public School, whereas the son of an ordinary blackboot in England would be able to attend the school."[113]

Manilal started a bilingual English-Hindi newspaper, *The Indian Settler*, in 1916, the first newspaper in the Indian community (Figure 2). It quickly became a vehicle for expressing Indian grievances and educating the community politically. Under Manilal's leadership, the British Indian Association of Fiji, founded in 1911, became an important channel of communication with the government and the outside world and helped make Manilal the most effective and widely respected leader of the Indians in the early years of this century. As such, he was also a thorn in the side of the government, which was determined to marginalize him. As far as the colonial government was concerned, Manilal was the "worst enemy of Indian progress in Fiji."[114] Consequently, when the governor nominated the first Indian member of the Legislative Council in 1916, it was not Manilal, but a wealthy but unlettered and pliant landowner, Badri Maharaj, from Rakiraki. The choice was widely criticized by Indians, but Manilal was not chosen in part on the technical ground that he was not a British subject, as the Letters Patent required, but a subject of the princely state of Baroda. Because of this snub, Manilal assumed a more confrontational stance in his dealings with the government, and the government began looking for a way to silence him. The opportunity came in 1920. Because of his alleged activity in the strike of that year, Manilal was served an order prohibiting his residence in all major Indian areas of the colony. Facing the almost certain prospect of financial ruin and political marginalization, he left Fiji.

Apolosi Nawai

Apolosi Nawai, too, was a charismatic man who fought the ethos and ideology of British colonialism. The causes he championed, in his inimitable way, have endeared him to thousands of his fellow Fijians, to many of whom he still is a legendary figure. These causes also earned him the wrath of the colonial establishment and the Fijian chiefs, and they eventually combined to defeat him and his vision for the future of the Fijian people. His opponents puzzled to the end whether Apolosi was "a freak of a genius, a great individualist in a land where communalism is still the native law, or whether he be a mere seditious imposter living at the expense of his brethren, or a puppet in the hands of unscrupulous agents."[115]

Reliable information on Apolosi's background is scanty, though he described himself as "a true Fijian." He was born in Nadi around 1876[116] and first came to public notice around 1914, as a result of his efforts to form the Viti Company, or Fiji Company. As early as 1908, as he later recalled, he had an "earnest desire to start in business because I was thinking of my friends who were so poor."[117] By 1911 he was urging Fijians to go into large-scale commercial agriculture—coconuts, bananas, maize, rice, and cane planting—"so that they should look after their money and also should not lease their lands in the dark." He launched his Fiji Company in 1914 with seven directors, all Europeans, and a capital of £10,000. Some of this capital—£3,000, which he described as a present—Apolosi used for himself. This led the European directors, eager to assert control over the venture, to charge him with fraud. When a warrant for his arrest was issued, Apolosi, who was then in the Yasawas, resisted, according to

The Indian Settler.

A MEDIUM FOR THE ADVOCACY OF THE INDIAN CAUSE IN FIJI

VOL. 1.—No. 3-4.   SUVA, FIJI, MARCH-APRIL, 1917.   Price One Shilling.

OURSELVES.

We are sorry that we have not ben able to supply our subscribers with their March number. We nad to change editors twice ere this, and the printers on whom we had relied for publication failed us at the eleventh hour. With considerable difficulty we have ben able to make other arrangements for printing and publishing; and we now have the pleasure of laying before the public our March and April issue amalgamated. We humbly hope that our shortcomings will be excused by our indulgent subscribers, who appreciate the difficulties of our task: for we know that they will relish the present number with double zest: of this we are sure.

CASTE IN FIJI.

The "Fiji Times" and the "Western Pacific Herald" have been both writing of late about the condition in Cumming Street. Whilst we agree with our contemporaries in deploring this condition, we cannot approve of some of the suggestions or remedies discussed. Some of the Fiji-made white aristocracy desire to segregate themselves from Indians, Fijians and Polynesians, and they suggest that these latter should be driven out of the township of Suva after business hours to leave these angelic beings in their paradise to rest. The idea of separate locations is no stranger to us. We have seen them in the Transvaal, and we may say that they are part and parcel of the existing Hindu civilisation in India. In the Transvaal Indians are made to live in separate streets outside towns, just as in Hindu India, the low castes such as "Bhangis, Mehtars or Chamars" are living in streets where no other castes live. But the Indian caste is not based on the degree of fairness possessed by the skin, nor on the money possessed, nor on the standard of comfort or luxury attain-

ed; but purely and simply on theocratic considerations solidified as birth-rights and birth-duties. The Kshatriya ruler of a kingdom is theocratically inferior to his Brahman cook, who cannot eat food touched by his master or his master's caste, and, therefore, there can be no idea of inter-marriage between the two stocks; but for purely social and political life there is no want of respect on the part of the higher caste towards the lower. Thus even a Mahommedan or a European Christian or Jew may get the best attention, first-class hospitality, the greatest respect from a Hindu of high caste; only the Mahommedan or European must not touch the food or drink and the family gods (idols in their place of worship) of that Hindu, no matter how humble or poor he may be.. So the Indian caste is not at all based on considerations of wealth or colour; on the contrary, the highest caste—the Brahmans—are expected to remain poor but proud in their learning and professorship of all knowledge, spiritual, secular, economic, political and moral. They are expected to devote their whole lives to the worship of Saraswati (the goddess of learning) and dominate the other castes purely and simply by their religious merit.

So that the Fijian caste system now proposed will have none of the redeeming features of the Hindu castes, and will only be distinction based on colour and wealth; and is it seriously meant that the "natives" in Cumming Street are behaving any worse than, for example, white people in the East End of London or similar parts in Sydney or corresponding areas of any European city in the world?

The remedy will be the same in each case. Educate these lower orders or their children, improve their economic, moral and sanitary condition, raise them step by step to a higher standard, by guaranteeing bet-

ter environments; without this what would the present Australian population have been? Judging by caste and birth where, would they be? The remedy surely is not segregation.

SWADESHI.
INCREASED DUTY ON ENGLISH COTTON GOODS IMPORTED IN INDIA.

SUPPORT OF HOME INDUSTRIES.

We are exceedingly pleased to learn from the latest cables that the tariff reform agitated for by the Indian Congress leaders for nearly half a century has approached realisation by the recent imposition of 7½ per cent. duty on imported cotton goods. This act of barest justice, though alone very late, is not therefore the less welcome, and it is one more peg on which to hang our hopes for the progress of the Indian people in India and outside India.

COME IN BOY.

Recently Mr. Manilal had occasion to attend the office of a well-known professional brother in Suva. Mr Manilal had been waiting outside for permission to enter, when the European clerk, who had not had the time to look carefully to ascertain who the visitor was—very likely he had only vaguely noticed some dark figure waiting outside—mechanically pronounced the words "Come in, boy," without raising his eyes from his desk, but when he saw it was Mr. Manilal he, of course, used the usual expressions of greeting in a proper manner, and most courteously went through the little business Mr. Manilal had occasion to transact. This incident shows once more the tendency—almost universal—to address all Indians as "boys." We might suggest that Indians should reply to such epithets by saying, "Yes, girls," and then this objectionable practice would receive a check.

Figure 2. (Courtesy National Archives of Fiji)

various contemporary accounts, and was jailed for eighteen months at Korovou. Once out of jail, Apolosi continued his efforts among Fijians and courted controversy and official wrath by making remarks that the government labeled seditious and considered were intended to bring it into contempt. According to government reports, Apolosi interfered with the performance of communal work by challenging the authority and power of government officials, enticing women to leave their homes to work for and live with him, supplying alcohol to Fijians who had no permit to consume it, and claiming supernatural powers for himself. As a result, he was exiled to Rotuma for seven years in 1917.

He returned from Rotuma in 1924 a disillusioned but undaunted man and resumed his activities under the watchful eyes of the government.[118] Over the next few years, Apolosi was accused of having sex with a girl under sixteen years of age (for this charge there was insufficient evidence for prosecution); of claiming to be the rightful king of Fiji; of prophesying the departure of Europeans from Fiji; of promising Fijians economic deliverance from Europeans; and of assuming supernatural powers in a manner reminiscent of the Tuka movement of the 1870s. These assorted claims and accusations and his grandiose gestures of power led to further detention in Rotuma, beginning on 14 January 1930. For the ensuing dozen years, Apolosi remained in detention. Soon after World War II reached the Pacific, he was deemed a security risk and in early 1942 was exiled to New Zealand. He died in 1946 on the small island of Yacata in the Koro Sea.

It is not necessary to dwell at length on Apolosi's alleged millenarian proclamations and proclivities. They were neither unique nor particularly dangerous. Visionary men, hounded by their government and rejected by the people they would lead, have, throughout history, claimed a measure of supernatural power to keep their efforts alive. Apolosi was no exception. Moreover, Apolosi should not be held responsible, as he was by the colonial government, for words uttered and disreputable deeds committed in his name by his followers. In any case, Apolosi disavowed the most exaggerated claims attributed to him, insisting that they were the work of his enemies. Nor is it necessary to highlight Apolosi's racist utterances about Indians. He was less subtle in these than other better educated Fijian leaders then or since, but he was not alone in wanting to "rid Fiji of Indians."[119]

At the heart of Apolosi's message was a desire to better the lives of the Fijian people. He wanted economic autonomy for them, and toward that end he worked to build a Fijian-owned company that would operate for the benefit of the Fijian people. The following resolutions, passed at a Viti Company meeting at Draubata in January 1915, manifest the flavor and direction of his thinking:

That we natives should make our contracts with the company with the idea
of keeping our lands in our own hands and all produce therefrom
both things found in the water and things that grow on land.
The company should have a store in every locality; these should be built
and there should be no dealings with Europeans therefrom.
The Government should be petitioned to raise rents and the prices on the
sale of land.

The Government should be petitioned to hand over the Crown grants.
The cleaning of towns and house buildings and similar (Government
   directed) work should be abolished.[120]

What these resolutions amount to is a program of economic autonomy
centering on keeping Fijian land in Fijian hands and restricting whatever
interfered with the achievement of that goal, whether the activity of the
colonial government or the tribal chiefs or the presence of Indian laborers
and intermediaries.

   Apolosi was especially concerned to remove from Fiji the rampant grip
of European commercial control. A letter written in 1914 expressing his
views to the chiefs conveys the spirit that pervaded his endeavor:

> The cause (or the beginning) of this thing is through the Europeans here in
> Fiji swindling us, the price of all our things are different, as we have seen in
> years past until the present day. Their swindling us will never cease. This is
> why I am writing to you my friends, the Chiefs of Fiji, to be good natured
> and stir (or move) yourselves with the spirit of confidence and let us help in
> helping this matter, to be use to your people, and to us in the sale of all our
> things."[121]

To accomplish his purpose, Apolosi worked to make Fijians more conscious of the role of their own apathy in perpetuating their problems. He
expressed his concerns at a meeting at Nakorovou in Tavua on 31 August
1917:

> Time passes, and with it passes opportunity. The worst of it is that you do not
> understand the use of time. You wake up and you chat with your wives.
> About 11 o'clock you get up and go and see your garden, and what do you
> accomplish?—Nothing; the time has simply passed. The older times were
> very different to this; and it is due to the apathy of the Chiefs. Please under-
> stand that I want what used to be done in the past to be done again now. Let
> us learn a lesson from the apathy of our ancestors. The result was that they
> were conquered. [The Chiefs] pay heed to the words of others; they do not
> consider the people dependent upon them. . . .
>   I beg you not to lease your land. I beg you to hand over to me control of
> your produce, to sell for you, and you will get good prices. Be energetic and
> get up early every morning and go and plant all kinds of produce and sell it to
> the Viti Company Limited, for your own good. The reason for our ignorance
> is due to our chiefs all throughout Fiji who sell their men. They give their
> men to be sold at 3/-each. How is this possible? It is done in ignorance and
> degeneracy. I see men working in Suva. They get 2/-each a day. The pay for
> your labour, carrying cases, is far less than the cost of the food of a horse in a
> stable. The Europeans call us fools. It is as though we laborers were wood. I
> beg you, my friends, stay in your own town, dig the soil—your own soil,
> make use of it. Take the great profit of it yourself for this is the time for it,

and the things we can do for our individual benefit in these days cannot be hidden from us. It is open to us to put money in the bank, to have cheque books, and over drafts of over 20 pounds."[122]

Apolosi concluded by saying, "I cannot turn left, right, forward, backward, up or down, with the crowd of enemies that are about us."

His enemies were many. First were the Europeans whose interests were directly threatened by the Fijian company. Apolosi continually argued that he was deliberately given bad advice by European advisors who wanted to sabotage his efforts. G. L. Barrow, one of the European traders living in the heart of the Apolosi territory in Colo West, was almost hysterical in his denunciation of Apolosi's Company: "I have had continual and continuous evidence of the disloyalty, dishonesty, rapacity, unscrupulous mendacity and malignant antagonism for the '*kai vavalagi*' and the Government and the white administration in state and Church which have characterized its propaganda and methods. The Fiji Produce Agency is a malignant cancer in the native body politic, which is daily and hourly eating deeper and deeper into the vitals of native loyalty and orderliness." The only solution to the problem as far as Barrow was concerned was disbanding the company.[123]

Many Fijian chiefs, especially those from coastal and maritime provinces who were loyal to the government, also opposed Apolosi. Apolosi accused them of undermining the interests of their own people, taking bribes from Indians for leases, and otherwise impeding the prosperity of the *taukei*. "The people of Fiji are in a bad plight because of the orders of their chiefs," Apolosi said. "Very few people are in a bad plight because of their own decisions about themselves. All this gives me great pain but I put up with my own bad treatment. Chiefs of Fiji look after themselves, never mind whether their people are in a bad state or not. The Chiefs' orders to their people are strong on account of their working in the Government."[124] Such remarks (and Apolosi's evident flair for flamboyant living) provoked widespread criticism from, among others, Ratu Sukuna, an articulate spokesman for the conservative chiefs: "The application of the principle [of equality] to a society that bristles, like all primitive societies, with inequality, is fundamentally unsound. It is historically precocious, logically fallacious, and practically pernicious."[125] Apolosi dreamed of Fijians competing effectively in the emerging arena of modern life, and Sukuna affirmed the colonial (and Polynesian) idea that Fiji's essence was chiefly hierarchy. Apolosi's inspirations were rooted in the less hierarchical, more Melanesian elements of Fiji's traditions.

The government itself was unable to cope with a man who questioned the foundations of European rule with his fierce insistence that "Fiji is for Fijians." Apolosi was working outside the accepted parameters of the colonial regime, to which his vision posed a threat. In 1914 the district commissioner of Lautoka, accustomed to expecting unquestioning subservience from Fijians and Indians, wrote that "from a purely native point of view the conduct of the so-called Company promoters is gross impertinence and is tantamount to contempt of the government and the authority of the native chiefs. These young men swagger through the country dressed up in smart clothes making the most foolish and impossible assertions."[126] To reassert its control, the government in 1917 passed an ordinance prohibiting any person or body of people from forming a Fijian company without the permission of the governor-in council.[127] Instead of encouraging Fijian enterprise, the colonial government was trying to extinguish it.

To the government's claim his program was subversive, Apolosi's reply was powerful:

> I have always wished with my whole heart to attain righteousness and cleanness, truth and wisdom, but I have not the strength to attain them as I have had no one to take an interest in me or hold me up or lead me out of this black darkness into which I had fallen. In this condition it was as though I were covered with worms and everything repulsive. Many saw me, laughed at me or mocked at me. It was as though they sucked my blood and wrung the water out of my soul and there was no place to which I could turn from this overwhelming darkness. The men who are righteous and clean, wise and sensible laughed at me and mocked me when I was about to sink into oblivion with the Viti Company Limited. They saw me with their eyes, but no man was merciful enough to give me a helping hand, and what I did I did without wisdom, enlightenment or sense.

If he were only given proper encouragement, Apolosi continued, "You will see what a useful and admirable man I will be, and how I will assist the carrying out of all useful orders which emanate from you, the hands of the government, for the better of the native population."[128] Some officials at the Colonial Office agreed. "An extraordinary man," one of them wrote, "whose energy and ability might have made him a useful instrument of government if it had been possible to direct them into proper channels." Another official felt that the colonial government had treated Apolosi with undue arbitrariness, taking extreme and "questionable" measures against him for minor breaches of the law. Apolosi "is by no means a perfect character," he wrote, but "one cannot feel satisfied that he has been entirely fairly treated, particularly when it is remembered that his periods of confinement have been the result of secret trials by the officials themselves."[129] Another official, however, called Apolosi a "sort of Fijian counterpart of the popular conception of Rasputin."

Apolosi died broken and dispirited, and historians have not always been kind to him. The tendency in recent years has been to blame him for his own failures by focusing on his grand, melodramatic gestures and the

intrinsic weaknesses of his program. But anyone who dared to think as
Apolosi did stood little chance of success in a world as rigidly codified as
colonial Fiji. It was not yet possible to challenge the system successfully, as
Apolosi and Manilal both sought to do. Rather, it was a place for those
who played the game according to rules established by the government.
Even so, it would be a mistake to see Apolosi and Manilal as failures.
Their fight encouraged others in later years. As legend and inspiration to
dissident Fijians, Apolosi subsequently became a more important figure
than he was in his own lifetime. Manilal's battles would be taken up soon
after he departed the scene.

World War I

Unfortunately for Apolosi and Manilal, their struggles coincided with
World War I, which was not a Pacific war in the sense that World War II
was twenty years later. As a member of the British Empire, Fiji felt its ebbs
and flows and contributed generously to the British war effort in both men
and money. The colony contributed altogether £600,777 to various patriotic funds, exclusive of costs borne by individuals raising funds to equip
and transport troops.[130] The Fijian people themselves contributed generously by raising funds through festivals and direct levies, though the contribution was not evenly acquired from all the provinces. In a not untypi-
cal incident, sixty-three people from Lomaloma and forty-four from
Mualevu in Lau sent fly whisks made from coconut fiber and tan woods on
their own initiative to be sold at auction for the benefit of the Fiji Contingent Fund. The *buli* of Lomaloma said of the incident, "This is but a small
offering. We are a poor people just now. Hurricanes have smitten us many
times, and the land has been withered by drought. Had we plenty of
money we would have sent it. Take, therefore, this small gift in the meantime."[131] Tailevu contributed to the Patriotic Fund in a similar spirit: "We
think of the women and men who are in distress in England on account of
their relations who have given their lives for us. We also think of our province in that our reputation should be maintained."[132] Lau and Lomaiviti
gave enough to purchase three motor ambulances for the British Red
Cross and subscribed periodically thereafter for their maintenance.
Cakaudrove provided sufficient funds to purchase equipment and maintain a cot at the Star and Garter Home for disabled soldiers and sailors.

In Rewa, the Provincial Council contributed £1,500 to buy a plane for
the Royal Flying Corps, requesting that it be named "Rewa, Fiji" and
bear the inscription "Presented by the natives of the Rewa Province, Colony of Fiji, for the use of the Royal Flying Corps."[133] In like manner,
Roko Tui Kadavu, Ratu Kiniavuai Nanovo, wrote the governor on 31
August 1914, offering five hundred to six hundred men to "go and fight at
Samoa and so help our British Government."[134] The offer was refused

because Fijians were enrolled only for "handling and transporting of cargo and handling punts and small boats."[135] Denied "the privilege of fighting side by side with the English soldiers of the King,"[136] Ratu Sukuna crossed the English Channel and joined the French army, in which he distinguished himself and won the *Medal Militaire*. About one hundred Fijians worked as members of the Labor Corps at Calais, but the British refused all offers by Fijians, Indians, and Part-Europeans to enroll in military service. In Fiji offers of platoons were not accepted, and some of those rejected went to New Zealand at their own expense, where they enlisted in the forces of the dominion.[137]

In areas where the Viti Company was strong, sentiments were quite different. There, British defeat was prophesied and eagerly awaited. In the Yasawas in 1918, for example, a rumor that the British had surrendered to the Germans was met with great rejoicing and beating of the *lali* 'wooden slit drum'. The expectation that now Fijians would pay no taxes and meet no other official obligations had allegedly been confirmed in a letter from a government official at Nadarivatu to one Sailosi. Such rumors were widespread. As one government official wrote, "If one is going to prosecute or banish all Fijians who spread rubbishy rumours or mouth largely idle disaffection, the gaols will be full and half the islands of the Western Pacific will have their Fijian exile."[138]

The response of Europeans in Fiji to the war effort was enthusiastic. The first contingent enlisted left for Europe on 31 December 1914. Altogether, 430 in a total population of 4,000 left Fiji voluntarily to join the military effort, 240 at their own expense. In total, 788 men of all nationalities from Fiji served in one military capacity or another, including 101 Fijians in the Transport Corps. These men saw action in practically every theater of war, from Mesopotamia to the North Sea and Africa, while Fiji medical service personnel also made their contribution. Though few, the Fiji men performed with distinction, winning more than one hundred commissions and thirty-four decorations. No women were permitted to serve.

In Fiji itself, German nationals or naturalized British subjects of German descent suffered the predictable fate of their counterparts in other allied areas. Local European planters from the Nadi area were indignant that Germans there were going about their business, planting with Fijian labor and enjoying British protection while England was fighting Germany.[139] They urged the government to intern German nationals and German-born naturalized British subjects. Though unsuccessful in that endeavor, they did force the governor to pass a bill that limited the movement of "aliens" in Fiji, restricted their residence, and curtailed certain of their freedoms, including the freedom to carry arms.

Twenty-six of the aliens were sent for internment to Australia or New Zealand and in the aftermath had their properties confiscated and their

businesses dissolved. Such, for example, was the fate of the firm of Heder-
man and Evers.[140] When the naturalized Germans returned from internment after the war, they were greeted with abuse: "No Huns Wanted,"
"Remember Lusitania," "No Squareheads in Fiji."[141] Many local Europeans supported forced repatriation of all Germans who had been
deported, and others thought that the German returnees should be denied
the right of naturalization and be prohibited from acquiring property and
the right to vote. Most of the Germans therefore went elsewhere, to Argen-
tina, Java, or Switzerland; the few who remained lived quietly.

World War I was a vicarious experience for most people in Fiji, though
some of its ripples did reach the islands. Contingency plans were drawn to
guard ports and strategic facilities and to evacuate men, women, and children by special CSR trains. Lautoka, the sugar town, had forty-four rifles
and eleven thousand rounds of ammunition for use in the event of
attack.[142] In addition, censorship was imposed on all forms of public communication, and trading with enemy aliens was prohibited, as was all
trade in arms and ammunition; passports were issued to track the movement of people.[143]

Fiji's request to mount an attack on German Samoa was not granted,
though ten men from the islands were members of the New Zealand Expe-
ditionary Force that went to Samoa; they proudly recalled later that one of
their number had hauled down the German flag in Apia.[144] Two other epi-
sodes in the war were much talked about in later years. One was the story
of the German warship *Seeädler,* commanded by Dresden-born Count Felix
von Luckner. This ship left the Atlantic, having sunk thirteen allied ships
there, for the Pacific, where, after sinking the schooner *A. B. Johnson,* it
was wrecked at Tahiti. Leaving some of his men there, von Luckner and
the rest of his crew made their way to Fiji in an open twenty-six-foot boat.
Arriving in Fijian waters, where they apparently intended to capture a
larger vessel in which to escape to Germany, von Luckner and his men
were trapped at Wakaya, eight miles east of Levuka, captured, and
handed over to allied forces.

Another story retold with much amusement in later years was how the
governor of Fiji had bluffed to lead potential German attackers away from
the islands.[145] Early on 15 September 1914, the wireless station in Suva
passed on to the governor a message intercepted between two German
ships of war about two hundred miles from Suva. The governor had just
learned in a coded message from Apia that Admiral von Spee had put into
the harbor with the *Scharnhorst* and the *Gneisenau,* guns trained on the town.
No shots had been fired, however, and an hour later, the ships headed in a
southwesterly direction toward Fiji. What if they attacked? The governor's
private secretary later recounted the fear that prospect created:

> It would mean town with red roofs peeping through the luxuriant green of
> tropic foliage, with but a handful of armed and harmless men, a crowd of

weakling Indians, of laughing and innocent Fijians, of refined and cultured
Europeans, men of position and ladies of quality, would become shambles,
the pink of the dawn would turn to crimson, the crimson of blood, red blood,
and the scarlet of tongues of flame, of devastating fire, ever swelling in volume, fanned and whipped by shrieking shell, the crash of explosives and the
rumble of falling masonry. Town of almost voluptuous loveliness transformed
with a spectacle of hideous ruin.[146]

To prevent that, the governor, thinking quickly, sent an open message:
"To Admiral H.M.S. *Australia.* Thanks for message. Shall expect you
tomorrow at daylight." The Germans picked up the message, accepted it
as authentic, and laughed at the governor for his carelessness. "Damn fool
of an English Governor, he gives the show away," the governor's secretary
later said, recalling the content of a German document. The Germans
quickly turned and headed for neutral waters, convinced they had the better of the episode, though in fact the *Australia* was two thousand miles away
and well beyond range of receiving cables from Fiji. The Germans had
fallen for the governor's "damn folly."

Influenza

Fiji was not as fortunate at the end of the war, when it was devastated by
an influenza epidemic that was a far greater tragedy for the islands than
World War I. The virus was introduced by the *Tulane,* returning to Fiji on
a voyage from Western Samoa and Tonga on 14 November 1918, though
it might already have been introduced by SS *Niagara,* which had arrived on
9 October from Vancouver and Honolulu with eighty-three cases of fever
of "unknown origin."[147] The first affected were Fijian laborers aboard the
Tulane, but soon the disease spread. Its impact was swift and merciless:
sudden fever, sore throat, inflammation of the lungs or bronchi, hemor-
rhaging in the lungs, coughing up of blood, and then death, usually within
three to four days of the appearance of the first symptoms. The effort to
combat the disease was hampered by harsh topography, unusually wet
weather, unfamiliarity with the disease, unwillingness or inability of the
infected to follow medical advice, and the absence of a third of Fiji's medical personnel at the war. Medical help from New Zealand arrived after the
epidemic was over, delayed by the dislocation of steamship service as a
result of labor troubles in Australia and New Zealand. The government
vessel, the *Ranadi,* was undergoing repairs. Nothing, it seemed, went
right.
    Eighty percent of all Fijians and Indians and 40 percent of the Europe-
ans in the islands were infected, and 8,149 deaths were reported. Among
the dead were 5,154 Fijians (5.66 percent of the Fijian population), 2,553
Indians (4.17 percent), 69 Europeans (1.4 percent), 76 Part-Europeans
(2.75 percent), and 293 others (6.93 percent).[148] These figures do not quite

tell the full story. The epidemic attacked the different age groups differently. Those under age fifteen who contracted the disease suffered lightly, as did those over forty-five. Particularly susceptible were men and women in the prime of life, and the incidence of death was highest "in robust males with an inclination to adiposity." As one official noted, "The loss to the country is increased by the fact that so large a percentage of the deaths occurred among those in the prime of life."[149]

Regional variations were evident. In Ba one out of every twelve Fijians died, but the more isolated Colo provinces escaped lightly. In Ovalau 90 percent of the population were infected, and 7.3 percent of the people of Levuka died.[150] In the islands of the Lomaiviti group, during the height of the epidemic, few villages had more than two or three persons capable of attending to others. In Taveuni the unindentured laboring population, alone and with little communal support, was particularly badly hit. In contrast, those on the plantations were largely insulated from the disease and had access to plantation hospitals; the employers had a very great interest in ensuring their survival.[151]

The epidemic opened up long-standing social fissures. The Nailaga people of Ba refused to come to the assistance of their old enemies from Bulu and took perverse pleasure in the latter's tragedy. "Nailaga was rather amused than grieved to learn of Bulu's troubles and deaths," wrote one official.[152] Indians everywhere complained bitterly of being neglected, a complaint the district commissioner of Rewa admitted to be valid,[153] but the colonial officials accused the Indians of "lamentable indifference to the suffering of their fellows." Fijian traditionalists took the opportunity to remind the government that the death rate among Fijians would have been much higher had it not been for the smooth working of the recently criticized communal system. On this point, Secretary of Native Affairs G. V. Maxwell wrote:

> Personally, I am convinced that the communal system and communal mode of life of the Fijians saved the race during the epidemic from practical extermination. We have in Suva an example of Fijians living independently in scattered dwellings. If it had not been for the European voluntary workers, I think that few of them would be alive today. In such conditions one household takes no interest whatever in the other. Where they live in native villages, the blood-tie is always there, and even if there are only half a dozen left unaffected by the disease, they will do something for their suffering relations."[154]

In fact, the effects of the communal system on the disease cannot be established one way or another. If the communal system provided support for those with the disease, the presence of so many people in a confined communal space might have encouraged its spread. In any case, Fiji was fortunate in this instance to escape the fate of Samoa, where the influenza epidemic killed an estimated 21 percent of the population, led to widespread dissatisfaction with New Zealand rule, and provided fuel for the Mau movement. Nevertheless, the epidemic left deep scars on the psyche of those who lived through it. It became a time marker. Subsequently, everyone reckoned age, experience, or circumstance in reference to the *badi bimari,* the big epidemic.

The first two decades of the twentieth century brought many changes to Fiji and its peoples. The Gordon-Thurston orthodoxy had been scrutinized, reexamined, and partly reformed. The ambitions of the planters had been contained, though within the framework of a larger role in the affairs in the colony. The idea of federation with New Zealand died a quiet, largely unmourned death. Indentured emigration had ended, despite much unheeded lament from the colony about the certain ruin it faced without an assured supply of cheap immigrant labor. Apolosi and Manilal, persistent thorns in the side of the government and the established order, had been subdued. However, like the issues they raised, they were harbingers of things to come. In the aftermath of the Great War, the players, but not the game, were changing in colonial Fiji.

2 The Foundations Challenged: 1920–1939

The year 1920 began on a historic note. On 1 January the indenture system for Indian labor was formally abolished, and all existing contracts were canceled. Thus ended an institution that had fundamentally altered the social and economic landscape of Fiji and deeply affected all who lived and worked within it. For the next two decades, Fiji would grapple with the implications and consequences of its termination. What role would the freed Indians play, or be allowed to play, in the colony that was now their home and in which they were no longer content to be just menial laborers but full British subjects demanding the rights and opportunities that status entitled them to? How would Fijians and Europeans react to the Indo-Fijians' demands and to the supposed encroachments on their own rights and privileges the demands entailed in the increasingly plural society of Fiji? Would the political system be opened up to accommodate the Indo-Fijians, and, if so, at what if any cost to others?

These questions dominated politics and public debate in the decades between the two world wars. Naturally, the Indo-Fijian community was in the vanguard of the movement for change, and Europeans fought hard to maintain their privileged position. For their part, Fijian leaders joined their European counterparts in the Legislative Council to stem the tide of change, though their concerns were largely parochial, involving problems of social and economic change affecting the Fijian community. To understand the interactions and rivalries between these three communities in the interwar years, it is necessary to understand the changing economic and social contexts in which those interactions and rivalries were played out.

The 1920s brought unprecedented changes in the structure of the sugar industry in Fiji. The Colonial Sugar Refining Company (CSR), long the dominant economic enterprise in the colony, became the sole miller of cane when it bought out the Penang Sugar Mill in 1926. During this period, the company also completed the transition from large plantations and estates to small farms as the basic unit of cane cultivation. In the late nineteenth century, the CSR had produced practically all its sugar cane with indentured labor. Beginning in 1909, however, it began leasing some of its plantations to independent contractors, mostly former officers, a practice that collapsed as a result of the labor shortage caused by the end of indentured immigration in 1916 and of the indentured labor system itself in 1920. After a further unsuccessful experiment with small Indo-Fijian planters on fifty- to eighty-acre parcels, the company decided to get out of cane cultivation. It divided its extensive holdings—132,886 acres of fee simple and leased land[1]—into ten-acre parcels, which it then leased to Indo-Fijian tenants. The transformation occurred rapidly. In 1925 in Fiji as a whole, the company itself cultivated 33,679 acres of cane compared with European planters' cultivation of 4,446 acres, CSR tenants' 6,905 acres, and independent (Indo-Fijian) contractors' 19,933 acres. By 1941, in contrast, the CSR cultivated only 3,153 acres and European planters 1,133 acres, while CSR tenants cultivated 46,521 acres and independent contractors 42,793 acres. Some 97 percent of all cane acreage was now in smallholdings, with CSR tenants accounting for 52 percent of the total and independent contractors 45 percent.[2]

At first sight, this change would suggest a fundamental restructuring of relationships in the sugar industry. Indo-Fijians were no longer mere employees of the company, as they had been during indenture, but independent producers of cane with personal stakes in the productivity of their farms.[3] However, the company viewed the change largely as a cost- and risk-sharing strategy: "We divide our risks with others, reduce the quantity of capital we have to invest, and settle a population on the land who would always be available for work in and about the mill and on the plantations."[4] The company was reluctant to relinquish its firm grip on the growers. As a result, its contract with them included specific provisions regarding the varieties of cane to be planted and the time and manner of planting and harvesting and stated that "crops must be tended to the complete satisfaction of the company."[5] The contracts also specified the company's right to unilaterally reduce the price it paid for cane if any action by the government increased the cost of producing sugar.

The company saw itself as a benign if paternalistic landlord providing security of tenure to its tenants and in return demanding the right to oversee their labor. Close supervision of the growers and tight control over their labor remained the hallmarks of the smallholding system and the sources of friction that soon plunged the colony into industrial strife. An interesting side effect of the new system was that the smallholding system considerably reduced the role and influence of Europeans in the rural sugar belt of Fiji, where they had once been prominent cultivators. The displaced or impoverished planters moved to urban centers and into civil service or commercial employment, ending whatever prospect there might have been for turning Fiji into a white-settler plantocracy.

Sugar remained the backbone of the colonial economy, as it would for several decades, but for a brief period in the 1920s, hopes for agricultural diversification were raised by the temporary success of experiments in producing other crops. An experiment in cotton production began in 1926, a joint venture of the government and the Empire Cotton Growing Cooperative. Two ginneries opened, one at Lautoka and another in the Sigatoka Valley, and between them they produced within a year 773,136 pounds of lint cotton valued at £74,343.[6] Also in 1926, pineapple cultivation was introduced in Tailevu and Nadi, and the fruit produced were considered equal if not superior in quality to Hawaiian pineapples.[7] A fledgling rubber industry appeared between 1923 and 1926, and sheep farming was started, producing wool thought by many to be equal to the best in Australia. Beef farming was also tried. The most successful of these experimental efforts, dairy farming, began at Tailevu as part of a scheme to rehabilitate demobilized soldiers, and is still prominent in that area.

Unfortunately, the hopes of economic diversification these experiments evidenced were dashed almost as soon as they were born, victims alike of the world-wide depression that began in the late 1920s and of the devastating hurricanes and floods that ravaged many parts of the colony at the same time. The rubber industry sagged, the pineapple and meat canneries closed, five hundred Indo-Fijian traders went out of business, European entrepreneurs faced bankruptcy, even the sugar industry declined. In 1928, a bumper year, Fiji exported 121,000 tons of sugar valued at £1,827,000; three years later, the totals were 68,000 tons exported with a value of £624,000.[8] The depressed circumstances reflected in these figures continued until the late 1930s, by when the dream of economic expansion and diversification had disappeared altogether.

One exception to these trends was the new gold mining industry. The most important initial discoveries of gold deposits were at Yanawai on the island of Vanua Levu, where production began under Mount Kasi Mines in 1932. By 1946 this mine had produced 63,592 ounces of gold and 4,850 ounces of silver with a combined value of £550,000.[9] Impressive as these figures were, they were quickly overshadowed by larger discoveries at Tavua. There, three mines were soon at work, the largest of which, the Emperor, during its first decade of operation produced 607,385 fine ounces of gold worth £5,556,558. Between 1932 and 1940, the proportion of gold in Fiji's total export trade rose from 1 percent to 40 percent; in 1941 and 1945, the value of gold exported exceeded that of sugar.[10] In 1939 the gold mining industry employed 1,493 workers, of whom 1,171 were Fijians.

The Tavua gold mines gave birth to one of three new townships that emerged during this period, the isolated and immigrant labor settlement of Vatukoula. The other new townships were Korovou, in Tailevu district, the result of the Settlement Scheme for Returned European soldiers started at the end of the war, and Nasea, in Labasa district, Vanua Levu's only township for many decades. Suva remained the urban center of the colony, but was no longer the largely European town it had once been.

Fijians and Indo-Fijians were now living there in increasing numbers and asking for a say in municipal affairs in the face of European determination to maintain their traditional supremacy.

Population and Its Politics

The 1920s and 1930s saw a rapid increase in the population of the colony. The absolute increase combined with differences in the rates of increase among ethnic groups to produce a shifting demographic mix and a new basis for social fear among some of the groups (see Table 1).

Several things emerge from the figures in Table 1. The most obvious is that for the first time since cession, the census of 1936 records an absolute increase in the Fijian population. The once alarming rate of decline had been arrested in the decade before 1921, though the upward curve was interrupted by the influenza epidemic of 1918. The 1936 figures put to rest the once widely held view that the Fijian people were facing extinction. However, the increase among Fijians was balanced by the much larger increase among Indo-Fijians. The Indo-Fijians were not yet a majority of the people in Fiji, but the relative rates of their increase and that of Fijians indicated that they soon might be. The disparity in the growth of the two communities was due not to differential birth rates—this rate was 35 per thousand for both of them in the 1930s—but to the great differences in death rates: 8.73 per thousand for Indo-Fijians and 23.08 for Fijians. This difference resulted from various factors, including disparities in general health, in immunity to introduced diseases, and in living conditions in the two communities.[11] Whatever its origins, the disparity in growth rates caused much concern among Europeans and Fijians, raising fears of Indo-Fijian domination of the colony and producing in turn a series of interesting political alliances and permutations designed to neutralize those fears.

Another demographic trend much noted at the time was the rapid increase of Part-Europeans, which added to the anxiety among Europeans, who were already fearful of being swamped demographically. This fear, together with the fear of Indo-Fijian domination, lay behind their

Table 1. Fiji's Population, 1921–1936

Ethnic Group	1921	1936	Increase	Rate/000
Fijian	84,475	97,961	13,176	156.0
Indo-Fijian	60,634	85,002	24,368	401.9
Part-European	2,781	4,574	1,793	644.7
European	3,878	4,028	150	38.7
Chinese	910	1,741	831	209.5

SOURCE: Compiled from Fiji census reports, 1921 and 1936.

effort to have the system of electing nongovernment members of the Legislative Council replaced by a system of nomination by the governor so that they could continue to dominate the political agenda of the colony. Because of their mixed ancestry, the Part-Europeans occupied an anomalous position on the social fringes of Fiji's racially compartmentalized, caste-conscious society. Their children were admitted reluctantly, if at all, to government-supported European schools, and Part-European men married to white women from Australia and New Zealand had to seek special permission to enter those countries.

The ambiguity of their position was symbolized by the controversy over their designation as a group. At first they were called "half-castes" and designated as such in the various censuses. By the 1930s, that term had acquired a pejorative connotation, indicating someone who was roughly hewn and lacking culture and sophistication by European standards. They then began to appear on paper, at least, as PENDs, People of European and Native Descent, or as PMENDs, People of Mixed European and Native Descent. As their numbers increased and the electorate expanded, so did their political influence among European politicians. Their participation in politics helped a little, at least outwardly, in representing their concerns and needs in the Legislative Council. Since World War II, they have been known as Part-Europeans and are referred to as such today, though for voting purposes after independence, they were lumped together with Europeans, Chinese, and "Others" as general electors.

The Chinese were another small but interesting component in the population of Fiji.[12] They began coming to the islands in scattered numbers in the closing decades of the nineteenth century; and at the time of cession, there were between twenty and forty of them, all engaged in the bêche-de-mer trade.[13] The majority of the Chinese immigrants, almost 90 percent of them,[14] came from the heavily populated regions of Kwangtung in southeast China, which had long sent emigrants to North America and Australia. In Fiji, as elsewhere, they were engaged in retail trade, market-gardening, laundering, baking, and other petty trades.

As the twentieth century progressed, the Chinese became concentrated in urban centers such as Levuka and Suva, but before that, they lived in rural areas such as Sigatoka, Tailevu, and Naitasiri, where they had sold Fijians such necessities as kerosene, bread, and tinned food, as well as trinkets and, on the side, illicit alcohol. Although they often lived apart from other groups, the Chinese adapted well to the needs and demands of the villages, often marrying Fijian women and raising families, much to the annoyance of some chiefs.[15] In Lau the district commissioner thought Chinese traders charged exorbitant rates for their goods and paid little for copra, though neither practice, he admitted, was restricted to Chinese.[16] Life was not easy for Chinese immigrants. They could not obtain liquor without a permit, were fingerprinted on arriving in the colony, were required to get certificates of identity that were valid for only a year and renewable for only six months, and were also routinely interrogated by the police about their business and personal matters.

The presence of the Chinese provoked a variety of responses. The Great Council of Chiefs expressed alarm over Chinese immigration and wanted a poll tax imposed to control or eliminate it.[17] Fijian chiefs such as Ratu Pope Seniloli preferred English to Chinese immigration because "contact with European methods served Fijians better" and because Fijians "could learn nothing of benefit or material use to themselves" from the Chinese. European politicians and members of the business community such as Maynard Hedstrom also opposed Chinese immigration because they believed it would diminish the prospects for European settlement (which by the 1920s were vanishing anyway) and add to the competition already faced by European merchants in Fiji.

The government vacillated. After the end of Indian indenture, there was some talk in official and commercial circles of importing Chinese to meet the anticipated shortage of labor, but the Colonial Office counseled against the idea, and it came to nothing. Introducing another racial group would only complicate an already complex situation, London feared. It would also alarm Australia and New Zealand by introducing "yellow labor so near [their] door." In any case, the Chinese would come only as free, not indentured, laborers, which would add to their cost.[18]

Still, the prospect of cheap Chinese labor was inviting, and in the early 1930s, Governor Sir Murchison Fletcher revived the idea. Chinese got along well with Fijians, Fletcher believed, and their industry and thrift might set good examples for the Fijians. They might also act as a "useful counter-balance to the Indians."[19] When the Colonial Office restated its opposition, Fletcher dropped the idea. In the following decades, the small numbers of Chinese in the islands continued to ply their trades away from the public gaze, but as independence approached in the 1960s, they began to look elsewhere, principally to North America and Australia, apprehensive of their future in an independent Fiji.

Fijian Society: Questions and Problems

Fijian society remained predominantly rural and governed by the rhythms of tradition. In most villages, the Programme of Work, which dictated what communal tasks were to be accomplished during which months of the year, controlled the pace of village life as well as the cycles of communal activity. On the surface, life went on as it always had, its rhythm punctuated by nothing more dramatic than building and repairing houses, making and maintaining village roads and bridges, planting and cultivating crops, keeping up provincial property—boats, offices and houses of provincial officials, medical substations, provincial schools and water supply systems, and whatever was necessary to keep the villages sanitary. Fijians continued to live in the old-style *bure* of walls and roof thatched with reeds, long grass, or sugar-cane leaves and with earthen floors raised a foot or two above ground level to ensure adequate drainage.[20] Work in the villages was still done communally, neighbors helping neighbors, whether clearing forests for planting, catching fish, preparing feasts, or doing whatever else could not be readily done alone. Tomorrow's tasks were announced by village criers at sundown today. The pace and intensity of daily work depended on fluctuating needs; no fixed routine was strictly adhered to.

Beneath the apparent calm and serenity were tensions that surfaced periodically, at meetings of the Great Council of Chiefs, for example. Concerns over sanitation and health led to the launching of the Child Welfare Scheme, financed by the Rockefeller Institute, and to the extensive Vaccination Campaign, which between 1929 and 1934 immunized nearly all Fijians against smallpox.[21] Similar concerns prompted efforts to curtail gambling, alcohol consumption, and other social vices. At the same time, the government, which regarded the communal life of Fijian villages as confining, proposed to create larger amalgamated communities in order to afford individual Fijians more social space and personal freedom. The governor explained the proposal to the Great Council of Chiefs in 1926: "It may mean of course the curtailment of your tribal liberties but the gain to all is surely worth the sacrifice—better medical attention, better educational facilities for your children, better houses to live in, improved sanitation, and the example of a cleaner, more energetic, and more diverse life."[22]

Still other problems faced Fijians in the 1920s. One involved Fijian women living in urban areas away from their people and working in questionable places of employment. Among such places were saloons, which numbered about sixty-five in the early 1920s—places of "evil joy," Ratu Jone Mataitini called them.[23] Distressed by this situation, Fijian leaders called for strict restrictions on the movement of women and girls away from the villages to urban areas. In 1923 and again in 1926, the Great Council of Chiefs passed resolutions demanding that Fijian women absenting themselves from their villages for more than twenty-eight days obtain the *buli*'s consent.[24] In 1933 the council attempted to prohibit married women from leaving their villages without the consent of their husbands, an effort the government vetoed on grounds that "coercion of women is not in accordance with modern principles."[25]

A more serious problem was the unsupervised and generally unrestricted recruitment of Fijian labor from the villages, which resulted in the neglect of communal tasks in the villages. The situation was reportedly so bad in Bua that few men were willing to remain in the villages, and a similar condition was reported in Ra.[26] Nonetheless, employment statistics do not support claims of a large-scale movement of Fijians into wagework.

In 1912, 1,250 Fijians—5.3 percent of all those of taxable age—were employed under the provisions of relevant labor ordinances, and in 1926, those figures were 2,051 and 8.7 percent. A decade later, in 1936, the census revealed that 1,002 Fijians were employed in mining, 375 in sugar planting, 436 in coconut and copra production, 416 in domestic service, and 1,161 in general laboring.

Why did Fijians accept being recruited for work outside their villages? Official sources and chiefly complaints sometimes suggest that labor recruiters ran rampant in the villages, enlisting unknowing Fijians against their will. Such suggestions seem unbelievable and have been largely discredited by scholars of the Pacific Islands labor trade.[27] Yet, work on the plantations was neither attractive nor easy. Quite the contrary. Many Fijians were employed there by the month, working without the assurances provided indentured Indians. Their contracts, such as they were, could be terminated with a month's notice by either party, but a laborer who gave notice was sometimes dismissed immediately without compensation. On some CSR plantations, laborers absent on the last day of the year forfeited all the money accrued to them. In addition, laborers could be prosecuted for not completing their tasks, for being absent without permission, or for any other reason given credence by their employers.[28]

In view of these conditions, it is not easy to explain why Fijians consented to such employment. Why, for example, did Fijians from Nadi travel to Ba to be recruited under the Masters and Servants Ordinance, sometimes under false names in order to avoid the provincial rates?[29] In Colo East, reported the district commissioner, younger Fijians showed apathy toward communal work and "endeavor[ed] to escape on every possible pretext to enable them to pursue more lucrative occupations," such as those offered by the CSR.[30] A substantial number of cases before provincial courts in Viti Levu involved the failure to observe the native regulations. In Colo East in 1921, of the 265 cases dealt with by the provincial court, 61 concerned the failure to perform communal duties, 48 involved the breach of native regulations, and 28 were about unlawful absence from the villages.[31]

Could it be that Fijians who contracted for such work did so because they actually disliked the regimented life of the villages and regarded its communal demands as excessive in contrast to perceived opportunities for a better life elsewhere? Was poverty an important reason? Did the example of free mobility of Indo-Fijians and their visible prosperity sharpen the Fijians' sense of immobility and economic stagnation, particularly in the more depressed areas, and impel them to seek whatever avenues of escape were available to them?[32] A contemporary observer noted:

> The breakdown of the native society and economic system is evidenced by the increasing difficulty of getting Fijians to do communal work. As people leave their villages to farm as individuals or to work for wages, it becomes very dis-

tasteful to those left behind to carry on the old ways of doing things. The time has gone when obedience to chiefly power was involuntary and when native regulations rarely had to be enforced by an order of court. Fijians now distrust or oppose the orders and supervision of their chiefs in planting and weeding native gardens. Nowadays, in the district courts, native magistrates are called on more and more to deal with offenses against the communal system. Scores of Fijians have been imprisoned for short terms for failure to carry out their communal obligations.[33]

The absence of young Fijian men from the villages was a problem, but these men had not necessarily broken away from their villages permanently. Perhaps they undertook outside work on a seasonal basis, returning to their villages to recuperate, to enjoy their earnings in the company of their friends and families, or to pay their debts. Whatever their reasons —and these are not mentioned in the records—Fijian workers left their villages without proper authorization, causing the elders great concern. Throughout the 1920s, the Great Council of Chiefs asked the government to impose a more stringent control on Fijian labor recruitment practices.

Fears of undermining the traditional Fijian order were fueled by a reopening of the debate over the basis and future directions of the government's Fijian (native) policy. The old Gordon-Thurston system, as reformed early in the century, was still intact, but changing circumstances rendered problematic the continued isolation and insulation of Fijians from the mainstream of island life. Acting Governor T. E. Fell, who came to Fiji from a background in colonial Africa, raised these issues in a direct way in 1922 and deserves to be quoted at length:

> The Fijian does not appear to have progressed materially with the rest of the world, since the Stanmore days. He has, to a large extent, been preserved as a somewhat attractive and picturesque figure in an atmosphere of communalism, and has changed apparently little since the "conquest" of Fiji by the missionaries, and the inauguration of vernacular schools. So far he is said to have been happy to remain in his old groove. Will he remain so as the world progresses round him? I doubt it. Rather, I fear a time may come when he will wish to know why he has been left behind, why facilities have not been afforded to him to enable him to strike out for himself like other people. If such a feeling becomes general, which in the future it may easily do, the race will certainly not be a happy one, and there will be considerable difficulty in store for the Government. If there are real signs of a change in attitude and thought on the part of the younger Fijian generation, is it not the duty of the Government, in addition to being a wise policy, to look ahead and meet the change, to steer it along in the direction of individualism, carefully preventing a too rapid movement which would not be in the interest either of the Fijian or his country?[34]

Building on the assumptions implicit in this statement, Fell suggested several innovations, among them making English compulsory in all government and government-assisted schools in order to broaden the horizon of Fijian youth; mandating agricultural training for Fijians while relaxing the native regulations requiring Fijians to do communal work; establishing technical schools for Fijians; permitting individual Fijians to hold agricultural land for their own use; creating a native cadet system for Fijians in government service; initiating a competitive apprenticeship system in the Public Works and Telegraph and Telephone Department for Fijians; and selecting one Fijian pupil each year through competitive examination for an overseas university education financed by government scholarship. Such measures, plus a gradual relaxation of communal regulations, Fell hoped, would make traditional policies gradually obsolete and hasten the time "for Fijians to be absorbed in the general scheme of Government, and not to remain in a semi-separate administration."

Fell presented his ideas not as policy recommendations but as a basis for discussion, and he invited comments from those with experience in Fijian affairs. Acting Colonial Secretary Islay McOwan responded that Fijians accepted the need for change and were, indeed, changing, but he suggested there was no need for haste. Invoking a traditional line of defense against proponents of change, he spoke paternalistically of "what appears to us the inherent vice of indolence but what, in reality, is the quiet and easy contentment of a people with few wants and simple taste." Other points were raised in defense of the old policy. Native policy, it was argued, "aims primarily at the preservation of the native race." Relaxation of communal obligations would not further that goal; it would instead provide Fijians the "opportunity to roam aimlessly and to loaf on new found friends in Suva or in the distant villages, rather than to engage in profitable pursuits." That, of course, would interrupt the progress already made. "It is not many decades since he was a savage of the most barbarous kind," McOwan said, "and from that condition he has been raised to a state, the docility and peacefulness of which are perhaps almost ideal."[35]

Official opinion was divided, and the upshot of the renewed debate on what was now an old subject was a compromise aimed at gradual change but no fundamental reorientation of policy. The office of secretary of native affairs was abolished in 1921 and its responsibilities transferred to the Colonial Secretariat; the district commissioners were placed in charge of provincial matters, assisted by *roko* in the administration of Fijian matters. Five years later, another governor, Sir Eyre Hutson, reversed these changes in response to pleas from the chiefs, but it was not until after World War II that the administrative structure of Fijian affairs was again in Fijian hands.[36] The goal of the government's "native policy," as it was called, was restated by Governor Sir Arthur Richards in 1937: "It is desirable to see that the healthy movement towards individualism does not completely destroy the authority of the chiefs, which must alter materially in scope or even in nature—by which I mean that the power and the need of detailed interference should slowly disappear leaving a real leader of free men and not a patriarch exercising through outworn custom a distasteful surveillance over the details of life."[37]

Whatever one thinks of that goal, it was eventually eclipsed by Ratu Sukuna's more conservative vision, which after World War II became the basis of renewed traditionalism in Fijian life. In the 1920s and 1930s, however, some progress was made in the effort to promote individualism. The 1933 Native Lands Occupation Ordinance enabled individual Fijian farmers, *galala*, to acquire security of tenure over portions of *mataqali* land, which they could cultivate outside their communal obligations and free from communal regulations.[38] Those farmers were also provided with some farming instruments, draught animals, and technical advice, in the hope that the efforts to promote individualism would achieve several goals. According to J. W. Coulter:

> It was believed that the standard of living would be raised by increasing the amount of food available and by giving the native a little purchasing power through the sale of "money crops." It was hoped that it would teach him to utilize his land to its fullest ability to produce. It was also hoped that it would increase the independence and self-respect of the native by making him less dependent on his chief for advice and leadership. In sum, it was thought that it would enable the Fijians to hold their own in the economic regime of the islands, which was being made more and more competitive by the increasing population of a foreign race with a new and alien culture.[39]

For a while, the prospects of the new policy looked bright. The farmers exempted from communal obligations grew cash crops of yaqona, maize, tobacco, and sugar cane. In Nadi the provincial council moved a resolution in 1926 requiring each able-bodied man to plant at least half an acre of marketable crops other than foodstuffs, and according to the district commissioner, the result was encouraging. The acreage planted as a result of the requirement totaled 225, of which 200 acres were in cane.[40] In the sugar cane belts by 1936, there were 1,131 Fijian tenants and nontenants of the CSR who together produced 36,422 tons of cane, which they sold for £27,017.[41] Governor Sir Murchison Fletcher was impressed with the work of Fijian cane farmers. He told the Great Council of Chiefs in 1931 that he was very pleased at the farmers' "surprising aptitude in the adoption of new methods and keen enthusiasm in making success of their work."[42] He also asked the chiefs to "assist our efforts and to do everything in your power to encourage your people to undertake the cultivation of cane." The chiefs, however, were not ones to advance a program aimed at undermining their own position in Fijian life.

The CSR, too, was coaxed into supporting the new program, not least because successful Fijian farmers promised to be useful counterweights against the Indo-Fijian farmers and laborers on whom the company then depended. In 1932 in Ba, the CSR began its experiment, providing seventy-two Fijian farmers with land, building materials, and daily wages of 1s 8d, and promising to assist them after twelve months of residence in applying for exemption from communal obligations. The idea, as the Reverend A. D. Lelean said, was to "wean him [the Fijian farmer] from the deadening effect of his communal habits of life"; and, by developing "initiative, discipline and knowledge of agriculture," to enable him to hold his own against the Indo-Fijian farmer and the threat the latter's success posed for long-term Fijian interests.[43]

Despite such efforts, the program fell far short of the hopes of its advocates. Governor Philip Mitchell offered one assessment of its results in 1944:

> I hope we have heard the last of this lunacy and that it is generally recognised that the village community is the basis of Fijian society and that for the Government to intervene to destroy it is stupid, if not indeed wicked. . . . Even if the exempted man succeeded in the sense that his sponsors understand success, that is to say even if he earned more money for himself with less obligations to his fellows, nothing would be proved which has not already been proved by the melancholy condition to which the same philosophy has brought Europe.[44]

Mitchell's melancholy assessment confirmed the views of those who had never expected the program to succeed in the first place. To the advocates of the traditional policy, the failure proved again that Fijians were unsuited to individual enterprise and belonged instead in their communal villages. That was the argument of Ratu Sukuna, among many others. By the 1930s, Sukuna, decorated soldier, Oxford-educated paramount chief, was the leading voice of conservative Fijian chiefly opinion. For Fijians, Sukuna said, independent farming is

> an experiment foreign in conception, novel in thought, and socially disruptive in form. [The communal villager] cannot by ukase be changed overnight into an individualist, nor can he in isolation find new vigour and moral purification; for still with the same outlook he cannot escape far from his fathers and the bonds of kinship. Freedom the new individualist does not understand. His word for it is "tu galala" which means freedom not in the sense of laissez faire but in the sense of freedom with an object.[45]

That was not the whole story, either. Fijian farmers starting out alone never had a fair chance to succeed. Culturally, they were poorly equipped to succeed individually. The thought of being alone, with the attendant risks of isolation, was not easy. Moreover, the farmers lacked knowledge of markets and prices and were without adequate transportation. Their children frequently remained away from the village schools, and they and their families were cut off from the cultural anchors in the *koro*. Their elders, the chiefs, whom they were likely to respect, opposed their efforts to become independent and advised them against it. The more successful *galala* were, the less likely they would be to contribute communal tribute or service to the village, thus undermining the prestige and authority of the chiefs.[46] To be successful in the face of these cultural and institutional odds, *galala* needed encouragement as well as guidance in all stages of farming. Both were missing. In the event that Fijian farmers faltered and failed, they, and they alone, had to bear the burden. As the district commissioner of Colo North and East said of the *galala* in 1937, "They must accept the responsibility if they decided to come into the scheme."

In the face of such attitudes, it is no wonder that the experiment failed. Had it been properly encouraged, the Fijian people might have been spared some of the problems they would encounter in the decades ahead.

Viti Cauravou

Despite the failures of the reform efforts, some of the support for those efforts came from within Fijian society itself. The most articulate and representative voice of this support was the Viti Cauravou 'Young Fijian Society'. Formed in 1923 by former students of Davuilevu and of Queen Victoria School, the society was intended as a forum for educated young Fijians to meet and discuss issues affecting themselves and other Fijians as well as to "engage in loyal exercises on such occasions as Empire Day, Cession Day, etc."[47] Soon after the society's formation, the social purposes displaced the patriotic ones, as its leaders began to consider alternatives to the limited changes permitted by colonial policy.

The Viti Cauravou became essentially a movement for Fijian cultural renewal and social rejuvenation aimed at placing the control of Fijian affairs in Fijian hands. In this respect, it was a spiritual successor of Apolosi's movement. A letter from the society stated its objectives: "We are rousing our people from their lethargy to go forward and work for our advancement. We are doing this owing to the large number of strangers who are coming into our midst and, because, if we remain inactive, and only watch their movement forward to better life, it will not be long before we are left behind in the march of progress."[48] Members of the society wanted Fijian youth educated in "first class schools in Fiji." They wanted Fijian farmers to have more control over what they produced and sold in order to curtail the "nefarious work of the [European and Chinese] traders." They sought to preserve the purity of the Fijian "race" by discouraging the "intermingling of our people by marriage with strangers, and, more especially with Asiatics" (by which they meant Indo-Fijians as well as Chinese). Fijians should be in perpetual possession of their land: "Our people should not be as strangers in their own land in these modern times."[49]

On the question of Fijian labor, a source of concern to Fijian chiefs and others in the 1920s, the Viti Cauravou stated that none of its members should sign on for less than £50 per annum. Members disobeying this directive would be expelled from the society. "It may be all right for strangers in our midst to indenture themselves as laborers," the society resolved at its annual meeting in October 1926, "but no true native owners of land should sign on. . . . We should devote ourselves towards the progress of our country."[50] The society also condemned the working conditions Fijian laborers endured on the plantations. They should be paid from the moment they received the order from the agent of the steamer to leave their villages. Their rations should be given properly and "not thrown about like animal feed." Proper records should be kept so that the workers would know exactly what was deducted from their wages by the employers. Planters should not "scruff and pull the ears of the men and otherwise ill-use them. . . . If we desire our people to work hard and diligently, [then] we should be taught to perform our parts in the proper spirit and that the old methods still displayed in these modern times" should be stopped.[51]

The society wanted other things too: an agricultural school for Fijian youths age sixteen and older and exemption of the students from communal work; improved education for Fijian girls—the "future mothers of the Fijian race"—in village and provincial schools to ensure that the "increase in the number of the native population will [not] be retarded"; establishment of a College of the South Sea Islands to provide tertiary education for qualified Fijian youth of both sexes; and the appointment to responsible positions in the colonial government of "competent" Fijians, that is, those who agreed with the society's objectives, rather than those who were "not fit and proper persons and do not behave in keeping with their positions as is expected of them by the people." Perhaps the most important of the society's proposals was that "rent" be paid to the Fijians by the owners of fee simple land. "Our hearts cry out," said the society, "at the great injustice that was done by the sale of our lands by our ancestors, for guns. Since the guns have been returned, why do not the lands revert to us? If it is impossible to return the lands to the rightful owners, something in the form of rents should be paid to them."[52]

Membership in the society was restricted to Fijians who were educated (literacy in English was highly desirable), had an account in the savings bank (to prove their thrift and industry), and were otherwise committed to improving themselves and the Fijian people ("drunkards, fornicators, thieves and habitual criminals" were specifically excluded).[53]

The ideals the Viti Cauravou encouraged—personal improvement, group pride, cultural integrity, economic development—were admirable. Yet, it failed to win the support of those who counted most. The society's call to prohibit liaisons between Fijian women and non-Fijian men, for example, which was supported by petitions signed by more than five thousand Fijians, was rejected by the Great Council of Chiefs in 1930 because such a prohibition was "derogatory to the dignity of Fijian womanhood and an unjustifiable restriction of liberty."[54] However, the rejection reflected more fundamental concerns. Chiefs such as Ratu Deve Togani-valu, Roko Tui Bua, thought the society was subversive of chiefly customs.[55] That was hardly the case, though the society did regard the constitution of the Great Council of Chiefs as "entirely wrong and out of date" and wanted the council enlarged to include twenty of its own members.[56] By insisting on competence in the administration of Fijian affairs, on the accountability of Fijian officials, and on educational and economic opportunities for all Fijians and not just those of the chiefly class, the society did threaten the privileged position of the chiefs. For the same reasons, it also threatened the political alliance between colonial officials and the chiefs, and thus the privileged position of Europeans, holders of fee simple land, and employers of Fijian labor. Regarding the *Viti Cauravou's* call to improve the conditions of Fijian workers on the plantations, Secretary for Native Affairs Islay McOwan wrote in 1926 that the society "should not interfere between the employer and his servant in the matter of wages which are fixed by mutual agreement," warning that any interference "will bring the Society into disfavour."[57] The governor agreed.

The combined opposition of chiefs and colonial officials ensured the failure of the Viti Cauravou. One may only speculate what might have happened had it succeeded. The educational and economic gap that separated Fijians and other groups in the colony might have narrowed, and the problem that gap later produced, including heightened racial animosity, might have been easier to resolve. In retrospect, the failure of the Viti Cauravou looks like a lost opportunity.

From Indians to Indo-Fijians

One development that caused much anxiety to all Fijians, whether members of the Viti Cauravou or not, was the rapid growth, economic advancement, and political assertiveness of the Indo-Fijian community. This development, or rather series of interlocking developments, set the tone for much of the political debate in Fiji in this period.

During this period of rapid Indo-Fijian population growth (from 60,635 in 1921 to 85,002 in 1936, an increase of 26.7 percent), an important aspect of the growth was the increase in the proportion of Fiji-born Indians (from 44.2 percent in 1921 to 71.6 percent in 1936).[58] This was a change of more than statistical significance. It signaled a profound social, cultural, and psychological transformation in the Indo-Fijian community. Before the 1920s, the Indo-Fijians tended to be socially isolated, economically dependent, culturally disoriented, and politically disorganized and voiceless. They lacked independent leadership of their own, their interests in the higher echelons of the colonial government being represented, insofar as they were represented at all, by the agent general of immigration and his staff. Perceived and treated by groups outside the government as "coolies," the Indo-Fijians were told to accept as permanent and proper their place at the bottom of the Fiji social hierarchy.

This began to change in the 1920s. Emerging from the shadows of the *girmit* experience, the Fiji-born Indians were different from their indentured parents or grandparents in social outlook and habits of thought. One colonial official observed in 1927 that the Fiji-born Indian "possesses a superior physique to that of his immigrant parents, [exhibits] greater intelligence, [and] practices a higher morality and demands a more advanced standard of living.[59] The differences in outlook and social organization arose in part because of the new competitive economic environment in which the Indo-Fijians found themselves and in part because the policies of the colonial government served to undermine the possibility of reconstituting the social order the Indian immigrants had known in their homeland. Where customs and caste conventions of the ancestral homeland persisted, they were largely in ceremonial form, as vicarious, sentimental links with a world far removed from them in time and place.[60] Both by choice as well as necessity, Indo-Fijians married across caste and occasionally even across religious lines. Indo-Fijian women enjoyed greater personal freedom than their sisters in India, though their marriages were still arranged by their parents, and they had to do the bulk of the household chores besides helping out in field work.

Indenture had taught its lessons well. The Fiji-born were more on their own, more individually oriented, more conscious of and sensitive to the relative deprivation they experienced in the larger society. India did not loom large in their consciousness, as it had perhaps done in the lives of the *girmitiya,* including my own grandfather, who even in old age still hoped to die in his *janmabhumi* 'motherland'. In contrast Fiji was the only home the new generation had, and they did not shy away from pursuing the rights and opportunities they thought were properly theirs. Intimately familiar with what the *girmitiya* had endured, they wanted to live in Fiji and do so with *izzat* 'honor' or 'dignity' and *insaf* 'justice' or 'fair play'.

The bulk of the Indo-Fijians in the 1920s and 1930s were still engaged in agricultural work. In 1936, 17,335 of the 25,190 employed adults worked in agriculture compared with only 1,728 in manufacturing and 1,011 in commerce and finance. Most of them were cane growers, either independent farmers or tenants of the CSR, and others cultivated rice, cotton, or bananas on their own. Most of them also grew vegetables for their own use or for sale in a local bazaar. Whatever work they did, however, they did with industry and conscientiousness. Failure was a word they dreaded like the plague. American geographer John Wesley Coulter captures their experience and mine, for I grew up on a small cane farm in rural Vanua Levu in the late 1950s and 1960s:

The regular work of Indian farmers in Fiji is in contrast to the irregular, easy-going life of the Fijians. The Oriental rises at half-past five, harnesses his oxen, and plows from six to eight. He breakfasts at home or in the field on *roti* and milk or tea *(roti* is bread made from flour fried in *ghee).* He resumes plow-ing until ten; at that time his oxen are unhitched to lie in the shade during the heat of the day. Shortly after ten he milks his cow, and from ten-thirty to twelve hoes weeds or cuts fodder along the ditches or roadside. At noon he lunches on rice, dal [dhal] or rice curry, and milk. In the early afternoon he hoes again, cuts more grass, or does odd jobs about the house. From three to five he plows. Supper at six consists of rice and curry and chutney and milk. There is smoking and conversation by kerosene lamp until bedtime at eight. In the evenings groups of Indians who have been working in the cane fields all day long trudge home in the dusk, carrying lunch pails.[61]

It was, by and large, a self-contained world of hard work and simple plea-sures, a world that endured until recent times.

Not all Indo-Fijians in this period were descended from *girmitiya.* In the 1920s and 1930s, small but steady numbers of free Indians migrated to Fiji. Among them were some repatriates who had returned to India from Fiji only to become disenchanted with life there. Most of the new immi-grants, however, were enterprising agriculturalists from the Punjab or artisans or petty traders from Gujarat. In 1921 there were 449 Punjabis and 324 Gujaratis in Fiji, and in 1936, 3,000 and 2,500, respectively.[62] Most of the immigrants in these groups were single males who, after estab-lishing themselves in Fiji, returned to India to get married. There was lit-tle cultural or social interaction between them and the descendants of the *girmitiya,* a circumstance that continued until well after the middle of the twentieth century.

Nearly all the Gujarati immigrants in Fiji lived in towns and engaged in such petty business activities as hawking, tailoring, laundering, boot or jewelry making, or merchandising. The most prominent Gujarati-owned companies today—Motibhais, Punjas, Narseys—are products of such humble beginnings. The Gujarati immigrants worked very long hours, so long in fact that even their fellow Indians, let alone European competitors, complained of the difficulty of competing with them. One North Indian court clerk remarked in 1935, for example, that the Gujaratis "take no rest, if they are not working with their front doors open they are continu-ing their labour inside the stores, this unfair competition is not in the inter-ests of the local Indians or traders and the sooner these people are made to take proper rest the better for them and the whole community."[63] More serious complaints came from the cane districts where Gujarati merchants charged mainly illiterate Indo-Fijian customers up to 20 percent more for goods on credit than for cash purchases and lent money to cash-starved farmers at exorbitant rates, often securing promissory notes for payment with standing crops.[64] Over the years, these practices generated strained feelings between the two groups, the effects of which have not yet disappeared.

The arrival of the immigrants introduced social and political divisions within the Indo-Fijian community of the sort that had never existed before. The divisions also energized local and then colony-wide politics, where they produced emotional contests in elections for the Legislative Council in the 1930s and 1940s. The Punjabis, especially Sikhs, were avid followers of the Ghadr movement, which was based in the Pacific Northwest of the United States and Canada and committed to overthrowing British rule in India by violent means.[65] (The word ghadr means turbulence or revolution.) The Gujaratis, on the other hand, were strongly nationalistic and avid followers of Mahatma Gandhi and his nonviolent approach to freeing the subcontinent of its British overlords. On a few occasions, much to the annoyance of the government, they organized partial *hartal* 'work stoppages' against British policies on the subcontinent.[66] Besides bringing a greater awareness of Indian nationalist politics to Fiji, the new immigration brought two young London-trained Gujarati lawyers, S. B. Patel and A. D. Patel, both brilliant and determined men. They arrived in 1927 and 1928, respectively, and their leadership later had a decisive influence on the course of Fijian politics. S. B. Patel, a quiet, reflective, scholarly man, remained in the background, advising, listening, mediating; A. D. Patel (no relation of S. B.) was a gifted orator and fearsome debater at home on the public stage, who became a major public figure in Fiji politics after World War II.

Growth and diversification compounded the tensions within the Indo-Fijian community in the late 1920s and 1930s. Cultural, religious, and social differences became more important as the post-indenture community groped for a reconstituted and more assuring identity. Hindu-Muslim conflict, virtually unheard of before the end of indenture, now erupted in wars of verbal abuse in which both sides distributed imported scurrilous, lurid accounts of the lives and alleged immoralities and misadventures of each other's saints and prophets.[67] *Rangila Rasul,* a vicious account of Prophet Muhammad's alleged moral and sexual misadventures, and *Rangila Rishi,* a vitriolic and slanderous tract about Swami Dayananda Saraswati (1824–1883), the founder in 1875 of the reformist Arya Samaj, so inflamed religious and communal passions that they were banned by the colonial government. Vishnu Deo, one of the leading Indo-Fijian leaders in the 1930s and 1940s who was also an ardent Arya Samaji, was convicted and fined for his role in publicizing some of the slanderous literature. Militant Muslims slaughtered cows in public to offend Hindu sensibilities, and Hindus, especially the more militant Arya Samajis, formed Sangathan movements in rural settlements to convert Muslims to Hinduism,[68] just as their fellow Arya Samajis were attempting to on the subcontinent. Even South Indian Indo-Fijians, late arrivals to Fiji and themselves victims of

North Indian cultural prejudice, formed Sangathan movements to convert to Hinduism South Indians of Muslim and Christian faiths.[69] Hindus and Muslims who associated with each other were sometimes fined by their respective communities and ostracized. Religious arguments about the contents and interpretations of the scriptures occasionally ended in fist fights, or more serious frays involving knives, crowbars, or car cranks; loud and abusive singing competitions were simultaneously staged by the two groups to further inflame religious passions.[70]

One result of this rancor and of Arya Samaj militancy was a demand for separate Muslim representation on the Legislative Council, a demand that continued for decades.[71] To support their demands, Muslims argued that in terms of history, culture, and religion, they were entirely different from other Indo-Fijians and deserved the same kind of special recognition in Fiji that Muslims in India were then demanding. The Muslims were a separate "community under the Moghuls in India," a petition said. "They were a community under the Nizams, Nawabs, Palegars and Naiks; they were a community during the time of the East India Company; they were a community under the British Crown." In effect, the petition continued, the Muslims "have been a community of people wherever they have been under the British rule including the Crown Colony of Kenya and Fiji."[72] In addition to separate political representation, many Muslim leaders demanded the teaching of Urdu in schools attended by Muslim children and at the Teachers Training College as well as the appointment of Muslims to statutory bodies and "wherever the interest of the Muslim community is concerned." More extreme members of that community wanted to remove the names of Muslims from Indo-Fijian electoral rolls and even boycott elections for the Legislative Council.

However, neither Hindus nor Muslims were homogeneous communities; both were divided by deep differences. Among the Hindus, there were bitter disputes between orthodox Sanatanis and reformist Arya Samajis concerning the meaning of texts and contexts in their scriptures and the place of idol worship in Hinduism.[73] The Sanatanis worshiped Lord Rama as a reincarnation of God and accepted the *Ramayana,* an epic about Rama's deeds, as a sacred text. The Samajis did not. Instead, as followers of Swami Dayananda Saraswati, they preached absolute adherence to the religion of the Vedic hymns, rejecting rituals and ceremonies that had accrued to the Hindu tradition. They boycotted each other's festivals and social events and rarely intermarried. Their differences spilled over into the political arena, where they supported different political agendas and social programs.

Among Muslims, an open war of words raged between the Sunni and the Shia sects of Islam. The Shia, the party of Ali, Muhammad's cousin and husband of his daughter Fatima, upheld the rights of the family of the Prophet to the religious and political leadership of the Muslim community.

The Sunni, literally meaning the majority community, refused to accept this view and accorded Ali the same status as the caliphs who succeeded Muhammad. On many occasions, the Sunni petitioned the government to ban certain Shia festivals, which they found "totally repugnant to the beliefs and susceptibilities of the Muslim."[74] These differences still persist, though they do not now arouse the passions they once did.

The growth and physical dispersal of the Indo-Fijian community, spurred in part by the CSR's decision to replace estate farming with smallholding systems and in part by the abolition of indenture, necessitated a reorganization of the machinery by which the government oversaw Indo-Fijian affairs. The administrative instrument of indenture had been the Suva-based agent general of immigration, assisted by resident inspectors of Indian immigrants in important district centers. This machinery was now obsolete and ineffective. At the behest of the government of India and over the initial objections of both the Fiji government and the Colonial Office, a secretary of Indian affairs was appointed in 1929 "to keep the Government of India supplied with correct information regarding the welfare and status of the Indian community generally".[75] (In 1937 the position was merged with that of the chief medical officer.) The secretary of Indian affairs was usually an experienced civil servant with knowledge of subcontinental affairs and of Indian culture and language, who functioned for the Indo-Fijian community much as the secretary of native affairs functioned for Fijians. The office was certainly useful in representing Indo-Fijian concerns and aspirations in the Executive Council, of which the secretary was an ex officio member.

The usefulness of the office was otherwise limited. The secretary was never able to win the confidence of all the quarreling factions among Indo-Fijians, many of whom felt that the secretary was first an advocate of government policies and only then a representative of Indo-Fijian concerns. They were justified in their suspicion. To illustrate, the Colonial Office asked Fiji in 1931, as it had asked other colonies, to look into the possibility of drafting trade union legislation to supervise the growth of "responsible" trade unions. Governor Fletcher refused, saying that such legislation "would be seized upon by the disloyal politician as a weapon for the furtherance of his own mischievous purposes," giving him the "opportunity of uniting by intimidation or cajolery ignorant and disaffected persons under the guise of a trade union, which would be duly registered." The secretary of Indian affairs agreed with the governor and went on to support the passage of a sedition bill to further emasculate the right of Indo-Fijian workers to unite themselves into trade unions.[76]

At the local level, changes in government machinery also occurred. District commissioners appointed advisory committees, beginning in the 1930s, as liaisons between the government and the villages and to help in such village-level concerns as signing burial certificates, attesting notices of marriage, resolving family and social disputes, and generally maintaining peace in the Indo-Fijian settlements. This experiment was modeled on the *panchayat* 'five-person council' system of rural India. More important than the advisory committees were the Indo-Fijian clerks, interpreters, and assistants to the district commissioners. These were individuals of some education, and in those days and localities where educated people were few in number, they exercised inordinate influence, regularly abusing their power. More often than not they acted as eyes and ears for the government in the districts, reporting on political and other trends in the Indo-Fijian community, thereby enabling the government to head off "trouble" in advance.[77] (In this respect, the Fijian administrative system, which also had its share of corrupt officials, better served the interests of the Fijian people.) The government had other Indo-Fijians in its service as well, among them Indo-Fijian politicians and other aspirants to public office who reported on their opponents to ingratiate themselves with the authorities and other well-placed officials, such as the inspector of Indian schools, A. W. MacMillan, who enjoyed the confidence of many Indo-Fijian parents and children.[78] The revamping of the administrative apparatus was a mixed blessing. It established more direct links between the government and the Indo-Fijian community than had previously existed, but it also facilitated a far greater penetration of the community by the government and its allies.

The 1920s and 1930s were times of unsettling change in the colony. Each of the major groups responded to these changes in its own way and according to its perceived interests. The resulting struggles were often portrayed in purely racial terms by officials who sought thereby to control them and preserve the status quo. But the issues behind the struggles were not primarily racial but social and economic, and collectively they challenged the legitimacy as well as the efficacy of European domination.

The 1920 Strike

Issues of economic inequality and social discrimination were most acutely felt in the urban working-class centers of Fiji. The people most adversely affected by the system of corporate control that dominated the economy were Indo-Fijians, the overwhelming majority of whom derived their livelihood as laborers or small cultivators. In indenture days, the demands of Indo-Fijians were easily shelved or deflected through legislative action, as in the 1880s, or crushed by force, as during the labor protest of 1907, in which a group of Punjabi and Pathan workers went on strike in Labasa to protest working conditions on the CSR plantations. (The strikers were arrested and dispersed to different parts of the colony.) The end of indenture in 1920 had changed both the economic and the political equations that had made that earlier result inevitable, and now emboldened Indo-Fijians again employed the strike weapon to get their grievances redressed.

The result was the first major strike in Fiji in the twentieth century. It began on 15 January 1920 in Suva when Indo-Fijian employees of the Public Works Department walked off the job, then spread at once to the large Indo-Fijian community at Rewa, and eventually lasted for two months.[79] The first group of workers struck when they were told abruptly that they would be required to work forty-eight hours a week instead of the customary forty-five. Besides rejecting this change, they demanded an increase in wages to 5 shillings per day because of recent increases in the cost of living. The government was reluctant to grant their demands, though its own Commission of Enquiry documented the economic disruptions caused by World War I and the inflation that followed it. Those disruptions had increased prices significantly, including those for such basic Indo-Fijian food items as rice, sharps, dhal, ghee (clarified butter), mustard oil, spices, and vegetables. The commission found that a weekly supply of basic Indo-Fijian food items that cost 5s 5d per week in 1914 cost 10s 1d in 1920, an increase that approached 100 percent.[80] During that period, the wages of unindentured Indo-Fijian laborers had remained constant around 2 shillings a day, while the wages of Europeans, Part-Europeans, and Fijians had increased.[81]

As the strike continued, positions hardened. The government ordered the striking workers back to work before it would consider their demands. The workers rejected the order, and angry and increasingly militant strikers staged marches in Suva and elsewhere. Governor Sir Cecil Rodwell, whose entire career as a colonial official had been spent in South Africa before he came to Fiji, took a hard-line position, convinced that political factors rather than genuine economic grievances were the real motive for the trouble, a stance adopted subsequently by other governors. Local Europeans were mobilized, and Fijians from Rewa and Navua were enrolled as special constables to maintain order, among them two hundred Fijians from Lau recruited under G. M. Hennings as an auxiliary unit to patrol strategic areas. In addition, military assistance from Australia and New Zealand was requested and received. Several confrontations took place between the police and the strikers, climaxing in a tragic encounter at the Samabula Bridge, in which one of the Indo-Fijian strikers was killed and several others wounded. This show of force won the day for the government, though at the expense of great political alienation in the Indo-Fijian community.

Company and *Kisan:* Round One

The 1920 strike was confined to southeastern Viti Levu. No sooner was it quelled than Indo-Fijian workers in western Viti Levu struck, this time against the CSR. The life of cane farmers and agricultural laborers in the west had never been easy. Regular credit facilities were virtually nonexistent there, and moneylenders routinely charged 30 to 40 percent interest, and even 60 to 80 percent was not unknown.[82] Moreover, the workers' relationship with the CSR was always fraught with difficulty. As the largest economic enterprise in the colony, the CSR was autonomous for all practical purposes. Even the government was partly dependent on the company for the conduct of its business. The Ba district commissioner, to illustrate, noted that government officials could use the CSR telephone line at company-specified "government time" but had to get company permission to use it at other times.[83] After the indenture system ended, the CSR continued to treat its Indo-Fijian tenants as it treated the *girmitiya*—as cheap labor to be controlled with a firm or brutal hand, as the occasion demanded.

This attitude helped induce the sugar strike, which occurred in 1921 in western Viti Levu. There, tenants and workers on CSR estates were demanding better wages (12 shillings a day), specified work hours, adequate housing, medical and pension benefits, educational facilities for their children, and small plots of land on which to keep milk cows.[84] Their situation was made worse in 1921 by the CSR's decision to alter its procedure in buying cane, no longer valuing it according to the sweetness of the cane of individual farmers but at a flat rate for farms grouped into 300- to 400-acre blocks.[85] Urging the governor to reject the pleas of the farmers and farm workers for higher wages and other things, the CSR advised that any concession would be harmful to industrial relations and would encourage labor idleness because Indo-Fijians "will only work long enough each week to produce [a subsistence] income and will idle the rest of the time." The author of this statement, CSR Manager Farquhar, continued: "Even if it were desirable to make wages in an educated democracy fluctuate up and down with the fortune of individual businesses—which we gravely doubt—there cannot, in our opinion, be any question that to thus attempt to regulate wages with ignorant and in many respects uncivilized people is wholly wrong."[86] The government was persuaded and sent a force that included 250 specially commissioned Fijian constables from Bau to intimidate the striking farmers into acquiescence. In the aftermath, the government, as usual, deported the "ring leaders" of the strike, among them Sadhu Basisth Muni, a recently arrived Sanatani priest who was falsely rumored to be an agent of Gandhi.[87] Some of the government's own officials and informers thought that the Sadhu was a gentle man of progressive views who exercised a moderating influence in the Indo-Fijian community.

One result of the strike was that the CSR began to court Fijian laborers more actively than it had done before, enlisting them under the Masters and Servants Act.[88] It donated money to Fijian churches and presented gifts to *buli* of several districts. *Bure* were put up at Lautoka for Fijian workers, and married couples were housed in separate quarters. Fijian laborers also received rations in addition to their regular pay. The CSR continued this policy throughout the 1920s, but with little success. It also threatened to close down its operations in Fiji if the government did not impose controls on the labor force. The governor did not take this threat seriously. He told the Colonial Office that "the real object of the Company in insinuating this possibility is to cause alarm to the Government and, if possible, to frighten us into supporting them in their policy as regards wages and Indians generally."[89]

Throughout the strike, the government maintained "an attitude of non-interference between employer and employed on the question of wages" and refused to take any part in negotiations between the striking workers and the CSR.[90] This was unfortunate because the farmers and workers were disorganized, partly because the government neutralized their leaders or deported them. Its tendency to see any industrial action by Indo-Fijians as the work of a few self-seeking agitators contributed further to the problem. The defeated Indo-Fijians realized that to protect their economic interests, they would have to become politically assertive. Thus was accentuated Fiji's "Indian problem," as it came to be known outside the Indo-Fijian community, a label that epitomized another unfortunate legacy of the strikes of 1920–1921, the exacerbation of racial tensions in the colony. By employing Fijian constables against striking Indo-Fijians, the colonial government had, wittingly or not, aroused latent hostilities that already existed between the two communities. Some Fijians from western Viti Levu wrote to the government seeking permission to form a native platoon so that they could be "prepared for and assist in any trouble that may arise in the future," a request that was sensibly refused.[91] The consequences of the exacerbation of racial tensions remained to be seen.

Education

Education was another issue that contributed to the swelling knot of group tension during the interwar years. For Indo-Fijians in the aftermath of indenture, education was a vital concern, a culturally validated avenue of escape from the economic and political bondage in which they found themselves. Of all the groups in the colony, Indo-Fijians were the most disadvantaged educationally, victims of both government and mission indifference. Interestingly, the Indo-Fijians' now-strenuous efforts to redress that imbalance paralleled those of the Viti Cauravou to correct a similar problem facing Fijians. Young and ambitious members of both groups were dissatisfied with the rudiments of standard education or vocational training that fitted them for traditional crafts at best. Instead, they demanded access to adequately funded English-language schooling of the sort and quality that would admit them to colonial life on an equal footing with other groups. Although information on the subject is scanty, there can be little doubt that the Part-Europeans needed and wanted the same thing. Education was an issue on which otherwise rival groups might have cooperated.

The government had never done much to educate non-Europeans. In 1909 Governor im Thurn appointed an education commission to look into matters of educational policy, but little came of its recommendations; in 1915, government expenditure on education totaled a mere £2,375.[92] In such a context, passage of an ordinance in 1916 establishing a colony-wide department of education under a superintendent of schools could mean very little. The government remained content to encourage and supervise voluntary, usually missionary, schools, rather than initiate measures of its own. This meager effort was directed toward maintaining ethnically segregated schools, on the grounds that "psychology and outlook in the various races are so fundamentally different"[93] as to make multiracial education impossible. This policy first came under critical scrutiny in the 1920s. The government's response to that scrutiny is an instructive instance of the disparity between profession and practice in colonial Fiji and of how the government worked behind the scenes to compromise its own apparent ideals. In the 1920s, education in Fiji was ostensibly run according to the 1916 Education Ordinance.[94] According to Section 7 of that ordinance,

> No applicant shall be refused admission into any school on account of the religious persuasion, nationality, race or language of such applicant or of either of his parents or guardians provided that this subsection shall not apply to the Public Schools in Suva and Levuka or to the Queen Victoria School at Nasinu or to any district in which in the opinion of the Board adequate provision exists for the education of scholars of different races in separate schools.

This statement appears much more reasonable on paper than did the actual operation of the school system it produced. For one thing, the qualifications and exceptions in the second part of the statement render the declaration of equality in the first part meaningless. For another, the Education Board consisted entirely of Europeans, who alone were responsible for setting policy and seeing that it was carried out. This meant among other things that they decided whether adequate facilities for separate education existed, without which racial coeducation was mandatory. For still another, no one in the government questioned the acts of the Education Board, including the ethnic results of its admission policies. As governor Eyre Hutson said in 1926, "If the Acting Superintendent of Schools is prepared to continue to accept responsibility in deciding all questions arising on applications for admission, he may continue his good offices in that direction; he should understand that the responsibility is a personal one and not imposed by me."[95] By so delegating responsibility in a critical area, Hutson and others in high office effectively removed themselves from any concern with education.

Despite this general indifference, there was some debate in high places concerning the nature and purpose of education in the primary schools. Acting Governor T. E. Fell felt that imperial responsibilities required that access to academic, English-language education be limited for non-Europeans. He wrote, rather convolutedly, in 1922:

> The matter of education is one which, in a Colony like Fiji, where the responsible race is numerically so inferior, is inseparable from considerations of the responsibilities of Empire. To impose upon the class which, in the circumstances, must naturally continue to lead, at any rate for many years to come, a form of education which, while progressive for native races, would be for them retrogressive is a step which would, in my opinion, lessen the value of that influence which alone can produce the standard qualifying for leadership, an influence which, if the Empire is to carry out its responsibilities amongst the native races of the Pacific must be left undisturbed.[96]

The education commission appointed to look into the school system in 1926 shared Fell's views. Schooling for the mass of Islanders "should be close to home and village life" and "adapted to the needs of rural workers getting their livelihood directly from the soil."[97] Governor Murchison Fletcher was of the same view. Only rudimentary English should be taught in primary schools, he said in 1931, as "indiscriminate teaching of English will lead the people away from their present contentment. They are asking for bread: will we give them a stone?" Fijians and Indo-Fijians were eager to learn English, the governor opined, "from mistaken ideas of the economic advantage to be derived therefrom."[98] Most Europeans supported the governor, but the Bishop of Polynesia disagreed. The knowledge of English among ordinary Indo-Fijians would lessen the influence of "agitators," check the propagation of "false ideas and superstition," and promote the advancement of European thought and culture. There was a political aspect to consider, too, the bishop continued. Without English, the Indo-Fijians "will continue to look to India for help and inspiration and will not identify themselves with the interests of the Colony as a whole."[99] The Colonial Office endorsed the policy of "gradual extension of English teaching on sound and practical lines,"[100] to make English the lingua franca of the colony.

While the desire of many Fijians for better educational facilities was neutralized by indifference within the Great Council of Chiefs, the efforts of Indo-Fijians in the same direction could not be so easily finessed. Facilities for educating Indo-Fijian children lagged behind those of all the other communities. In 1932, for example, 109 Fijian schools received some form of financial assistance from the government compared with only 6 government and 37 assisted schools for Indo-Fijians.[101] Only two years earlier, in 1930, the first of their schools, the Natabua Indian School, had added a secondary department. Even so modest an advance came without the encouragement of high officials. Governor Fletcher, for example, wanted to reorganize the educational bureaucracy by, among other things, replacing the director of education with a much lower level superintendent of education. He also resisted efforts to upgrade Indo-Fijian education, proposing that such upgrading be contingent on enactment of a special tax on specifically Indian agricultural products so Indo-Fijians would have to pay for it.[102]

The Colonial Office, however, rejected Fletcher's proposal on these matters, reminding him that as facilities for the education of Indo-Fijian children were not as extensive as they were for Fijian children, "the necessity for further extension of effective Indian education should be clearly recognized." The colonial government could not "divest itself of ultimate moral responsibility" for the extension and the improvement of Indo-Fijian education. Fletcher, the Colonial Office noted, "seems rather hurt by the fact that the Indians are more vocal than the Fijians." But, it continued, "it is hardly a matter for condemnation if a community expresses audibly its desire for more and better education."[103] One official at the Colonial Office regretted Fletcher's hostile attitude toward the Indo-Fijian community: "All this racial discrimination," he said, "is bad for Fiji and is sowing race-hatred."[104]

In the 1930s, some efforts were made to improve the educational system in the colony, especially regarding the registration of schools and of new teachers and the prescribing and approving of syllabi and teaching standards. In all, there was much apparent movement but few practical results. Between 1931 and 1939, net government spending on education dropped from 5.8 percent to 4.7 percent of all government expenditure, though the total enrollment in primary schools rose from 23,000 to 30,000 students.[105] Nonetheless, the government made sure, as the exam paper in Figure 3 illustrates, that the syllabus in the primary schools remained parochial and limited to the memorization of dates, facts, and events of the British Empire. Respect for authority, fulfillment of duty, discipline, pride in the achievements of British culture and civilization—these were the values that the colonial curricula fostered.

Electoral Representation

Competing political aspirations also produced conflict between ethnic and racial communities in Fiji. Concerning the three major groups in Fiji, as J. R. Pearson, the first secretary of Indian affairs, said in 1928, the problem was that Indo-Fijians were impatient for change, Europeans too resistant to it, and Fijians too willing to side with the Europeans in order to restrain the Indo-Fijians.[106] The resultant political infighting revolved around the issue of democratic representation on municipal councils on the local level and on the Legislative Council on the colonial level. Non-Europeans had been effectively excluded from voting in municipal elections by a 1901 ordinance that restricted the franchise to men of property who could also read, write, and speak English. When enacted, this ordinance probably disenfranchised few men who owned property and paid a meaningful amount of taxes. By the 1920s, however, non-Europeans outnumbered Europeans in Suva, and they paid a substantial proportion of all municipal taxes. By 1921, for example, the population of Suva, which totaled 12,982, included 1,753 Europeans, 7,246 Indo-Fijians, and 1,981 Fijians. In Levuka, to cite a different kind of example, Indo-Fijians were assessed the education rates even though Indo-Fijian children were excluded from the Levuka Public School.[107]

At the level of the Legislative Council, the situation was equally arbitrary and inequitable. In 1920 the council consisted of twenty-one members, among whom eleven were nominated officials, seven elected unofficial members (all Europeans), and two Fijian chiefs appointed by the governor from a panel chosen by the Great Council of Chiefs. There was also provision for an additional nonofficial nominated member (for Indo-Fijians since 1916). The right to vote for council members at this time was restricted to literate British subjects of European descent, who were 21 years of age or older, possessed property with a net value of £20 or more, or had a net yearly income of £120 or more. In 1923 as a result of pressure from a number of Indo-Fijian organizations, the government proposed to amend the Letters Patent to include two representatives of the Indo-Fijian community.

Reactions to the Indo-Fijian–led efforts to expand the franchise were predictable. Europeans of all persuasions were vehemently opposed because any expansion would benefit Indo-Fijians more than any other group and would, they said, amount to government endorsement of Indo-Fijian political aspirations. A meeting of Europeans convened in 1923 by solicitor J. C. Dive declared that Europeans "will resist, and will also encourage the native Fijians to resist with all means at their disposal, the contemplated attempt to admit Indian residents of Fiji to the body politic or to granting to them any measure—however small—of political status."[108] Similarly, Henry Marks, a leading local merchant and member of the Legislative Council, told visiting Secretary of State L. S. Amery in 1927 that if the policy was to "foster and encourage the Indians of this Colony, then we are starting 100 years too soon."[109] "We have the Indians here and we want to make the best of it," Marks said, which meant among other things teaching them "we are the Colony and not the Indians."[110] Fijian chiefs were equally opposed to expanding Indo-Fijian voting rights and political participation. Roko Tui Ba, Ratu Epeli Ganilau, did not

FRIDAY, 12TH NOVEMBER, 1937.   Index No.........
Time: 2.00—2.45
Marks: 100.

General Knowledge.

Write your examination number at the top right hand corner.

Before you begin number your paper 1 to 50.

If you do not know the answer to a question, leave it blank, do not guess.

---

1. The ex-King of England, Edward VIII, is now known as...

2. What great event took place in England on 12th May this year?...................................

3. ...., the capital of Spain, has been heavily bombarded this year.

4. Who is the heir to the throne of England?...

5. The present Governor of Fiji is..

6. Major Joske and (a)...and (b)...............................
   were the Fiji representatives to the coronation.

7. Name two great works of the Fiji Government during 1936 and 1937 to help traffic on Viti
   Levu..

8. The last Olympic games, where athletes from many countries compete, were held in..............

9. ....was Prime Minister of England when King Edward VIII
   abdicated.

10. ....is now Prime Minister of England.

11. The red cross of St.., the white cross of St. Andrew and the
    red cross of St. Patrick make up the Union Jack.

12. On the East side of the Sahara desert flows the famous river.....................................

13. ....a British possession in the Mediterranean, is a steep rocky
    Peninsula joined to the mainland of Spain by a sand isthmus.

14. Mount......................................7,318 feet, is the highest mountain in Australia.

15. Coolgardie and Kalgoorlie, in Western Australia, are noted for the production of.................

16. ....is the largest city of New Zealand.

17. ....is the chief export of New Zealand.

18. The Rocky mountains are on the west of..

19. The cold waters of the Labrador current, meeting the warm waters of the.........................
    to the South of Newfoundland cause dense fogs off the coast.

20. ....was the capital of Fiji before Suva.

21. Fiji sends her copra to..

22. ....is obtained from the juice of certain trees in the Equatorial
    Rain Forest. It is collected from the wild trees in the Amazon and Congo river basins
    and from plantations in the Malay Peninsula and Ceylon.

23. ....is the chief export of Fiji.

24. Where is the Deccan Plateau?..

25. Before men lived in tents or huts, they made homes for themselves in...............................

26. The..in Egypt are thousands of years old and were built by the ancient Kings to be used as tombs.

27. ...., the best known of the Roman governors, encouraged the Britons to build houses, towns, and markets.

28. ....a famous Roman Emperor, was born in Britain, and it was during his reign that the Christian Faith became a recognised religion of the Roman Empire.

29. To establish Christianity in England, Pope Gregory sent a band of missionaries to England under a monk named...

30. ....a great religious teacher of the 7th century was born at Mecca.

31. Charles the Great revived the Roman Empire and it came to be known as the.....................

32. Duke William of Normandy invaded England in the year........................and became King William I of England.

33. The travels of...to China and the East aroused men's interest in those countries in the 13th century.

34. ...., was a famous Italian Sculptor, Painter, and Architect who was born in 1475 and died in 1564.

35. ....was the brave French Commander who was killed in the same battle as General Wolfe.

36. ....won the province of Bengal and laid the foundations of the British Empire in India.

37. On June 18th, 1815,...was defeated by the Duke of Wellington at Waterloo.

38. In 1917, British troops, under General..captured Jerusalem.

39. The..Department was responsible for the work of the construction of the Rewa Bridge.

40. Bills become law when they have been passed by the....................................Council, and the Governor has given his assent.

41. The..Court is the highest in the Colony and hears appeals from lower courts.

42. ....duty is a tax levied on goods brought from overseas and must be paid before the goods are received by the importer.

43. If the hard outside covering of our teeth, called....................................is injured, the teeth soon decay.

44. The way to keep teeth from decaying is to keep them..............................

45. Habits are formed by...not by talking.

46. We should not....................................hard immediately before or after a meal.

47. If our clothes should take fire, we should not start to....................................

48. One way in which the skin regulates the heat of the body is by the........................glands.

49. Plenty of pure...................................inside and outside our body is necessary for its health.

50. Name two chief ways in which diseases may be spread...

51n37—300

Figure 3. Primary school leaving examination. (Courtesy National Archives of Fiji)

want Indo-Fijians, who he said had come from the lowest classes in India, to be socially or politically equal to the Fijians. "It is safe to anticipate," he said in 1922, "that if the Indians in Fiji will be given more political rights than us Fijians, it will be the commencement of disaffection in our minds, and we strongly object to being ruled by Indians, as we always have regarded British rule to be the sole foundation of honour, justice and fairness."[111]

This opposition to Indo-Fijian enfranchisement compounded the government's difficulties. While officials generally sympathized with the opposition, they could not altogether disregard Indo-Fijian political aspirations, especially while they were negotiating with the government of India for the resumption of immigration to the colony. Wrote T. E. Fell in 1922:

> We cannot do without our Indians, and from the Colony's point of view it is essential we should settle them as placidly and loyally as possible by giving them reasonable political status. The imperial point of view is a far larger one. The Government of India puts a ban on us as undesirable. We are under no obligation to her. We might say "We will treat Indians fairly, but we will do so according to our lights and we wish no further interference from you." Such a policy would be disastrous from the Imperial point of view. We are a pawn in a great game. The prize to be won is that of India, emerging from her present upheaval, as an integral portion of the Empire; on Dominion lines, to stick to us for all time. Possibly I am not so optimistic about the ultimate result, but we can afford to play no false card to increase chances of losing it.[112]

The Indian government had been concerned to protect the political interests of the Indo-Fijians. Its Colonies Committee had raised the issue in 1924, protesting that two representatives for a large and growing community were not enough.[113] How could they be, it reiterated in 1927, when 3,878 Europeans had seven members in the Legislative Council while 60,634 Indo-Fijians, who cultivated 44,378 acres of land and owned 36,000 head of stock, were to have only two?[114] The proposal to allocate only two seats to Indo-Fijians, it said, was unfair and "intended to assign an inferior status to Indians as compared with their British fellow-subjects, and to limit the growth of their political influence in the Colony." The government of India wanted a minimum of three seats for Indo-Fijians. The long-term goal, it continued, should be the abolition of communal franchise (in which each racial group voted for its own candidates separately) and its replacement by a common franchise (one person, one vote, one value). If this was not practicable, there should be communal representation on the basis of equality among the three main groups. When the Suva government pleaded provisions of the Deed of Cession that pledged the government to protect Fijian interests, the Indian government responded that it had "no desire to question" either the deed or the interests of the Fijian people. But it wondered, since "the elective representation on the Legislative Council at present enjoyed by the European community is presumably regarded as not inconsistent with the terms of the Deed of Cession," how it could "be argued that the grant of a similar status to their Indian fellow-subjects would infringe those terms."[115]

The argument was hard to rebut, and the Colonial Office made no direct effort to do so. It remained adamant, however, pointing to its special obligations to the Fijian people, "the discharge of which forms the first obligation of the Government in all matters relating to the Colony and its administration."[116] In the Letters Patent that arrived in the colony in 1929, Indo-Fijians and Fijians were each given three seats on the Legislative Council, to be filled by communal election, and European representation was decreased from seven to six seats, creating an artificial appearance of parity between Fijians and Indo-Fijians on the one hand and Europeans on the other. The property qualification for Indo-Fijian councilors was fixed at annual incomes of £120 compared with £200 for Europeans, and the literacy qualification for Indo-Fijian voters could now be met in Hindi, Urdu, Tamil, Telugu, or Gurumukhi.

These compromises failed to satisfy Indo-Fijian leaders. On being seated in the Legislative Council in 1929 and after raising a multitude of questions concerning Indo-Fijian grievances, the inaugural Indo-Fijian council members staged a walkout when their motion for a common franchise for all voters was defeated.[117] In moving the motion, Vishnu Deo repeated the now standard litany of arguments against communal voting: it was racially divisive, discriminatory toward Indo-Fijians, and inconsistent with pledges of political equality made to overseas Indians by the imperial government. Common roll voting, on the other hand, would unite races behind common purposes, diminish racial and religious barriers, encourage candidates to appeal to all elements of the population, and allay the fears Europeans and Fijians had of Indo-Fijian domination. S. B. Patel, who had played an important behind-the-scenes role in the decision to boycott the Legislative Council, wrote to his friend H. S. Polak in London:

It is the recognition of the principle of the common franchise for all His Majesty's subjects in the Colony that we are looking for. We stand for the Colony as a whole and not for any one section of it. We do not wish or desire to dominate. We do not want to see the Fijian suffer. His interest in the Colony is paramount and we want to maintain it and help him towards the achievement of elective representative in place of nomination. We do not want to predominate. We do not want any special or lower franchise qualifications. All we want is the recognition of the principle of common equal rights. We should not mind if we had only 100 voters, provided we had a common franchise. We should not even mind if a European represented us, so long as he was elected on a common ticket.[118]

These views did not impress Europeans and Fijian chiefs who saw the demand for a common franchise as nothing more than an attempt by Indo-Fijians to dominate the political order in Fiji. As J. J. Ragg told Ratu Pope Seniloli in 1921, the Indo-Fijians' demand for equality "is only a velvet covering for the steel claws underneath waiting for the opportunity to grab, cling to tenaciously, and finally control the whole or any portion of the earth in which these races have settled themselves."[119] Ragg urged the Ratu to "make it plain, with no uncertain voice, that you, the owners of this country, will not tolerate any franchise to the alien Asiatic British subject or otherwise, which would give him an equal voice with your own in the Councils of the Government of this Colony." Not surprisingly, Ragg did not see European control of the political and economic affairs of the colony as inimical to the interest of the *taukei*.

While European opposition to common franchise is understandable, that not all Indo-Fijians favored a common voting roll calls for some comment. Muslims, a minority in the Indo-Fijian population, opposed the idea because they feared being lost in the Hindu majority; so also did some orthodox Sanatani Hindus, who saw common voting as a device by which well-organized, militant Arya Samajis hoped to dominate Indo-Fijian politics. Representatives of these groups joined with conservative Europeans in the Legislative Council to have all council members appointed by the governor rather than elected. In 1935 K. B. Singh, an India-born, Nausori-based, politically ambitious schoolteacher moved a motion in the council for an appointed body, thus underlining the fact that cultural, religious, and personal concerns played a larger role in Indo-Fijian political thinking than did opposition to Fijian and European demands.

Those demands intensified as Indo-Fijian activism increased. In 1933 the Great Council of Chiefs approved a statement insisting that "the immigrant Indian population should neither directly nor indirectly have any part or direction of matters affecting the interests of the Fijian race."[120] Two years later, Ratu Sukuna, by then the most articulate and important Fijian leader, said that such things as democracy, elections, and majority rule were alien and incomprehensible to the Fijian people, who had lived for ages honoring their natural leaders as the best judges of all matters of state and of everything else of vital importance to them. The Crown Colony form of government, in which governance was entirely in the hands of the governor assisted by the advice of nominated or "natural" leaders of the respective communities, was best suited to the temperament of the Fijian people, being, as it was, "above the influences of local interests and prejudices." Democracy, which Indo-Fijians were demanding, would bring not peace but "nefarious and ruinous consequences."

Listening to the democratic clamour of the past months, [Sukuna continued] one question repeatedly comes up in our minds, for what did our fathers cede this country? They did so in order to secure for themselves, their people and posterity, a form of government that would ensure peace and happiness, justice and prosperity. Systems or institutions that fail in human experience to produce these things are not for us. For after all, the moral justification of representative government lies in its power to do good, and to achieve something of this the elements that contribute to it must all be present. We have come to the parting of ways and, looking ahead in the light not only of our interests but also of those to whom we handed over this country, we choose, with the full support of native conservative and liberal opinion, the system of nomination believing that along this road, and along it alone, the principle of trusteeship of the Fijian race can be preserved and the paramountcy of native interest secured.[121]

Such views effectively closed the door on political dialogue, not only between Indo-Fijians and Fijians, but between tradition-oriented Fijians like Sukuna and members of the Viti Cauravou, who preferred a more open political system among Fijians despite their opposition to the extension of political rights to Indo-Fijians. They almost certainly would have opposed another of Ratu Sukuna's proposals to have the Great Council of Chiefs nominate Europeans to represent Fijians in the Legislative Council, a proposal that even the government found retrogressive.[122]

Ratu Sukuna's views regarding the advantages of the nominative system found unexpectedly vigorous support among some leading Muslim Indo-Fijians, whose distrust of Hindus outweighed their suspicion of Europeans. In a memorandum, one of their number, Ra District Clerk A. G. Sahu Khan, told Governor Fletcher of their support for a nominated over an elected Legislative Council:

Members chosen on the elective principle possess a positive vice for they always dance to the music of the ring-leaders amongst their constituents, and often aim at getting cheap applause and thus sustaining their popularity amongst the masses, even if it be at the expense of their own community's welfare. De facto, the elective principle as compared with the nominative principle, simply transfers the power of selection from the head of the Administration to the garrulous "soap-box orator."[123]

Such support strengthened the hands of Fletcher, who opposed common voting and thought the campaign for it the work of a handful of agitators with little support among Indo-Fijians, whom he characterized as a "prosperous and contented community" of people with "no interest in or comprehension of political controversies."[124] Those of them who supported a common roll were, in his view, dupes of local politicians who were themselves the "uninformed tool of an extraneous organization, which is dangerously seeking opportunity to use the Colony for the purposes of its world-wide attack upon the British raj."[125]

Before he decided that a completely nominated council was the best way to neutralize the Indo-Fijian campaign on behalf of a common roll, Fletcher considered several other possibilities. One was the introduction of Chinese immigrants to counter the Indo-Fijian influence, a proposal that, as already noted, the Colonial Office vetoed. Another was to give Muslim Indo-Fijians a Legislative Council seat of their own, a proposal many Muslims heartily endorsed and which Fletcher thought would dilute the effectiveness of the "radical" Indo-Fijians. The Colonial Office, on the advice of the government of India, rejected this proposal on the grounds that the Muslims were too few to merit one of only three seats reserved for Indo-Fijians. Moreover, a separate seat for Muslims would institutional-ize, and therefore exacerbate, the friction between Hindus and Muslims. And it would not satisfy the government of India, which still supported the principle of a common voting roll.[126]

With these options foreclosed, Fletcher fell back to the position advo-cated by the two groups on whom he had to depend, the Fijian chiefs and the Europeans—replacing the elective council with a nominated one. Like the chiefs and the Europeans, he came to regard a nominated council as the only attainable alternative to the much-feared political domination of Fiji by the Indo-Fijians, perhaps in alliance with the small but growing community of Part-Europeans. The nominated council also had the advantage of support from some Indo-Fijian Muslim, Sanatani, and Christian leaders, as a means of protecting their interests in the larger Indo-Fijian community. The Indo-Fijian majority, however, remained adamant in their support of a common voting roll and an elective council. As two of their most important leaders, A. D. Patel and Vishnu Deo, said, "What we say and what we aspire to is that we have a right to criti-cize, a right to advise, a right to express our aspirations and our needs through the representatives elected by us in the government of this Col-ony."[127] This was the position of the government of India, which warned that the institution of a nominated council would likely increase political unrest among Indo-Fijians to the embarrassment of the Fiji government. C. F. Andrews voiced the opinion of many Indo-Fijians when he predicted that a nominated council "would accentuate the dictatorial powers of the Government and would encourage favouritism and flattery of the worst kind."[128]

Faced with irreconcilable alternatives, the Colonial Office effected a compromise in 1937. Again, the Legislative Council was reconstituted and enlarged. The new council would consist of thirty-one members, sixteen of whom were ex officio members of the colonial government. The remaining fifteen seats were divided equally among Fijians, Europeans, and Indo-Fijians. Three each of the Indo-Fijian and European seats were elected and others nominated, and all five Fijian seats were to be filled by the governor from a list of ten names submitted by the Great Council of Chiefs. One of the nominated Indo-Fijian seats came in practice to be reserved for Muslims. Indo-Fijians were disappointed with this arrangement, but acquiesced in it in part because it met at least one of their goals—representative parity with Europeans and Fijians. The Fijian chiefs accepted it because they effectively chose their own representatives in their own way; and the Europeans agreed to it as the best they could hope for under the circumstances. As they said at their political meetings, government control was preferable to "Indian control." The presence of an official majority and nominated members meant the colonial government's position would remain unchallenged. The new system lasted basically unchanged, though not unchallenged, for three decades.

The structure and composition of the municipal councils were also concerns of Indo-Fijians, and, in turn, of the government of India. The latter's Colonies Committee supported the introduction of a ward system in Suva elections and a simple educational test in Indo-Fijian vernacular languages as well as in English to qualify Indo-Fijians to vote in municipal elections. These proposals produced at the local level a political division that replicated the one just described at the colonial level. Europeans, who had built Suva, or so they said, insisted that they not have to share power there with Indo-Fijians, only recently removed from indentured life on the plantations. The influx of Indo-Fijians, they charged, was already threatening sanitary conditions in Suva and threatening, too, the trust Fijians had placed in Europeans. Henry Scott, a former advocate of European colonization and of the alienation of Fijian land, imagined disillusioned Fijians admonishing their fellow whites this way: "You Europeans have betrayed the trust we reposed in you, the Government has betrayed the trust reposed in it, a trust that is as great as it is possible to be."[129]

The members of the Viti Cauravou expressed similar views. At a meeting in the Suva Town Hall in October 1933, a group of them resolved that Indo-Fijians should be excluded from municipal affairs forever and "strongly urg[ed] that at no time in the future will it be made possible for [Indo-Fijians] to be appointed to positions of leadership in the Colony."[130] Why? Indo-Fijians, the members of the Viti Cauravou explained, "have been the cause of some big happenings in this Colony." In addition, "India is under Britain—Britain is not under India; therefore it is not right that one belonging to India should rule over the Europeans but that Indians in Fiji should be subject to Europeans." This logic pleased both the local Europeans as well as the Fijians, whose Great Council of Chiefs endorsed the view that municipal councils should consist entirely of members nominated by the governor.[131]

Governor Fletcher agreed with these sentiments and passed them on to the Colonial Office in 1935. His contemptuous view of the Indo-Fijians was apparent. Indo-Fijians, he told London, had come "from the most ignorant and backward part of the people of India," and recent events elsewhere in the world showed the "danger of placing power in the hands of an untutored people".[132] "I believe," he said, "that the point of view of an Indian in all parts of the world is largely coloured by his resentment that, no matter what his standing in terms of wealth or culture, the European persists in ignoring his social existence, but be this as it may, the important point with the local Indians is, not constitutional forms, but a determination that he shall get what the European has got, and that he should be granted all round equality of status."[133] Fijians and Europeans, he said, would never accept this; they would instead see it as an act of betrayal of the Deed of Cession.

Fletcher's arguments brought a perplexed reaction from the India Office, which questioned his assertion that only English-speaking people were "capable of taking an intelligent interest in municipal affairs and closely affected by their management." Noting also that the literary qualification for Indo-Fijian voters for the Legislative Council could be met in any of *five* Indo-Fijian languages (Hindi, Urdu, Tamil, Telugu, and Gurumukhi), as well as in English, the India Office continued: "It is difficult to see why a man whose education is considered sufficient to give him a part in the management of the affairs of the whole Colony, is not capable of taking part in the management of local affairs." Insistence on a knowledge of English was curious, as the government "insisted on electors being literate in a language which it is doing its best to prevent them from learning. So long as most of the Indians have had no opportunity of learning English, it seems only fair that literacy in their language should be allowed as a qualification."[134]

Concerning the Deed of Cession, an exasperated official at the Colonial Office minuted: "It seems to be impossible to explain to Sir Murchison Fletcher that granting the Indians a further measure of control in the towns, where Fijian interests are very small, is a very different thing from granting a control over the colony." Countering Fletcher's argument about the "political immaturity" of the Indo-Fijians, he said, "A few generations ago, it could have been said, and was said, that the British people were incapable of governing themselves, and I don't think we can permanently maintain the position that there are certain races which are for ever unfit to administer their own affairs. Certainly we cannot take that line as regards Indians, in view of political developments in India itself." This official concluded: "We shall never reach agreement with the Fiji government in its present temper."[135]

In the end, however, the colonial government prevailed. Faced with a choice between an expanded municipal franchise with more local control of municipal government on the one hand, and central government control of municipal government on the other, it chose the latter. Not all Europeans endorsed the choice. Among those who did not were Alport Barker, publisher of the *Fiji Times,* and a large number of the ratepayers. Even Sir Philip Goldfinch, head of the CSR, was opposed to centralized control of municipal government, but went along with the new policy because, he said, "the half-caste argument had persuaded him."[136] (He meant the increase in the Part-European population and its implication for European dominance.) In any case, on 1 January 1936, the previously elected Suva Municipal Council was replaced by a town board of seven ex officio members of the municipal government and six unofficial members, two each representing Europeans, Fijians, and Indo-Fijians, all six appointed by the governor. This system remained in place for a decade.

Land and Land Tenure

If political representation was one major source of conflict in Fiji, land tenure was another, and it acquired special urgency in the late 1920s and early 1930s, as Indo-Fijian agriculturalists spread through the colony. Until then, while large-scale European colonization was still a possibility, alienation of Fijian land had been a larger issue than land tenure. The demand for the sale of Fijian land was then led by European politicians and planters, among them Maynard Hedstrom, a prominent local businessman and member of the Legislative Council. Hedstrom considered Fijians "primitive and undeveloped," lower on the evolutionary scale than even Africans, and unfit to be judged by European standards. He wrote the Colonial Office accordingly in 1923:

> I suggest that it is a mistake to think that every change of policy should depend upon the consent of the natives—the position of the Government with regard to the Fijians is analogous to that of the guardian of a child who is heir to an estate. The guardian will do everything possible in the interests of the estate and the heir, but each step forward will not depend necessarily upon the consent of the child. We Colonists recognize the paramount duty of the Government is to protect the interests of the native but that does not mean that he should be allowed through caprice, or through lack of knowledge, to hinder and obstruct the natural development of the Colony—which development, wisely controlled, must be in the best interests of the native land owners.[137]

Governor Cecil Rodwell was also inclined to the view that reform was needed in Fijian land policy. He therefore asked the Colonial Office to authorize the sale of Crown land in the colony, subject to approval by the secretary of state. By doing so, he advised, the government would generate revenue from one of its principal assets, while the security of freehold tenure would spur increased productivity and additional investment.[138] The proposal would also benefit the Fijian people. According to Rodwell:

> The natives are awakening to the fact that they have far more land upon their hands than can possibly be required, either for their present or for their future needs, and that by keeping it out of the market they are losing a con-

siderable revenue which might be made available for educational development, the extension of medical facilities and the general improvement of their
condition.[139]

Some Fijian chiefs and provincial leaders also favored the idea of long-
term leasing of land; Bua and Cakaudrove, but not Macuata, told the governor in 1923 that he could even sell their land.[140] At a special meeting of
the Natewa Provincial Council, all the *buli* of the districts in Vanua Levu
adopted a resolution reading in part, "We approve of the Government
selling on our behalf all our leased lands in Vanua Levu and to pay[ing]
the interests on the proceeds to the owners at 6 monthly periods."[141] A
similar resolution was passed at Nabouwalu on 8 June 1923, at a meeting
attended by the *buli, tūraga ni qali, tūraga ni mataqali, tūraga ni koro,* and
native stipendiary magistrate. None other than Ratu Deve Toganivalu,
the Roko Tui Bua, said: "What is the use of your land lying idle and being
in a state of poverty? It would be far better if you gave your land to be
leased or sold, and thus acquire money. It is no use doing nothing with
waste land of no use to you."[142] Selling land, he continued, would mean
big bank deposits and good interest rates. It would also attract European
settlers, from whom Fijians could benefit through example and through
training in improved agricultural methods.

Not all Fijians accepted these views. Those who did not were especially
strong in the west. A decade earlier, when the government urged Fijians to
hand over their unused land for leasing, the Sabeto Fijians rejected the
proposal, saying they themselves might one day become cultivators. "We
think of our descendants and we foresee what will happen to them," said
the western chiefs, among them Tui Dreketi and Tui Nadroga.[143] The people of Nailaga and Bulu were more forthright. "Where would we reside?"
they asked in response to the lease proposal. "Our wives and children—
are they to live in goats' hiding places?" they continued when asked to
hand over surplus land.[144] These sentiments were as strongly held in 1923
as they had been in 1916.

Officials at the Native Secretariat also opposed the sale of Fijian land.
They pointed to the self-serving nature of European claims for more
freehold land and to the illusion behind the hope that Europeans would
ever settle in large numbers in Fiji. Eyre Hutson, then the colonial secretary, had pointed this out as early as 1917: "No European can clear and
cultivate land here without coloured labor. The Fijian will not serve as an
agricultural laborer for the wages likely to be offered, and therefore the
planter is dependent on cheap imported labour." Making land available
for sale would open the way not for settlers but for speculators, and government oversight would do nothing to prevent the inevitable corruption
that would invite. At no real risk to the speculators, Hutson said, the
Fijian "sells his birthright for a mess of pottage. He takes one bribe and
loses the control of his land forever."[145] Fell made the same point in 1923:

"If we allow the native land to be sold we may be letting the Fijian receive a momentary consideration for what future generations might never cease regretting they had parted with."[146]

Once again, European civil servants proved better guardians of Fijian interests than some of the Fijian chiefs. The Colonial Office accepted their argument and rejected the proposal to permit the sale of Fijian land. Responding to the Hedstrom petition in 1923, officials in London pointed out that there was no shortage of land available in Fiji for development. In any case, they argued, "there is at present no development to obstruct; and there is not likely to be until Fiji is able to compete as a field for the investment of outside capital, with colonies less remote and offering great attraction." Europeans already owned 20 percent of the land in Fiji and 35 percent of the cultivated area. The picture "of a congested European agricultural community, struggling to break down the barriers which exclude them from rich but sparsely populated native reserves, is not in accordance with reality," colonial officials concluded, ending the last serious effort to open Fijian land for sale.[147]

By the mid-1920s, a new source of pressure on Fijian land was beginning to come from Indo-Fijian tenants as they spread around the country following the end of indenture. The Indo-Fijians sought not to buy land but to systematize leasing procedures and realize security of long-term tenure. The existing leasing procedures were cumbersome and frustrating in the extreme. The would-be lessor applied to the commissioner of lands in Suva or to the commissioner in whose district the land was located. The commissioner notified the local *buli*, who in turn brought the application before a meeting of the District Council, at which the Fijian owners expressed their views on the proposed lease. These the *buli* then conveyed to the district commissioner, who communicated them and his own recommendations on the proposed lease and his estimate of the rental value of the land involved to the government. There, the by-now considerable file was reviewed jointly by the commissioner of lands and the secretary of native affairs. If they approved, the lease was then sold at public auction to the highest bidder.

In the 1920s, the procedure was simplified somewhat, but many of its irrational elements remained. The concerned *mataqali* head might still want a "little something" to agree to the lease, and he might also play one potential tenant against another. In Nadi these problems were so acute that the district commissioner reported that bribery was sometimes the only way an Indo-Fijian tenant could secure a lease.[148] Even bribery did not work, for there was no guarantee, after a chief had been bribed, that the District Council or the colonial government would approve the lease. Another problem with this system was that because tenants naturally wanted only the best land, many undesirable parcels remained unused.

One source of pressure to change the system was the CSR. By the

1930s, nearly half of the sugar cane in the islands was grown on land leased from Fijians. In 1934, to illustrate, 4,100 farmers leased 45,500 acres from the company, while 4,600 leased 35,000 acres from Fijians. By this time, agricultural development in the colony was threatened by the uncertainties of short-term leases as well as the failure of Fijians to turn to cane growing in large numbers. Sir Philip Goldfinch therefore urged that "any sign of the 'dog in the manger' attitude on the part of the land owners must be obliterated with a firm policy of the Crown."[149] That is, Fijians must become cane farmers or lease their land to those who would, which in this case meant Indo-Fijian farmers.

There was also pressure from Indo-Fijian cane growers, who were increasingly leasing more Fijian land. Issues of land tenure were raised at virtually every conference of Indo-Fijian leaders. They were concerned for more secure leases, full compensation for improvements made on the land when expired leases reverted to Fijian owners, and legislation governing relations between landlords and tenants. In addressing these issues, Indo-Fijians had the support of the Imperial Indian Citizenship Association of Bombay[150] as well as the government of India, which expressed concerns in 1935 that the system of limited leases "creates insecurity of tenure which leaves the Indian lessee very much at the mercy of the Fijian landlord." This, in turn, threatened the well-being of the colony, which "must largely depend upon a satisfactory adjustment of [Indo-Fijian] rights and opportunities in relation to agricultural land."[151]

Fijian thinking showed an awareness of these pressures as well as the emotions that land issues always generated in the islands. At the 1930 meeting of the Great Council of Chiefs, there was talk of asking for the return to Fijian hands of all lands sold before cession; of having all land of extinct *mataqali* returned to the *yavusa;* and of refusing to pay any compensation for improvements made by tenants when the leases expired and reverted to Fijians.[152] Ratu Sukuna raised other prospects. Speaking on the land question in the Legislative Council in 1933, he said: "The Indian community, having shown us the way and given us the example, can hardly expect to continue to hold all the agricultural land in the sugar districts, in places where the plough mints money. They will recognize that Natives, in their own country, have a right to some of the good things of this life, and it is for this reconciliation of community interests . . . that I plead."[153] This was a legitimate, but in the circumstances disingenuous, argument. Sukuna was an opponent of *galala* farming and an advocate of traditional forms of subsistence farming for Fijians. In addition, despite government encouragement, Fijians had little success as cane farmers. That was one reason why in 1934 the chiefs adopted a measure directing that when leases expired on cane lands, the lands would be leased again by the government for the owner's benefit if the owner did not return the land to cane cultivation.[154]

Initially, the colonial government had been reluctant to pressure Fijians into leasing their unused land. As late as 1935, Suva told the Colonial Office that criticism of the system was exaggerated, that most chiefs were leasing their lands, and that those who were not leasing intended themselves to enter the world of commercial cultivation. The last prospect, the government explained, was the "symptom of a movement which is healthy and worthy of encouragement, and any action on the part of the Government to thwart the ambition of the Fijian to produce another economic crop may tend to shake his confidence in Government."[155]

Despite this commitment to Fijians, the government was already taking steps, such as revising the Real Property Ordinance of 1876, to help tenants on their lands. These steps included provisions for reducing rent during the term of lease contracts of both Fijian and Crown lands, relief from excessive rent during emergencies, and greater statutory protection for subtenants. Restrictions on Indo-Fijian residence in certain areas not close to the district officers were also relaxed, and the prohibition against Indo-Fijian farmers owning more than ten acres of agricultural land, which was difficult to enforce in any case, was removed. In addition, procedures for applying for leases were streamlined. Applications would be considered on their merit and approved subject only to the quality of the land and the tenant's ability to work it. Similarly, regulations limiting leases to Indo-Fijians to twenty-one years were abolished and replaced by others that fixed leases at twenty-one years with an option for renewal for another nine years if at least a quarter of the leased land had been under continuous cultivation.[156]

Such piecemeal efforts, though important, were not enough to satisfy the Indo-Fijian farmers or their advocates in and out of the government of India. To satisfy that government, the Suva government would have to intervene more actively to reconcile the competing economic interests of Indo-Fijians and other groups in Fiji. Accordingly, the Suva government told the Great Council of Chiefs in 1936 that it would take a greater role in the "stewardship of native lands," for purposes of promoting continuity of policy and security of tenure while also ensuring ample land to meet the needs of Fijians.[157] By this time, the Fijian chiefs themselves had concluded that leasing policy needed reform to remove the corruption that had crept into its operation and given landowners a bad name. Unless they took the lead, Ratu Sukuna told the chiefs in 1936, the government would enact its own reforms. There were other considerations, too, Sukuna said:

> We cannot in these days adopt an attitude that will conflict with the welfare of those who like ourselves wish to live peacefully and increase the wealth of the Colony. We are doing our part here and so are they. We want to live; they do the same. You should realize that money causes a close inter-relation of interests. If other communities are poor, we too remain poor. If they prosper, we also prosper. But if we obstruct other people without reason from using our lands, following the laggards there will be no prosperity. Strife will overtake

us, and before we realize the position, we shall be faced with a situation beyond our control, and certainly not to our liking. . . . You must remember that Fiji of today is not what it used to be. We are not the sole inhabitants; there are now Indians and Europeans.[158]

This conciliatory attitude facilitated the government's efforts to reform land policy, including the regularizing of leasing procedures. The first draft of the new Native Lands Ordinance was completed in 1937, and the finished version was enacted three years later, placing the entire responsibility for leasing of all Fijian land in the hands of a statutory body, the Native Land Trust Board, and providing for the reservation of sufficient land to meet the needs of Fijians. With that, the land question was settled for more than a generation.

The Colonial World

During the interwar years, Fiji was a quintessential British colony, its government closed, its life compartmentalized along sharply drawn lines. The Colonial Office in London, which consisted of senior former colonial administrators from throughout the British Empire, maintained a close supervision of the colony's affairs. Virtually every decision the government in Suva made, every policy change it considered, had to be approved by London. On many matters, the Colonial Office was guided by the governor's advice, but there were many issues—education, land policy, and electoral representation—on which his advice was rejected or modified. In all matters affecting the Indo-Fijian community, the Colonial Office had to consult the India Office, which in turn was in touch with the government of India. As a result, the views of the Indian government carried weight in Fijian affairs—the subcontinent was, after all, the "jewel in the British Crown." Rarely did the Colonial Office adopt a policy of concern to Indo-Fijians that the India Office opposed. In the event of an irreconcilable difference of opinion between the two, the dispute went to the British cabinet, which neither of them wanted. In many ways, the India Office's role in safeguarding the interests of the Indo-Fijians was not unlike that of the Deed of Cession for Fijians. That role declined after World War II and vanished altogether when India achieved independence in 1947. In contrast, the symbolic significance of the deed for Fijians increased notably.

In Fiji itself, governors occupied an undisputed place atop the colonial hierarchy. The governors varied greatly in background and experience. Some, such as Sir Arthur Gordon and Sir Everard im Thurn, were innovative men with academic turns of mind, and the authority of one like Sir John Thurston rested on his long residence in Fiji. Many twentieth-century governors came to Fiji with backgrounds in colonial administration in Africa and elsewhere and attempted to use their previous experience in formulating policies in Fiji. With the parameters of action imposed on Fiji's governors by the Deed of Cession and reaffirmed regularly by the Colonial Office, they had little opportunity for initiatives of their own. Their effectiveness was further reduced because none of them stayed on beyond their usual five-year terms. For the most part, they were occupied with routine matters of administration.

In this task, they were assisted by the two branches of the colonial legislature, the Legislative and the Executive councils. The former consisted of a permanent majority of ex officio members (heads of government departments) and a minority of elected members representing the three major population groups in the islands. In debating government policy and articulating the views and interests of those population groups, the Legislative Council functioned like a caricature of the Westminster tradition; it was a caricature because the government was always assured of majority votes for any legislation it chose to put forward. The Executive Council, consisting of the governor, select heads of major government departments, and a few appointed European members, functioned as the cabinet. Non-Europeans joined this body after World War II. This structure lasted until the mid-1960s.

The colonial officials were expected to conduct themselves with the decorum and dignity befitting members of "the greatest Empire the world has ever known," an empire that "stands for all that is good in the modern world."[159] To this end, London mandated a precise, uniform code of conduct for all its colonial representatives. Confidential reports on senior civil servants were regularly sent to London. These officials, indeed all members of the civil service, were required to observe political neutrality and could not express an opinion on any matter of public or political importance without the approval of the secretary of state. Those who breached the code were variously demoted and transferred to remote parts of the empire, involuntarily retired and pensioned off, reprimanded, or dismissed from the service, depending on the severity of the offense and the social status of the offender. The district commissioners, the government's most senior representatives in the provinces, were required to pass language examinations in either Hindi or Fijian, depending on the location of their posting; junior officials were likewise encouraged to acquaint themselves with the language and customs of the majority ethnic group in their area.

All agencies of the government had roles to play in fostering the ideals the empire attached to itself—loyalty, self-sacrifice, and endurance. The schools, for example, staged colony-wide celebrations of Empire Day, the sovereign's birthday, and Cession Day. A celebration is illustrated in the circular that the director of education sent to head teachers of all government and assisted schools, describing ceremonies to be staged in commemoration of Empire Day in 1929 (Figure 4). The aim of the observance, as

FROM THE DIRECTOR OF EDUCATION.

TO HEAD TEACHERS OF GOVERNMENT AND ASSISTED SCHOOLS.

Subject : EMPIRE DAY, 24TH MAY, 1929.

26th April, 1929.

LAST year Empire Day was more generally observed than in former years, but it is the Acting Governor's wish that celebrations should be held in all schools throughout the Colony

It is suggested that the morning session be devoted to teaching the children some of the main facts of the growth and extent of the Empire to which they belong, and to awakening a deep interest in and an emulation of those civic virtues of loyalty, self-sacrifice and endurance which have been such assets in building up the Empire.

Lord Meath, the founder of the Empire Day movement, says:—" It is intended that Empire Day celebrations shall be an outward sign of an inner awakening of the peoples of the British Empire to the serious duties and responsibilities which lie at their door."

You will aid to fulfil the spirit of this intention if your lessons are planned to promote in your pupils' minds a deeper sense of patriotism, a stricter self-discipline, a hardier endurance, a deeper respect for others and a strict obedience to lawful authority. The history of the development of the Empire contains the names of explorers and navigators whose lives exemplify one or other of these virtues.

For the juniors it is suggested that the history of the Union Jack should be taken and the moral that " Union is strength " emphasised. Such a lesson might be followed by crayon drawings and, time permitting, talks on the daily life and habits and customs of the children of other parts of the Empire. It should be explained that the 24th of May was selected as Empire Day because it is the birthday of the Queen and Empress of India during whose reign the Empire was consolidated. Further, they should learn the rallying cry of " For God, Duty and Empire."

In all schools the National Anthem should be learnt and in those schools where it is appropriate, Kipling's Recessional or " Dear Land of the Morning " should be learnt and recited or sung at the opening of the celebrations.

The afternoon session should be devoted to the usual celebrations and the following programme is suggested:—

1. Assembly of children outside the school.
2. Unfurling and saluting the Union Jack.
3. National Anthem.
4. Address by the District Commissioner or the School Manager or a prominent citizen or the Head Teacher, emphasising our glorious heritage and the privileges it brings.
5. Recitation of patriotic poetry.
6. Cheers for the Empire.
7. Sports.

A programme such as this will need to be carefully organised, so you are requested to give it your early attention.

In those districts where several schools and the Government Station are located it is desired that the Head Teachers form a committee to make definite arrangements for a combined celebration to which the District Commissioner should be invited to deliver an address to the children. Details concerning the programme, arrangements for the collection and allocation of sports' subscriptions for prizes and the programme of sports' events should be agreed upon well in advance.

A short report of the celebrations held and of the number of children attending should be forwarded to the Director.

Copies of the pieces of patriotic poetry referred to above are attached for the use of those teachers who are not acquainted with them.

A. H. PHILLIPS,
for Director of Education.

ANNEXURE.

―――――

GOD SAVE THE KING.

God save our Gracious King,
Long live our noble King,
        God Save the King !
Send him victorious,
Happy and glorious,
Long to reign over us,
        God Save the King !

Thy choicest gifts in store,
On him be pleased to pour,
        Long may he reign !
May he defend our laws,
And ever give us cause,
To sing with heart and voice,
        God Save the King !

FIJIAN HYMN.

Dear land of the morning,
Child of the sun returning,
From thy bounty giving
All that we require,
Thee do our souls adore.

Sweet land and precious,
Rich land and gracious,
Under thy cloudless skies,
And o'er thy hills and seas
Do we find peaceful days.

Beautiful land of love,
O ! land of mirth and song,
If ever thou art wronged,
Glory 'twill be for us
To suffer and to die.

RECESSIONAL.
(1897.)
Printed by kind permission of
Mr. RUDYARD KIPLING, LL.D., D.Litt.

God of our fathers, known of old,
        Lord of our far-flung battle-line,
Beneath Whose awful Hand we hold
        Dominion over palm and pine—
Lord God of Hosts, be with us yet,
Lest we forget—lest we forget !

The tumult and the shouting dies;
        The captains and kings depart:
Still stands Thine ancient sacrifice,
        An humble and a contrite heart.
Lord God of Hosts, be with us yet,
Lest we forget—lest we forget !

Far-called, our navies melt away;
        On dune and headland sinks the fire:
Lo, all our pomp of yesterday
        Is one with Nineveh and Tyre !
Judge of the Nations, spare us yet,
Lest we forget—lest we forget !

If, drunk with sight of power, we loose
        Wild tongues that have not Thee in awe
Such boastings as the Gentiles use,
        Or lesser breeds without the Law—
Lord God of Hosts, be with us yet,
Lest we forget—lest we forget !

For heathen heart that puts her trust
        In reeking tube and iron shard,
All valiant dust that builds on dust,
        And guarding, calls not Thee to guard,
For frantic boast and foolish word—
Thy Mercy on Thy People, Lord !
                                        Amen.

Figure 4. Empire Day memorandum. *(Courtesy National Archives of Fiji)*

the circular says, was to instill in students "a deeper sense of patriotism, a stricter self-discipline, a harder endurance, a deeper respect for others and a strict obedience to lawful authority"—in short, to produce law-abiding colonists loyal to "their" imperial heritage. Such observances, varying only in detail, continued well into the 1960s, as I well remember, when colony-wide essay competitions were held to describe the achievements of colonial rule or the significance of the Deed of Cession (or the important contribution of the CSR to the development of Fiji).

In the larger society, Europeans were a small, privileged minority at the top of the social hierarchy. They were not a homogeneous group, for there were significant internal differences among them of rank, power, and prestige according to wealth, occupation, place of residence, and country of origin.[160] The ranking English civil servants, for example, were generally the elite of the elite, especially in their own estimation, and they and resident urban professionals lived lives of social exclusiveness. Many Australians and New Zealanders, on the other hand, jostled for whatever advantages, social and economic, they could get. The New Zealanders thought of themselves as better, more refined representatives of colonial English culture, and the Australians were generally less respectful of the rituals and protocols of colonial life. The urban, professional Europeans had little social interaction with other racial groups, but rural planters and traders interacted rather more freely with Fijians and Indo-Fijians, even often speaking their languages.

Still, there were privileges Europeans enjoyed because they were Europeans. In urban areas, they lived in all-European neighborhoods from which other ethnic groups were effectively excluded, neighborhoods such as Toorak, named after a fashionable Melbourne suburb, Suva Point, and Muanikau in Suva. The best wards in hospitals were reserved for Europeans, as was access to all supervisory and managerial positions in the civil service—non-Europeans, for example, could hold no position beyond the level of a grade two clerk until after World War II. Europeans were likewise entitled to trial by jury in all cases at law, but non-Europeans were not. Europeans could drink alcohol without restrictions, whereas Fijian men even of rank and Indo-Fijian men of "good standing" had to have special liquor permits. Fijian and Indo-Fijian men were expected to take their hats off as a mark of respect for Europeans and to retreat to the back of passenger trains to make way for European travelers.

These forms of petty discrimination were, in a way, resented as much as more serious forms of restriction, especially by Indo-Fijians. They might not drink alcohol, for example, and many did not for cultural or religious reasons, but they resented having to seek a permit while Europeans did not. Proud of their ancient heritage and civilization and resentful of their enforced place at the bottom of the colonial hierarchy, the Indo-Fijians had no choice but to resist the European-dominated colonial order. In this they were unlike Fijians, many of whom openly admired Europeans and European civilization. As Ratu Sukuna stated in the Legislative Council in 1947:

> Indians, like ourselves, have much to gain from European teaching on the practical approach to life. This approach, based on the humanities, refined by Christianity, steeled by economic and political encounters, tempered by defeats and victories, this approach, I say, has proved itself, especially in the

case of the British pattern, as the only effective approach to life. The attitude of mind created by this experience, by meeting and overcoming of difficulties in the vicissitudes of life, has in the course of centuries produced the spirit of co-operation, of moderation and of tolerance.[161]

This appreciation of things British facilitated the political coalition between European and Fijian leaders that emerged in this period. Another facilitator was fear of Indo-Fijian dominance.

Fijians and Indo-Fijians viewed each other warily, often through the prisms of prejudice and stereotypes. For the most part, Fijians watched with suspicion and even hostility as Indo-Fijians established a securer footing in Fiji and articulated their demands for equal political and other rights. Many feared that Indo-Fijians could progress only at their expense. Indo-Fijians, in turn, regarded Fijians as people crippled by the weight of traditional obligations and chiefly exactions, needlessly standing in the way of their progress. Where they lived in proximity, the two groups engaged in some cultural borrowing and adaptation, but there was almost no intermarriage. Government policy did nothing to encourage the two groups to cross each other's boundaries. On the contrary, it effectively excluded Indo-Fijians from residence in Fijian villages, even where they were accepted by Fijians, because, officials argued, their presence encouraged gambling and quarreling among the Fijians. Indo-Fijians did not understand the art of communal living and found it impossible to submit to the Native Regulations governing Fijian life.[162] Even those Indo-Fijians who were accepted by the Fijian villagers were forced to leave. In addition, the government excluded Fijian and Indo-Fijian children from each other's schools even in places where they lived as neighbors. The gulf between the two communities that resulted from culture, language, and religion was exacerbated by government policy, which made no attempt to draw them together "into truly common bonds of citizenship."[163]

3   For King and Country: 1939–1959

On the eve of World War II, a bit of doggerel appeared in the *Fiji Times*.
Titled "To Whom It May Concern," it went:

> Please be kind to Britain
>   She isn't very strong
> Her Navy is inefficient
>   Her Army has all gone wrong
> Her ARP* is useless
>   Her Air Force is too small
> Her people so degenerate
>   She has no morale at all
> She doesn't want to fight you
>   She's so convinced you will win
> She'll let you take her empire
>   If it will save her skin
> She's old, decayed and senile
>   And you have strength and youth
> So please be kind to Britain
>   Don't keep abusing Britain
> Or you may learn the truth.[1]

---

*Air Raid Precaution

The "truth" was what Britain encountered in the war and in its aftermath.
The war signaled the dramatic decline of British power, absolutely as well
as relatively, and with it the fading glory of an empire that was never as
strong or viable as it appeared. The empire's secret was that the "natives"
had always been restless, and once its vulnerability was clear, they turned
on the empire. India, the cornerstone of the empire, led the way with independence in 1947, followed in turn by other Asian and African colonies,
and finally by insular possessions, protectorates, and dependencies around
the globe. For Britain as well as the peoples of its once far-flung empire,
the world would never be the same again.

The impact of the war on Fiji was far less direct or immediately apparent. Not a single shot was fired on Fijian soil for the defense of Fijian lives and property; nor, except for a brief period in 1942 when the islands seemed to be within reach of Japanese aggression, was the colony in any danger. Yet in many significant ways the war cast a long, dark shadow over Fiji and left in its wake a legacy as troubling as it had brought to other Pacific islands that came into the vortex of the fighting itself. The people of Fiji divided sharply over the meaning and purpose of the war and over matters of loyalty and disloyalty to the empire and the war effort; these divisions exacerbated the ethnic and political tensions already troubling the islands. Nonetheless, the war enlarged Fiji's position in the southwestern Pacific and brought Islanders in closer contact with the outside world than they had ever been before. New values and ideas crept into the colony, and the changes they helped to induce are among the foundations of modern Fiji. Many roots of contemporary Fiji can be traced to events that immediately followed the war.

War

News of mounting tension in Europe and rumors of war had been circulating in Fiji in early 1939. Schoolchildren already knew the names and alleged deeds of Hitler and Mussolini and of the British Lion carrying the flag of freedom and justice in the face of great odds. The headline in the *Fiji Times* on 4 September signaled the climax of the mounting tension: "England At War." Fiji, like the rest of the empire, was at war, too. That night at 8 o'clock the governor spoke to the colony by radio on the outbreak of war. "If the principle of 'might is right' were established throughout the world," he said, quoting the words of King George VI, "the freedom of our own country and the whole of the British Commonwealth of Nations would be in danger. But far more than this, the peoples of the world would be kept in bondage of fear; and all hope of settled peace and security of justice and liberty among nations, would be ended. This is the ultimate issue that confronts us."[2]

A day later, the governor announced several emergency measures to put the colony on a war footing. Censorship was imposed on all postal and telegraphic communication, the movement of enemy aliens in Fiji restricted, and a Necessary Foodstuff and Controls Committee appointed to prevent profiteering.[3] Among Europeans in the colony, there was understandable anxiety about the role they knew they would be called on to play in the event of actual fighting in or near Fiji and about the fate of their families and friends "back home," in England, Australia, or New Zealand. Among Fijians and Indo-Fijians, the initial concerns were less pointed and less enduring; it was, after all, difficult to remain constantly on alert about events taking place on the other side of the world. By early 1940, a sem-

blance of normalcy had returned to Suva, as the *Fiji Times* indicated edito-
rially in January:

> Wars come and go, as also do cycles of boom and depression, and when we
> depart this world we leave it in very much the same state as we came in,
> whether we be paupers or millionaires. It is not bad individual policy to
> endeavour to live as well and as comfortably as possible within one's means
> in hail, rain or fine. And it is nice to be able to do business with people. Most
> likely they will come back and do the same with you.[4]

Despite this mood of business-as-usual, Fiji was ill-prepared to defend
itself. The colony had had no regular military force since the departure of
the Royal Engineers in 1878. In late 1939, the government had at its disposal four separate companies of volunteer infantry that had only recently
been amalgamated under a single command. When the war began, this
nucleus was augmented substantially, after which forces were deployed
strategically throughout the colony. One group of soldiers was placed in
the Suva area, and another, financed in part by the CSR and the Emperor
Gold Mines, on the western side of Viti Levu to guard the sugar mills and
the gold mines in Tavua. In addition, there was a small Indo-Fijian platoon based in Rewa, first established in 1934, but disbanded just before
the war for reasons that will be discussed later. Altogether, 11,000 men
from Fiji served in the military during the war, a total that peaked in
August 1943 when 8,513 men were in uniform. Of these, 1,070 were local
Europeans, 808 were New Zealanders attached to the Fiji Defence Forces,
6,371 Fijians (of whom 3,083 were in the Labour Corps), and 264 Indo-
Fijians (158 of whom were in the Labour Corps).[5]

In addition to shoring up the defense forces, the government constructed air raid shelters, slit trenches in Suva and other areas considered
vulnerable, recruited auxiliary fire-fighting units, and secured emergency
water supplies and medical facilities in blast-proof shelters. The civilian
population in Suva and Lautoka was carefully instructed on the use of
these emergency supplies and on what to do in the event of an attack (see
Figure 5). In Fijian villages, the *tūraga ni koro,* or village leaders, were
coached to beat the *lali,* a slit drum, if and when prearranged signals
announced the arrival of the enemy. In towns, that dreadful news was to be
spread by telegraphic signals, also prearranged and circulated among the
populace. In Suva the population was prepared for the expected emergency through regular drills and blackouts that were repeated every week.[6]

Almost as soon as the war began, the government took measures to
increase revenues to support the imperial war effort. On 7 September
1939, the Legislative Council voted a supplementary budget of £15,000, of
which £12,172 was to pay for the increased military and naval forces and
the rest to cover the special expenses created by administering the intern-

SUVA DISTRICT

AIR-RAID

SHELTERS

Plans of the Town of Suva showing the Air-raid Shelters are on exhibition at the General Post Office, the Town Hall, and Police Headquarters.

The shelters are listed below for the information of the general public.

Take steps NOW to select the most suitable shelter nearest your home also to the place where you work.

Preparations are in hand to make these public shelters gas-proof and the general public will shortly be instructed as to what to do in the event of gas bombs being used in an air-raid. If you have a private shelter you can make it gas-proof by hanging at each entrance a "gas curtain", i.e. a blanket or carpet weighted down with wooden cross pieces or slats, and with one foot trailing along the ground. When not in use the blanket should be rolled up and tied in position but in emergency it must be let down and kept wet.

If you have a private shelter, make sure that its location is known to your Warden.

DISTRIBUTION OF SHELTERS.

MARKS' PARK.
WAIMANU ROAD (opposite Lilac Theatre).
NINA STREET.
MARKS LANE.
ELLERY STREET.
RODWELL ROAD.
SEA LARK HILL.
FORSTER STREET.
GIRLS' GRAMMAR SCHOOL.
DISRAELI ROAD.
HOLLAND STREET.
HOLLAND STREET (under Mission School).
CAKOBAU ROAD.
VICTORIA PARK.

PRINCES ROAD.
RESERVOIR ROAD.
POOR HOUSE.
C.W.M. HOSPITAL.
EXTENSION STREET.
HUON STREET.
BROWN STREET.
DOMAIN ROAD WEST.
GLADSTONE ROAD.
HERBERT STREET.
REWA STREET.
KNOLLYS STREET.
SWALLOWS CAVE.
TAMAVUA BY-PASS.
WAIMANU ROAD.

Police Headquarters,
9th February, 1942.

J. E. WORKMAN,
Commissioner of Police.

Figure 5. *(Courtesy National Archives of Fiji)*

ment camps, the censorship program, and the collection and storage of emergency supplies.[7] Early in 1940, individual and residential taxes were increased by 25 percent and corporate income taxes by 50 percent.[8] By early 1942, these increases had produced £110,000 in additional revenues, of which £40,000 were collected in just one day, including £10,000 each from the CSR, Emperor Gold Mines, and Loloma Gold Mines.[9]

This was no mean effort for a financially strapped colony in a remote part of the British Empire. Eventually, Fiji's total war expenditure amounted to nearly £5 million, the largest of any comparable colony in the empire, and nearly half the total local revenue (£9,250,000) raised during the war years.[10] Voluntary contributions enlarged this contribution in significant but unknown amounts. The Patriotic Knitting and Sewing Society, led mostly by European women, was an active and effective raiser of private funds. Fijian men and women, to cite another example, performed *meke* and *taralalā,* and Indo-Fijians staged soccer and singing competitions to raise funds for the war. Following the example of the Rewa Fijians in World War I, Indo-Fijians raised enough money on their own to buy a fighter bomber for the Royal Air Force, which they asked to be named the *Fiji Indian,* just as the one in 1917 had been called the *Rewa.*[11]

News of the war and progress on fronts around the world was not always easy to come by. The *Fiji Times,* ever the imperial cheerleader, carried stories of heroic Allied efforts in the face of great odds. In rural areas, where there was little news and even less interest in the war, radio carried the news in Fijian and Hindustani for a few hours on selected days. In rural towns such as Ba, Lautoka, and Labasa, loudspeakers were installed at strategic marketplaces to broadcast radio coverage. By 1944, when the war had receded from the Pacific, there were five thousand licensed radio sets in the islands and presumably several times that many listeners to the radio news. In addition, a great many propaganda pamphlets were printed and widely circulated in villages and schools throughout Fiji.[12] Among the notable titles in Fijian were:

A Kedra Magiti Na Kai Jamani ("Food for the Germans"), an illustrated booklet depicting German plunder of food supplies in conquered Europe.
Yalogaga Nai Tekiteki Ni Veigauna ("Gallantry—the Garland of All Ages"), a booklet describing the acts of bravery of various decoration winners.
A Dromu Ni Siga Ena Veivanua Vakatali ("The Sun Sets on the Italian Empire"), a booklet describing Allied victories against Italy and culminating in the expulsion of the Axis powers from Italy's African colonies.
Ko Itila: Lasulasu ka Dauveidabui ("Hitler: Liar and Deceiver").

Such literature no doubt had its effect in Fijian villages, where loyalty to the British monarch, the highest chief of all, was already strong. As some of the Fijian recruits put it jokingly, they would eat Her Majesty's enemy if they caught up with him, and not *vakadua* 'right at once', but piece by piece, "beginning with the little finger on Monday and proceeding with the rest."[13]

Indo-Fijians showed no such enthusiasm for the war or for the British cause. They read the government periodical *Vijay* 'Victory', which praised Allied gallantry and just as regularly foresaw the imminent collapse of enemy forces. War propaganda material imported from India circulated among people living in towns and surrounding villages. Propaganda films were very popular. Among the notable films was *Desert Victory,* on the Allied conquest of North Africa, and it, like other cinema fare, was regularly accompanied by news of the war reflecting Allied views of things.[14] All this kept the people of Fiji in touch with the world of war far away, though for much of the time the war itself remained a remote and relatively abstract event. For Fijians and Indo-Fijians alike, but especially for Indo-Fijians who lived in scattered settlements and had few readily accessible means of communication with the world outside, the rhythms of life were what they had been before talk of war had ever been heard.

The War in Nadi

The place in Fiji most affected by the war, not directly from combat or occupation but from the presence of Allied forces, was Nadi.[15] A sleepy, dusty little sugar town before the war, Nadi received the first contingent of New Zealand troops in November 1940; their numbers were augmented at the end of 1941, when New Zealand assumed responsibility for the defense of the colony. After the onset of the Pacific War following the Japanese attack on Pearl Harbor on 7 December 1941, much larger forces, eventually totaling 8,000 troops, mostly Americans, also arrived. For a time, Nadi was home for a large number of infantrymen, a fighter aerodrome, a trans-Pacific airport, and a command station, as well as the base for coastal, field, and antiaircraft artillery units.

The resulting concentration of activity and people, including large numbers of laborers from Fiji itself, had an immediate impact on the local residents. Many Indo-Fijian tenants on the fringes of the town were evicted and surrounding Fijian villages uprooted to make room for war-related construction work, including accommodations for the troops. All the evicted Indo-Fijian families had to fend for themselves; many of their members wandered about town, finding casual or war-related employment in Nadi, or living off relatives. Some of the families were moved to Namaka or to the Sabeto valley, where their intrusion was actively resented by local Fijians, who sometimes terrorized them, going into their homes and demanding food while the men were away at work. In Namaka the use of Fijian land to settle the displaced tenants angered the Fijians there, and the result was sometimes violence.[16] These incidents left an aftermath of bitterness that added to the already strained relations between the two groups.

Nor were relations always smooth between the Fijian laborers who came into Nadi during the war and the local *taukei*. Indeed, within the Labour Corps itself, Fijians from different provinces did not get along well. Problems of insubordination and "defective loyalty"[17] were exacerbated by inadequate rations and housing facilities and inordinate delays in repatriation arrangements for the workers. Equally important, Fijian workers did not take kindly to supervision by men who were not their traditional leaders. Things began to work smoothly only after a proposal by Labour Officer Ratu George Toganivalu was adopted to divide Fijians according to their provincial origins and into smaller subgroups belonging to the same or related *vanua*. Following this reorganization, men from Kadavu, Macuata, Colo East, and other parts of Viti Levu worked at Namaka; those from Bua dominated the Fijian labor force at the Lautoka wharf; and those from Lau, Cakaudrove, and Lomaiviti took over the aerodrome servicing at Laucala Bay.

Another kind of problem stemmed from the black marketeering and vices of various sorts that mushroomed in the rapidly growing, overwhelmingly male environment. Men of all races and classes were involved. An illicit liquor trade thrived in areas close to military camps, and homemade brew with such revealing names as *tēvoro* 'devil', *siviyara* 'plow', *Fiji Airways,* and *kaukamea* 'iron' was available to anyone who could afford it and risk its aftereffects, including arrest by the police.[18] More important, for people of all races and social classes, the prices of basic goods soared. Kerosene wick lamps used in all rural households, to cite an example, jumped from the prewar price of 4s 6d to 24s 6d. Similarly, Fijian landlords demanded double the prewar prices for building materials. A hundred bamboos cut and delivered for 10 shillings before the war, for example, now went for 20 shillings. Local shopkeepers began charging different prices to different customers for the same item. Petrol lighters, which sold for sixpence before the war, now sold for 2s 6d to Europeans, 3s 6d to New Zealanders, and 4s 6d to Americans. Shopkeepers regularly charged the local people more than the price set by the government.[19] They could refuse to give receipts for goods purchased, and a customer insisting on a receipt could be told that stocks were exhausted; in any case, enough pliant witnesses could easily be produced to swear to the propriety of a particular transaction. The Gujarati merchants of western Viti Levu, it was widely said at the time, were among the worst offenders in overpricing.[20]

The war also energized some local "industries." In addition to the illicit liquor trade, prostitution was so widespread that American medical authorities had to encourage "waitresses" to submit to weekly medical examinations. The theft of benzine by lorry and taxi drivers, to circumvent fuel rationing, became sufficiently extensive to constitute a prosperous trade. Fijians at the Native Labour Compound became adept at roping stray and even domesticated horses and selling them to soldiers for recreation: "on the spot for cash and no receipt is given, no names are asked."[21] Some daring Indo-Fijians, probably in return for some unsavory favor, made away with .45 US Colt pistols, Springfield rifles, explosives, detonators, and many rounds of ammunition, which they later used for hunting.

In some places, Fijians did brisk business with the military. The people of Serua province were organized into a camouflage-net producing unit. Between December 1941 and June 1942, they produced 81,875 square fathoms of netting from *vau* bark, enough to cover sixty-seven and a half acres of land, and delivered them to the Royal Artillery and to the New Zealand Air Force base at Suva. Others, including Fijians from Beqa, supplied 2 to 3 tons of *dalo, kumala,* and other foodstuffs each week to the soldiers based at Namaka.[22] The infusion of cash into the hitherto largely subsistence Fijian economy brought about its own changes. In some *koro* on the western side of Viti Levu, tinned fish, meat, and biscuits began to replace traditional items of exchange. There also Fijians neglected their communal duties and relied instead on their own individual labor for food. Some *koro* surrounding Nadi became "dollar conscious" as trinkets that had fetched only a few pennies before the war were snatched up for handsome prices by the departing soldiers.

At first, the white soldier was a novelty for many Fijians and Indo-Fijians, for most of the white people they had encountered before the war were civil servants or officials of the CSR, people who did not as a rule do manual work. As contact increased, novelty gave way to familiarity. When Fijians in the Civil Construction Unit learned that their New Zealand coworkers were paid more per hour than they themselves earned for the whole day, even though the Kiwis "set a standard of efficiency far below the customary ruling in this country," the Fijians quickly learned to adjust. In no time, they became adept at implementing the go-slow policy.[23] Contact also removed some of the awe with which Fijians and Indo-Fijians had viewed white people before the war. As District Commissioner Western J. Judd wrote, "Contact with New Zealand and American personnel on a basis of social equality has had a profound effect on their [the locals'] moral character and in their conduct toward Europeans in general."[24]

The locals especially liked the Americans, who were outwardly friendly, impatient with rituals, and frequently critical of British colonialism. The Americans, one official said, were "strangers with novel viewpoints and unfamiliar ways," whose presence "caused a silent but far from painless upheaval in the lives of all the communities." "Why don't you give them independence if they [the locals] want it?" some of the Americans asked colonial officials, adding somewhat less than accurately: "That's what we did in the Philippines and see how they are fighting for us." The Americans' "keep-the-change" attitude made a particularly favorable impression on the locals. American soldiers thronged the streets, hotels, and cinema houses in towns, paid high prices for meals and souvenirs and laundry work, and shared cigarettes and chocolates. They also got drunk in public, which went against the colonial social protocol, and they were persistent suitors. As one official stated, "Women and liquor seem to be their dominant interests."[25] Inebriated, the Americans talked freely about their war experiences in the Pacific, much to the annoyance of many local sahibs, who did nothing but wait for an order to serve in the war, which never came. To them, the Americans' claim that they had "been through hell on Guadalcanal has become a phrase of derision rather than honour." The bitterness was understandable for men from New Zealand, who received taunting letters from women at home for "lotus eating while their brothers in arms have fought" in North Africa and the Middle East.[26] Americans fed up with Fiji and the war said: "We want to go home." New Zealanders fed up with idling in Fiji said, "We are fed up with this place. We want to go to Libya."[27]

To counter possible breaches of security that the Americans' free talk could cause, Alport Barker, chairman of the Suva City Council, warned local hosts of American soldiers to be circumspect. "When you are in the company of an American soldier or sailor, either in your own home or elsewhere," he said in a memo, "don't ask him questions about his work. If he starts to talk about it, swallow your curiosity and encourage him to change the subject." "Loose talk," he continued "has cost us enough lives already in this war."[28] The local sahibs, used to having their own way, were understandably upset by the unregulated social intercourse between the local people and the outsiders. "The result of all this has been to give many Europeans a feeling that they have been rudely shaken out of what was, after all, not such a bad frying pan into what may prove a thoroughly uncomfortable fire."[29] For them, being outnumbered and socially eclipsed by the Americans was hard to take, especially as both Fijians and Indo-Fijians were aware and appreciated that the strength of the Americans was winning the war in the Pacific. The feeling of insignificance was grave enough for one member of the Legislative Council to say "We're swamped. We don't mean a thing now. We don't count at all."[30]

This was an exaggeration, of course. Likewise, the Australians and New Zealanders were scarcely of one mind on all things. As the war wore on, frustration mounted and splits emerged among them. Some of this was aired on Radio Australia, which was regularly received in Fiji and was accused by some local Englishmen of being "intent on stirring up anti-English feeling and driving as hefty a wedge as possible between Canberra and Whitehall."[31] Even the ever-loyal *Fiji Times* accused the British Lion of "deserting its cubs and leaving them to be devoured by the Japanese tiger" and John Bull of "sitting tight and secure in his little island, accepting heroic sacrifices in blood and treasure from his children but unwilling to take any risk on their behalf in return."[32] These words of war among Europeans left no lasting legacy in Fiji.

For King and Country

By late 1942, the war in the southwest Pacific was virtually over. With the Allied recapture of the Solomons from the Japanese and steady progress in Papua New Guinea, the danger to Fiji had passed. Gradually, the foreign soldiers began to depart. New Zealand armed forces, however, which had assumed responsibility for Fiji's defense at the beginning of the war, established a small air base at Laucala Bay near Suva and remained there till the mid-1960s. After they left the islands, the base became the home in 1968 of the newly opened University of the South Pacific.

Demobilized Fijian soldiers and others engaged in military-related work returned to their villages to resume their subsistence life-style. Of Fiji's 262 war dead, Fijians numbered 139, 29 of whom were killed in action while the rest died from wounds, sickness, and disease. The soldiers returned as heroes, many decorated for their performance in the jungles of Guadalcanal.[33] The highest award, the Victoria Cross, was presented posthumously to Corporal Sefanaia Sukanaivalu in November 1944 for his bravery in the Solomon Islands campaign. British war propaganda painted the Fijians as hell-bent on killing, "ruthless, splendidly trained fighting men who think nothing of walking 15 miles off a trail to kill a handful of Japanese," for whom the "mere threat to keep [them] from going on patrol constitutes all the discipline necessary."[34] Such a portrayal led the principal of Waitaki High School in New Zealand to request that selected Fijian boys be refused admission to his school because "the Fijians were savages." Fijians were formidable jungle fighters, but people like Viliame Lomasalatu were rare exceptions. According to stories related to Fijian scholar Asesela Ravuvu, Lomasalatu had vowed before leaving Fiji that he would eat the first Japanese soldier he killed. He was dragged away by his noncommissioned men, but not before he had managed to scoop out an eyeball of a dead Japanese soldier with his penknife.[35]

The colonial government praised the Fijian people and their leaders for their splendid war effort. "Out of the evil of war has come some good to the Fijian people," J. F. Nicoll, the acting governor, told the Great Council of Chiefs in November 1944, "for it has enabled you to prove to yourselves and to others that you are a sound people, able and willing to shoulder your full share of the burden of war."[36] Such patronizing rhetoric about the need for indigenous peoples to "prove" themselves, to meet the standards set by whites, was a constant refrain in colonial thinking in Fiji through much of this century. But the government's words did not match its deeds when the question of rehabilitating the returned soldiers arose. At first officials were inclined to do nothing at all, hoping that the communal system would take care of the needs of the returned soldiers. This attitude led Ian Thompson, a captain in the Fiji Infantry Regiment and later an important public figure in Fiji, to complain that "we are simply shutting our eyes, shifting the onus, and in the military parlance passing the buck."[37]

In the end, the government made a token gesture of appreciation for the Fijians' war efforts—it was no more than a token gesture—by providing the returned soldiers free passage to their homes along with a few implements and tools, a six-month exemption from communal duties, and some medical benefits.[38] The returned soldiers were disappointed, for many had been led to believe that they would receive better recognition for their sacrifices made both on the battlefields and at home by having to neglect their gardens and family concerns. As one Fijian observer said, "To many Fijian ex-servicemen, 'rehabilitation' was a farcical institution which had once supplied them with an axe, a spade, a fork and a knife, and no more. This institution became a matter of ridicule rather than satisfaction among Fijian veterans."[39]

The Fijians responded generously and enthusiastically to the call to fight for the empire in distant places in part because the government needed Fijian soldiers and made strenuous efforts to recruit them into service. It portrayed the war in terms that suggested that Fijians were fighting for the preservation of their way of life. In his first radio broadcast to the Fijian people, the governor said:

> In these islands you have a beautiful heritage handed down to you by your forefathers, islands which for better protection your Chiefs ceded to Her Majesty Queen Victoria of beloved memory. As in the other case of the Empire, this war is being fought to keep you in possession of your islands and of your hearths, in enjoyment of your native institutions and those the Government has given you, in brief, of the priceless things of the body and of the soul that the enemy had taken away from all the conquered countries.[40]

Such exhortations had a powerful impact on many rural Fijians, who had no means nor any reason to question the governor's words. Furthermore, Fijians were no strangers to warfare. Bravery and courage in battle were values on which their society placed great emphasis. For young men in Fiji, as in much of Melanesia, physical prowess demonstrated in war was an important rite of passage. No honor was greater than being permitted to fight to protect home and hearth.

The government's recruitment campaign was extremely well organized and helped by the hierarchical organization of Fijian society. Instructions from the advisor on native affairs at the headquarters in Suva were conveyed to the district commissioners, who, in turn, through descending chains of command, passed them on to the *roko, buli,* and *tūraga ni koro.* The separate administrative system for the Fijians facilitated the coordination of Fijian efforts throughout the colony.[41] Led by their local leaders, Fijian provinces reportedly vied with one another to produce the highest numbers of qualified recruits. According to one observer, the quota for some districts was exceeded "as young men could not bear the shame of not participating in such a community effort [as recruitment] or losing face when men returned from the war. It was a source of honour and pride to the *buli* and his people if they were well represented and none of their soldiers were rejected by the recruiting officer."[42]

Prominent Fijian chiefs, such as Ratu Tiale Vuiyasawa, Ratu George Tuisawau, and Ratu Etuate Mataitini, spearheaded the recruitment effort, contributing to its success. However, Ratu Sukuna's presence on the recruiting campaign made the major difference because he was, by virtue of his high birth, experience, and Western education, the undisputed leader of the Fijian people.[43] He toured the villages in military uniform

Fijian recruits during World War II being inspected by Ratu Sukuna, whose active encouragement ensured ready Fijian participation in the war effort. *(Courtesy Fiji Ministry of Information)*

and exhorted young Fijian men to enlist for service. *"Eda na sega ni kilai na taukei kevaka e na sega mada ni dave e liu na noda dra,"* he told the village chiefs, "Fijians will never be recognized unless our blood is shed first."[44] The colonial rhetoric that Fijians had to "prove" themselves to be men worthy of European respect echoed in Sukuna's words. Sukuna was also enthusiastic because he was an unabashed Anglophile to whom the best things of modern life, such as good government and education and refined culture, came from England. Having been the beneficiary of an elite English education and colonial patronage, he naturally volunteered his efforts to protect those things that had enhanced his power and status.

Other motives, often unstated but unmistakable, were behind Sukuna's support for the war effort. He hoped to harness the vigorous display of Fijian loyalty to the British to rein in the forces of change that were beginning to impinge on Fijian society. Indo-Fijians were demanding more secure leases to Fijian land and the opening up of the political system. There were pressures from the government of India and from the Colonial Office that neither the government nor its supporters could ignore. Elements within Fijian society itself were demanding more participation in the administration of their affairs. An active support for the war effort, Sukuna probably reasoned, would win the sympathy of the colonial administration and contain the forces of change and pressures for reform. Sukuna was not disappointed. He reminded a Great Council of Chiefs meeting in 1945 of the many recent improvements in provincial hospitals and medical practitioners' and nurses' quarters, of the new installations of water supplies, and of the campaign to combat tuberculosis and filariasis and elephantiasis. "All these things have come to pass," he said, "because you [chiefs] provided manpower for the war effort and in memory of those who lost their lives in action."[45] Even more satisfying for him were the changes that the government implemented in Fijian administration after the war.

In contrast to the Fijian response, the Indo-Fijian war effort was unenthusiastic and conditional. Since this is a subject of considerable controversy in Fiji, it bears detailed examination.[46] The conventional view among most people is that Indo-Fijians did not rally behind the war effort because of the government's refusal to grant them the same conditions of service as were provided to European soldiers. That is a part of the answer. The Indian Central War Committee formed by the governor, which consisted of some of the most important Indo-Fijian leaders, including Vishnu Deo, A. D. Patel, A. R. Sahu Khan, and Dr. Girin Mukherji, did insist that non-European soldiers receive the 3s 0d per day and the separation allowance of 3s 0d for wife and 1s 6d per child that Europeans were receiving.[47] Equal pay, equal worth, equal risk was their principle. The committee members told the governor that they would, of course, fight to defend Fiji if it were attacked, but their people were unwilling to fight for the empire in other parts of the world unless the government acknowledged the principle of equality between Europeans and non-Europeans. The government, supported by Europeans, refused to act on their demand, which dampened the effort to recruit Indo-Fijians for the war effort.

While this demand for equality was one factor in discouraging Indo-Fijian effort, there were others as well. The government's reluctance to enlist Indo-Fijians as soldiers was among them. Just as the government had rejected Manilal's request to form an Indo-Fijian platoon in 1916 "to take part in the responsibilities of the Empire at such a critical time as the present,"[48] it was equally reluctant to establish an Indo-Fijian platoon in 1930 when Indo-Fijians once again approached the government, largely because of Fijian and European opposition. It did, however, establish a small unit in Rewa in 1934, but disbanded it in 1940, ostensibly because of the shortage of equipment but in fact because of the opposition of European officers. "It was a matter of personal regret to me," the governor told members of the Indian Central War Committee in 1942, "that military considerations at the time should have necessitated the disbandment of the Indian Platoon, which had given eight years of voluntary service in the Fiji Defence Forces. . . . The disbandment was not due in any sense to unwillingness on the part of the Indians to serve in the armed forces of the colony."[49]

Soon after the outbreak of the war, South Indians approached the governor through A. D. Patel, general manager of the Sangam, the umbrella organization of that community, and offered a volunteer corps to do first-aid work and to "act as social servants in case of any emergency."[50] For this, they requested training and equipment. The government did not act on the offer. A prominent Indo-Fijian leader, Chattur Singh, approached the governor on several occasions to enlist two of his sons in the army and the navy, but was turned down each time on the ground that the military was short of equipment. When Singh complained, the governor, Sir Philip Mitchell, told him, "I am the Commander-in-Chief, but I cannot rule the army."[51] A group of about forty Indo-Fijians from Ba volunteered to enlist in 1942 when the governor visited the district, but were turned down by European officers for various reasons. Similarly, the government refused the offer of fifty Indo-Fijian Muslims, who volunteered their services without conditions, refusing to make equal compensation an issue as the "mercenary spirit" was deemed to be alien to Islam.[52] Faced with this situation, some part–Indo-Fijians, with such names as John Brown, went to New Zealand and enlisted in the Maori regiments.

The government was reluctant to enlist Indo-Fijians as soldiers for several reasons. One was the opposition of Fijians and particularly of Europeans to giving Indo-Fijians any military training. Events in India, such as Gandhi's Quit India campaign, the gathering pace of the nationalist movement, and Subhas Chandra Bose's collaboration with the Japanese to oust the British from India, deeply colored their assessment of the loyalty of the Indo-Fijians. The Indo-Fijians were held responsible for events on the Indian subcontinent, events neither the Fijians nor the Europeans could fathom but which they detested intensely. Contributing to this view were the memories of the strikes of the 1920s, which had pitched Fijians and Europeans against Indo-Fijians, who were regarded by Fijians, Europeans, and the colonial government as "treacherous and ungrateful."[53] Giving Indo-Fijians military training could lead to greater trouble in the future. The government shared these views. In 1931, over the criticism of the Colonial Office, it passed the Sedition Bill to monitor political activity in the Indo-Fijian community.[54] In addition to all these factors was the government's view that Indo-Fijians would not make good soldiers anyway, being unable to submit "themselves to the controls, restrictions and rigours of life in a strictly disciplined force, to accept without complaint the restrictions of individual rights and convenience inevitable in a disciplined communal life, to accept and obey unquestioningly, the orders of superior officers and especially to have the capacity rapidly to assimilate to complicated training which is the lot of modern soldiers."[55]

The most important contribution the Indo-Fijians could make to the war effort, the governor told them, was to increase the production of foodstuffs. Fiji was an agricultural colony, he said, "composed of islands which in the nature of things do not produce munitions of war and whose peasant farmers in these circumstances could probably best help the war effort by pursuing their own vocation." "I assure you" he told members of the Indian Central War Committee, "and I ask you to carry that assurance back to your Districts when you return—that the efforts of the Indians in Fiji in response to Government appeals for the growing of foodstuffs and the maintenance of essential agricultural interests have been not one of the least important contributions made to the prosecution of the war."[56] In his radio appeal to the Indo-Fijian community, the governor asked them "in the first place to increase the general level of production by working with increased effort in whatever may be their normal employment, and in the second to fit themselves individually for any special responsibility for which they may be selected."[57]

This attitude explains why the government's attempt to recruit limited numbers of Indo-Fijians for war work was poorly organized. The dispersal of Indo-Fijian settlements was a hindrance to recruitment, but the government's choice of recruitment officers compounded the problem. One of them, K. B. Singh, had little credibility in the Indo-Fijian community. Having gone against the wishes of the majority of Indo-Fijians in 1935, he had voted, with Fijians and Europeans, to replace the elected Legislative Council with a nominated one. He had also privately urged the governor to increase political surveillance of the Indo-Fijian leaders and offered himself for intelligence work if the government took him into its confidence.[58] Another leading recruiter was M. T. Khan, a prominent Lautoka businessman and president of the Kisan Sangh, an organization engaged in a bitter struggle with rival organizations for the control of the Indo-Fijian cane growers. Since the government regarded Khan and his organization as more loyal, it worked through them. The result was the alienation of very large sections of the Indo-Fijian community. The government's efforts to recruit Indo-Fijians for war work were doomed, if not by design then certainly by inexplicable ineptness.

There were other reasons for failure. The CSR was opposed to the government recruiting Indo-Fijians, many of whom were its tenants and workers. The CSR manager at Lautoka, E. H. Griffith, told District Commissioner Western J. Judd in 1943 that recruitment was hurting the sugar industry and should be discontinued. The District Officer Nadroga was accordingly instructed by Judd that "on no account are tenants to be permitted to leave their farms to join the Labour Battalion."[59] The CSR attorney, H. K. Irving, wrote to the colonial secretary in 1943 that "in view of the serious shortage of labour over the past year it seems quite irrational to recruit from those engaged in the sugar industry."[60] The CSR tenants were bound to the company by agreement, which prohibited them from leaving their farms for more than two months at a time. Absence for a longer period was a breach of contract, which could result in the expulsion of the tenants. The Indo-Fijians were caught in a difficult situation. The choice between enlisting for war work on the one hand and keeping their farms on the other was no choice at all.

Membership in the British Empire was no badge of honor for the Indo-Fijians. Local Europeans owed their power and prestige to British colonialism, and Fijian chiefs were grateful for the security and privileges they and their people enjoyed as a result of British policies. The Indo-Fijians, on the other hand, and with good reason, remembered *girmit* and the racial humiliations and denigrations of everyday life. Fighting in the war to them meant fighting to uphold a system that was oppressive and humiliating. The British propaganda that the war was being waged to protect freedom and liberty sounded hypocritical. The readers of the *Fiji Samachar* believed that the war was being fought to preserve British colonialism; that the British Empire was a "white race empire" in which only whites could move freely; that justice in the abstract was quite different from the practical realities they encountered in their daily lives:

> Indians seem to have been born into this world to be ever at the pleasure of the "great lords." When plantation labour was needed in the Colonies, Indians were shipped abroad like so many sheep and goats. When mention is made of rights, then horns are shown. When any country has to be enslaved, Indians are praised and Indian troops are sent first to the trenches. But as soon as mention is made of equality of treatment, then those who make the claim are branded as seditionists and are flung in gaol.[61]

Much was said during the war years about the Indo-Fijians' alleged seditious activities. It is true that many Indo-Fijian households with radios did listen to the Tokyo-based Radio Azad in the predawn hours and heard Japanese propaganda about Asian solidarity against European racism and colonialism. Some local leaders did receive banned Indian newspapers. And to the four hundred Sikhs gathered at the Tagi *gurudwara* (Sikh temple) in Tavua in 1942, General Dwyer, the notorious perpetrator of the Jallanianwallah Bagh massacre, was not a hero but a criminal.[62] But it is not true, as some "loyal" Indo-Fijian intelligence operatives told colonial officials, that leaders such as A. D. Patel were actually "hopeful that the Japanese would invade the island" or that "Mr Patel was even dreaming of a Japanese wife."[63] The truth was that whatever their political sympathies and ideological predispositions, the Indo-Fijians were neither seditious nor disloyal. Only the Fijians' exuberant war effort and colonial-European propaganda made them appear so. As A. W. MacMillan, the inspector of Indian schools who worked as an intelligence agent for the government, wrote in 1942 after an exhaustive tour of western Viti Levu, "If opposition to the war effort exists it is not conspicuous, and I have found no trace of it." It had been a "great and reassuring pleasure," he said, "to observe among the simple peasantry a loyalty to the Govern-

Victory celebrations, Victoria parade, Suva, 1946. A Chinese float is in procession. Note the Carnegie Library building at left; today it houses the Suva City Library. (*Courtesy Fiji Ministry of Information*)

ment here and a fervent hope that the Allied Nations will ultimately be victorious."[64]

Company and *Kisan:* Round Two

For most Indo-Fijian farmers and laborers, the real enemies were not the Japanese or the Germans, but poverty, indebtedness, and the CSR. The company was the economic juggernaut of the colony, and for most Indo-Fijians, its de facto ruler as well. Over the years, it had become accustomed to having things its way, dictating terms to its tenants and cane contractors and extracting concessions from the government. The company's threat to pull out of Fiji if its freedom to operate as it pleased was in any way endangered was a powerful deterrent to government intervention in its affairs, even where such intervention was in the broader interests of the colony. By the late 1930s, however, the situation was changing. Cane was grown by a new postindenture generation of Indo-Fijian farmers, who were more conscious and assertive of their rights. This new assertiveness, together with a rising cost of living, pressure on the land caused by population growth, decline in per capita incomes, and the attitude of the CSR, brought the farmers into confrontation with the company, climaxing in a major strike in the sugar industry in 1943.[65] Coming as it did during the war, this strike fueled new fires of racial hostility in the colony.

From the farmers' point of view, a large part of the problem in the sugar industry lay in its organizational structure. The CSR strictly regulated all aspects of sugar production in Fiji. This was necessary, it said, to promote efficiency and sound management, without which the industry would fail. It was in the interests of the farmers themselves, the CSR argued, that the company maintain strict control, without which the fragmentation of landholdings that had "impoverished so much of Asia [would] very soon develop with Indian farmers in Fiji," leading them to the "centuries-old tendency . . . to get themselves into a hopeless position with the money-lenders."[66] The farmers saw the situation differently. As A. D. Patel said, "The relation between the Company and the growers was strongly reminiscent of the relationship of barons and serfs during the medieval ages. They had to take what was given to them and be thankful for the small mercies whether they liked it or not."[67] Governor Sir Harry Luke was of a similar view. The company's attitude, he said, was: "We have fixed the price of cane at what we consider to be a just and reasonable level, and we have laid down certain conditions which we require you to accept. We are not prepared to enter into any argument on the subject and we expect you to rely upon the Company's good faith."[68]

The farmers' grievances coalesced around a number of issues. One was the tenancy agreement between the company and its Indo-Fijian tenants, which left them entirely at the mercy of the company. No vegetables for home consumption could be planted on the land leased from the CSR, and no poultry or milking cows could be kept on it without the company's permission. The tenants wanted a proper sublease that would give them greater freedom. Furthermore, the leased land had to be cultivated according to strict guidelines enforced by the company; tenants who breached them were usually punished, even expelled. The company alone determined the varieties of cane the farmers could grow; that cane had to be "tended and harvested to the complete satisfaction of the Company, and cane must be cut level with the ground." The company insisted that right-of-way on the land it leased to its tenants "be given when required by the Company for the removal of crops grown on neighbouring areas" without compensation. And the company appointed its own sirdars 'cane gang foremen' without consulting the *kisan*. It also required farmers to supply labor from time to time to work on the company's tramway and in the mills and fields. It paid the wages of the workers, but the growers had to provide an adequate bonus to compensate the workers for absence from home.[69]

The workers also argued that wages in the sugar industry, at the rate of 2s 2d per working day, were insufficient to provide even the basic necessities of life to themselves and their families. The farmers opposed the company's method of paying for cane, which was at a flat rate per ton based on the percentage of cane sugar (p.o.c.s.) and an additional three-shilling "bonus" that it could withdraw at its discretion. None of the farmers could understand the p.o.c.s system; they wanted a minimum flat rate of 16s 6d per ton. They demanded more payment for their cane because most of them were in straitened circumstances. Indebtedness was a major problem for the farmers, who had to borrow money to lease a piece of land and then borrow some more, usually at exorbitant rates, to plant crops and meet their usual social obligations. The problem was especially acute in the late 1930s when the per capita incomes in the cane areas "were almost certainly in decline."[70] The CSR did advance money to farmers at 5 percent interest, which was considerably lower than what the Indo-Fijian money-lenders charged. But very few farmers were able to avail themselves of the credit because the company advanced money only on standing crops and even then on a very conservative estimate, so that farmers were not able to get sufficient money to meet all their needs.

Many farmers also charged that the company did not credit them with the full weight of the cane they sent to the mill or with the full percentage of sugar in their cane. They had no opportunity to check the accuracy of the figures the company provided, and no representatives of the *kisan* were present when the weight and quality of cane were determined, leaving room for the suspicion that the company was profiteering at their expense. The farmers wanted the p.o.c.s. system abolished.

In 1939 the company introduced two additional changes that further alienated the farmers working on its leased lands. One was the system of rotational cultivation of cane. In theory, this was a sound principle of soil management, but sound theory meant little to Indo-Fijian farmers struggling with the problems created by a declining income. Their rents were high, they were already in debt, and their only hope of making ends meet was to cultivate all the land they could. To pay rent on land without any return on it would simply worsen their already precarious financial situation. The farmers said they would agree to crop rotation if the blocks were increased to sixteen acres from the usual eight acres, which the company refused to do. Another cause of dissatisfaction was the system of harvesting by area rather than by the readiness of the crop. This meant that growers whose cane was not ready for harvest because of low density of sugar content had no option but to have their cane cut if it was in the area being harvested. Farmers missed out on a good return because of the new procedure. The suggestion that they be paid a price based on the average density for the area was rejected by farmers with good crops.

These and similar grievances had been present for the previous two decades, but the farmers were too disorganized and internally divided and controlled by the company to do much about their situation. That changed in November 1937 when farmers formed the Fiji Kisan Sangh, or Farmers' Association, under the leadership of M. T. Khan and Ayodhya Prasad.[71] Its objective was to unite the farmers in one properly constituted organization, which could also negotiate directly with the CSR from a position of strength. Although initially the task proved difficult because CSR tenants feared reprisals from the company, the Sangh was able to claim, within a year of its establishment, the membership of nearly three-quarters of all the cane farmers in the western and central divisions of Viti Levu. In other words, it became a force that could not be ignored, not least because the Colonial Office itself had been urging the government, though unsuccessfully, to encourage the growth of "responsible" trade unions in the colony "in advance of the need for it, rather than defer action until the matter may perhaps have become the subject of political controversy."[72]

In the beginning, the CSR refused to acknowledge the existence of the Sangh and forbade its officers to have any formal or informal contacts with the Sangh's officials, saying that it would listen to complaints only when these were brought forward by individuals.[73] The company had long viewed any industrial legislation in the colony as a "grave mistake, . . . fraught with serious consequences to the future welfare of the Colony, with its varied races and interests" and likely to "sow the seeds of discord and industrial strife."[74] However, the Sangh's existence was an accomplished fact that was acknowledged by the government itself. On 22 May 1939 the governor received a deputation from the Sangh, though technically as a body of men rather than as representatives of an organization; the farmers presented their grievances regarding wages, tenancy arrangements with

Rural market scene in Fiji in the 1940s, with Indo-Fijian buyers and sellers in typical garb. *(Courtesy Fiji Ministry of Information)*

the CSR, and other matters.[75] In 1941, because of government pressure and a realistic assessment of the situation, the CSR recognized the Kisan Sangh as a legitimate representative organization of cane farmers.

The recognition produced some results. The Sangh was able to negotiate a ten-year contract with the company. For its part, the company met some of the farmers' demands, agreeing to improve the delivery of fertilizer, reducing interest on advances to 4 percent, and allowing the farmers to have a representative at the mill weighbridge to check the weight of cane. It also agreed to give farmers written receipts for cane proceeds, allowed them to grow some food crops on their leaseholds, and reduced the daily working hours in mills from twelve to eight.[76] The Kisan Sangh was given the responsibility for appointing sirdars and for the harvesting and delivery of cane to the mills. In return, the Sangh agreed to cooperate with the company to settle disputes among farmers, increase the efficiency of the harvesting program, and persuade its members to bear losses that occurred in the industry.

Just when the Kisan Sangh seemed to be consolidating its position, a rival farmers' organization, the Akhil Fiji Krishak Maha Sangh (All Fiji Farmers' Association), was formed in June 1941. Its leaders were A. D. Patel and Swami Rudrananda, the head of the Ramakrishna Mission in Fiji. The formation of this body has frequently been seen as an attempt by

Patel to divide the farmers for his own personal political ends. (Patel was defeated in the legislative election in 1937 by a North Indian law clerk.) It has also been suggested that because the Kisan Sangh's efforts to establish cooperative stores threatened the interests of Gujarati merchants, Patel, a Gujarati, deliberately set out to destroy the farmers' unity to protect Gujarati commercial interests.[77]

These views, which were widely shared by colonial officials and others, are both inaccurate and misleading. Part of the problem lay with the Kisan Sangh itself. Having won recognition by the CSR, it began to use intimidation, "terrorist methods,"[78] in the words of one observer, to increase its membership and to finance its cooperative stores by, among other things, demanding that farmers pay one penny on each ton of cane harvested to the Sangh. It also appointed its own members as sirdar, dismissing many who had been sirdar for several years. Its cooperative stores failed to deliver the goods. In addition, its conciliatory attitude toward the CSR as "a loyal opposition to the company"[79] disenchanted many. The Kisan Sangh's support came principally from the North Indian community, many of whom held leases from the company, were more prosperous, and stood to lose more from any confrontation with the company. The Maha Sangh, on the other hand, derived its support from South Indians, many of whom were wage-paid cane cutters, had few good leases of their own, and were generally poorer than the North Indians. They had little interest in the existing order, but stood to gain from a militant stand against the company.[80] Whatever the reasons and motivations behind the formation of the Maha Sangh, the two rival organizations were bitterly divided, splitting the Indo-Fijian cane farming community for decades.

Meanwhile, the situation of the farmers continued to worsen in the late 1930s and early 1940s, as they faced a large increase in their cost of living and the heavy expenditure involved in cultivating cane. In March 1943 the Kisan Sangh asked the company to increase the price of cane above the formula agreed in the contract. The company refused. On 22 June 1943, the Maha Sangh wrote to the colonial secretary, alerting the government to the problem facing the farmers. "Considering the tremendous rise in the price of live-stock, agricultural tools and implements, exorbitant repair charges and almost prohibitive cost of harvesting coupled with high cost of living," it said, "unless the price of cane is varied, it is impossible for the growers to carry on with sugar cultivation." The farmers, it continued, might "have to by force of present circumstances altogether give up cultivation of sugar cane and resort to crops which would ensure them a reasonable margin of profit and a decent standard of living."[81]

At first the government was reluctant to mediate the dispute. The governor told a farmers' gathering in Lautoka in July 1943 that "the cane was theirs and if they wished they could let it rot in the fields. . . . For that matter," he said, the farmers "could shoot their working animals and burn their own houses, so long as they were careful to burn their own and not other people's."[82] This attitude, which stiffened the resolve of the already distrustful farmers, did not last long. After some careful second thoughts, the government agreed to appoint a commission of inquiry in July 1943, consisting of the attorney general; a European member of the Legislative Council, H. H. Ragg; and an Indo-Fijian accountant, A. L. Patel. They were to investigate whether there had been a large increase in the cost of living as the farmers claimed. The Kisan Sangh supported the appointment of the commission, but the Maha Sangh members and other farmers' groups refused to appear before it to give evidence. They wanted a court of arbitration that could make final and binding recommendations, rather than a commission whose findings would not be binding on the parties to the dispute. They viewed the appointment of a commission as a stalling tactic by the government, an exercise designed to prove the view that the Indo-Fijian cane farmers were not as badly off as they claimed.[83]

The commission's findings bore out the farmers' suspicion in that they showed that the increase in the price of cane since 1939 had kept pace with the aggregate increase in the cost of living.[84] The commission's assessment of what it cost an average farmer to subsist was absurdly low, its prescription fit, the farmers said, for "the animal standard of life," leaving no margin for meeting the normal social and cultural obligations of life, the expenses for educating children, and the cost of hiring occasional laborers to cut cane or help with general farm work.[85] According to the commission's findings, a farmer with a family of six (including himself) could live on a weekly ration of 2.5 pounds of potatoes, 2 pounds of onions, 0.5 bottle of ghee, 0.75 bottle of cooking oil, 7 pounds of sugar, 0.25 pounds of tea, 4 pounds of dahl (lentils), 1.5 pounds of salt, 5 ounces of garlic and other condiments, 9 pounds of rice, and 18 pounds of sharps. As for clothing, he could do with two pairs of khaki trousers and shirts, a pair of canvas shoes, and two singlets a year, and his four children between them could manage with six khaki shorts and shirts and six singlets. As for household utensils, the commission thought that four enamel plates, mugs, and bowls, one hurricane lamp, one basting spoon, one frying pan, and two billy cans should be sufficient. The farmers protested. Said A. D. Patel:

> We growers are also human beings. We also live in society. We also have to meet our social, economic and religious obligations and keep up social appearances just the same as any other people. We have to educate our children and give them better opportunities in life. We have to entertain friends and relations and visit them on occasions. We have to dress up properly befitting our status in the community and meet a host of social expenses in a modest way. . . . We have as much right to be prosperous and happy as anybody in the world with decent housing and better comforts.[86]

The heart of the matter, Patel said, was "not on how little the farmer can manage to live, but how much at the present price of sugar and other by-products of cane, the Company can afford to pay, after making a due allowance for a margin of profit which can be considered fair and just during war time. . . . If the Company is making more profit now than what it was making before the war," he said, "then there is no justice in saying that the growers must sacrifice so that the Company's share holders may prosper."[87] The company told the governor in September 1943 that it was not a philanthropic organization but a commercial venture that wanted to make a profit, and it was not making the profits its critics alleged. The company had an obligation to make a profit for its shareholders, Patel agreed. But he argued that the company had "ignored the patent fact that the sole aim of the growers in producing sugar cane is also to make profit. . . . Unless the growers obtain a reasonable margin of profit consistent with the work and capital they put in and the risk and patient waiting they take in the production of cane," he argued, "there is no justification for them to continue producing cane."[88] The government was privately inclined to agree with this view, but it did not act. Nevertheless, the governor advised the secretary of state that "neither you nor this Government should approve or appear to approve or be satisfied with standard of living as expressed in Commission Report for very damaging use could be made of that by press in UK and even US."[89]

The rejection of the commission and its recommendations by the farmers had set the stage for a prolonged strike.[90] Many tortuous and difficult negotiations took place between the government (and its designated agent, Ratu Sukuna) and the growers' leaders, especially A. D. Patel, S. B. Patel, and Swami Rudrananda, though there were none directly between the growers and the company itself.[91] They all failed to break the deadlock. The CSR refused to increase the price of cane and wages, believing that when the war was over, prewar conditions would return and it would face tough competition from other sugar-producing areas such as Java.[92] At various times during the negotiations, the farmers offered to sell their cane directly to the government, which, they said, could then decide what "fair and just" price it would pay for the cane. But the CSR was opposed, and the government did not act.

As the weeks went by, feelings on both sides hardened. The government's advice to the farmers was "that you harvest your cane and plant new crops of cane, working with zeal to repair the damage and loss which have been done; that you await patiently and lawfully the decisions which the Secretary of State is now deliberating and accept them loyally in the confidence that they will be based on full consideration of your views."[93] Local European and Fijian opinion was solidly behind the government, the governor cabled the secretary of state for the colonies, and all advisors

A. D. Patel and Swami Rudrananda of the Ramakrishna Mission, lifelong friends who worked together in the Sangam (a South Indian organization) and for the sugar cane farmers. They were the joint leaders of the 1943 cane strike and were together again in the 1960 strike. *(Courtesy Mrs. Leela Patel, Nadi, Fiji)*

"agreed that Patel and Swami should now be left to sink in the quicksands that are forming round them."[94] The CSR was convinced that the strike would collapse under the stress of the financial difficulties the farmers faced. At the end of seven months, facing defeat, for the company had sufficient resources to outlast its opponents, the farmers agreed to harvest under protest. By then only a small portion of the cane was left for harvesting. Altogether, 332,669 tons of green cane and 101,499 tons of burned cane were harvested, and 322,552 tons of green cane and 68,081 tons of burned cane were left in the fields. The farmers lost an estimated £1 million in income from cane.

Early in 1944, a commission of inquiry headed by Professor C. Y. Shephard, of the Imperial College of Tropical Agriculture in Trinidad, was appointed to look into the problems in the sugar industry.[95] The farmers, who had agreed to appear before the commission, repeated a number of their previous demands, which would require the CSR to add the value of molasses and bagasse to the price of sugar when calculating the price of cane, allow farmers to choose from a variety of canes to plant (so that they could choose cane that was better suited to the soil conditions of their farms), and permit farmers to grow food crops on a quarter of their farm's area. The company, on the other hand, concentrated its efforts on showing that it had not made the profits its critics alleged.[96] The commission found that the cost of living of Indo-Fijian workers had risen by 115 percent between 1939 and 1943, but the average price of cane had risen by only 50 percent. The farmers were, indeed, deeply in debt, it concluded. Using figures provided by the company, it agreed that the company had not made substantial profits, but that it could afford to pay more for the cane than it was prepared to. Nevertheless, the commission advised against increasing the contract price of cane. Finally, and perhaps most important, it proposed the establishment of a sugar board with an independent chair to oversee matters in the industry.

Although generally pleased with the report, the company rejected the major recommendation regarding the setting up of a sugar board and urged the government to do likewise. In this it was successful. The Maha Sangh rejected the report's findings about the company's profits, saying they were based on false and misleading figures, but accepted those provisions that gave the government and the growers a voice in the future management of the industry.[97] In a private note to S. Caine of the Colonial Office, Shephard praised the man who had been vilified as the chief villain of the piece, A. D. Patel, the leader of the Maha Sangh. "I was impressed by A. D. Patel's intelligence, and believe he will mellow under responsibility. He will make a most useful member of the Sugar Board."[98] The colonial government would never countenance that advice, though in the Indo-Fijian community, Patel's prestige was high, and he was elected to the Legislative Council later that year (1944). The government accepted the report and its moderate and quietly pro-CSR tone. Privately, though, Governor Mitchell told Shephard that the current price of sugar cane was too low and did "not give a proper return to the grower nor permit of a standard of living of which we ought to approve."[99] He also told the secretary of state that the company should be asked to modify the 1940 agreement—which it had refused to do before—and offer a slightly higher price for cane.[100]

The strike caused hardship all round, especially for the farmers for whom cane cultivation was often the only source of livelihood. It sowed seeds of suspicion between the company and the *kisan,* and it split up the farmers' movement into two bitterly opposed factions. There were other effects as well. The government was embarrassed at not being able to handle the CSR, although it knew the company to be dictatorial and heavy-handed in its dealings with the farmers.[101] Fijians were angry at the effects of the strike. Ratu Edward Cakobau and Ratu Sukuna criticized the strike leaders, accusing them of holding a pistol at the colony's head for selfish reasons, of singing hymns of hate while Rome burned. Both demanded that the government requisition the crop and offered Fijian cane cutters to do it.[102] Ratu Sukuna suggested that Fijian leases might be in jeopardy if the farmers continued their strike, a threat that would be heard time and again in subsequent years. The government posted soldiers in the western districts during the strike, apparently to preserve law and order for those farmers who wanted to harvest. This deeply embittered the farmers against the government, whose reluctance to get the CSR to the bargaining table was seen as an act of collusion between the two. As A. D. Patel said, the company was the tyrannical mother-in-law and the government its dutiful daughter-in-law. The CSR emerged victorious in 1943, but the fundamental issues had not been resolved. They surfaced again and embroiled the industry in yet another round of dispute seventeen years later.

Native Land and Fijian Affairs

The war years saw profound and far-reaching institutional consolidation of the Fijian Administration, ending almost two decades of official vacillation and uncertainty and laying the foundations for the next several decades. The land question was finally resolved in 1940 with the creation of a statutory organization, the Native Land Trust Board.[103] The board consisted of the governor as chair, the secretary for Fijian affairs, a Fijian nominated by the governor, and the directors of Land and of Agriculture. The acceptance of the governor as chair reflected the trust the Fijian people placed in the office and its holder as the protector of Fijian rights. The alienation of Fijian land, by sale, transfer, or exchange, was forbidden except to the Crown. The board became the sole agency for leasing and administering Fijian land. It retained 25 percent of the rent on leases for administrative costs and paid the rest to the landowners according to specified criteria.

The Native Lands and Fisheries Commission was empowered to prepare definitive records on the ownership of Fijian lands, assist in the surveying of unsurveyed lands, maintain a periodically updated Vola ni Kawa Bula 'Register of Native Owners', and settle disputes regarding the headship of landowning units or groups of landowning units. The commission was also charged to ensure that enough land remained in Fijian hands for agricultural purposes and for the use of future generations of Fijians. To this end, the commissioner was empowered to ascertain the lands needed for use by Fijians and to embark on a program of reservation. The task, which was intended to be completed within two to five years, took nearly two decades and caused much friction when long-settled tenants had to move elsewhere because their land had been placed in reserve. The disenchantment was all the greater when productive agricultural land reverted to bush, laying the foundations of an enduring grievance among Indo-Fijian tenants and farmers.

Nevertheless, for all its problems, the establishment of the Native Land Trust Board and the passage of the Lands Ordinance was a milestone in modern Fijian history and was certainly a concession by Fijians to the demands of a multiracial Fiji. When questions about land tenure were raised later, Sukuna said, with some justification:

> The Fijian owner is frequently blamed for retarding settlement. If the truth be known he has done a great deal, probably more than any other section of the community, at any rate measured in ethical terms. He has given up his right of bargaining, dear to the heart of every one of us; he has abandoned premiums; he has slowly swallowed the sentiment . . . the attachment to land; he has also handed over the control of his inheritance to a Board. These, Sir, are acts of goodwill and co-operation which, I believe, are unmatched in our time.[104]

This concession and Fijian support for the war effort did not go unnoticed or unrewarded. It strengthened the hand of those who upheld the Gordon-Thurston system. Wrote Advisor on Native Affairs Pennfather in 1943:

> We have been accused of nursing the Fijian in our manner of native administration, but I challenge anyone to say that there is a finer native in the Empire, physically and morally, than the Fijian, and there certainly is not a more loyal one, as has been proved by their wonderful war effort. I think a fatherly Government which has looked after the Fijians, to the best of its ability has helped no little in bringing this about. There does not appear to have been much wrong with our Native Policy up to the present.[105]

The Conference of District Commissioners reached a similar conclusion. At their meeting in 1943, the commissioners concluded that instead of encouraging the Fijians to go their own ways, "it is imperative to maintain the closest possible connection between the individual and the land"; that "any tendency towards disintegration of Fijian village society" should be discouraged; that exemption, or *galala,* should be discontinued as it led to misunderstanding; and that village life should be improved through amalgamation and better housing and social services.[106]

The Great Council of Chiefs, with Oxford-educated high chief Ratu Sukuna at its head, heartily endorsed these views. Thus in 1944 there came into existence a reversionary system of Fijian administration that was to remain in place for two decades. It was a singular and dramatic attempt to stem the tide of change taking place in Fiji after the war, to revert Fijian society to its traditional principles of organization: to a society, which, in Sukuna's words, was "based not on contract and freedom but on consanguinity and status," with "common descent, common faith, and common interest," and held together on the one hand by "shrewdness, tact and forbearance and on the other loyalty, obedience and reverence."[107] The resultant creation of a government within a government once again placed the responsibility for administering Fijian society in

Ratu Lala Sukuna and Adi Maraia. In the background is Maurice Scott. Easily the most distinguished *taukei* leader in the twentieth century, Sukuna filled several important roles during his lifetime, becoming the Speaker of the Legislative Council in 1956. He died in 1958. *(Courtesy Fiji Ministry of Information)*

Fijian hands, insulating the Fijian community from the mainstream of Fiji's colonial life and restricting opportunities for cross-cultural contacts. It left a legacy of deep political, social, and economic implications for the Fijian people and would be the subject of much debate, at least among the makers of colonial policy, in the late 1950s and early 1960s.

The most important feature of the revamped Fijian administration was the creation in 1944 of an all-powerful Fijian Affairs Board, which replaced the much larger Native Regulations Board.[108] Consisting of the secretary of Fijian Affairs (Sukuna) as chair, all Fijian members of the Legislative Council (five altogether), and a legal advisor appointed by the governor, the board was, in effect, the executive and administrative arm of the Great Council of Chiefs. It made regulations regarding the welfare of the Fijian people and the observance of customary rights, ceremonies, obligations, conduct, and communal services; defined the powers and procedures and jurisdiction of Fijian courts in civil and criminal matters; and appointed district and provincial officials *(buli* and *roko)*. It was also given the first right of review over any legislation that affected "in any important matter the rights and interests of Fijians and especially any Bill imposing taxes to be paid by them or relating to their Chiefs, local authorities or land." The board still exists, though its composition has changed in response to altered political circumstances.

The Great Council of Chiefs retained its old functions, but was expanded in 1948 to include, in addition to the *roko* of the provinces, six chiefs nominated by the governor and two representatives (instead of only one) from all provinces with a population of over ten thousand. Designated chiefs, such as the head of a *matanitū* or *vanua,* were entitled to demand certain personal services from their people, such as building their house or planting their garden, making mats and tapa, supplying visitors with food and the chief with turtle, and transport. By amalgamation, the number of provinces was reduced from nineteen to fourteen, six of which were new (Ba, Nadroga/Navosa, Naitasiri, Serua, Ra, and Tailevu).[109] The *roko,* appointed by the governor in consultation with the Fijian Affairs Board, became the effective head of Fijian affairs at the provincial level, in place of the (European) district commissioner. This change removed the former administrative ambiguity about where the ultimate authority in local administration resided. Each province had its own provincial court with two Fijian magistrates and one European magistrate to try offenses against Fijian Affairs Board regulations and impose a penalty of up to £10 or two months imprisonment. The powers of the District (Tikina) Council were also expanded. It could now "make orders to be obeyed by all Fijians within the area of its authority," giving it almost total control over the regulation of village affairs, reinforced by strict penal sanctions for any breach of village regulations.

Since the focus was on village-based communal development, the

Native Regulations restricted opportunities for migration and employment in towns. It was unlawful for Fijians to remain in an industrial or a
closely settled area for more than seven days. As to the *galala,* the promising smallholders promoted by hopeful administrators a decade before,
they could petition for commutation of all the required social service rates
(taxes) on a yearly basis, and if successful, each paid a commutation rate of
£1, in addition to all levies under the Native Regulations. As agriculturalists, and to keep their exemptions alive, each had to maintain at least three
acres of land, with two additional acres for cattle, and a minimum yearly
income of £50. All decisions on commutation were now to be made by a
special Provincial Council of local Fijians and not the governor, who had
made them in the past.

The Fijian Affairs Board regulations were important in a number of
ways, not the least because of the precision and detail with which they
attempted to regulate Fijian rural life. Every aspect was codified with sanctions, including regulations about the size and shape of houses that could
be constructed, procedures for the clearing of land by burning and the provision of family food crops, and in the 1920s and 1930s, even one regulation prohibiting the consumption of *yaqona* during certain hours (11 PM to
6 AM) and by men under eighteen years and women with young children.
The provincial officials were probably not required to interpret the regulations literally, but there was grumbling about overadministration among
many *taukei* as the regulations began to take effect.

Colonial officials justified imposing the regulations this way:

> First, they secure the continuance of the Fijian communal system and the
> customs and observances traditionally associated with that system. In the
> complex structure of society in Fiji, resulting from the influx of non-indige-
> nous races, it has long been recognised that legislation must intervene to rein-
> force the moral and customary sanctions which in earlier times bound Fijians
> together in the communal fold. Secondly, they provide a simple code of civil
> and criminal law comprehensible both to Fijian magistrates and people and
> adaptable to situations arising in the communal way of life, enforcing in some
> instances traditional Fijian moral standards. Thirdly, they enable cases to be
> heard locally and justice to be speedily carried out.[110]

At one level, there can be little argument with the intended thrust of the
regulations and the system they sought to uphold. After all, they seemed to
be putting the administration of Fijian life back where it properly
belonged, in the hands of the Fijian people themselves. But underpinning
the approach was the assumption of homogeneity across the Fijian social
and economic landscape, which was as misleading as it was problematic.
Ratu Sukuna's tranquil, well-knit, cohesive Fijian society, isolated from
modern needs and aspirations and forces of change, progressing steadily
under the wise, time-tested leadership of chiefs—"The Fijian is still at

heart a subsistence agriculturalist with a simple conception of life—his clan institution and the thatched houses of his boyhood, his land and the peace and leisure of his *koro*"[111]—did exist, especially in the maritime provinces and other parts of Fiji isolated from a competitive cash economy and a multiracial population.

In western Viti Levu and around *koro* fringing Indo-Fijian settlements, there was another reality, however, in which the needs and the aspirations, already whetted by modern communication, the war, and contact with other groups, were different. Whereas in Lau, for example, the traditional structure remained relatively intact, in Nadi or Ba and other such places, it did not. As one contemporary observer said, in these areas, "a sense of frustration accompanies this reversion to the old order and as the new clothes grow ragged the present semi-communal system loses more and more of its flavour. The natives have tasted the easier fruits of individualism and in increasing numbers are looking towards 'exemption' as prisoners might look to parole."[112] There was no provision for variation and flexibility in the regulations, and the gap widened with time. Indo-Fijians entered the world of business, commercial agriculture, or modern education, coming to terms with the demands of the larger world. Under the new regulations, the Fijians, in contrast, began to retreat to the succor of a traditional village life whose foundations were not as secure as they once had been. For the Fijian people, the dilemmas were clear. R. S. MacDougal, who reviewed the operation of the Fijian Provincial Administration in the mid-1950s, wrote:

> I have seen for myself how their system of land tenure discourages development, how some of their customs and traditions encourage thriftlessness, and how personal initiative is stifled. Some have already been changed, others must be if the Fijians are to make progress in a very competitive world, if their children are to be better educated, if they are to enjoy a higher standard of living, and above all, if they are to hold their place in a group of islands which are rapidly ceasing to be isolated from the world, and in which more than one race is living.[113]

The glaring differences, and the need to catch up with others, would be one of the major challenges facing the next generation of Fijian leaders, who were beginning to learn the ropes in Ratu Sukuna's very large shadow.

The Politics of the Deed of Cession

The war and the industrial disputes, the profiteering activities of some Indo-Fijian merchants during the war, the illegal possession of firearms and explosives obtained mostly from the American forces—all had their

predictable effects on race relations in the colony.[114] These were further
strained by the fact that during the war years, the Indo-Fijians surpassed
the Fijians as the largest ethnic group in the colony, their numbers in 1946
standing at 130,000 and 119,000, respectively.[115] Against the background
of Indo-Fijian demands for political parity, more secure leases, and
removal of racial discrimination in employment, this increase intensified
underlying ill-feeling between the two communities, reinforced fears of
Indo-Fijian dominance, and provoked hostile reactions from others. "It is
becoming a not uncommon thing among young Fijians, many of whom
have had training in arms, to talk of the day when they will fight and kill
Indians," reported the governor to the Colonial Office in 1945.[116]

Among Europeans, racial prejudice apart, competition from Indo-
Fijian merchants, launderers, tailors, and house servants demanding
higher rates of pay caused hostility. In addition, political developments on
the Indian subcontinent, the gathering pace of the independence movement there, and the specter of England's imperial decline provoked resentment among local Europeans who regarded the Indo-Fijians as collaborators in the movement to bring about the collapse of the British Empire.
However, there was another side to the issue. As the governor told the
Colonial Office at the end of the war, the Indo-Fijian was also a victim of
prejudice because "there is a reluctance on the part of many Europeans
and Fijians to recognise that the Indians, 80 percent of whom were born in
Fiji, must be regarded as a permanent part of the population and that the
Indian cane farmers contribute very substantially to the economic life of
the Colony."[117]

Fijian and European attitudes toward the Indo-Fijians were forcefully
aired in the now famous "Deed of Cession Debate" in the Legislative
Council in July 1946. It is perhaps the finest debate in the annals of Fiji's
colonial history, illuminated with inspired flourishes of rhetorical brilliance
from its leading participants. The motion by A. A. Ragg stated:

> The time has arrived in view of the great increase in the non-Fijian inhabit-
> ants and its consequential political development to emphasise the terms of the
> Deed of Cession to assure that the interests of the Fijian race are safeguarded
> and a guarantee be given that Fiji is to be preserved and kept as a Fijian
> country for all time.

Ragg had been forced to take up the cudgel on behalf of the Fijian people
because, he said, they were "impotent to help themselves."[118] The Fijians
needed help to compete with non-Fijians (he meant Indo-Fijians) because
they lacked "character" to cope with life's pressures: "Those who know
natives well," he said, "know what they most lack, and what, if they are to
be true men, they must somehow acquire, are the qualities of mind and
soul that are expressed in the word 'character.' " Character was what the

Fijians lacked. "We, who work for and among them," he continued, "know, too painfully, how deficient in all manly qualities they are. Courage, honour, firmness, pure ambition, truthfulness, unselfishness—these and kindred qualities are all too rare." Still, Fijians as a race of people were not entirely to blame; they were simply victims of circumstances, of a destructive communal environment, fostered by the government, which stifled individual effort and initiative.

Ragg, then, was not defending colonial policy toward Fijians; nor was he defending traditional, or communal, society. His vision was of a new society, more along the lines that the Viti Cauravou had proposed in the 1920s and 1930s than the one Sukuna was following. Said Ragg, "Herd men together like sheep, take away from them all incentive and ambition, impose on them a legal code that stops all outlet for individual effort, stifle all expressions of individual opinion, and the result, most assuredly, will be the annihilation of all character and the production of a placid race of mental and moral invertebrates." This was what the colonial policy was in danger of producing. H. B. Gibson also made a plea to revive *galala* and abolish traditional ceremonies, which, in his view, were extravagant and a drain on the resources and energy of the Fijian people. Even H. H. Ragg, not entirely in agreement with A. A. Ragg's call to abolish Fijian communal customs, was convinced that Fijian salvation lay in following the "gospel of work," the virtues of thrift, industry, and enterprise.

European members who spoke in favor of the motion were sometimes disingenuous. Some of them had been fellow travelers with other Europeans who, as late as the 1930s, had agitated for the sale of native land in the name of economic development. Indeed, in the course of the debate, Gibson urged the government to consider encouraging European settlement in Fiji, lamenting that Fiji "is a Colony for Europeans but European settlement here has never been encouraged." More Europeans, especially New Zealanders, should be appointed to government positions, "and gradually by and large we will get an increasing number of European people in the Colony and we will counter-balance this evil and we will save our Fijian friends from the fear of being swamped which they say to us is a very real fear." He saw no contradiction in what he was proposing. There was also the realization that European privilege could most effectively be maintained by a coalition of convenience with Fijian interests even if, as in A. A. Ragg's case, European perception of Fijian interest was at variance with Sukuna's.

Fijian reaction was equally predictable, though less windy. Supporting Ragg, Ratu Tiale W. T. Vuiyasawa, Ratu George C. Tuisawau, Ratu George B. Toganivalu, and Ratu Etuate N. Mataitini all sought renewed assurance that the promise of the Deed of Cession was not being neglected. How is the government going to reconcile Indo-Fijian demands for parity with the principle of trusteeship for Fijians? asked Ratu George Toganivalu. What steps would it take to deal with Indo-Fijian demands for more land? "We Fijians have heard of an English King called Canute," said Ratu Etuate, "and we do not propose to follow his example nor can we, as representatives of our people, sit idly by." In a debate a year later, Ratu George Toganivalu pleaded for Fijian and European unity. Turning to European members, he said, "We acknowledge you as our superiors intellectually. We do not want to be separated, and we ask for your full support. We believe that if, in Fiji, the European and the Fijian are separated, both will fall."[119] The Fijian Affairs Board on 19 July 1946 also lent its voice to the expressed fears of Indo-Fijian economic and political domination and adverse effects on everyday Fijian life, urging the government to "adopt a firm attitude towards the Indians in order that the interest of the Fijian race remains pre-eminent in the Colony."[120]

A. D. Patel and Vishnu Deo led the Indo-Fijian counter-attack. They made essentially three points. The first was to state the obvious fact that the "non-Fijian inhabitants" mentioned in the text of the motion actually meant Indo-Fijians, suggesting that the motion was essentially an anti–Indo-Fijian tirade. Vishnu Deo argued that if the Indo-Fijian presence in Fiji was a threat to the terms of the Deed of Cession, then Europeans were partly responsible. "If immigration to this Colony by people who are materially useful was against the terms of the Deed of Cession," he asked, "why did not the European Members then think about that? Was it because their own interests were to be served by immigration from India that they wanted to shut their eyes to it, or was it really a breach of the terms of the Deed of Cession?" Who was dominating whom, he continued, when 45 percent of the jobs in the civil service were held by Europeans, 40 percent by Fijians, and only 15 percent by Indo-Fijians; or when Europeans had long dominated the membership of the Legislative Council and had even proposed to remove legislation protecting Fijian land? Furthermore, Vishnu Deo pointed out that the decline in the Fijian population and other associated problems had little to do with Indo-Fijians. The European death rate was 3.97 per thousand; Part-European, 7.27 per thousand; Fijian, 15.31 per thousand; and Indian, 7.39 per thousand. "Is it the fault of the Indian community that the death rate of the Fijians is higher than their own?" he asked. In any case, he added, tongue-in-cheek, the deed "did not advocate non-Fijian birth control."

In an impressive contribution to the debate, Patel carefully analyzed the deed clause by clause, pointing out that its terms were not in need of reemphasizing: "So far as the desires of the people who ceded this country to the British are concerned," he said, "those desires are scrupulously fulfilled." The Europeans, not the Indo-Fijians, had threatened Fijian interests. They had "gobbled up half a million acres of freehold land from the Fijian owners." He emphasized that Indo-Fijians had themselves advocated that Fijian interests should always remain paramount, "that where those interests come into conflict with our interests, we readily agree to make our interests subservient to theirs." Indo-Fijians and Fijians had rather more in common than was apparent; both, he said, were victims of the "obnoxious and odious racial discrimination that prevails in Government Service." The Fijian people, Patel argued, had little to fear from Indo-Fijians:

> We came and undertook to work under a system which, thank God, saved the Fijian race from the infamy of coming under. . . . As a matter of fact, if anything, the coming of my people to this country gave the Fijians their honour, their prestige, nay indeed their very soul. Otherwise I have no hesitation in saying that the Fijians of this Colony would have met with the same fate that some other indigenous races in parts of Africa met. I would ask my honourable colleagues to consider that aspect of it before they condemn my people.

The government was caught in a dilemma for, implicitly, the motion was a criticism of its own policies and attitudes. There was another aspect, as well. As Governor Grantham reported to the Colonial Office in 1946, "I do not wish to minimize the seriousness of the Indian problem, though apart from the relative growth in populations, it might be better termed the Fijian problem since it is rather a question of raising the Fijian so that he is able to hold his own with the Indian in the modern world, than of holding back the Indian so that he does not outstrip the more easy-going Fijian."[121] In the end, a diluted and innocuous version of the motion was passed, affirming that the "non-Fijian inhabitants of this Colony stand by the terms of the Deed of Cession and shall consider that document as a Charter of the Fijian people."

Race Relations in the 1950s

A. A. Ragg was still unsatisfied. He carried on his crusade against the imminent Indo-Fijian threats to Fijian interests well into the 1950s, petitioning the Colonial Office and corresponding with important public figures in Britain, with his alarmist rhetoric, calling the Fijian administration a dictatorship worse than communist Russia and making detailed proposals on how to limit the size of the Indo-Fijian population.[122] If Indo-Fijian population growth remained unchecked, Ragg projected that by the year 2000, Indo-Fijians would number 835,000, Fijians 425,000, and others 148,000 (see Figure 6). To avert this disaster, he proposed shutting down all permanent immigration from India and China, repatriating (with some compensation) Indo-Fijians and Chinese at an annual rate of 12,000 and 200, respectively, beginning with sixteen-year-old males and fourteen-year-old females chosen by ballot, with all the leases thus vacated to revert to Fijians for a small sum paid for the unexpired portion of the lease. Euro-

Figure 6. A cartoon from the 1950s: "Fate of the Fijians." *(Courtesy National Archives of Fiji)*

peans did not pose a threat to Fijians, Ragg said; in any case, they had a right to be in Fiji because they had discovered the islands, introduced stable government, protected the Fijians, and promoted the economic development of the colony. But the other races had to go. Unless the British government took immediate steps to act on his proposals, Ragg warned, "a day will come in the not too distant future when we shall have to get troops from Australia and New Zealand to shoot down the Fijians to protect the Indians."[123]

Ragg was not alone among Europeans in advocating the repatriation of the Indo-Fijians. R. W. Robson, the longtime publisher of *Pacific Islands Monthly,* was equally forthright and tactless. "If it is considered cruel to return them to India," he wrote in 1953, "why not transport them to the fertile, depopulated groups in Polynesia—Marquesas. They would probably end by clawing each other to death, within ten years: but at least we could count on a quiet and decent future for Fiji."[124] A. W. MacMillan, London Missionary Society preacher and longtime inspector of Indian schools in Fiji, offered another alternative. Writing to Ragg in August 1952 from retirement in Tauranga, New Zealand, MacMillan wondered if it might not be a good idea to settle Indo-Fijians in New Guinea:

New Guinea is the largest island in the world, 1500 miles in length, with great river basins like the Fly and the Sepik, with mountains up to 15,000 feet; and capable of carrying a population of from 30 to 50 millions, and become another wealth producing Java or Sumatra. Left empty as it is, with perhaps two or three million primitive natives scattered along its crocodile-like length, it is sure to be a tempting bait for Asian expansionists. I think an Asian Power [is] likely to attempt to seize it this century. Any obstinate policy to keep it unoccupied will be provocative and be bound to lead to trouble. Why not populate it in ways that will develop its resources, help hungry Asia, and regulate immigration so as to prevent New Guinea from falling into the hands of Communist China or Japan?[125]

Such a colonization scheme could be carried out under Commonwealth supervision. Even India, Pakistan, and Ceylon could be persuaded "to associate themselves with us and the Dutch to go and do in New Guinea what our brave pioneers have done in distant lands, and with that challenge give them a definite outlet for migration, rather than have to face the recurring demand for admission to Commonwealth countries on terms of equality." The ingenuity of the proposal was matched only by the irony that it was being advocated by a man who had been entrusted to look after the education of Indo-Fijian children.

The Colonial Office shared Ragg's concerns about the rate of Indo-Fijian population increase, but thought his projections wildly exaggerated. It could not countenance the idea of repatriating a people who had lived in Fiji for two or three generations and who knew no other home than Fiji. In any case, the Indo-Fijians had expressed no desire to leave Fiji. They played an important part in Fiji's economic life, which would suffer if they were to leave. The real solution to the problem, the Colonial Office said, lay not in repatriating any one group but in promoting "improved methods of agriculture, food production and land husbandry, and these are pursued by the Fiji Government."[126]

Such racial feelings and phobias infected political discourse in the colony throughout the 1950s. Frustrated by continued Indo-Fijian demands for constitutional change, increased elected representation in the Legislative Council, and universal adult franchise without property or gender qualifications,[127] Europeans adopted an even more reactionary attitude toward the Indo-Fijian community. A *Fiji Times* letter writer called the Indian "a blight which his adopted country would gain to get rid of."[128] A. J. C. Foster, in a thoughtful series of articles on the "Future of Fiji," wrote in 1957, "The European to a very great extent, regards the Indians as just one step from coolies."[129]

Fijian editorial writers expressed uneasiness about Indo-Fijian progress and aspirations and deep apprehension about the place of their own people in the larger scheme of things. "What intensifies this uneasiness is that Indians tend to disregard the affairs of this Colony and the British Empire

and concern themselves of their own interest and in the interest of India,"
said the *Volagauna*.[130] Feeling under siege, these Fijians rejected advice to
modify and change aspects of the neotraditional Fijian system:

> Those who wish us to take this step are probably of the opinion that our
> progress is very slow; that we are staggering under the yoke of communalism
> and that other races are marching ahead of us. There is no such burden in the
> communal system to hinder our struggle; their references are correct but it
> would be unwise to make the change at this stage, i.e., to abolish the Native
> Regulations. This will lead to the complete destruction of the communal
> structure that ties us together; it will definitely destroy the Fijian way of life of
> working together. This will also make it easier for other races to do whatever
> they like in our midst.[131]

A survey in the mid-1950s found that 63 percent of the Fijians interviewed expressed complete intolerance of the presence of Indo-Fijians, and
25 percent wanted them to remain in the colony, but only on terms favorable to the Fijians. On the question of self-government in cooperation with
Indo-Fijians, a majority of the Fijian respondents were completely
opposed.[132] Reflecting this defensive mood, the Great Council of Chiefs in
1954 rejected the government's proposal to have two of the Fijian representatives to the Legislative Council elected on communal franchise. This
defense of traditionalism was tempered by the awareness of the need to
have a new and articulate Fijian leadership to explain and defend the
Fijian position. Furthermore, the conservative view was not widely shared
across the Fijian community. As one Fijian stated: "We want representatives—whether chief or commoner—who are capable of expressing our
views clearly and fearlessly in the Legislative Council and not those who
are idle and reactionary."[133] Fortunately, this view was heeded, and
Ravuama Vunivalu, one of the ablest Fijians of his generation and a commoner, entered the Legislative Council in the 1950s.

The Indo-Fijian community, for the most part preoccupied with its own
internal economic affairs and cultural and social disputes, was, of course,
aware of much of the public comment about the problem their presence
had supposedly caused in Fiji, though not about the drastic solution that
its critics were proposing. European criticism was dismissed as sour
grapes, coming from a group whose economic stranglehold over the colony
was beginning to be challenged, as yet in a minor way, by the Indo-Fijian
business class. Not surprisingly, Indo-Fijians held the Europeans and the
colonial policy of ethnic compartmentalization responsible for the unhappy state of race relations in the colony. This is how the *Fiji Samachar*
described the issue in 1962:

> Who told us that there are separate schools for us? Who built boys and girls
> grammar schools separately and restricted Fiji and Indian boys and girls

Ratu K. K. T. Mara in ceremonial dress, 1955. He was then emerging as a future
Fijian leader. *(Courtesy Fiji Ministry of Information)*

from studying there? Who built the Indian and Fijian Affairs departments
separately? Who forced us to fill in government forms stating that we were
Indians? Friends, you have told us that at every step we are Indians.
Through you people we were not able to unite with the Fijians. You did not
allow us to study together and sit together. Suva Youth Centre is open today.
You are thinking of this today but it is too late. You did not allow our children
in the Suva Sea Bath. What if Indian, Fijian and European children had
eaten together and swum together? Their unity and co-operation would have
increased and they would have grown up together and considered the future
of the colony together. They would have done a lot for the welfare of the Colony, but my friends we have been separated at every step and we have been
prevented from making progress in the Colony and the results will be suffered by our children.[134]

The Fijians' problems, the Indo-Fijian leaders argued, were caused not
by the progress made by the Indo-Fijians, but by an overprotective colonial government and the rigid strictures of the Fijian administration,
which governed every aspect of Fijians' lives. As an editorial in the *Pacific
Review* argued: "Government should know that mothers commonly
believe that over-protection is better than no protection. [But] if the child
is not given the chance to walk just because it might fall, then what should
be our opinion of such mothers?"[135] Structures and institutions useful to
the Fijians of the nineteenth century had lost their relevance in the modern
world. "It is high time," the editorial concluded, that "Fijians are freed
from that iron cage which was built for their forefathers." While Fijian editorial writers advised their readers to adhere to tradition and customary
ways, their Indo-Fijian counterparts emphasized the virtues of endurance
and endeavor: "Nothing useful can be achieved without the application of
what these words imply. A man without endurance will be a rolling stone
and if he does not try, he will not be of any use to the world. Endure and
try, try and try again; you will succeed at last."[136]

The government maintained a low profile during this long and acrimonious debate in which the contents and implications of the Deed of Cession
were once again invoked, particularly by Ragg and other like-minded
Europeans, to suggest that the government had been derelict in its duty
to the Fijian people. Finally, in 1957 Governor Sir Ronald Garvey took
up Ragg's challenge in a Cession Day speech that provides instructive
glimpses into official thinking and deserves to be quoted at length:

> Surely the true intention of this Deed, acknowledged and accepted by the
> chiefs who were parties to it, was that Fiji should be developed so as to take a
> significant place in the affairs of the world but that, in the process, the rights
> and interests of the Fijian people should be respected. To read into the Deed
> more than that, to suggest, for instance, that the rights and interests of the
> Fijians should predominate over everything else, does no service either to the
> Fijian people or to their country. The view, for the Fijians, would mean com-

plete protection and no self-respecting individual race wants that because, ultimately, it means that those subject to it will end up as museum pieces. The Indians are equally eligible to have their interests respected. By their work and enterprise, the Indians in Fiji have made a great contribution to the development and prosperity of their country, and to the welfare of its people. They are an essential part of the community and it is unrealistic to suppose that they are not or to imagine that the position of Fijians in the world today would benefit by their absence.[137]

The debates in the press forced the colonial government to consider steps to identify impediments to the progress of the colony. To this end, it instituted two important commissions of inquiry, one to examine the problems of the colony as a whole and another to dissect the social and economic problems facing the Fijian community in particular.

War in Malaya

In this emotionally charged atmosphere, the Fijians were once again called to fight for the cause of the British Empire, this time against the Communist insurgency in Malaya. The Indo-Fijians wanted to enlist, but Acting Governor A. F. R. Stoddart thought "soldierly qualities [were] lacking among Indians,"[138] and did not pursue their offer. The Europeans, too, were disappointed, saying that "any call for sacrifice for Malaya should somehow have gone to the Colony as a whole and not the Fijians alone."[139] The Fijians had become victims of their proud military record. The first battalion of the Fiji Military Forces, which had been reconstituted early in 1950 under a 1948 defense agreement between Fiji and New Zealand, left in January 1952, initially on a commission for two years, though that was later extended to four. By 1953 there were 850 men from Fiji in Malaya, of whom 800 were Fijians (0.6 percent of the total Fijian population). Their record for bravery and skill in jungle warfare was, expectedly, exceptional. As a Malayan commander stated: "Of all the troops of many races who have been for a long time fighting the menace of the Communist terrorists in Malaya, none have gained greater respect, admiration and affection than the First Battalion, Fiji Infantry Regiment."[140] They killed 175 Chinese, captured 3, and had 1 surrender, and they covered themselves in medals: two Orders of the British Empire, one Member of the British Empire, one British Empire Medal, two Military Crosses, two Distinguished Conduct Medals, five Military Medals, and twenty-four Mentions in Despatches.

Why were Fijian soldiers going to Malaya? One reason was that their chiefs told them to. As during World War II, so too in the 1950s, the chiefs spearheaded the effort to enlist Fijian men for service. Many of them, such as Ratu Penaia Ganilau, were commissioned officers who went to Malaya. The rationale for the war was explained by the governor:

Off to Malaya, 1954. Fijian soldiers fought against communists there from 1952 to 1956. *(Courtesy Fiji Ministry of Information)*

Fiji will welcome the opportunity to take an active part in defeating this insidious threat to law and order in Her Majesty's realm. For the dangers arising from the activities of the terrorists now operating in Malaya, and the evil forces of which they are the tools, are not limited to the confines of one territory. They are part of an attack on the well-being—and even the very existence—of the British comity of nations and of all freedom-loving people.[141]

Service in Malaya was good for the Fijian people, the governor said. The young Fijian soldier (average age twenty-two) would come back "home a better man than when he went away. . . . Having returned from the wars, having seen something of the world and satisfied his natural and commendable curiosity, he will be all the more ready to settle down in the koro, marry the sweetheart of his choice and, as they come along, tell his children—with pride—how he helped to win the war for freedom in Malaya."[142]

Besides a solid reputation for ability in jungle warfare, the Fijians gained little. Able-bodied men spent valuable time away from their families (for whom little or no official assistance was provided while the husband was away), neglecting their gardens at a time when other groups in Fiji were forging ahead in the economic field and in the professions. In 1958, while there were plenty of Fijian men with the experience of jungle warfare and with medals on their chests, there was no professionally qualified Fijian lawyer and only one qualified dentist and one medical doctor. By contrast, there were thirty-eight Indo-Fijian lawyers, twelve doctors, and eight dentists practicing in Fiji.[143] Even the *Fiji Times* was forced to the unhappy conclusion that the "material benefits to the Fijians in return for helping make Malaya safe for some sort of independence are paltry. The rates of pay for private soldiers [3s 9d per day] and the allowance for wives [2s 0d] are extremity of parsimony, and the scope of rehabilitation is still a subject of some doubt."[144] The returning servicemen did receive some simple agricultural tools (a spade, fork, axe, cane knife, and file) and some personal items (a mosquito net, a blanket, two pairs of shorts, two shirts, and one set of eating utensils—for two or more years of active service in Malaya!) and exemption from communal duties for six months immediately following discharge.[145] These paltry gestures hardly compensated for the loss of productive time in a period of rapid change. The social and economic costs of the Malayan war to Fiji, and to the Fijian people in particular, were significant, if unrealized at the time.

Social Change

By the 1950s, the face of contemporary Fiji was beginning to emerge with the laying of foundations for developments that became an integral part of Fiji's life in the next decade. A regular and scheduled system of public transportation began to take shape. In Suva the Atomic Power Bus Service began regular runs from the Bank of New South Wales building in central Suva to the Colonial War Memorial Hospital and parts of suburban Suva in 1948. Pacific and Sunbeam bus companies ran the round-the-island bus service, beginning in the late 1940s. By 1957 there were about 7000 cars (Morris Minor, Austin, Cambridge, Humber) plying the roads. With 30,000 people, Suva was declared a city in 1953, after being a town for 72 years. In the same year the colony played host to a warm royal tour of the islands by the recently crowned Queen Elizabeth and the Duke of Edinburgh.[146] Three years later, living up to its new image and its responsibility to multiracial taxpayers, the city opened its once exclusively European Suva Sea Baths to all races, though mixed bathing at the beaches had been occurring for a decade or more. Suva's affairs had once again, since January 1949, been managed by a fully elected council, replacing the system of official nomination to the Town Board started in the 1930s. In the Supreme Court of Fiji, Fijians and Indo-Fijians were now allowed to sit as assessors. Organized, colony-wide multiracial sports competitions in rugby, soccer, tennis, hockey, and cricket began to take place. The now-established interdistrict football competition for the Lloyd Farebrother Trophy became a major annual event in the colony.

On the other side of the island, the wartime aerodrome at Nadi was declared an international airport in May 1950 after a proposal to have one at Suva Point was judged too expensive. Nadi rapidly became the transit point for TEAL (Tasman Empire Airways Limited, now Air New Zealand), Pan American Airways, and Qantas. The growth in air traffic was phenomenal: in 1945, only 4 civilian aircraft had landed in Fiji; by 1948, 765 had landed. Internally, Fiji Airways, formed in 1954, linked the two main islands, though for another ten years the plane journey remained a luxury for most people in the colony. From the sea came magnificent white cruise liners with such magical names (to young school children such as myself) as *Mariposa, Oriana, Oronsay, Stella Polaris, Lurline,* and the *City of Los Angeles,* carrying tourists in search of tranquil paradise. Fiji was rapidly establishing itself as the hub of the Pacific.

Something of an information revolution was also taking place in the colony. The Fiji Broadcasting Commission was launched in 1954 as a statutory organization controlled by unofficial members—the first of its type in the British Empire—and began regular trilingual transmission. The outside world in the form of news and cultural events began to enter an unprecedented number of homes. Programming presented a problem to the officials, as the poem by commission member E. R. Bevington indicates in a lighthearted way. The schedule for 16 November 1954 is shown in Table 2.

Over the next decade, programs would be expanded considerably, with more Fijian and Indo-Fijian cultural and religious items featured on the

Birthpangs of the Fiji Broadcasting Commission
E. R. Bevington

A Broadcasting Commission
With powers of transmission
Is hard work for all concerned

For tastes differ greatly
And even the saintly
Do not like their tastes spurned

Some like the charms
of Haydn and Brahms
While others are less easy to please

Some like hot jazz
While others have fads
About crooners who draw heavy fees

The vernacular sessions
Are major transgressions
To those who are strange to Fiji

While Indians and natives
Are nothing but plaintive
For songs of indigenous glee

The talks are not fun
To those who have done
A hard day of work at the bench

They expect to relax
And not hear the facts
Of the decline in the use of good French

The programme's too dull
There's not enough sport
And the standard of culture is bad

The programme's too long
There's not enough song
Or there's not enough news to be had

The high-brow and the low-brow
The know-all and know-how
They all could do better they think

But the poor old Commission
Must keep up tradition
And give what it can or go sink.

Table 2. Daily Schedule of the Fiji Broadcasting Commission

Morning

6:30 AM	Devotional service, breakfast session
7:00–8:00	News and Weather
8:45	Fijian Programme
9:15	Ballads Old and New
9:45	Popular Vocalists
10:00	Close down

Afternoon

12:00 noon	Luncheon Music
12:30 PM	News, Weather, Shipping
1:00	Music by Geri Galian
1:15	Songs by the Fontaine Sisters
1:30	News, Weather, Shipping
1:45	Presenting the Les Brown Group
2:00	Close down

Late Afternoon and Evening

4:00 PM	Latin Americana
4:15	Variety Singers
4:30	Indian Programme
5:15	Round the Town with Our Shopping Reporter
5:30	Waltz Time
5:45	Theatre Fun
6:00	The Melachrino Strings
6:15	Public Relations News Letter
6:30	News, Weather, Shipping
6:45	Drama of Medicine
7:00	Question Mark
7:15	Special Assignment
7:30	Hit Parade
8:00	Indian Programme
9:00	News, Weather, Shipping, Station Notices
9:15	World Affairs
9:30	World Theatre (BBC)
10:30	Close

SOURCE: *Fiji Times,* 16 November 1954.

This bus provided the first regular bus service in Suva in the early 1950s. Note the election poster for the Legislative Council. *(Courtesy Fiji Ministry of Information)*

A moment in time: Central Suva, 1955. Note the Burns Philp store in the background and the Bank of New South Wales at left. *(Courtesy Fiji Ministry of Information)*

Queen Elizabeth II at Suva Wharf, 1953. On her left is Governor Sir Ronald Garvey. The Duke of Edinburgh is behind her. *(Courtesy Fiji Ministry of Information)*

air. The radio would long remain the most important, in many cases the only, source of news for most households in Fiji.

The years following the war also saw a large growth in the number of local newspapers (Table 3).

As the only daily, the *Fiji Times* exercised a great deal of influence on public opinion in the colony. Australian-owned (from the 1950s onward) and politically conservative, it remained an organ of the colonial Fijian and European establishment. In the 1960s, under the editorship of New Zealand–born former Public Relations Officer Leonard Usher, the newspaper became a sympathetic friend of the Alliance Party and a bitter critic of those who opposed the colonial establishment, often headlining stories from such trouble spots as Guyana to suggest what might happen to Fiji if the people and policies it championed were not heeded. The *Fiji Times'* national rival was the *Pacific Review*. Under the influence of A. D. Patel, this weekly later became the acknowledged voice of the Federation Party. Among its more venturesome activities, unparalleled in the annals of Fijian journalism, was the publication in Fijian of stories from Indian scriptures and legends, including translations of the *Ramayana*. For a time the newspaper was edited by a young Fijian chief, Ratu Mosese Varese-kete. The various Hindi newspapers were the organs of different political

Cruise liners at Suva Harbour in the 1950s. The Lami hills are in the background. (*Courtesy Fiji Ministry of Information*)

Table 3. Newspapers Established in Fiji by the Late 1950s

Newspaper	Language	Frequency
Fiji Times	English	daily
Pacific Review	English/Fijian	weekly
Volagauna	Fijian	fortnightly
Nai Lalakai	Fijian	weekly
Na Mata	Fijian	monthly
Jagriti	Hindi	every three weeks
Shanti Dut	Hindi	weekly
Fiji Samachar	Hindi	weekly
Jai Fiji	Hindi	weekly
Kisan Mitra	Hindi	weekly
Sangam	Tamil	monthly

SOURCE: CSO files.

factions and cultural groups within the Indian community, and the Fijian newspapers for the most part echoed established opinions of that community.

The existence of so many newspapers made for lively and remarkably well-informed debate about the colony's social and political affairs. No other Pacific Island colony, and probably no other comparable British colony anywhere in the world, could boast such active and diverse print media. In some respects, the Fiji media were far ahead of their more established metropolitan counterparts. There could not have been many newspapers in the world that ran an editorial on nuclear testing as the *Jagriti* did in 1957:

> People living in the vicinity of the [Pacific] islands where the atom and hydrogen bombs have been tested are afflicted with hazardous diseases. Full information has not been given so far about them. Nations engaged in testing these bombs in the Pacific should realize the value of the lives of people settled in this part of the world. They, too, are human beings, not "guinea pigs."[147]

Education

An important reason for the presence of so many newspapers in Fiji was the expansion of primary and secondary education in the years following the war. The blueprint for educational development was provided by the Stephens Report of 1944, which had recommended, among other things, the expansion and improvement of educational facilities, greater government involvement in educational administration, improved training of teachers, and their absorption into the civil service.[148] In 1947 the Nasinu Teachers' Training College was established near Suva, and in 1948 all registered teachers became civil servants. District education offices were established in each of the three administrative divisions of the colony, the Eastern, the Central, and the Northern. In the mid-1950s, further progress was made with the strengthening of postprimary education and the granting of overseas scholarships to a select number of students.[149]

By 1955 there were some 310 Fijian and 149 Indo-Fijian schools in the colony, with 60,223 children in primary schools and 2,462 in secondary. Each sizeable Indo-Fijian settlement had a modest primary school of its own, often run by such cultural and religious organizations as the Sangam, Sanatan Dharam, Arya Samaj, and the Fiji Muslim League. Among secondary schools, the government-run Natabua High in Lautoka and Ramakrishna mission's Sri Vivekananda High in Nadi (established in 1949) played an especially prominent role in educating a whole generation of Indo-Fijian professionals in Fiji. The Indo-Fijian thirst for better education found annual expression at conferences organized by the Fiji Teachers' Union. An example of the kinds of issues raised by Indo-Fijian teachers is provided by the Fiji Teachers' Union's 1953 resolutions, which included demands for the establishment of a Fiji university college affiliated with the University of New Zealand, provision for nursery and kindergarten classes in heavily populated areas, and the upgrading of training and provision of periods of study leave for teachers.[150]

In the Fijian community, too, many important advances were made in the educational field. The Fijian Provincial Schools were consolidated at the Ratu Kadavulevu Intermediate School in Tailevu. Adi Cakobau School was established for Fijian girls in 1948 and moved to its present rustic location at Sawani in southeastern Viti Levu in 1956. Perhaps the most important development of all was the establishment of a permanent home for the Queen Victoria School. Established in Nasinu in 1907 at the behest of Fijian chiefs "for the express purpose of teaching in English the adoption of English ideas and habits,"[151] the school had fallen victim to World War II when its buildings were used to billet New Zealand soldiers and house the 8th General Hospital of the US Army, while the students were banished to the frugal but picturesque isolation of Nanukuloa in Ra.[152] In July 1950, Governor Sir Brian Freeston laid the foundation stones of the new school at Matavatucou in Tailevu, on 205 acres of beautiful, sea-lapped land donated by Sir Henry Scott, as a "fitting acknowledgement both of the wartime loss of the original school and of the great sacrifice rendered by the Fijian people to the war effort of the Empire and the Mother Country."[153] The school was formally opened in 1953.

The aim of the reestablished Queen Victoria School was defined as twofold:

to give its pupils an academic education in a broad and modern sense which will fit them to take up posts in the various civil services—educational, medical and administrative—and enable the best of them to proceed abroad for further training, either immediately after leaving school or after a period in the public service: and yet to centre this discipline of the mind in an environment reflecting the predominantly agricultural life of the community and calling for a practical approach to the problem of life and social and economic co-operation in Fiji."[154]

In at least one important respect, the physical location and the educational mission of the Queen Victoria School were seriously flawed. The Fijian boys spent their formative years in an isolated, rural, and predominantly Fijian setting with no opportunity for contact with other groups. Their vision remained narrow, focused on Fijian ethos and ideals, uninformed and uninfluenced by any real understanding of the cultural values and aspirations of other people in Fiji's plural society. In their later years, the students of Queen Victoria School, more than those of any other Fijian school, were called on to fulfill roles (as educators, administrators, public figures) on a wider stage requiring cross-cultural skills that they sorely lacked. The same was true of Indo-Fijian children attending predominantly Indo-Fijian schools in the cane belts of Fiji. It was mainly in mission schools, such as those run by the Marist Brothers, that schoolchildren from different racial groups studied and played together, but such opportunities were rare.

Education in primary schools was, for the most part, rudimentary and vocational. In the lower grades, much of the instruction was in the vernacular, but pupils in the higher grades were taught in English. A whole generation of Fiji's primary school pupils in the 1940s and 1950s grew up on the *New Method Readers,* a series used in most tropical British colonies in Africa and the West Indies. They read beautifully written stories about King Arthur, Ulysses, and the Cyclops, about desert crossing in Egypt, Rip van Winkle, Rama and Sita, and England's four seasons, often memorized by heart. A middle-aged bus driver in Labasa, who presented me with a tattered copy of his primary school *New Method Reader* early in 1990, took great pride in reciting the stirring lines of Lord Tennyson's "Ulysses," which he had learned in primary school:

> Though much is taken, much abides; and though
> We are not now that strength which in old days
> Moved earth and heaven; that which we are, we are;
> Made weak by time and fate, but strong in will
> To strive, to seek, to find, and not to yield.

The words aptly captured his tenacious approach to life.

By the 1960s, the *New Method Readers* were replaced by the *Oxford African Readers,* so that primary schoolchildren of my generation grew up reading about African witch doctors, tribes, and life-styles, about "our" South African Uncle Smith taking a cruise liner to England, and about a fat Sokoloko Bengosay desperately trying various tricks to make herself look thin and pretty. For the most part, stories about English and Asian societies had been dropped. Not until the 1970s did the primary school curriculum acquire a more local (and Pacific) orientation.

In senior secondary schools, all the instruction was in English. Their curriculum, heavily academic and exam-oriented, was set by Cambridge University. In the 1940s and 1950s, the plays of Shakespeare were regular fare, *Macbeth* and *The Merchant of Venice* being particular favorites. The novels of Charles Dickens, Thomas Hardy, Jane Austin, and Robert Louis Stevenson were prescribed regularly, and students of Latin were expected to read Cicero's *Correspondence,* Virgil's *Aneid,* and Ovid's *Metamorphosis.* Students of Greek read Xenophon's *Anabasis,* Demosthenes' *Philippic,* Homer's *Odyssey,* and Euripides' *Cyclops.* History students preparing for the higher qualifying examination in 1951 were required to be familiar with a large number of topics, ranging from the history of Fiji and the organization of the colonial government to British imperial history and the history of the Renaissance and the Reformation. A representative exam paper indicates just how much a student was expected to know—or cram —to pass the exam (see Figure 7).

In the 1960s, many senior Fiji secondary schools would change from the Cambridge Certificate to the New Zealand School Certificate system, with a corresponding restructuring of the curriculum. History students continued to study such topics as the unification of Italy and Germany, the causes of World War I and the French Revolution, and the rise of the trade union movement in Britain (though, mercifully, not the history of the Tudors and the Stuarts). They also learned about the rise of the Liberal Party in New Zealand, the life of Sir Apirana Ngata, the economic policies of Sir Julius Vogel, the history of refrigerated transportation in New Zealand, and the history of the convict settlement of Australia. In literature, the works of Katherine Mansfield, James K. Baxter, and A. R. D. Fairburn found a place in the traditional list of more established English writers. In some secondary schools, the novels of John Steinbeck *(Grapes of Wrath),* J. D. Salinger *(Catcher in the Rye),* Ernest Hemingway *(The Old Man and the Sea* and *For Whom the Bell Tolls),* Patrick White *(Voss),* and D. H. Lawrence *(Sons and Lovers)* and the poems of T. S. Eliot were part of the English curriculum. The curriculum of the 1970s would have a much more South Pacific and Fijian orientation.

The colonial educational orientation had its share of critics who argued that the curriculum promoted a "false sense of values" among Fiji's school children.[155] The criticism was valid and reinforced because local history

Paper No. Q. 9.

QUALIFYING EXAMINATION.

Thursday, 8th. November, 1951.

HISTORY.

Time: 9.00 - 10.30
Marks: 100

ADVICE TO ALL CANDIDATES:-

A. Read the questions carefully.
B. Answer the questions BRIEFLY, giving only IMPORTANT facts.
C. Check your answers to see that you have answered all questions FULLY.
D. Do not waste time.

SECTION A:- Answer EITHER Question 1 OR Question 2 and ONE other.

1. Write a brief account of how government has developed mentioning particularly (a) early forms of government (b) government in the Middle Ages (c) modern forms of government.

(25 marks)

2. (a) What do you mean by the Industrial Revolution?
    (b) Name five inventions or discoveries made during the 19th. and 20th. centuries and say by whom they were made.
    (c) What was the effect of the Industrial Revolution on (1) trade (2) the people (3) agriculture (4) industry (5) communications?

(25 marks)

3. EITHER (a) Name three ways by which each of the following peoples improved civilization and culture:- The Egyptians; the Greeks; the Romans.
    OR (b) Write brief notes about any two of the following:- (1) The Renaissance (2) The Reformation (3) The Middle Ages (4) Great Religions of the World.

(15 marks)

4. (a) Write a sentence or two about the discoveries of:- Drake; daGama; Columbus.
    (b) Write a sentence of two about:- Shakespeare; Michael Angelo; Darwin.
    (c) Who were:- Tasman; Cook; Sir George Grey?

(15 marks)

SECTION B:- Answer Questions 5 AND 6 and any TWO others.

5. Write one or two good sentences on each of the following to show what they had to do with the history of Fiji:- (a) Ma'afu (b) The Missions (c) Sir Hercules Robinson (d) The Deed of Cession (e) The Coming of the Indians to Fiji.

(20 marks)

6. Explain briefly the difference between any five of the following:- (a) An Ordinance and a Regulation. (b) Common Law and Statute Law (c) A Magistrate's Court and the Supreme Court (d) The Executive Council and the Legislative Council. (e) Rates and Taxes (f) A Direct Tax and an Indirect Tax (g) A Colony and a Dominion.

(20 marks)

7. Describe <u>briefly</u> how any <u>three</u> of the following became great nations:- Germany; Italy; Russia; China; Japan.
(10 marks)
8. Describe <u>briefly</u> how any <u>three</u> of the following became a part of the British Empire:- South Africa; Canada; New Zealand; Australia.   (10 marks)
9. Write brief notes on the following:- Stalin, Roosevelt; Bernard Shaw; Churchill; Ghandi.   (10 marks)
10. Write a <u>brief</u> account of <u>either</u> World War I <u>or</u> World War II.   (10 marks)

Figure 7. Qualifying examination paper, 1951. *(Courtesy National Archives of Fiji)*

and culture were completely ignored. However, there was method in the madness of learning in tropical Fiji about England's changing seasons or about the great exploits of King Arthur and his band of merry men. The intent clearly was to foster pride in the culture and history of the colonizer and in the great accomplishments of the mighty British Empire. Through classroom instruction and the performance of certain rituals, such as the daily hoisting and saluting of the Union Jack and singing the "national" anthem ("God Save the Queen"), Fiji's schoolchildren were made to feel a part of a much larger entity that was in the vanguard of world civilization, in which students might hope to participate in the distant future. There were some unintended, and, from the colonizer's point of view, unwelcome consequences as well. Exposure to great works of literature and the broad sweep of human history, rudimentary though it was, sharpened the students' sense of grievance and deprivation in a society based on unequal principles, and heightened their expectations of a better life. No longer content to pick up crumbs from the table, these school leavers would be looking for well-paying positions in the civil service and taking up jobs in the professions, particularly medicine and law. They were the role models and leaders of the next generation.

The years after the war were a time of immense change in Fiji. The war had taken its toll and left its mark on the political and psychological landscape of the colony. The practice of unquestioned racial segregation and white supremacy had entered its last throes. The fate of the Fijian people in their own country, a subject discussed with unprecedented vigor in this period, had emerged as a central issue that could no longer be ignored. The winds of decolonization and independence sweeping Asia and Africa were approaching the Pacific, with dramatic consequences for Fiji. In the field of industrial relations, the peace and tranquillity of the previous decade or so were about to be shattered. As the silent 1950s drew to a close, the turbulent 1960s were on the horizon.

4 Winds of Change: 1959–1969

"We are not as stupid as that [to ask for independence]," said the man who would be prime minister, Ratu K. K. T. Mara, to American reporter Homer Bigart in 1961. "What would we get out of it? We can't even pay for our own food. We would have to pay for everything. There would be no advantage in independence."[1] Yet, at almost the same time as Mara was airing these views, Britain was quietly charting a course for internal self-government for Fiji, the first step in the direction of eventual independence in 1970. The process and politics of dismantling colonialism in Fiji dominated the decade, laying bare the tensions and contradictions deeply imbedded in the colony's polity and society.

Other changes were no less significant during this period. The CSR, long the economic colossus of colonial Fiji, closed down its operations after being unable to accept the verdict of an independent inquiry into the sugar industry. Gone, too, would be the long-established and sometimes moribund separate Fijian administration in response to pressures for change from within the Fijian community itself as well as criticism from outside. High drama characterized the industrial strikes of 1959 and 1960; the tensions of elections and by-elections; the suspense of the marathon trial of Mohammed Apisai Tora, Fiji's self-styled Fidel Castro (among many other things) in connection with the burning down of the Koro Levu Beach hotel; the excitement of the inaugural South Pacific Games in Suva in 1963. Alongside these events less dramatic, but equally important, changes were taking place, such as the opening of the University of the South Pacific in 1968 at the former Royal New Zealand Air Force base at Laucala Bay; the introduction of decimal currency in 1969; the abolition in the same year of all race- and gender-based discriminatory liquor legislation; and the introduction of universal adult franchise. Almost as fascinating as the substance of these changes was the unanticipated speed and unpredictability with which they occurred. Many aspects of the Fijian scene in 1969 would not have been recognizable to an observer living in 1960.

Fittingly enough perhaps, a decade of such great turbulence began on an unsettled note, first in the European commercial sector in Suva and then with much greater impact some months later in the sugar industry in western Viti Levu. The 1959 and 1960 strikes shared many features. Both pitched local people against foreign multinational companies. Both were portrayed at the time, by the government and other vested interests, as unnecessary disruptions led by irresponsible men exploiting their fellow workers and farmers to promote their own political careers. Both failed to achieve their objectives. Perhaps most important, both strikes and the emotions they engendered exercised a profound influence on social and political developments, and on race relations in Fiji, in ways that, for better or worse, shaped the course of its subsequent history.

The 1959 Strike

The December 1959 strike took place in the oil industry, involving the Wholesale and Retail General Workers' Union and Shell Oil and Vacuum Oil companies. Led by the union's energetic mixed-race general secretary, James Anthony, and its Lautoka-branch president, Mohammed Apisai Tora, the strike was a dramatic event that shook the city of Suva to its foundations, along with the colonial establishment and conventional wisdom about Fiji. By the 1950s, neither the idea of trade unionism nor the instrument of strike to redress industrial grievance was new in Fiji. By 1955, there were thirty-one registered industrial associations in the colony, covering workers in a variety of occupations and sectors of the economy: airports, commerce, gold mines, sugar mills, pastoral farming, the timber industry, the Public Works Department, municipalities, and sailors, stevedores, teachers, and fire fighters.[2] By then, too, there existed an umbrella organization, the Fiji Industrial Workers' Congress, which convened annual conferences and made "appeals to all concerned to drop discrimination and allow equal pay for equal work in quality and quantity and equal privileges in respect of leave."[3] Such resolutions in the prewar period would have been unthinkable and would almost certainly have invited retribution from the colonial government.

In 1955, Fiji faced six strikes in various industries. A strike in the gold mines July 1957 involved 1,138 men and lasted several days. In July 1957, the Chini Mazdur Sangh (Fiji Sugar Workers' Union) organized lightning strikes at the Ba, Lautoka, and Rakiraki sugar mills to demand more pay and better benefits and working conditions for its members. Still, for workers to stage a strike in the 1950s was to risk a great deal. The expatriate companies were strong and used to having their way; the colonial government was frequently their ally; and working class solidarity could not always be taken for granted or easily forged. The Wholesale and Retail General Workers' Union was to discover this at first hand in its industrial struggle over better conditions for petrol and gas workers.

The strike began at 8:00 AM on Monday, 7 December 1959, when members of the Wholesale and Retail Workers' General Union walked off their jobs after failing to have wages raised to £6 per week.[4] (The oil companies had agreed to raise wages from £3 0s 6d to £3 10s 0d per week.) An attempt by the commissioner of labor to get workers back on the job as a precondition for negotiations had also ended in failure. The situation worsened the following day when the government issued a statement condemning the strike and, to all intents and purposes, aligning itself with the companies. Tension mounted, and conditions in Suva deteriorated rapidly the next day as feelings hardened on both sides. To preserve solidarity and prevent dissension and slippage of support in their ranks, the union members reportedly threatened and intimidated some of their more accommodating comrades, and the police provided protection for those individuals and companies, such as Burns Philp, that wanted gas.

The climax came late in the afternoon of 9 December when police refused James Anthony permission to address a large gathering of increasingly restive and militant workers. When the crowd, determined to hear their leaders, refused to disperse, saying, "We want a meeting," and began making threatening gestures at the police, a riot squad of forty constables commanded by Superintendent Mersh threw smoke grenades into their midst. The grenades were met with an avalanche of stones hurled angrily at the baton-charging police. Angered and provoked, stone-throwing youths rampaged through the city, aiming their stones principally at European shops and cars and other suspected collaborators. Law and order in Suva deteriorated to such an extent that its inhabitants spent the night in fear. Next morning they woke to find empty shops and the streets in central Suva littered with broken glass.

The next day, schools were closed, a curfew was declared, the Fiji Military Forces were brought out in force, and "responsible" Fijian and Indo-Fijian leaders were asked by the government to use their appeal to end the violence. Nevertheless, isolated instances of violence continued in the city's neighborhood, and buses and taxis were prevented from running. By midafternoon of 10 December, the scene of action had shifted from the streets to Albert Park, where Fijian and Indo-Fijian leaders addressed a large gathering of strikers and sympathizers. Anthony, Tora, and others followed the next day, apparently dissociating themselves from their more eager stone-throwing members. An important development that ended the strike had taken place behind the scenes. Anthony was given sleeping draughts to recover from exhaustion at the Colonial War Memorial Hospital. In his temporary absence, the president of the union, Ratu Meli Gonewai, heeded the advice of Ratu Mara to accept mediation by the Fiji Industrial Workers' Congress. When he found out the terms on which his members had agreed to return to work, Anthony protested vigorously, doing "all he could to prevent any agreement except on the Union's original terms." By then it was too late. The strike had been broken. After arbitration, wages were raised from £3 0s 6d to £4 11s 4d.

An official inquiry into the "disturbances" was conducted by Chief Justice A. G. Lowe. Not surprisingly, it exonerated the police of all charges of excessive and premeditated use of violence against the strikers, but accused union members and their sympathizers of harassing those who attempted to cross the picket line to obtain gas. There can be little doubt that threat was used, though no evidence was found of the strike leaders sanctioning such behavior. It would be surprising if strong-arm tactics were not used by some of the members to coerce solidarity in the face of official threats and reprisals and latent divisions among the workers. On the fundamental issues, the inquiry found in the workers' favor and concluded that the urban workers had good cause to resort to industrial action. Wages had not increased at all since 1955 while an "appreciable rise in cost had taken place in the four years to December, 1959, particularly for Fijian City dwellers for whom, apparently, no index is prepared." It noted further that "many lower paid workers, mostly married men with families but more particularly workers who were not members of any Union, found difficulty in making ends meet on the wages they received." The strike was not a plot by Communist-sympathizing union leaders who were determined to wreck the European-dominated economy, as was claimed by many employers at the time and later.

The inquiry concluded that the union had struck only after the government's announcement had appeared to place it on the side of the company. The inquiry found that the union "had for some considerable time, and with patience, attempted to get the local oil companies to discuss the question of wages and conditions of employment." Even when the companies employed delaying tactics, the union "agreed to delay matters so long as they had some negotiations and agreement was reached on the conditions to be embodied in any arrangement between the parties." The companies, used to having their way, and dismissive of the potential for sustained industrial action, had continued to stall. Delays were aggravated because local company officials had to seek guidance from their head offices in Australia, which were largely ignorant of local grievances and sentiments. The inquiry noted that in the circumstances, "it is not unnatural that the Union executive felt, after doing what they could for four months to get negotiations started, that they could not succeed with their wages claim to any reasonable degree unless they took definite and unilateral action, which they did at a time when they were resentful at their treatment by the Oil Companies." The local company officials and their overseas patrons had to bear the bulk of the responsibility for the crisis.

The government, too, was criticized for the manner in which it had handled the strike. The inquiry found that the government's condemnation of the strike a day after it had started was ill advised. The commissioner of labor should have issued the official statement, not the government itself, though the commissioner was largely unaware of the correspondence between the union and the companies. "The Government statement was almost tantamount to saying that the Union should have continued in its endeavour to bring about the negotiations which they had sought, without any success whatever, for so long," the inquiry noted. "At one stage during the correspondence, Mr Anthony had consulted the Labour Department and had received certain advice, which was followed but which, in the event, proved to be of no avail." Precipitate and ill-considered government action added fuel to the fire.

The government had good reason to be more apprehensive about this strike than others in the past. For the first time in Fiji's history, a strike had a multiracial character, as was evident in both the striking workers and their active sympathizers, as well as in the union leadership: Anthony, the self-admitted brains behind the strike, was a mixed-race young man of twenty-four, and Ratu Meli and Apisai Tora were Fijians, the former a chief and the latter a Fijian Muhammadan convert. For Fijian and Indo-Fijian workers to find common cause in their deprivation and to then jointly take action to alleviate their situation went against the policy and practice of ethnic compartmentalization. In its external manifestations, the strike appeared to be anti-European. Certainly, European shops, cars, and other property were especially targeted by enraged strikers rampaging through the streets of Suva, though some Indo-Fijian bus operators were also threatened. This incipient Fijian–Indo-Fijian solidarity threatened European economic and political interests and the informal European-Fijian coalition that had developed over the previous decades.

The Fijian–Indo-Fijian solidarity also threatened Fijian chiefs, whose position depended on their control of the Fijian people. Any Fijian class association with Indo-Fijians went against the traditional view that the Fijians' future lay not in towns or urban employment, but in the secure framework of Fijian communal life under responsible chiefly leadership. The chiefs rallied behind the government and their European friends. "If ever a country of the British Commonwealth needed the steadying force of firm, sympathetic and knowledgeable leadership," the *Fiji Times* editorialized, "that country is the colony of Fiji today."[5] Ratu Mara, Ratu George Cakobau, and many other chiefs addressed the rally at Albert Park on the afternoon of 10 December, telling the gathering that what had happened was wrong and should not be repeated. "Don't bite the hand that feeds you," said Ratu George, echoing the sentiment of other chiefs.[6] A strident Semesa Sikivou, a Fijian member of the Legislative Council, expressed his outrage at what his people had done:

> I am ashamed to see what we Fijians have done. We have a reputation in sports, in games and in war, but what has happened now has brought about a black mark which will stand forever. I am sad to see that some Fijians have fought the very ones they have given their protection to. I never dreamt that I would live to see the day on which a Fijian would stone the white men, to

whom the Fijians' forefathers ceded this country. Let me make it clear to you. Those people of Britain are your best friends. They are your best neighbours. They are the ones closest to us and the ones who stand to help us. I warn you: be very, very careful. Do not accept any advice that comes to you from foreign people.[7]

The advice was effective, for soon afterward racially segregated trade unions began to emerge in Fiji. Early in April 1960, the constitution of the Fiji Stevedores' Union restricted membership of the organization to ethnic Fijians only. Ratu Meli Gonewai, formerly the president of the Wholesale and Retail Workers' Union, formed his own union, the Fiji Oil Workers, claiming that workers had to work harmoniously with their employers and that "the intrusion of outside influences into the union's affairs was a great danger and diverted attention of members from the real objects of trade unionism."[8] The Fijians in the Public Works Department formed the Fiji Public Employees Workers' Union, which was open to all races except Indo-Fijians.[9] George Suguturaga formed a Suva-based Municipal Native Workers' Union early in 1960, which was to be "managed and controlled solely by Fijians."[10] Among other Fijians-only unions that emerged in this period were the Fijian Domestic, Restaurant and Allied Workers' Union, the Lautoka Municipal Council Workers' Union, the Fijian Engineering Workers' Union, and the South Pacific Sugar Workers' Union.[11]

Compounding the problem for Fiji's working class people was that in the aftermath of the strike, the trade union movement was left leaderless. The two strike leaders went their separate ways. Anthony was enticed into accepting a scholarship to study in Hawai'i, where he remained in self-imposed exile. His co-adjutor in the strike, Apisai Tora, lost his bearings and flirted with one cause after another, excoriating chiefs for oppressing ordinary Fijians at one point and calling for the expulsion of Indo-Fijians from Fiji at another. The once-promising foundation of a racially integrated working class movement slipped, and what appeared once to have the potential to become a turning point in modern Fijian history remained an aberration, at least for the next two decades, until the emergence of the Fiji Labour Party in the mid-1980s.

Company and *Kisan:* Round Three

Much the same sort of problems faced the sugar-cane farmers as those encountered by the industrial workers of Suva: a powerful company, headquartered in Sydney, reluctant to negotiate with the farmers except on its own terms and emboldened in its dealings with them by the silent support of the expatriate-dominated colonial government. Once again, the cane farmers had to resort to the strike weapon to redress their grievances. Their strike, which began in July 1960, was a less violent affair than the

"Don't bite the hand that feeds you: Beware of foreign influences." Ratu Mara addressing a crowd at Albert Park, 10 December 1959. On Mara's right is Ratu George Cakobau, and on his left Ratu Edward Cakobau. *(Courtesy Fiji Ministry of Information)*

Company and *kisan*, Sigatoka Valley, early 1960s. A *kulmbar*'s (overseer's) typical posture and garb. On left is a typical Indo-Fijian dwelling in the sugar belt. *(Courtesy Fiji Ministry of Information)*

In the cane fields in the 1960s, cane is loaded onto CSR-supplied trucks, the main method of transporting cane to the mills. *(Courtesy Fiji Ministry of Information)*

Suva strike, but in the long run it had far greater impact on the course of colonial economy and politics. The principal cause of the strike was the failure of the company and the cane farmers to arrive at a mutually satisfactory agreement. How and why this came about must be considered in the light of certain long-term developments in the 1950s.

On the whole, the 1950s had been a good decade for the farmers.[12] The yields of cane were slightly higher than they had been in the 1940s, in part because of the introduction of new hybrid varieties of cane. The average yield of cane had increased from 18.2 tons per acre in 1941–1945 and 20.2 in 1950 to 21.6 in 1956–1960. The price of sugar exports had increased from £32 3s per ton in 1950 to £39 5s per ton in 1959, raising the average income for cane farmers from £223 in 1950 to £540 in 1959.

This apparent trend toward prosperity was offset by a number of problems. First, population increase far exceeded the increase in the area of land under cane. The average cane acreage had increased from 90,816 acres to 160,732 acres (an increase of 77 percent) between 1946 and 1956, whereas the Indo-Fijian population had increased from 100,943 to 193,464 (91 percent) in the same period. Much of this population growth had to be absorbed on the farms because of limited outside employment opportunities. For the farmers, this situation was compounded by the substantial rise in the pay of farm substitutes (hired workers) during the decade, on some CSR estates from 2s 6½d per ton to 7s 0d per ton, an increase of nearly 300 percent. The CSR's policy discouraging the diversification of farming on its leases meant that most Indo-Fijians had to depend for their livelihood on income from sugar cane.

Yet another problem was the resettlement of Indo-Fijian cane farmers whose lands had fallen within Fijian reserves. Often the displaced tenants were settled on smaller plots of generally marginal agricultural land that gave lower yields than those obtained on the more established farms. Moreover, many newly resettled farmers did not have access to tramlines and had to provide their own transport to the mills, which added to their costs. Their profit from cane was considerably lower than that of farmers close to the tramlines. This sharpened their sense of grievance.

The CSR's efforts to resettle the displaced farmers angered the more established farmers. The ten-year cane contract between the company and the farmers was due for renegotiation, and the farmers concluded that by adding some 3,000 new (lorry) contractors and extending the area of cane cultivation, despite the limitations placed on the production and sale of sugar by the Commonwealth and International Sugar Agreements, the company was surreptitiously strengthening its negotiating position against them. As the Cane Growers' Federation Committee told Under Secretary of State for the Colonies Julian Amery in July 1960,

> We believe that this was deliberately done to weaken the bargaining position of the growers in the negotiations for a new contract in 1960. These new con-

tractors had to make their own roads and deliver their cane to the Company by lorry transport at their own cost. Thus the Company obtained cane from these new contractors at a cheaper price and at the same time created a rival block of sugar cane growers with a view to us[ing] them if necessary against the growers who were already producing cane in the old areas."[13]

In any case, the company had managed to increase the amount of surplus sugar from 24,000 tons at the end of the 1958 crushing season to 110,000 tons at the end of the 1959 season.

The accumulation of surplus sugar was one fortification that the company had erected to defend its position from any future strike. Another was the revaluation of its assets in Fiji. Anticipating demand for a better contract from the farmers, the CSR had revalued its assets in Fiji—though not in Australia—from £5,895,521 to £13,030,370. The company's chief manager was told:

For your information, our main reason for acquiring this valuation is the ever-present possibility that some situation could arise in Fiji which would lead to an investigation, or some form of arbitration, in which it could be necessary to produce information. An up-to-date valuation would also be a considerable advantage to us in future negotiation in connection with the CSA [Commonwealth Sugar Agreement].[14]

The revaluation was a repetition of the company's actions in 1949, just before negotiating a new contract in 1950.

Thus fortified, in October 1959 the CSR circulated a draft of the new contract to farmers.[15] From the farmers' point of view, the terms of the contract were severe, differing in several important respects from the expiring contract. Believing that Fiji had reached an optimum level of cane production that could be catered for within the existing international commitments, the company had decided on complete control of cane production by insisting on buying cane from the farmers on a tonnage rather than an acreage basis. In this way, the company could strictly regulate production to meet its marketing requirements. It also altered the price scale of the old agreement in anticipation of future sugar market uncertainties and fluctuating cane yields producing varying amounts of sugar. The expiring agreement, the company said, had worked to its disadvantage, by providing for "too sharp a rate of increase in cane price with price of sugar and insufficient discount for cane yielding less sugar."[16]

These two provisions, the control of production on a tonnage basis and the new formula for sharing the proceeds of the cane, were the main differences between the expiring contract and the new, but not the only ones. The company could limit the quantity of cane to be milled to balance sugar production against available market demand, storage capacity, and stocks (irrespective of whether it had encouraged additional production in the first place); reserve the power to unilaterally terminate the contract for a variety of reasons; and decide the variety of cane that farmers could plant and the procedure for delivering it to specified points on the tramline. It could also pass on to the farmer all the liability for delay in crushing cane caused by mechanical failure; damage to plants, machinery, or buildings; industrial dispute; or nonarrival or shortage of ships, fuel, sacks, or other commodities. All the risks and sanctions were on the growers' side.

Apprehending prolonged and difficult negotiations with the company, the various cane farmers' associations—Akhil Fiji Krishak Maha Sangh, Vishal Krishak Sangh, Vanua Levu Farmers' Union, and the Kisan Sangh—submerged their internal differences and formed an umbrella organization called the Federation of Cane Growers' Association in 1959.[17] They prepared a draft contract of their own and submitted it to the CSR in November 1959. Among other things, the draft stipulated that the company buy cane from the farmers on an acreage rather than a tonnage basis, as it had done for the past fifty years, and keep the mills open until all the farmers' allotted quota of cane had been cut.

There were other provisions, too. The company should give thirty instead of seven days' eviction notice to its tenants who had breached their contracts. Furthermore, the farmers should be given the choice of planting any one of the varieties of cane approved by the company; one of the farmers' representatives should be at the mill weighbridge to check weights and be allowed to inspect the weighbridge at reasonable intervals during the crushing season; a definite timetable for the prompt payment of proceeds should be set, with 75 percent of the price to be paid within thirty days of the delivery of cane, 15 percent fourteen days after the end of the crushing season, and the remaining 10 percent on 30 April following the crushing season. The farmers should also be given the right to inspect the company's statement of account to see how the price of cane was determined for that crushing season, including information on the quantity and price of sugar by-products (such as molasses) sold by the company. In essence, the growers wanted more openness, greater accountability on the part of the company, and access to some of the records of sugar production.

The Federation leaders met with company representatives on 5–6 January 1960, but the meeting broke down when the company refused to accept the farmers' proposal that to use up all the surplus cane, farmers should not plant any new cane in 1960. This proposal, if accepted, would clearly have weakened the company's stand. By the time the groups met next, on 3 February 1960, the company had hardened its attitude.[18] It would accept cane only on a tonnage basis, and it would not operate any of its mills beyond 15 January. Federation leader A. D. Patel remonstrated with the company: How would an illiterate farmer know precisely how to produce the exact tonnage of cane required by the quota? What would happen to the tonnage outside the quota? Why should the farmers alone have to bear the cost of delays caused by hurricanes and other natural disasters? And he questioned the provision that required the growers to bear the increased cost of transportation if any regulation came into effect varying the conditions of transporting cane to the mill or transporting sugar for shipment or to storage at the port of shipment.

At their next meeting, on 14 March 1960, the company withdrew its previous draft contract and submitted a new one. The term of the new contract was reduced from ten years to two years. Several new conditions were added that, among other things, enabled the company to compel all farmers to deliver their cane to the mills at their own cost by lorry contract. The farmers rejected the offer, but offered new terms, including the suggestion that 80 percent of the farmers' cane be cut on an acreage basis and the rest on terms acceptable to all the farmers, before any of the mills closed. The CSR disagreed and declared a deadlock in the sugar industry.

On 7 May, the governor met the members of the Federation Committee at Lautoka and suggested the appointment of a commission of inquiry. This proposal was rejected by the farmers, partly because of their previous experience with such commissions (as in 1943). They knew that in such an exercise, the company could not be forced to produce its records before the commission—which, as it turned out, was what happened during the Eve Commission hearings in 1960. Instead, the farmers wanted independent arbitration that could make binding recommendations on both the company and the farmers.[19] On 8–9 June, the farmers met the governor and offered to sell sufficient cane to manufacture 199,000 tons of sugar under the 1950–1960 contract, but the company would accept this proposal only if the farmers agreed to the appointment of a commission of inquiry.

Throughout July, several negotiations were attempted without success. The government remained confused and unable to make decisive choices.[20] Several proposals were mooted privately in official circles to break the deadlock. It was suggested, for instance, that the sugar industry be nationalized, but this would mean expropriation of private property with compensation that could run into millions of dollars, not to mention certain opposition to the idea both in Fiji and overseas. The sugar industry could be declared an essential service, but the Essential Services Arbitration Act was concerned with disputes connected with the terms and conditions of employment, whereas the sugar dispute was about the buying and selling of a commodity. The government could declare a state of emergency, requisition all sugar cane, and employ gangs for compulsory cutting; however, this would have been unlawful because there was no mutiny or rebellion in the colony. The government could, of course, subsidize the farmers, but it would be wrong in principle for it to use the taxpayers' money to subsidize one or both parties to a dispute. In the end, however, it decided to do nothing. The governor told the colony in September 1960 that he "can no more force the company into buying cane on growers' terms than it can force the farmers into selling their cane on company's terms."[21]

As the negotiations continued for months, with no resolution in prospect, the farmers' solidarity began to weaken. The Kisan Sangh and the Vanua Levu Cane Farmers' Union, led by Ayodhya Prasad, J. P. Bayly, D. S. Sharma, Shiu Nath, and Vijay Singh, and Fijian farmers advised by John Falvey on 24 July signed a separate list of terms and conditions with the company, including an agreement to harvest enough cane on a tonnage basis to produce 199,000 tons of sugar, with the standing crop to be added to the next year's quota. They agreed with the CSR, somewhat reluctantly, that all mills would close on 22 January. Most farmers rejected the agreement, insisting that both the first and second rounds be cut on an acreage basis and that mills be kept running till an equal share of all the farmers' cane was cut. Patel made a last-minute counteroffer to the governor, inviting him to decide the percentage of area to be harvested from each of the farmers on an area basis; not surprisingly, the governor rejected the offer, saying that it would divide the farmers and lead to practical difficulties later on.[22] For all practical purposes, the July agreement had broken the back of the strike, arousing enormous acrimony in the Indo-Fijian community that would later spill over into the political arena. In the end, the Federation used Under Secretary of State for the Colonies Julian Amery's visit to Fiji on 15 October 1960 and his promise to look into the sugar industry to call off the strike. By then all the mills were crushing cane in any case. Disunity had defeated the farmers once again.

A commission of inquiry under Sir Malcolm Trustram Eve, QC, was appointed to look into the sugar industry.[23] Eve was an establishment lawyer.[24] Among other things, he was the first church estates commissioner of the Church of England, the independent chair of the Cement Makers' Federation, and a director of the Yorkshire Insurance Company. He saw his task as removing a "bee from the bonnets [of the CSR]," not as embarking on a searching inquiry into the company's operations, as the growers had hoped. He was assisted by J. S. Wheatley of the Colonial Office and by an accountant, J. M. Bennett, who was a partner of his London firm's Australian branch, some of whose own members were helping the CSR prepare its case to the Eve Commission! This indirect association may not have affected his work for the commission, but Moynagh has noted that Bennett " 'nodded vigorously' when told privately by Dixon [CSR general manager] that whatever happened the enquiry must not let Patel 'come out on top.' "[25] The CSR prepared a separate confidential paper for the commission, outlining Patel's political history and alleging that he had always worked against the farmers' interests for his own political advantage.

The detailed submissions the various parties made to the inquiry need not be elaborated here.[26] The CSR argued that nothing was seriously wrong with the organization, structure, and operation of the sugar industry, the strike being caused "by political considerations" on the part of the farmers' leaders. From the company's point of view, the main problem was that the price of cane was too high, and the yield of sugar from cane had declined. A large part of the problem also lay with the growers themselves, too many of whom were careless with their savings and expected their large families to make a profitable living from cane proceeds. If anyone was entitled to a sympathetic consideration, it was the company, not the farmers. The farmers, the company said, "have been receiving a larger share of the industry's total income than was intended or can be justified for the future and . . . as a result, the millers' share of the gross income had dwindled to such an extent that its profits are inadequate and unsatisfactory." The Federation, on the other hand, demanded a greater share of the industry's proceeds and a long-term contract with the company, drew the attention of the inquiry to the problem of indebtedness among farmers, and called for the creation of a statutory sugar board to supervise and, if need be, intervene in the affairs of the sugar industry because of its central importance to the colonial economy. To break the monopoly of the CSR, which operated by remote control from Sydney, and to provide employment in rural areas, the Federation asked the commission to rule in favor of small cooperative sugar mills.

The farmers were deeply disappointed with Eve's report, which was published in 1961.[27] "Can't trust Eve" was a refrain heard at many a farmers' rally in western Viti Levu. The commission found nothing seriously wrong with the CSR's operations except the way it had dealt with the farmers, especially in its refusal to share information about the cost of sugar production. Eve endorsed the CSR's proposal to create a wholly owned, Fiji-based subsidiary to manage the company's Fiji operations. This led to the creation in 1962 of South Pacific Sugar Mills Limited. The CSR also convinced the commission to have production controlled on a tonnage rather than an acreage basis, and that the company deserved more proceeds from the industry than it had taken in the 1950s. The commission recommended that the company receive 30 percent of the net proceeds of sugar to cover its basic sugar-making costs, and it gave 82.5 percent of the balance to the farmers and 17.5 percent to the company.[28] The company could not have asked for a better insurance policy.

Among its other recommendations, the inquiry suggested implementing Shephard's 1944 recommendation regarding a sugar advisory council under an independent chair. Because of the CSR's opposition, however, the inquiry rejected the farmers' proposal to give the board sufficient powers to impose a settlement if no agreement could be reached voluntarily between the farmers and the company. Similarly, their proposal for cooperative, farmer-owned sugar mills was rejected outright as impractical and unnecessary, as also was the suggestion to have production control on an acreage basis. Their proposals for divesting the sugar quota for Fiji from the company and investing it in the government and enacting legislation to control monopolies, as was the practice in Britain, were rejected. As Moynagh has noted, the Eve inquiry was "an astute political exercise. Under the guise of impartiality, a report which was distinctly favourable to the CSR had been produced."[29]

Eve also obliged the CSR in another way by singling out A. D. Patel, the leader of the Federation Committee, as the chief villain of the piece. In a passage that became standard fare in anti-Federation and anti-Patel speeches in the Legislative Council and elsewhere in the colony, Eve wrote that Patel's "conduct has been so obviously against the interests of the growers as to lead us to advise them that his policies at the time should not have been followed. We hope that his future conduct may change and that he will show a far greater sense of responsibility to the country of his adoption. We are satisfied that this leader is a very able man, and that he could provide sorely needed leadership of the right kind."[30]

This was a predictable indictment that leaves many questions unanswered, the most obvious of which is why eleven thousand Indo-Fijian farmers out of twelve thousand would follow Patel to the end if what he was doing was perceived to be against their interest. Patel was not exactly an unknown figure, having been the principal leader of the 1943 strike. Furthermore, if Patel had been an agent of the Gujarati business community, as was widely alleged by his opponents,[31] how would members of the business community benefit from the ruin of the farmers? Finally, if the strike was a part of Patel's political agenda, then why did he and his associates publicly declare their intention not to stand for election to the Legislative Council in 1960?

Patel had been reluctantly drawn into the negotiations with the company because of the pleas of cane farmers and leaders such as S. M. Koya and James Madhavan.[32] Having been defeated in the Legislative Council election by Tulsi Ram Sharma in 1950 and Ayodhya Prasad in 1953, Patel had been devoting most of his time to his law practice—he was the colony's leading criminal lawyer—and to education and social welfare, especially in the South Indian community. The farmers knew that to confront the CSR, they needed skillful and intelligent leadership, and Patel was the one man who could provide that. Eve's attack on Patel backfired, for Patel emerged from the strike with his stature enhanced and his credibility among the farmers intact; it soon became clear, even to those who were opposed to Patel, that Eve's formula was not in the farmers' interest. A. D. Patel would go on to win the 1963 election for the Legislative Council by defeating his bitter rival, Ayodhya Prasad of the Kisan Sangh, and become the principal figure in Fiji politics for much of the decade. Another Federation leader, S. M. Koya, who emerged on the public scene for the first time during the strike, also became an important leader of the Indo-Fijian community in the 1960s. The CSR had won this round, but the farmers would triumph in another contest between company and *kisan* a decade later.

An important political outcome of the strike was the launching of the Federation Party in 1963 from the foundations laid by the Federation of Cane Growers. The party's base, naturally enough, was in the Indo-Fijian farming community in the sugar belt of northwest Viti Levu, though by the mid-1960s, branches had been opened throughout Fiji. The Kisan Sangh and the Vanua Levu Farmers' Union, led by Ayodhya Prasad and Vijay Singh, respectively, which had signed the agreement of 24 July, and others variously dissatisfied with Federation policies or with Patel personally, formed the core of Indo-Fijian supporters of the Alliance Party, which emerged in late 1965. The strike had provided yet another source of bitter division in the Indo-Fijian community. It caused other divisions as well.

At the start of the negotiations, and during the early stages of the strike, all the farmers' unions, Fijian and Indo-Fijian, were represented by the Federation Committee. Soon afterward, however, a moribund union of Fijian cane farmers was revived, and two new unions of Fijians emerged in Ba and Sigatoka, dissociating themselves from the larger umbrella organization. This development, which was publicly endorsed by the Fijian administration and weakened the farmers' unity further, was bad enough. But the public offer to the government from Fijian ex-servicemen and even the Great Council of Chiefs to "assist in the preservation of law and order and in the protection, if necessary, of cane farmers who are prepared to harvest their crops" worsened the situation.[33]

Race had once again entered the picture, pitting Fijians against Indo-Fijians. The government's posting of security forces, almost entirely Fijians, in the already emotionally charged cane districts, a tactic it had employed in 1943 and in the early 1920s, served to further alienate the growers from the government. Europeans demanded severe punishment for the strike leaders. One of them said, "When a child fails to respond to coercion, there is only one solution, a good hearty wallop."[34] The *Fiji Times* editorialized: "Already there are jackals discernible, prowling hungrily on the edges of Fiji's distorted economy. Let us recognise them, and deal with them, while we have the opportunity . . . and before we do anything else."[35] The strike leaders, in its view, were nothing more than "self-seeking, politically ambitious, emotionally twisted grabbers after power by lies and intimidation."[36] Ravuama Vunivalu, fifth Fijian member of the Legislative Council, agreed, urging the Fijian people "to take a firm and positive stand on the matter, whatever the cost." The "so-called [Indo-Fijian] leaders and their kind [should] be sent back to where they came from, lock, stock and barrel."[37] Ratu Meli Gonewai, the erstwhile multiracial trade union leader, George Suguturaga, and Livai Volavola (later mayor of Suva) wrote to the governor saying that "as natives of Fiji seeing the crisis now almost overtaking Fiji, we cannot keep quiet any longer and let this thing go on. . . . We would rather die than to let these people go ahead with what they are doing."[38] With such talk of retribution filling the air, coming hard on the heels of the 1959 industrial strike in Suva, an unsettled road ahead unfortunately looked assured.

Commissions of Inquiry

Both Europeans and Indo-Fijians were shaken and disillusioned by the strikes of 1959 and 1960. The Fijians, for the most part, were still predominantly in the subsistence sector, largely outside the orbit of commercial activity in the colony. Although this might have been considered desirable in the earlier part of the century among those who wished to preserve "the Fijian way of life," by the 1950s the Fijians' isolation and absence from the commercial sector had become a major problem for the colony's policy-makers. By then, the plural society of Fiji had become firmly enmeshed with the wider global economy, and the Fijian people, even if they wanted to, could not afford the luxury of economic, social, and political isolation from the broader affairs of the colony. Nor could they be immune to the effects of the economic advancement of other people in the colony. Why were Fijian people lagging behind other communities in the economic field when they held the greater proportion of the natural resources of the colony in their hands? How should these, especially land, be developed in ways that advanced the general welfare of the colony while ensuring that the *taukei* were not disadvantaged? This was a pressing issue throughout the 1950s.

To examine these and related matters, Professor O. H. K. Spate of the Australian National University was appointed in June 1958 to conduct a comprehensive investigation. His terms of inquiry were broad ranging. He was asked, first, to "assemble and assess such data as can be obtained on the economic activity of Fijian producers, with special attention to the effects of their social organization on that activity"; and, second, to consider "how far the Fijians' social organization may be a limiting factor in their economic activity, and to suggest in what ways change in that organization might be desirable."[39]

Spate was a renowned human geographer of the Indian subcontinent and a gifted scholar uniquely qualified for the task. After a year's investigation, during the course of which he visited scores of villages and talked tc Fijians from all walks of life, he produced a prescient, unsentimental report. Fijians were severely lagging behind other communities in the economic field, his inquiries confirmed, the chief cause of which was not the success of other ethnic groups but the static social institutions and practices within Fijian society itself. The conflict between custom and money "is at the root of the problem," Spate argued. Chiefly leadership along traditional lines was unable to guide the Fijian people in the modern context, he continued:

Professor Spate with Ratu George Cakobau, the paramount chief of Fiji, 1966.
(Courtesy Professor O. H. K. Spate)

The functions of the chief as a real leader lost much of their point with the suppression of warfare and the introduction of machinery to settle land disputes, but constant emphasis seems to have led to an abstract loyalty *in vacuo,* to leaders who have nowhere to lead to in the old terms and, having become a sheltered aristocracy, too often lack the skills or the inclination to lead in the new ways. Hence, in some areas, a dreary negativism: the people have become conditioned to wait for a lead which is never given.

Fijian society was at the crossroads, "with horizons widened by the war in Malaya, with the increased mobility of the bus, with the constant irritant stimulus of the Indians, with new needs for money on all hands, the rot—or the ferment—set in," most evidently in urban areas and in *koro* in areas of commercial agriculture, which most acutely faced the "unresolved conflict of contract and money against kinship and status." The process of change was irreversible, and unless it was guided carefully and with foresight, Fijian society would break "into a confusion giving no stable foundation to build on."

The choices facing the Fijian people were "rigid authoritarian collectivism," which was no choice at all, or a "community of independent farmers, living or working on holdings heritable, and alienable at least among Fijians, but retaining in each village of Old Tikina area a common centre —church, school, guesthouse, parish hall, chiefly residence—where the old dignity which the *koro* is so rapidly losing might be recaptured . . . a community less the old frustrations (though doubtless with its own), but no less rich in real satisfactions." In short, the encouragement of a system of *galala* farming that the old conservative wisdom had deemed undesirable and pronounced a failure.

Spate had diagnosed the problem trenchantly and offered recommendations that, if accepted, might have loosened the skewers of traditionalism to pave the way for a gradual, progressive Fijian participation in the larger economy and society. Spate was not alone, however, in arguing that Fijian society was at the crossroads. Many other academics in the 1960s, such as anthropologist Cyril Belshaw and geographer R. F. Watters, offered similar prognoses, though perhaps less elegantly than Spate.[40] Fijian anthropologist Rusiate Nayacakalou, the first Fijian to obtain a doctorate (at the London School of Economics under the supervision of Raymond Firth), concluded that it was a monstrous nonsense to think that his people could have it both ways.[41] Even the government was inclined to Spate's view. Governor Sir Kenneth Maddocks told the Great Council of Chiefs meeting in August 1960:

Much has been achieved in the past by your traditional communal system and in some areas this system is still producing excellent results. But a money economy and a new standard of living have changed the pattern of life in these islands. I am sure that the way forward lies in individual initiative and enterprise amongst Fijians and in the development of a tough and self reliant body of independent farmers.[42]

A Ballad of Economic Development Vaka Viti
Profeta Spate

Said the *Bose-ni-Tikina* to the Roko Tui Wau,
"We don't like the way you're running things, there's going to be a row,
So there'll be no more *solevu* for the old *yasana* clique,
Or you'll find we've gone *galala* by the middle of next week."

In wrath the *Roko* marshalled his forces for the war,
All his *Buli* stout around him, and *tūraga* by the score;
Every *Ratu,* every *Tui* in the Province joined his band,
For he meant to show these rebels there was Custom in the Land.

Now the *Bose-ni-Tikina* knew the thing it had to do,
It had made the proper presents, in the proper quarter too—
To Ratu Viliame, the Progressive EDO,
"The rising man on FAB" said people in the know.

Now Ratu Viliame was Progressive as could be;
He had talked all night with Doctor Spate, the whisky flowing free;
They'd unscrambled *mataqali, kerekere* they'd deplored,
And they'd solved the basic problem with a Free Yaqona Board!

"From the tiresome bonds of Custom if only we were free,
And our still more tiresome *Buli,* how Developed we should be!
Financial Aid is needed, but we're sure we will make good,
For Profeta Spate has met us, and he *thinks* he thinks we could."

So Ratu Viliame approved this splendid plan—
It would make his reputation as a Most Progressive Man—
And the *Roko* and his minions failed in their fell attempt
For each village that he visited had got itself Exempt!

Now *Floreat Yaqona!* Every *rārā* was the site
Of *magiti* on the grandest scale, *taralalā* every night—
Till Ratu Viliame *read* Professor Spate's Report
And next week the whole *Tikina* was up before the Court!

(Spate 1991, 117)

Bose-ni-Tikina, *tikina* council; *solevu,* feast and presentation; *yasana,* ruling local chiefly group; *Ratu, Tui, Tūraga,* chiefly titles; *kerekere,* custom of borrowing at will from kin; *rārā,* village greens; *magiti,* feast; *taralalā,* informal dance. Other terms explained in text.

Before the recommendations and implications of the Spate Report could be properly digested, another more wide-ranging commission of inquiry into population trends and natural resources in the colony began under the leadership of Sir Alan Burns, a former governor of Nigeria. The commission received numerous submissions, both oral and written, from all segments of Fiji society, which reflected their own interests and perceptions of the problems afflicting Fiji. Indo-Fijian farmers demanded greater security of land tenure and a speedy demarcation of reserve boundaries, a process that had dragged on for nearly two decades instead of the proposed two years, causing much hardship and friction all round. Other groups advocated easing the stays of the Fijian administration and more active and planned exploitation of the natural resources of the colony.

The views of the Great Council of Chiefs were, for obvious reasons, the most important.[43] The chiefs and their people "severally and jointly reaffirm and pledge their loyalty to the Crown and their unshakable faith in the continued honouring of those pledges embodied in the Deed of Cession and re-iterated from time to time," their submission began. Fijian interest must remain paramount in Fiji, they reminded Sir Alan. On the question of land, the chiefs reminded the commission that while the Fijian people owned 83 percent of all the land in the colony, 2 million of the 3.75 million acres of Fijian land were rough, mountainous, and practically useless for agricultural purposes. A large portion of the good cultivable land, 300,000 acres out of 500,000 acres, was leased to non-Fijians. The chiefs suggested that besides opening up land, the commission should consider greater development of secondary industry in which Fijians should have a bigger share to balance the national trend. The chiefs noted that "with the Fijian outstripped in numbers and in commercial enterprises, the land in his possession is his sole hope of economic advancement: and to be without this in his own country would be disastrous." No land sales should be permitted for public purposes except in exceptional circumstances to the Crown. Before making more Fijian land available to non-Fijians, the chiefs argued, the government and the Native Land Trust Board should take steps "to curb the general abuse of the land which is prevalent in the Colony—abuses which take the form of bad cultivation methods, overstocking and indiscriminate burning of bush." If need be, *talāsiga* 'sunbaked' lands, some 250,000 acres on gently undulating hills, should be considered for agricultural development.

On the sensitive subject of population trends in the colony, the chiefs recommended stricter control of immigration, both Indo-Fijian and Pacific Islander. They also lamented a "conspicuous lack of any organized endeavour by the Indian leaders and people generally to encourage among themselves methods of birth control or family planning." Making matters worse for everyone, they argued, was the apparent indifference of the Indo-Fijian community to this important issue. On the question of impedi-

ments to Fijian economic development, the chiefs pointed out that the
communal system was not responsible for Fijians' lagging behind other
communities. There were other reasons. "Lack of finance is our weakness," they said. "Without it there can be no talk of developing the land.
With it nothing is impossible." Accordingly, the chiefs wanted more funds
to be made available to the Native Land Trust Board and even to individual Fijians so that they could improve their land and encourage greater
production.

Clearly, the Burns Commission had a tall and complex agenda in reconciling these competing claims and interests to chart the course for a new
Fiji. Its recommendations were far ranging, and the government agreed
with most of them.[44] It accepted that Fijians had the same right as other
British subjects to enjoy their freedom and liberty; that Fijian land ownership rights should be secure and unchallenged; that the process of
declaring reserves should be accelerated; that immigration should be controlled but not completely stopped; and that the independent Fijian farmer
should be encouraged by the government and steps taken to promote agricultural development in the colony. Other suggestions were more problematic. The commission's recommendation to modify the structure of the
Fijian administration was accepted with reservation. The recommendations that the governor should cease to be the chair of the Native Land
Trust Board, that the board itself be placed under the authority of the legislature, and that the title of secretary for Fijian affairs should be changed
to secretary of local government were rejected because they were unacceptable to the Great Council of Chiefs.[45]

Many Indo-Fijians gave the Burns Report a lukewarm reception, arguing that it had not gone far enough. Its prescriptions, argued an editorial
in the *Pacific Review,* were "more in the nature of a tonic rather than a
medicine."[46] Common Fijian reaction to the report, coming as it did on
the heels of the Spate Report, which had also pointed to stark choices facing the Fijian people, was one of dismay and anxiety. At a meeting in Suva
Town Hall in March 1960, one speaker said, "We are afraid of the place
Sir Alan is trying to take us." Ratu Penaia Lala interjected at one point,
"If we eat strange food we will suffer from indigestion."[47] The strongest
feelings were expressed against the recommendation to abolish the Fijian
administration in letters to the vernacular press. In a typical letter,
S. Mala of Sawakasa wrote to the *Volagauna* to say that "the Fijian Administration may perhaps be described as the cord that binds a Fijian canoe
together. Take away this cord and the canoe sinks."[48] M. N. Rokoua
shared that sentiment: "To accept the abolishment of the Fijian Administration would also mean the destruction of that brick wall of defence bar-
ring non-Fijians from devouring reserve lands. Where will we turn to for
assistance if we lose this inheritance?"[49]

Ratu Mara agreed, and his words carried weight, for by the early 1960s, he had already emerged as the best educated and most articulate of the post-Sukuna generation of Fijian chiefs. "I venture to say that the main point of this criticism of the Fijian Administration is that those people in this Colony who are ambitious and hungry for power have found a stumbling block in the Fijian Administration which has authority over half the population," he said. "Abolish this authority and people without leaders will flock to them. That is what they want, and I think the commission was beguiled by these people."[50] The colonial government, Mara asserted, appeared to be ignorant of the Fijian social system and tended to "borrow too much of the experience of officers from Africa to be used in Fiji." The Burns Report, he quipped, was a report about the Fijian people, written by Europeans for the benefit of Indo-Fijians.

Fijian fears were genuine and powerfully expressed. Caught in a bewildering whirlpool of criticism and facing an uncertain future, the Fijian people were harking back to the simple life of legend and myth, uncomplicated by the problems of living in a competitive modern environment. That era, however, was rapidly vanishing beyond recall, especially in areas that had been touched by the forces of the modern world and contact with other communities. Even high chiefs opposed to the suggested changes realized that the choice facing their people was not a choice between the past and the present, but the stark reality of adapting to an environment to which they were latecomers, one they could no longer ignore, or could ignore only at their own peril. This realization led to the eventual dismantling of the rigid structure of the Fijian administration in the late 1960s.

Toward Self-Government

For many Fijian leaders, the call for changes in the most cherished institutions of their society could not have come at a worse time. The Spate and Burns reports coincided with moves afoot in Britain to give colonies a greater measure of self-government as a step toward eventual full independence. A debate in the British House of Commons had resolved in 1959 that Britain should "evolve a positive policy for those smaller territories where difficulties might arise in regard to the achievement of complete independence within the Commonwealth."[51] Fiji was one of those colonies.

Governor Sir Kenneth Maddocks, correctly reading the signals, informed the Colonial Office in 1961 that Fiji's constitutional structure, which had remained unaltered for twenty-four years, was ready for change.[52] Among the changes he proposed, which the Colonial Office approved, were extending franchise to women, removing property and income qualifications for all voters, and implementing the membership system whereby unofficial elected members joined the Executive Council, supervised groups of government departments, and accepted collective responsibility for the council's decisions. This new system, it was hoped, would provide valuable training for selected members of the Legislative Council and enable civil servants to work in an administrative setup that would prepare them for a full-fledged ministerial form of government later in the decade. While announcing these changes, Maddocks emphasized in his 1961 Cession Day address that both he and the Colonial Office would stand firmly by the Deed of Cession and "subsequent promises that were made regarding the ownership of Fijian land [and] continue to take into account the need to safeguard legitimate Fijian interests."

The constitutional proposals were debated in the Legislative Council. Indo-Fijian and European members were guardedly optimistic, but the Fijian members expressed deep apprehension because they were not certain precisely what changes the proposals might bring. Said Ravuama Vunivalu: *"Na vatu ga e cere e dau seva na ua, ia ua vatu e dromu e dau vorovoro waqa."* (The high rock that is clear of the water is washed by the waves, but the one that is submerged beneath the tide is the one that wrecks our boats.)[53] Ratu Mara echoed this sentiment and explained why his people were anxious:

> Undefined constitutional changes conjure up all sorts of political perils in the minds of Fijians. It can throw up on the screen of one's mind the Congo, Algeria, Cyprus, Cuba or even the partition of India and Pakistan. The Fijian people should not be condemned for their apprehension of the devastation and disaster of the changing winds of constitutional change. It is probably the inherent reaction of island people to run to shelter when the winds of change gather force. In this context the only shelter the Fijians know is the present constitution, as Government has not been explicit in its proposed constitutional change. They should be pitied rather than condemned for preferring the devil they know to the one they do not know.[54]

Ratu Penaia Ganilau went a step further. "When independence comes to Fiji," he told the Legislative Council debate in December 1961, "let the British Government return Fiji to the Fijians in the spirit in which the Fijians gave Fiji to Great Britain."[55] Ratu Penaia probably meant what he said, though later, other Fijian chiefs indicated that this was really a rhetorical flourish, a bargaining strategy, to extract maximum concessions from the government and other communities during constitutional negotiations.[56]

Two years later, when it became clear that constitutional changes would come to Fiji whether its people were prepared for them or not, members of the Fijian Affairs Board met at Wakaya Island to prepare a statement of

Fijian preconditions for constitutional negotiations. This statement, which was never formally published, but was quoted and misquoted throughout the decade, was addressed to Nigel Fisher, then parliamentary under secretary of state for the colonies. Prepared on 17 January 1963, the statement was signed by all the Fijian members of the Legislative Council (Mara, Ganilau, Sikivou, Ravuama Vunivalu, George Cakobau); A. C. Reid, chair of the Fijian Affairs Board; and J. N. Falvey and R. M. Major, its legal and financial advisors, respectively. It is reproduced in its entirety as Figure 8. This powerful plea for paramountcy of Fijian interests, endorsed by the full Great Council of Chiefs two years later,[57] was as timely as it was effective. As Sir Derek Jakeway said in 1965, Britain had no intention whatsoever of putting Fijians "under the heels of an immigrant community,"[58] a remark that was "acclaimed with gratified hearts by the Fijians."[59]

In 1963 a new order in council enlarged the size of the colonial legislature. The number of official (that is, government) members was increased from sixteen to nineteen, and the number of unofficial members increased from fifteen to eighteen, giving the three main communities six representatives each in the Legislative Council, four to be elected on racial rolls and two nominated by the governor, in the case of the Fijians from a list presented by the Great Council of Chiefs. As the election for the Legislative Council approached and the pace of local political activity intensified, a number of quasipolitical parties suddenly appeared on the scene. The Fijian Association, formed in 1956 with the assistance of Fijian Affairs Board Legal Advisor Sir Maurice Scott, changed its name to the Fijian Peoples' United Party in March 1962, "in keeping with the present trends," and sent officials to Fijian villages to explain the mechanics of the impending election.[60]

In the absence of a solid umbrella organization, however, Fijian political opinion was far from united. Isikeli Nadalo founded the Fijian National Party, an outgrowth of a Sigatoka Fijian cane farmers' union, which called for balanced economic and social development and an open mind to political change. Apimeleki Ramatau Mataka formed the Bula Talei Communist Party, which, he claimed, had about one thousand members in four villages in Nadroga. The party was "communistic in theory and practice," he said, and aimed to "retrieve the Fijian people from the alien doctrine of private property to the traditional communal ownership."[61] Apisai Tora founded the Fijian Western Democratic Party,[62] which, as its name suggests, was both regionalist and populist in rhetoric and ideology. Tora wanted to strengthen Fijian land rights, to see all freehold land "deceitfully bought" and "improperly obtained" by Europeans returned to Fijian landowners, and to secure more economic development in western Fiji.

OFFICE OF THE FIJIAN AFFAIRS BOARD
SUVA, FIJI.

17th January, 1963.

The Honourable Mr. Nigel Fisher M.C., M.P.,
Parliamentary Under Secretary of State for the
        Colonies.

Sir,

    We desire to place before you the following representations.

    We consider that the Act of Cession had, for the Fijian people, a
special implication. It was this. They envisaged their country as attached
to the Crown - an integral part of the United Kingdom. Her Majesty's title,
decided by the Chiefs after Cession, is "Queen of Fiji and Britain" (Radi ni
Viti kei Beritania) and the Council of Chiefs have from the beginning
jealously maintained their right of directly addressing the Sovereign on the
occasion of their meetings. It is the Fijian view that the possibility of
severance of this link with the Crown - a link forged in a spirit of mutual
trust and goodwill - should never be contemplated.

    This special relationship would appear to have its closest
parallel in the constitutional links between the Channel Islands or the Isle
of Man and the United Kingdom. It is submitted that before any further
constitutional change is considered and certainly before there is any move
towards internal self government, the terms of the special relationship
between Fiji and the United Kingdom should be clarified and codified along the
lines of the relationship between the United Kingdom and the Channel Islands
or the Isle of Man.

    We propose a new constitutional instrument which would embody this
understanding of the relationship and would make provision for the
safeguarding of Fijian interests, building on and strengthening the spirit and
substance of the Deed of Cession.

    There would have to be a precise restatement of the guarantees on
Fijian land ownership. We visualize that the Native Land Trust legislation
should not be changed or added to without the prior consent of the Sovereign
and the agreement of the Council of Chiefs. We also stand by the expressed
desire of the High Chiefs in the preamble to the Deed of Cession that Fiji
should be a Christian state and that therefore no constitutional or
administrative changes should take place that would deviate from that
intention. The provision in the Fijian Affairs Ordinance that all legislation
affecting Fijian rights and interests should be referred to the Fijian Affairs
Board or, on the recommendation of the Board, to the Council of Chiefs, should
be retained, and likewise the Governor's direction to the Public Service
Commission to Work towards a balance of the races in the Civil Service.

    Subject to a satisfactory solution of the issues we have raised in
the foregoing memorial, we would be prepared to initiate, in co-operation with
the other principal races, further moves towards internal self government. In
this regard we wish to remind you of the terms of the resolution passed at the
last session of the Legislative Council which records the insistence of the
Fijian people that the initiative for any constitutional change should come
from them.

Yours faithfully,

(Sgd.)	K. K. T. Mara	1st. F.M.	(Sgd.) A.C.Reid Chairman.
"	P. K. Ganilau	2nd. F.M.	
"	S. Sikivou	3rd. F.M.	" J.N.Falvey Legal Adviser.
"	R.Vunivalu	4th. F.M.	" R.M.Major Financial Adviser.
"	G.K. Cakobau	5th. F.M.	

Figure 8. The Wakaya letter. *(A. D. Patel papers)*

He presented himself as a successor to Apolosi Nawai, whose name he frequently invoked, as the true champion of common people and western Fijians. He wanted to assert greater control over the Native Land Trust Board and the "yaqona-mixers to be seen in [its] precincts." He appealed to western pride and identity; for too long had the leadership in Fijian society been in the hands of easterners: "They do not come to serve but to be served." He himself came "from the humble surroundings of a Fijian village, one who knows what it is to be ignored by snobbish officials, what it is to be discouraged by feudalistic Rokos and Fijian chiefs and what it is to be straitjacketed by the system under which you and I live." Tora was the quintessential chameleon of Fijian politics, who changed his colors and political loyalties several times before the decade was over.

The best-organized and most effective political party in Fiji in 1963 was the Federation, which, as seen earlier, had emerged from a loose federation of cane growers' associations formed on the eve of the 1960 sugar dispute. Unlike European and Fijian leaders to whom the idea of representative government was fraught with difficulties, the Federation leaders advocated a more rapid pace of constitutional development leading to full internal self-government, compulsory education, and compensation to tenants whose land had been put into reserves. Their overarching political ideology was "one-nationism."

The 1963 election was a historic event for several reasons. It was the first time that elections were fought on the basis of universal adult franchise. There were no property qualifications for voters or candidates. Most important, it was the first time the ballot box had reached the Fijian people, giving them the power to elect their own political representatives to the Legislative Council.[63] This change had not come easily or without opposition from many Fijian chiefs, to whose power direct voting represented a potential threat. There are interesting images of Fijian voters facing the ballot box for the first time: a Fijian woman claps her hands ceremoniously (cobo), puts the paper in the box, claps her hands again, and then, hunched, walks slowly out of the room; a Fijian man writes his candidate's name on the blackboard instead of using the ballot box; Ratu William Toganivalu bows respectfully to his superior chief and political opponent, Ratu Penaia Ganilau.[64]

The election results held few surprises. The voter turnout was extremely high: among Europeans, 84.2 percent (2,435 registered out of 2,892); among Fijians, 76.1 percent (25,559 out of 33,584); and among Indo-Fijians, 88.3 percent (31,907 out of 36,137). Ratu Mara's seat was uncontested in the eastern constituency, his traditional political base. In the southern Fijian constituency, university-educated sitting member of the council, Semesa Sikivou, won (10,152) over Livai Volavola (2,600) and A. Waqabaca (228). In the western constituency, Cakaudrove high chief Ratu Penaia Ganilau triumphed easily (7,347 of 11,133 votes) over

Tora (1,496), Nadalo (659), Peniasi Naqasima (1,434), and Ratu William Toganivalu (197).

The real drama of the elections was in northwest Viti Levu, where emotions engendered by the 1960 strike were still raw. The election was seen, in effect, as a referendum on the strike and on Patel's role in it. All the Federation candidates won, though Koya only narrowly beat future Alliance minister James Shankar Singh, who came from Ba and had deep family roots there. Koya's victory was a historic achievement, for it was the first time that a Muslim had been elected on universal franchise, disproving the claim of the Muslim separatists that Hindus would never support Muslim candidates. Much attention focused on the western constituency contested by Federation leader A. D. Patel against the Kisan Sangh candidate Deo Sharma. Patel won handily, capturing 6,244 of the 9,662 votes cast to Sharma's 3,346. His political and industrial stand vindicated, Patel emerged from the elections as the acknowledged leader of the Indo-Fijian community, occupying the niche that Ratu Sukuna had occupied among the Fijians.

In July 1964, following the elections, the membership system was introduced in Fiji as a small but significant step in the direction of internal self-government. For the first time, the Executive Council had a majority of unofficial members (six), the only official members on it being the attorney general, the colonial secretary, and the secretaries for Finance and Fijian Affairs. For the first time, too, three elected members, representing the three major ethnic groups in the colony, were given the responsibility of administering the colony under the overall authority of the governor. A. D. Patel was appointed member for Social Services (under whom came education, medical services, correctional services, labor, social welfare); Ratu Mara, member for Natural Resources (agriculture, land, forests, fisheries, minerals, cooperatives); and John Falvey, member for Communications and Works (tourism, transport, civil aviation, electricity).

Important though this development was, it was overshadowed by other issues and problems in the next hectic two years. One was the preparations for, and debate over, issues to be covered at the coming constitutional conference in 1965; another was the perceived need for a political party that could serve as an umbrella organization for Europeans, Fijians, and non-Federation Indo-Fijians and that could compete effectively with the Federation Party.

By the mid-1960s, a number of quasi-political parties existed in Fiji, in addition to the ones already mentioned. Among these were the Rotuma Convention, the Suva Rotuman Association, the Tonga Association, the Fiji Chinese Association, the Kuo Min Tang (Fiji Branch), and the General Electors' Association. Muslims advocating separate representation for their community and opposed to the idea of a common electoral roll formed the Fiji Muslim Political Front. Ayodhoya Prasad launched his

From left: J. N. Falvey, Member for communication, Ratu K. K. T. Mara, Member for Natural Resources, and A. D. Patel, Member for Social Services, in the Legislative Council chambers, July 1964. *(Courtesy Fiji Ministry of Information)*

National Congress of Fiji, which broadly represented the social and economic interests of the members of the Kisan Sangh, while A. I. N. Deoki and other leading Indo-Fijians in Suva revived the Indian Association of Fiji. There also existed a Fiji Labour Party, whose political creed was democratic socialism.[65] In his Cession Day message to the colony in 1965, Jakeway urged the different groups to form a multiracial political party, which, in his view, the Federation was not. Such a political party, Jakeway said, would "encourage political alliances which cut across barriers of race and which will provide a firm and enduring basis on which all the communities of Fiji can move forward in partnership towards the full control of their common destiny."[66]

Such direct political intervention by the governor was unprecedented in Fiji, but it went unremarked at the time. Conversation with those acquainted with the subject indicates that the governor played a significant behind-the-scenes role in getting the non-Federation groups to think of forming a political alliance. He personally told Mara to "jump on the bandwagon [or] you'll be sorry for yourself."[67] In any event, a new political party, which called itself the Alliance, was formed on 12 March 1966. According to some sources, the name was suggested by Jakeway himself,

Governor Jakeway at Cicia Island, 17 May 1967. This photograph provoked much adverse comment at the United Nations. Some members captioned it "Brown Man's Burden." *(Courtesy Fiji Ministry of Information)*

who had the Malaysian model in mind. The strongest spoke in the Alliance wheel was, and long remained, the Fijian Association, some of whose members had actually wished for a completely separate political party to advocate specifically Fijian interests. Europeans and "Others" eventually came under the General Electors' Association, while Indo-Fijians formed the Indian Alliance. Early in 1966, then, Fiji had two major political organizations with rival visions and agendas.

While these developments were taking place in the colony, its constitutional problems began attracting international attention, which threw yet one more complication into an already complex situation. In July 1963, the Soviet Union pressed the United Nations General Committee on Colonialism to send a fact-finding mission to Fiji. Its chief delegate to the committee, Vladimir Brykin, accused Britain of "cutting off" the people of Fiji from contact with the outside world and giving the UN extremely sparse information about the colony, charging further that Fiji was a "classical, old-time colony, with unlimited powers in the hands of the Governor."[68] Independent Afro-Asian nations joined in the debate, asking Britain to speed up the decolonization process. The following year, in November 1964, delegates from these developing nations drafted a resolution calling for the reaffirmation of the "inalienable right of the people of Fiji to self-determination and national sovereignty," and the Committee on Colonialism passed a resolution, with the United Kingdom, United States, and Australia abstaining, calling on Britain to "take immediate steps to hand over power unconditionally to the people of Fiji."[69] Britain's defense was that the peoples of Fiji differed greatly from one another in their political interests and aspirations, and it would take a long time before they were "united in a common effort for the common good."[70]

Among those in Fiji who advocated the United Nations General Assembly's intervention was Apisai Tora. On 17 June 1963, he and Malelei Raibe wrote to U Thant, the UN secretary-general, describing the political situation in Fiji. The colony, they said, was "governed along the classical Colonial formula. [Europeans] had complete political and economic domination over the indigenous people, the immigrant Indo-Fijians, Chinese and others." They said the practice of allowing Fijian civil servants to contest elections "was so gross in British Parliamentary practice that it leaves us speechless." They drew the United Nations' attention to problems facing the ordinary Fijians. "In Fiji the primary need by the indigenous people is freedom from some form of oppression imposed within not from without the present regime. That is to say the Fijian man in the street although inarticulate needs to be freed immediately from the Stultifying effects of the Fijian regulation so that he may enjoy the fundamental liberties now enjoyed by other communities living in Fiji and basic to the Constitution of your parent body—the United Nations Organization." Finally, they urged the secretary-general not to meet with Ratu Penaia Ganilau and Ratu George Cakobau, who were visiting the United Nations. The only case these two chiefs would put forward, Tora and Raibe said, "would be for the vested interests which is composed of the Fijian Aristocracy, Australian capital investment and a handful of white settlers stubbornly clinging to the last vestiges of lost Brittanic Glory against all the compelling lessons of history."[71]

This petition provides insights into the thinking of a colorful Fijian personality and perhaps also of some dissident Fijians, but it did not reflect the feelings of most Fijian people. *Nai Lalakai* commented that the United Nations' "frequent reference to colonialism is but an indication of the envy they have for the efficient way in which Britain has guided and advised our country for many years."[72] "The desire for prompt independence," *Vakalelewa ni Pacifica* said, "is similar to a young boy who wants to get married when he is not self-supporting. It is obvious that he will get married when he is well off. Similarly, the time of independence will come but all the necessities good for independence are not in hand yet."[73] Ratu Penaia Ganilau, the subject of Tora's scorn, was angry because United Nations resolutions ignored "the repeatedly expressed desires of the native Fijians to retain protection. . . . We know Fiji, they don't," he said in

1964. "We know the kind of future we want. They don't. We treasure the trust that was expressed in the signing of the Deed of Cession. They have never heard of the Deed of Cession."[74] As far as he was concerned, he would be glad if he never heard from the UN Committee on Colonialism again. A year earlier, all six Fijian members of the Legislative Council had resolved that the committee should not "interfere in our affairs unless we, the people of this country, seek its assistance through our acknowledged leaders. . . . We do not desire their interference," they said, "nor are we impressed with their much publicized utterances. We refuse to be dragooned into making rapid and ill-conceived political changes."[75]

For their part, the Europeans poured scorn on the Committee on Colonialism. The *Fiji Times,* borrowing from Shakespeare, said that "the twaddle talked in the United Nations Committee on Colonialism [was like] a tale told by an idiot . . . full of sound and fury signifying nothing."[76] The Federation leaders for the most part refrained from making public statements on the issues raised at the United Nations, though privately they must have welcomed the criticism of colonial practices in Fiji. A. D. Patel told close political colleagues that if a UN delegation were to visit Fiji, he would take it first to a Fijian village to show what little progress Britain had made in improving the health and sanitary conditions of the average Fijian.[77] The deliberations at the United Nations may not have produced direct results in Fiji, but they kept an important issue alive in the international forum and put Britain in the politically embarrassing position of having continually to justify why it was not granting immediate independence to Fiji.

The 1965 Constitutional Conference

In the early 1960s, relations between the principal political groups were tense, but with the constitutional conference scheduled for 1965, leaders of the major groups began to seek ways to begin a dialogue before going to London. Patel took the lead and circulated a memorandum inviting members of the Legislative Council to discuss points that might be raised at the conference.[78] Some progress was made in the informal discussions that took place in Suva. All members of the council agreed, for example, that Fijian landownership rights were inviolate, and the issue of these rights was not to be raised, though conditions under which land was leased could be. They also agreed that links with the Crown should be maintained and that independence would not be an immediate aim.

However, the discussions became stalemated on the question of the method of election. Patel urged the introduction of the common roll method of voting, of which he had long been an advocate, arguing that "it is only through making one nation out of Fiji that we can achieve the sort of future we want for everybody." A common roll would encourage the development of parties along national rather than racial lines and promote the growth of national consciousness. Communal rolls, on the other hand, he maintained, fostered communal loyalties and magnified communal differences: "Success in politics will depend exactly on reflecting communal interests and prejudices. Compromise will be rendered difficult, and relative party strength may be frozen for long periods of time because a party can grow only with an increase in the size of the community upon which it is based."

These were prophetic words from a person who fully apprehended the ravages of communalism on the Indian subcontinent. The failure to break ethnic barriers and transcend communal consciousness, which a common roll would have facilitated, would come back to haunt and eventually consume Fiji. Many Fijians, distrustful of its political implications, especially supposed Indo-Fijian dominance and the erosion of Fijian paramountcy, and already feeling stampeded into directions that until recently had seemed unthinkable, opposed the very idea of a common roll. As the readers of the Fijian vernacular, *Nai Lalakai,* understood the concept, the common roll meant that

> there will no longer be representatives for the Fijians, as a race, in the Legislative Council. There will be no European representatives, as they are a minority race. It follows that a majority of the members of the Legislative Council, assuming that common roll is applied to Fiji, will be Indians because they are numerically superior. They have the maximum votes in most of the constituencies in Fiji. Decisions in Legislative Council will be decided by a show of hands which is a situation where Mr Patel will thereby realize his aims concerning lands and the leasing of lands. Moves can also be made to abolish the laws and ordinances of the Native Lands and Fisheries Commission and also the Fijian Affairs Ordinance on which the Fijian Administration is based. These are some of the things which can be done by Mr Patel and his followers if a common roll is accepted. If this is not so then what really lies behind the proposal to have a common roll?[79]

Fijians will have a common roll, went a popular refrain around the *yaqona* bowl, when the eel grows hair or when the *balabala* flowers (which it never does).

Reports of the confidential constitutional discussions among the leaders began to appear in distorted form in the *Fiji Times,* which had managed to inject itself into the political deliberations, not as an independent instrument, but as a partisan on the side of the Alliance. The editor, L. G. Usher, was a notable figure in Alliance circles. The leaks suggested that by insisting on certain points, Patel and his colleagues were bent on wrecking the preconstitution talks and were behaving in an unstatesmanlike manner, all in contrast to the behavior of the Fijian and European members of the Alliance Party. Angered, the Federation leaders discontinued the talks, preferring to negotiate the outstanding points in London. Their decision was severely criticized in the local media as the action of "petulant and arrogant children."[80] Nor were many non-Federation Indo-Fijian leaders happy,[81] but Patel argued that withdrawal was justified not only by the leaks that had "created an atmosphere of mistrust and misunderstanding among the people of Fiji," but also because "nearly all the remaining subjects for discussion are controversial and on which it is very unlikely any agreement would be reached in Fiji."[82]

In April 1965, Eireen White, under secretary of state for the colonies, visited Fiji to acquaint herself with local feelings and views before the start of the constitutional conference. She heard a range of opinion.[83] Muslims repeated their perennial demand for separate representation, once again on the grounds that in every important cultural, social, and religious way, they constituted a group of people separate from Hindus. If Muslims were to be given separate seats, argued Ratu Jone Mataitini, then the three Fijian confederacies should also be accorded separate representation. Emosi Vuakatangane, later an Alliance politician, wanted the prime minister of independent Fiji to be always a Fijian. Some Fijian women such as Suliana Kaloumaira, Amelia Rokotuivuna, and Taufa Bale advocated the partial introduction of a common roll, long-term leases for Indo-Fijian tenants, and the abolition of the monopoly on political power of the Great Council of Chiefs. Tora's Fijian Democratic Party was advocating in May 1965, at a meeting ironically in the Kisan Sangh Hall in Lautoka, of all places, that "if Fiji and Fijian interests are to be protected, then the quickest possible way should be found to send Indians away to other countries," citing the examples of Burma and Ceylon as precedents. The Great Council of Chiefs reiterated the terms of the Wakaya letter, as also did the Fijian Association. A closed-door meeting of the association held at the Ratu Sukuna Memorial School in January 1965 resolved, "Since Cession we have never demanded anything from Britain. There has been too much spoon-feeding and we have always waited for decisions to be made for us. Those are now things of the past. These days we know what we want, and we must demand them."[84]

Who should be allowed to participate in the conference itself became a matter of public debate. The Fijian Democratic Party resolved at a meeting in the Suva Town Hall in June 1965 that Indo-Fijians should be excluded from the conference. "The Deed of Cession was signed by only two people, Her Majesty's representatives and the Fijians," it was said. "That instrument has never been amended in any way up to now. The conference in London will have plenty to do with changing it, and as such it is only right that only the signatories to the Deed should take part in the deliberations."[85] A *Volagauna* correspondent agreed, but added another reason: "The Fijians and Europeans are benevolent and patient and are not greedy [like the Indo-Fijians]. They can evenly distribute things so that peace and harmony can prevail in Fiji. They both belong to the Christian faith. They act like Christians and they will never wish to deprive anybody else of what is rightfully theirs."[86] The Colonial Office, of course, would have none of this.

The conference started in London in July. John Falvey, leading the European delegation, argued that "there are many people in Fiji who are well content with our present and quite new constitution [and only a] few who are seriously critical of the administration of our country since 1874, when sovereignty was ceded to Her Majesty Queen Victoria."[87] Not one member of his delegation, he said, "is here to demand independence for our country." All they wanted was limited self-government with continuing links to the Crown. Ratu Mara agreed. "We have declared that independence is not our goal because we have never found any sound or valid reason to attenuate, let alone abandon, our historical and happy association with the United Kingdom." He hoped that the United Kingdom "will share with us our prosperous future, as she has always willingly and unstintingly shared our past and our present." Patel, on the other hand, could not disagree more. "Political liberty, equality and fraternity rank foremost among the good things of life and mankind all over the world cherishes and holds these ideals close to its heart," he said, and "Fiji is no exception." He wanted political freedom in Fiji to combat poverty and illiteracy and the rule of democracy along the lines enjoyed by the dominions in the British Commonwealth. He also hoped that the result of the conference might "well mark the beginning of the end of a form of government which stands universally condemned in the modern world."

That was not to be. Still, the conference produced several major steps toward more internal self-government.[88] For the first time—there were many firsts in the 1960s—the constitution provided for a majority-elected Legislative Council and the end of nomination of unofficial members. The only nominated members retained were the attorney general, the financial secretary, and the colonial secretary. Chinese, Rotumans, and Pacific Islanders were given the franchise for the first time, the Chinese being placed on the European roll and the other two groups on the Fijian roll. A ministerial form of government was to be introduced and a bill of rights was to be incorporated into the constitution, though it did not provide protection from racial discrimination in civil service appointments. The governor was required to consult a newly created Public Service Commission in the appointment of civil servants, though not for the most senior positions in government, such as those of colonial secretary, financial secretary, attorney general, secretary for Fijian Affairs, and commissioner of police, whose appointments remained the responsibility of the Colonial Office. Most important, the conference provided for an expanded Legislative Council of 36 members: 14 Fijians (9 elected on communal votes, 3 elected on multiracial cross-voting, and 2 nominated by the Great Council of

Chiefs); 12 Indo-Fijians (9 communal and 3 cross-voting); and 10 Europeans and Others (7 communal and 3 cross-voting). The system of cross-voting was seen as a limited concession to the principle of a common roll, in which multiracial electorates voted for seats reserved for candidates of different races.

Fijian and European delegates were satisfied with the outcome of the conference. Mara cabled Fiji: *"Ni yalovinka ni kakua ni taqaya, na veika kece koni taqayataka e seqa ni yaco, sa nomuni na lagilagi."* (Don't be concerned. All that you were concerned about did not materialize. The victory is yours).[89] Fijian rights remained intact; the link with the Crown was maintained, the common roll issue had been put on a very dimly lit back burner, and, on top of it all, Fijians had emerged from the conference with more seats than either of the other two groups.[90] The principle of Fijian paramountcy in Fiji's body politic had been recognized and restated. That was as it should be, argued Ratu Edward Cakobau, because Fijian interest was "fundamental and it must gain priority."[91]

Fijian delegates returned to Fiji to elaborate ceremonies of welcome jointly organized, at the suggestion of Adi Litia Lalabalavu and Ratu Naulivou, by the three confederacies of Kubuna, Burebasaga, and Tovata, ceremonies that were normally performed for chiefs individually by the people in their separate confederacies.[92] The symbolic message of Fijian political unity could not have been more powerfully expressed. The Europeans, a tiny minority in the total population, had retained their privileged position and, indeed, the balance of power in the new legislature. By supporting the Fijians, they had reinvigorated a coalition that was to pay a nice political dividend later. Mara appreciated their "magnanimity." "I am very pleased indeed at the way particularly Europeans have behaved," he said upon returning to Fiji. "We have gained two seats more in the outcome at the expense of the Europeans. This proves to me that greater love hath no man than he lay down his life for his fellow man, and this is what the Europeans have done for the Fijians at this conference."[93] To the Federation, he said: "This constant pin-pricking, the constant endeavour to drive a wedge between Fijians and Europeans is not only stupid but fruitless. Speaking as a representative of the Fijian people, I can say that it [the Federation] will never achieve its ends."[94]

The Federation Party, however, was bitterly disappointed because it had lost out on virtually every major point. Indo-Fijians had lost the parity with Fijians that they had enjoyed since the 1920s. As Patel said, in the new constitutional arrangement, "The chiefs are given a seat in the Pullman car in this constitutional train. The Europeans are given a seat in the first class, the Fijian people are given a seat in the second class and the Indians are given a seat in the third class."[95] The common roll found no practical support and neither did the party's counterproposal for an electoral system that combined communal, common, and cross-voting rolls.[96]

The Indo-Fijian community found itself more politically isolated than before the conference and more electorally segregated from the other groups. The Fijian roll, for instance, was expanded to include all the other Pacific Islanders and the European roll enlarged to accommodate the Chinese. Why should the Chinese be on European rolls, when they had culturally less in common with Europeans than had Indo-Fijians?

The Federation also felt that Britain had not played a fair mediating role at the conference, preoccupied as it was with the crisis in Aden. By not impressing upon the Fijian and European delegates the desirability of introducing an electoral procedure "as the first step towards altering Fiji's present system whereby at least some members of the Legislature should be eligible for election regardless of race under a common franchise," the Federation leaders argued, the United Kingdom delegation had encouraged the Europeans and Fijians "to believe [that] rejection by them of the constitutional proposals to the unreasonable detriment of the Indian community would be adopted by Great Britain without due regard to the requirement of fair play and justice to all communities." The Federation called the composition of the legislature and the method of election "unjust, unfair, impracticable, and undemocratic," widening the chasm between the different communities.[97] "They will harden the existing racial division and make practical integration of the different communities, which is vitally necessary to the building of a politically homogenous and democratic nation, extremely difficult, if not impossible." Knowledgeable independent observers agreed that if Britain had applied more pressure on the Fijians and Europeans, a more equitable electoral system could have been devised. Wrote Professor J. W. Davidson, "There is reason for believing that the Fijians could have been persuaded to abandon their demand for greater representation in the legislature than that of the Indians and to accept a simple common roll procedure for the election of the nine members to be returned by voters of all communities."[98]

Elections and By-elections

Fifteen months after the conference, Fiji went through another election in September 1966. This was a very important contest, for it was the first time an election was fought on party lines, between the Federation Party and the Alliance. Both parties clung to their past positions: Federation for independence and self-government and the introduction of a common roll with the ultimate goal of "one country, one nation, one people," and the Alliance for gradual political change and the retention of communal rolls. Both parties won handily among their traditional constituencies: the Alliance won 65.25 percent (26,981 out of 41,344) of the Fijian communal votes, and the Federation likewise garnered 65.25 percent (43,075 out of 66,009) of the Indo-Fijian communal votes.[99] Altogether, the Alliance won twenty-two seats to the Federation's nine.

The system of representation produced a result the government privately favored. The Fijian chiefs and Europeans, too, were pleased, for now in power, they could exercise some control over the pace of constitutional change, which had thus far emanated largely from the Colonial Office in London. As the leader of the victorious Alliance Party, Ratu Mara was appointed the leader of Government Business, while retaining his Natural Resources portfolio. Vijay Singh was appointed member for Social Services and Charles Stinson, member for Communications and Works. Three other elected Alliance members, Ratu Penaia Ganilau, Ratu Edward Cakobau, and K. S. Reddy, were co-opted to the Executive Council. This arrangement lasted a year until 1 September 1967, when Mara was appointed chief minister and a ministerial style of government was introduced.

This undoubted success for the Colonial-Alliance government was seen as an act of betrayal by the Federation. Anthony Greenwood, secretary of state for the colonies, had led them to believe that the 1965 constitutional arrangement was to be a temporary measure, to be revised and reexamined a few years after its promulgation. Now, however, it seemed to be acquiring a more permanent life. A visiting official from the Colonial Office, a Mr. Bowden, told Patel in 1967 that since the constitution was working well, he did not see any reason for another conference anytime soon.[100] This angered the Federation leaders deeply. Then, rubbing salt into the wound, the government began making unilateral decisions on issues that had hitherto required a bipartisan approach. For example, the governor introduced the ministerial system of government without even mentioning it to the opposition.[101] The ethnic imbalance in the Council of Ministers was another issue. Of the nine ministers, seven were Europeans, two Fijian chiefs, and only one Indo-Fijian (Vijay Singh). Where was justice in this allocation, the Federation charged, when Fijians and Indo-Fijians constituted 94 percent of the population and Europeans only 6 percent? Altogether, it looked certain that if constitutional change did not take place immediately, the Federation and the entire Indo-Fijian community would be consigned to "the wilderness of frustrated and possibly endless opposition"[102] in a country further segregated into racially based electoral compartments.

On 1 September 1967, exactly a year after the elections, Patel moved a motion in the Legislative Council that

undemocratic, iniquitous and unjust provisions characterize the existing constitutional and electoral laws of Fiji and their operation have caused alarm in the minds of right thinking people and have hampered the political advancement of Fiji along democratic lines and this House therefore is of the opinion that Her Majesty's Government of the United Kingdom should call a constitutional conference immediately to ensure that a new constitution is worked out and based on true democratic principles without any bias or distinction on the grounds of colour, race, religion or place of origin or vested interest, either political, economic, social or other so that Fiji may attain self-government and become a nation with honour, dignity and responsibility as soon as possible.[103]

If this was not done, Patel argued, Fiji faced a hard and tragic future. He reiterated his view that "racial attitudes will stiffen, divisions will become still more rigid and defined and when the real time comes, people of this colony will find it almost impossible to break all the rigid barriers in order to unite the various communities of this country and lead them to nationhood." The subsequent history of Fiji would show just how accurate Patel was in his prognosis.

The Alliance attack on the motion was led, interestingly enough, not by Mara, the leader of the Alliance, or any other Fijian leader, but by Vijay Singh, who repeated his party's view on the desirability of maintaining the communal roll and a gradual move toward more self-government under steady Alliance leadership.[104] The debate was emotionally charged, with its full share of rancor, pettiness, sarcasm, innuendos, and allegations. The Alliance leaders were portrayed by the opposition as the stooges of big business and other vested interests, and the Federation leaders were portrayed in turn as irresponsible and opportunistic anti-Fijian wolves in sheep's clothing. The partly dead horse of the Indo-Fijians' war record was reanimated, and the politics of the 1960 sugar-cane strike were dredged up.

Singh, a Ba-born, England-trained lawyer, sharp and articulate, was in full flight, accusing the Federation of bad faith, sabotage, and lack of patriotism. To illustrate his point that the Federation had done little to promote racial integration while always bemoaning its absence, Singh told a story about John and Mary. John asks, "Mary, if you wasn't what you is, what would you be?"

Mary: "Why, John, I would like to be an American beauty." Then she asks John, "If you wasn't what you is, what would you like to be?" ["Puppet, puppet," interjected opposition members].

"I would like to be an octopus."

"Why would you like to be an octopus?"

"So I could put all my hundred arms around you."

"John, you ain't even putting the two arms you already got."

In the middle of this barbed reply, the Federation Party walked out of the legislative chamber amid shouts of "puppets" and "cowards" hurled freely across the floor. "They were absent in 1943," Singh pressed on, "they were absent in war and they are absent in peace. I wonder where they propose to fight the constitutional battles." Mara was furious: "We will not be diverted from our task by wild, unreasoned, unfounded and childish behaviour such as we have just seen."

The Federation had hoped that the walkout from the Legislative Council would cause the Colonial Office to intervene by arranging another con-stitutional conference. But the Colonial Office failed to oblige. For obvious political reasons, the Colonial-Alliance government was not prepared to encourage political reconciliation, hoping that an effective performance in government by them might take some of the wind from Patel's sails. When the Federation boycotted three successive sessions of the Legislative Coun-cil, writs for by-election were issued and elections scheduled for August 1968. The by-election was to be a referendum on several issues: A. D. Patel's leadership of the Federation Party and of the Indo-Fijian commu-nity generally, Ratu Mara's and the Alliance's appeal among the Indo-Fijians, and the Federation's political platform generally.

It was a tense campaign. The Federation Party attacked the "diehard colonialist supremacists," the "notorious colonial policy of divide and rule," the domination of the civil service by expatriates, and the "wicked lie" that the Federation Party was anti-European (as opposed to anti-European colonialism). It repeated its standard call for the introduction of a common roll, social welfare, the equitable distribution of wealth, and the nationalization of the gold-mining industry.[105] These were platforms that the Fiji Labour Party would advocate in the mid-1980s. At the same time, the Federation also attempted to broaden its base among the Fijian people. This effort met with some success. The once (and future) anti–Indo-Fijian Apisai Tora, and Isikeli Nadalo, both western Fijians, began talks to merge their National Democratic Party with the Federation, thus injecting the word national into its name to make it the National Federation Party (NFP). This marriage of political convenience took place in November 1968, giving the disaffected Tora a platform and the Federation a hope of increased Fijian support. Ratu Julian Toganivalu, a high chief and brother of three notable Toganivalus (William, David, Josua) in the Alliance Party, joined the NFP as its organizing secretary and personal assistant to Patel. Ratu Mosese Varasekete, half brother to Ro Lala, and Tui Dreketi (Ratu Mara's wife) also joined the party. The Federation emphasized the need for Fijian–Indo-Fijian solidarity against the "white colonialist domi-nated Alliance Party" and advocated immediate independence for Fiji:

> This Party's aim is to work for immediate independence and to set up a dem-ocratic republic with a parliamentary government within the British Com-monwealth. In order to maintain a link with the past a person who is ethni-cally a Fijian will be elected as the Head of the State by a plebiscite based on adult suffrage at five yearly intervals. To preserve connection with Great Britain, independent Fiji will seek membership of the British Common-wealth.[106]

With this platform, the NFP hoped to accomplish three goals in one sweep. By providing for a permanent Fijian head of state, it would assuage Fijian feeling about the paramountcy of their interests in Fiji. By maintaining political and constitutional links with Great Britain, it would blunt the criticism of those who feared the idea of a republic. And by insisting on a universal plebiscite, it would introduce the principle of a common roll, so that the head of the republic represented all the people of Fiji and not just a section of them.

The Alliance rejected the platform, arguing that the provision for a permanent Fijian head of state was racially discriminatory as it prevented members of other ethnic groups from aspiring to that high office! The real reason, probably, was that the stipulation of universal franchise posed a threat to the prospects of high chiefs, for such a broad-based election might elect a commoner or a chief who was not from the traditionally dominant maritime provinces. In short, it threatened the balance of power within Fijian society. The Alliance strategy, instead, was to paint the NFP as essentially anti-Fijian and to shore up Ratu Mara as the only person capable of leading Fiji. An editorial eulogy in *Jai Fiji* captured this well: "People have faith in him. He occupies a special place in the hearts of the people for the integrity, ability and impartiality with which he has worked in the Alliance's short administration. The people are aware that he is engaged in building one nation. He abhors vanity and disruption."[107] A. D. Patel, in contrast, was painted as an uncompromising, antiwhite dictator of his party's policy.

The results of the by-elections were dramatic.[108] All of the nine Federation candidates were returned with increased majorities in all the Indo-Fijian communal constituencies. The NFP captured 78.6 percent of the votes cast (46,960 out of 59,780), and the Alliance managed only 12,820, or 21.4 percent of the votes.[109] Two of its candidates lost their electoral deposits by winning less than 10 percent of the total votes cast in their constituencies. Unremarkably, perhaps, Patel himself was returned with the largest margin of votes of all the candidates, 7,903 to 2,772, defeating Manikam Pillay, an established South Indian lawyer-politician in Nadi. The results underscored Patel's stature as the dominant figure in his party and the NFP's appeal among the Indo-Fijians. It also became clear that the party could no longer be ignored in any future political developments. As K. C. Ramrakha recalled, the results of the by-election meant that the Alliance "would have to come to terms with us."[110]

The margin of the NFP victory stunned the Alliance. Mara felt personally betrayed and hurt that his new role as chief minister counted for so little at the polls. His people were saddened that they had made so many concessions on such things as land, but these did not seem to be appreciated. "Let there be no violence," he said, "but let it be clearly understood that Fijian people . . . cannot and must not be ignored."[111] *Volagauna* acutely expressed the dilemma of the average Fijian. "The present change is too swift for the Fijian and he does not quite understand what is being done or what part he is to play," it said. "He is suddenly grabbed by the hand and thrust into an unknown situation without knowing where he is being led."[112] From the other side of the political divide, a correspondent of *Jagriti* responded to the charge that the NFP was promoting racial polarization. The people who make this charge "forget that the Government enforced communal roll," he said. "Now when Indians have elected their able Indian candidates under the communal system, a false accusation is brought against them that the Indians have deceived the Fijians. If Indians do not vote for their party, then who should they vote for?"[113]

As racial violence threatened to erupt in the country, Mara told Frank Rennie, then commander of the Royal Fiji Military Forces, during a game of golf, "We might let things take their course for a while," and retreated to Lau, returning to claim center stage again when the threatening storm clouds cleared from the horizon.[114] Throughout Viti Levu, a militant Fijian Association organized large rallies to vent the Fijian reaction and sense of betrayal at the election results.[115] Laws regarding land should be tightened; leases to Indo-Fijian tenants should not be renewed or should be renewed at increased rentals; even the Agricultural Landlords and Tenants Ordinance (ALTO) should be reconsidered. In Suva a two-thousand-strong Fijian Association meeting passed a resolution that "the control of the country should be returned to Fijian hands, by force if need be."[116] Independence in any form was to be firmly rejected. In Vatukoula three thousand Fijians roared disapproval of independence and a common roll, ALTO and renewal of leases, going so far as to suggest that "ways and means should be sought to deport all Indians from Fiji." At a rally in Ba, typical of many, Sakiasi Waqanivavalagi, later an Alliance cabinet member, led an angry procession of Fijians clad in black. The black attire, he said, symbolized the funeral of Fijian–Indo-Fijian relations.[117] For a while it seemed that Fiji was on the brink of a racial conflagration.

Fortunately, these passions subsided without any major incident. At the first session of the Legislative Council after the by-elections, A. D. Patel moved a motion to renovate deteriorating historical sites on the island of Bau, the political center of Fijian society and the home of the Vunivalu. It was a sensitive gesture of reconciliation, atonement in the view of some, which helped to diffuse tension and dampen extremist racial rhetoric.[118] The NFP, Patel seemed to say, had nothing against the Fijian people, their traditional leaders, institutions, and values, only against a system that had kept the two major ethnic groups divided from each other for so long.

From the other side, too, came words of caution. Ratu Edward Cakobau, perhaps the most widely loved Fijian chief in this century, said in his Cession Day speech in 1968:

> I do not question the need for change for to stand still means stagnation.
> What I do suggest is that we have been carried along at too fast a pace—a

pace not of our choice; a pace which has not given us time to take accurate bearings; and I suggest that it would not be a bad thing if all of us, Fijians and others, found out where we are; become familiar with our present surroundings and try to chart some of the hazards ahead before pressing on too quickly into the unknown.[119]

For his part, Governor Sir Derek Jakeway confirmed that further discussions on the next step in constitutional development would take place within the life of the existing legislature. These, he said, would be all-important for Fiji's future, and they "should not be rushed nor should they be unduly delayed."[120] All the racially threatening clouds of 1968 had produced at least one silver lining.

By early 1969, tempers on all sides had cooled, and a semblance of normalcy returned to Fiji. Ratu Sir Kamesese Mara, who was knighted in January 1969, told a Ba Jaycees meeting in May that all Fiji residents should be called Fijians, which would help foster a feeling of nationalism,[121] a suggestion warmly welcomed by Patel, who himself had made the same point in the Legislative Council on 29 August 1967. A joint Federation-Alliance group agreed in December that "it would be difficult to find a more appropriate name than Fijian"[122] for all Fiji's peoples, but the subject was left open for further discussion. Eventually, the Great Council of Chiefs' opposition killed the idea. Exploratory talks were underway for a possible joint Federation-Alliance approach to negotiating the new sugarcane contract, as also were talks between the two political parties on the future directions of constitutional change.

The End of an Era

Besides this growing feeling of rapprochement between Fijians and Indo-Fijians, to the unease of some and the consternation of others, there were other developments that ushered in fundamental changes in Fiji. Among the most important of them were the much-needed reforms in the old system of the Fijian administration. These reforms had been advocated by both the Spate and the Burns commissions of inquiry, and the initial reaction of the Fijian leaders and the Great Council of Chiefs had been negative. Obviously, the uncertainty surrounding the fate of an institution that had become a deeply embedded part of the Fijian way of life affected Fijian responses to the political climate in the colony in the 1960s. But the changing social and economic realities in Fijian society itself and "whispered complaints" in the Fijian villages made changes not only desirable but also inevitable.[123] As Ratu Penaia Ganilau, minister for Fijian Affairs, noted in 1967, there was a "fundamental, unavoidable conflict of ideas between the traditional and modern principles of government," and choices had to be made.

Paramount Fijian chiefs in Tonga. From left: Ratu Edward Cakobau, Adi Laisa Ganilau, Ratu George Cakobau, Adi Lala Mara, Ratu Mara, Lelea (George) Cakobau, and Ratu Penaia Ganilau, at the Royal Palace, Nukualofa, July 1968. *(Courtesy Fiji Ministry of Information)*

The people were now educated; there were new opportunities before them; urban migration increased and the people could make a living outside the village system; there was a great reshuffle of population and new forms of association emerged such as the co-operative society, the trade union, the credit union, the social and sporting clubs and the less formal associations in which the people now found niches for themselves. In the country areas an expansion of production of the old crops and the emergence of new ones for cultivation demanded new patterns of activity and organization. Women's activities took on a new significance and the churches, schools and youth organizations gave a different colour to rural life. The conflict with tradition permeated all aspects of Fijian life—social, political and economic.[124]

It was impossible to hold back the clock of culture. After wide-ranging debates at all levels of Fijian society, many aspects of the Sukuna-envisioned, postwar Fijian Administration were gradually abolished. The control of the Fijian magistracy was shifted to the Judicial Department; the separate Fijian courts were abolished along with Fijian divorce courts and the criminal offenses code of the Fijian Regulations; the Medical Department, rather than the native health inspector, was to look after the health of the Fijian villages; the Provincial Constabulary was shifted to the Police

Department; and many other minute regulations that had governed the lives of all Fijians, such as social service regulations and those dealing with transport and with the work of the Native Lands Commission, were also abolished. The provincial local government was to be based on modern democratic principles rather than on traditional lines, with members of the Provincial Councils directly elected by the people living in the *tikina* that they sought to represent. Again the words of Ratu Penaia are worth quoting at length:

> Fijians are objecting to being regarded as anthropological curiosities and a community apart from the broad community in which they live. Similarly, they want to play a fuller part in the modern life of the colony, and many see that this can be done through the life of the Fijian Administration provided the Administration can be re-organized in accordance with the accepted principles of modern democratic life, including its responsibilities, functions and duties. Fijians object to what I may refer to as "cotton wool legislation," and want to tackle modern life by being allowed to face the hard facts of such life, free from paternalism, however well meant, and from especially protective legislation.[125]

These were wise words, which, if sincerely meant and implemented, contained the potential to lay the foundations of a new kind of Fijian society.

Another institution that had dominated the life of Fiji for nearly a century was also about to come to an end, the Colonial Sugar Refining Company. The ten-year cane contract based on the recommendations of the Eve Commission was up for renegotiation. All the farmers, Fijians and Indo-Fijians, members of the Federation of Cane Growers and of the Kisan Sangh, were agreed that the expiring contract had worked to their great disadvantage. None of them, not even the CSR's own counsel, R. G. Kermode, fully understood its terms![126] The cumbersome and expensive administrative machinery of the sugar industry did not serve the farmers' interests.[127] Learning from their experiences in 1943 and 1960, the farmers insisted on independent arbitration to decide the terms of the new contract, rather than a commission of inquiry. A. D. Patel recommended that Lord Denning, Britain's master of the rolls,[128] be invited to arbitrate. As Denning was one of the most eminent jurists in the British Commonwealth, other groups could hardly reject his name. Patel was aware of Denning's reputation for making law as much as interpreting it and was convinced that if all the facts were properly presented, the farmers were bound to get a better contract.

Denning accepted the invitation, and arbitration proceedings began at Lautoka in August 1969. The CSR wanted to retain the Eve contract governing the growing, harvesting, and purchase of cane, arguing that it had produced stability in the industry, and urged Denning to make only minor variations in it. Denning, however, rejected this view, arguing that he had been asked to "settle [all the] terms [of the dispute] which will be just and equitable and will be fair to all parties."[129] The Federation of Cane Growers, and the Alliance Contract Committee as well, called the contract a "killer" that had pushed farmers into debt and bankruptcy and called for its termination. Both sides produced a voluminous amount of evidence in support of their positions.[130]

As it turned out, Denning agreed with the claims of the growers.[131] He rejected the Eve formula advocated by the company and recommended a new contract that gave the growers 65 percent and the millers 35 percent of the proceeds of sale, each paying their own costs, instead of the 57.75 to 42.25 ratio of the Eve formula. The sale, Denning said, should include not only sugar but also the proceeds of molasses and other by-products, as the farmers had demanded all along. The growers were also given the power to appoint a qualified accountant to examine the books and accounts of the millers, something the company had successfully resisted in the past. Finally, the growers were to receive a guaranteed minimum price of $7.75 per ton of cane, $5.75 paid within five weeks of delivery and the remaining $2 within six weeks of the end of the crushing season. In nearly all respects, the Denning Report contradicted the recommendations of the

Lord Denning at Lautoka. On his right is Robert McNeill, independent accountant advising Denning. McNeill died a few months later. *(Courtesy Fiji Ministry of Information)*

Eve Commission and found in favor of the farmers. The man who throughout the 1960s had been reviled for his militancy by Sir Malcolm Trustram Eve, and many others besides, received Denning's fulsome praise. A. D. Patel, Denning said, "was intellectually the most brilliant, as a character the most honourable, and as an advocate, the most persuasive. Quick in mind, fluent in speech, he stood out above all." It was Patel's "persuasive advocacy," Denning said, that had led him to his report.[132]

Denning was aware of the ripples his award would cause. If he had erred at all, he said, he had erred on the side of the farmers because the company throughout the 1960s had enjoyed a first-class innings. He wrote in conclusion:

> During all these years the costs of the millers have been covered, they have received considerable contributions to their capital improvements and, in addition, they have had good reward. They have not gone short. But the growers have. In settling the terms of the new contract, I have tried to restore the balance. I have tried to give the growers the reasonable remuneration which the Commonwealth Sugar Agreement intended that they should have. I hope this will not deter the millers from continuing their good work for Fiji and for the sugar industry in Fiji. The great public companies of today owe a duty, not only to their shareholders to make a profit, but to the people amongst whom they live and work, to do their best for them. Every responsible shareholder recognizes this. If the sugar industry in Fiji is to prosper, the bitterness of the past must be removed. Growers and millers must work together in a spirit of mutual trust and good will—as befits partners. Let this new contract be the foundation on which to build.[133]

That was not to be. The CSR was deeply upset by Denning's comments on its activities as well as the formula he recommended. It produced a written rebuttal outlining supposed errors of fact and judgment in his award, arguing that the new contract would expose the millers to high risks and burdens "which a commercial enterprise should not properly be called upon to bear."[134] This was to no avail. Still, in many quarters within the CSR the report was greeted with a sigh of relief. Independence was imminent, and it would look awkward for an expatriate multinational to dominate Fiji's economy in the way it had done for nearly a century. It would be better to depart with a negotiated settlement, which is what happened in 1973. A golden handshake worth $10 million ended the life of the CSR in Fiji.[135] The sugar industry was placed in the hands of a statutory organization, the Fiji Sugar Corporation.

Proceeding apace with the Denning arbitration were government-encouraged constitutional negotiations for independence between the Alliance and the NFP.[136] The discussion had begun in some secrecy in May 1969 under the leadership of Ratu Mara and A. D. Patel.[137] Both sides stated their positions. Patel would attend the first session only, as he died on 1 October 1969. His oft-repeated view stated at the outset of the negotiations was that Fiji was ready for immediate independence on the basis of universal adult franchise within the Commonwealth. Ratu Mara for the Alliance argued that Fiji was ready for immediate and full internal self-government, without a common roll, and with a firm and guaranteed protection of basic Fijian rights.

Negotiations continued for several months as both parties explored possibilities of compromise on divisive issues. The transcripts clearly indicate that the NFP was in an especially conciliatory, concession-making mood, sobered perhaps by the experience of the 1968 by-elections and now under the less surefooted leadership of Siddiq Koya. The NFP also wanted to assure the Fijians that it had no desire to undermine their interests.[138] To this end, it discarded its republican platform and agreed with the Alliance's proposal for dominion status. Faced with Alliance intransigence and predictions of violence should a common roll be imposed, the NFP also dropped its once rock-solid adherence to the common roll principle. It agreed to go into independence without an election, giving the Alliance the uncontested advantage of leading the nation into independence. It also initiated the idea, readily accepted by the Alliance, without any quid pro quo, of giving the Great Council of Chiefs weight to safeguard Fijian interests in the proposed Upper House. The Deed of Cession was to receive a special mention in the preamble of the new constitution, but not Salisbury's dispatch. For its part, the Alliance discarded its opposition to independence and adopted a liberal stance on the issue of citizenship, dropping its negotiating tactic of threatening to grant a "belonger status" to nonnatives.

The words in the transcript convey the air of excitement, solemn purpose, and political maneuvering that attended these confidential proceedings. They also show the long distance that had been traveled on the constitutional path in such a short time. One example will suffice. On 6 November 1968, a group of chiefs, including George Cakobau, L. K. Mara, E. Vitu L. Qiolevu, and K. K. T. Mara, had reportedly petitioned the Queen to return the country at independence to the hands of Fijian chiefs.[139] Now, a few months later, they were negotiating terms for independence that would ensure a place for all the residents of Fiji. The Fijian Association did an even more remarkable somersault. Its leaders were participating in constitutional negotiations on one day and on another expressing themselves to be "of the firm opinion that only the Fijian people and Great Britain should discuss matters affecting Fiji and that other races which did not participate in the Deed of Cession should not take part in the constitutional conference."[140]

When Lord Shepherd, minister of state for Foreign and Commonwealth Affairs, visited Fiji between 26 January and 2 February 1970 to ascertain at first hand the status of the constitutional negotiations between the two parties, he found that many basic issues about the broad structure and function of the dominion government and the role and responsibilities of its different branches had already been agreed upon.[141] The unresolved issues regarding the exact structure and composition of parliament, and the method of election to it, were left for discussion in London.

The penultimate conference paving the way for Fiji's independence was held at Marlborough House in London in April 1970. The result was a compromise—some said a compromised—constitution. Fiji was to have a bicameral legislature with an appointed Upper House (Senate) and a fully elected Lower House (House of Representatives). The latter consisted of 52 seats, with 22 each reserved for Fijians and Indo-Fijians and 8 for the General Electors (Europeans, Part-Europeans, Chinese, and Others). Of the 22 seats reserved for Fijians and Indo-Fijians, 12 were to be contested on communal votes and the remaining 10 on national seats (which meant that the candidates themselves were required to be ethnic Fijians, Indo-Fijians, and General Electors, but they were elected by all registered voters). In the Lower House, then, Fijians and Indo-Fijians received electoral parity (42.3 percent of the seats each), and the General Electors, a very small component of the total population (around 4 percent at the time of independence), retained their privileged position.

The paramountcy of Fijian interests was explicitly recognized in the Senate. Its 22 seats were allocated as follows: 8 for the nominees of the Great Council of Chiefs, 7 for the prime minister's nominees, 6 for the leader of the opposition's, and 1 for the Council of Rotuma. At any given time, ethnic Fijians made up a half or more of the Senate, as both the prime minister's and the leader of the opposition's nominees invariably consisted of a number of Fijians. More important than numbers were the veto powers that the Great Council of Chiefs' nominees were given over all legislation affecting Fijian interests and privileges. Section 68 of the constitution provided that the consent of six of the eight Great Council of Chiefs' nominees was required for the passage of any legislation relating to the Fijian Affairs Ordinance, the Fijian Development Ordinance, the Native Lands Ordinance, the Native Lands Trust Ordinance, the Rotuma Ordinance, the Agricultural Landlord and Tenant Ordinance, the Banaban Lands and Settlement Ordinance, and the Rotuma Lands Ordinance. In short, Fijian rights and interests were given such watertight protection that none other than the Fijian chiefs themselves could alter or amend legislation pertaining to them. A firmer guarantee of protection could not be devised. As Ratu William Toganivalu, a leading member of the Alliance Party, said in a 1982 parliamentary debate:

> I consider that we Fijian people have come out better under the terms and conditions of this constitution than the other races. . . . I would refer mem-

bers to the entrenched clauses in the constitution wherein is embedded and safeguarded the very things that are dear to us. The constitution is perhaps the best in the world when you consider it in the context of the multiracial society we have here.[142]

On one important question, however, the two parties were unable to reach an agreement at the conference. This was the method of election for the House of Representatives, that is, the number of seats to be contested on a communal and national or common roll basis. To break the stalemate, leaders of both the parties agreed that the method of election adopted at the conference was an "interim solution" designed to provide for the first House of Representatives elected after independence. A permanent basis was to be provided by a duly appointed commission of inquiry. Nothing was set in stone forever, Shepherd, the British delegate to the conference, told the delegates. "The constitution is a living creature, subject to growth, susceptible to change," he told them. "It is a sign of life, vigour and maturity to be ready for change when change is required."[143] We shall soon see just how ready for change Fiji was after independence.

The 1960s was a decade of profound change in the political and economic life of Fiji. Once unthinkable changes took place with unprecedented speed and led Fiji in directions that had once appeared unimaginable. It was a time of great irony, too. A decade that had started on a note of discord and despair ended on a note of compromise and conciliation. Organizations and individuals with entrenched views and conservative vision embraced change, albeit somewhat reluctantly and largely on their own terms. There was also sad irony in A. D. Patel's dying without seeing the fruits of his lifelong struggle, for he had played a seminal role in instigating these changes leading to the demise of colonialism and the departure of the CSR. He died as he would have wished, though, in the course of duty, representing the cane farmers before the Denning arbitration. Another man who had seen no great advantage in gaining independence would reap its fruits for many years to come.

5 *The Center Cannot Hold: 1970–1987*

The Union Jack was lowered for the last time at dusk on Friday, 9 October 1970. The new sky-blue flag of the independent Dominion of Fiji, with a miniature of the colonial flag in the top left-hand corner and bearing Fiji's coat of arms with its dove of peace, was not raised until ten the next morning, some thirteen hours later. This unusual delay was intended to symbolize the respect that both parties accorded the transfer of power. Fiji was not marking the end of British rule so much as celebrating the birth of a new nation. "We have a long and close association with Britain," said new

Flying the Fiji flag. Independence Day celebrations at Albert Park, 10 October 1970. A Fijian *meke* 'action-song' is being performed. *(Courtesy Fiji Ministry of Information)*

Prince Charles at Albert Park, 10 October 1970. On Mara's left is Fatafehi Tu'ipe-lehake of Tonga, Tupua Tamasese Leolofi III and his wife, Rita Tamesese. At extreme left is Sir Keith Holyoke of New Zealand, and to his left is Adi Lady Lala Mara. *(Courtesy Fiji Ministry of Information)*

Prime Minister Ratu Sir Kamisese Mara: "We became dependent in a warm spirit of friendliness and trust and we become independent in the same warm spirit. . . . Nothing that is happening today," he told a youthful Prince Charles, "can change the warm feelings of our people for the Crown, the United Kingdom and its people."[1] Caution, continuity, and continued links with the colonial past rather than fundamental change in new directions would be the hallmark of the postcolonial years.

Independence was celebrated with aplomb and splendor, with impressive and solemn Fijian ceremonies of Cavuikelekele, Qaloqalovi, Yaqona Vakaturaga, and Wase ni Yaqona performed for Prince Charles, who personally handed the Instrument of Independence to Ratu Mara, formally terminating the Deed of Cession. Hundreds of distinguished guests from around the world were present to wish the young nation well. Throughout the country, schools closed for celebration. Flower shows, traditional performances, prayers, and sporting activities continued for a week. Above all else, there was a widespread feeling of relief. Fiji, it seemed, had come a long way from the dark, violence-threatening days of the 1968 by-elections; and a momentous change had been accomplished without a much-feared and much-prophesied political upheaval. This optimistic mood was captured in a poem by a high school student from Labasa:

> There's a new life in view
> There's gold in the blue
> There's hope in the hearts of men
> Fiji is on the way
> To a happier day
> For the road is open again[2]

Yet, beneath the bubble of public celebration, deeper fears remained unarticulated.[3] Fundamental questions about the structure and sharing of power, the thorny problems of land tenure, the structure of the electoral system, and the goals of development remained unresolved. Fiji had traveled the road to independence rather hurriedly and somewhat secretively. The public were never informed, much less consulted in advance, about the agreements that took Fiji into independence. No real attempt had been made to build a solid basis of public support for the new order, the whole process being engineered from the top. Because of this, many of the problems mentioned would continue to surface throughout the dominion years and eventually consume the nation.

The principal political failure of postcolonial Fiji during its first two decades was the unwillingness of its leaders to recognize the changed and changing realities of Fiji's society and politics. New problems and issues defying simple racial or political categorization arose and demanded bold and imaginative responses and leadership. These were absent in the aging, entrenched leaders, convinced of their fundamental right to govern and unwilling to share power with others except on their own terms.

The changes in this period were enormous: improved communication, airstrips on the outer islands, upgraded roads girdling the two major islands, and improved interisland shipping. All reduced isolation and increased contact among the people, with attendant consequences. Rural electrification programs brought modern amenities and modern technology to areas that had long remained untouched by modern forces of change. Expanded cultivation of cash crops, such as sugar cane in the Seqaqa district on the island of Vanua Levu and pine plantations greening the hills of western Viti Levu, brought unexpected economic opportunities and fostered attitudes sometimes in direct conflict with traditional values. The radio, and later video, boom brought many new images from across the ocean, creating new expectations and tastes. It was a time, too, when the borders of Fiji were crossed with unprecedented frequency. Tourists arrived in ever larger numbers, increasing from a yearly average of 15,000 in the 1960s to 186,000 in the 1970s, making tourism the principal source of the country's revenue, and increasing the gross domestic product per capita from a mere \$369 in 1970 to \$1415 in 1980.[4] There was movement in the other direction as well, as thousands of skilled people, mostly Indo-Fijians apprehensive about their prospects in Fiji or with their eyes set on greener pastures, left for America, Australia, Canada, and New Zealand, in that order of popularity.[5]

Within Fiji, there were significant movements of population, as well as obvious population increase. The number of ethnic Fijians increased from 202,176 in 1966 to 342,965 in 1988, and the Indo-Fijian population in the same period increased from 240,960 to 341,141.[6] The number of ethnic Fijians surpassed that of Indo-Fijians, reversing a forty-year trend. Emigration and a lower birth rate among the Indo-Fijian population, resulting from an effective family planning program in the community, made this change possible. The pattern of Indo-Fijian decline will continue in the years to come, and it is not likely that the indigenous Fijians will ever again be surpassed—or will allow themselves to be surpassed—by another ethnic group. The political and social implications of that demographic dominance for Fiji's society, especially with the threat of Indo-Fijian dominance diminishing, will bear close watching.

Proceeding apace with population increase was the drift to urban areas. In 1966, Fijians living in urban areas numbered 48,205 (23.8 percent of the Fijian population). In 1988, the number of urban Fijians had increased to 107,780, or 31.4 percent of the Fijian population. The number of urban Indo-Fijians in the same period increased from 88,979 (36.9 percent of the Indo-Fijian population) to 144,533 (42.4 percent). By 1988, a total of 277,025 Fiji citizens (38.7 percent of the population) lived in urban areas. In the late 1980s, more than half the urban Fijians—70,000—lived in and around Suva, large numbers in the crowded, low-cost housing neighborhoods of Raiwaqa, Nabua, and Lami.

For many of these people, the change from rural to urban life was more than simply a change of physical location. It meant entering a world of modern multiracial living far removed in both time and space from the communal confines of their *koro*. It also meant contact with the usual frustrations of urban life, such as unemployment, overcrowding in low-cost housing divisions such as those in Raiwaqa, Suva, the breakdown of traditional values and status patterns, and the transition to the demands of wage earning and the cash economy. The multiracial work force to which the urban dwellers belonged created alliances and coalitions that cut across traditional boundaries. Multiracial schools, social clubs, voluntary associations, and sporting activities—soccer, once an Indo-Fijian game, was now dominated by Fijian players—produced a consciousness that appeared to diminish the role of race as an important factor in national life. At the University of the South Pacific in Suva, students came into contact with new ideologies that provided them with a vision of the world that contrasted sharply with the one they had left behind.

Together, all these changes and transformations began to alter the fabric of Fiji's society and politics. In particular, they called into question the edifice of a public life and political system constructed on the pillars of communalism and racial separation. This complex and changing substratum underlay the political developments of the postcolonial era.

The 1970s: Tentative Honeymoon

During the 1970s, it seemed that a just and fair multiracial democracy could be made to work in Fiji. In the warm afterglow of the peaceful transition to independence, Fiji's political leaders appeared determined to prove the cynics and prophets of doom wrong about the future of the young nation. The close personal rapport established between Ratu Mara and Siddiq Koya, leader of the opposition, set the tone of political discourse in the country.[7] Mara took Koya along to regional and international meetings to prove that genuine multiracial cooperation existed in Fiji. Mara also asked Koya to chair the Tenth South Pacific Conference in Suva, the first and only Indo-Fijian to have been given such prominence at this important gathering of regional Pacific Island leaders. Vijay Singh, later to become the first Indo-Fijian knight, headed the Fiji delegation. Koya was an important member of the Fiji delegation to the Tongan independence celebrations, where he cut a colorful figure: rotund and bula-shirted, donning a coconut leaf hat and sipping coconut milk in the company of other equally rotund, flower-bedecked Pacific leaders. A joint parliamentary committee negotiated the deal with the CSR that resulted in a $10 million final golden handshake for the company. R. D. Patel of the National Federation Party (NFP) accompanied Agriculture Minister Doug Brown to Washington to lobby for a larger quota of the US sugar market. And occasional, though not really serious, talks were held about a possible coalition government.[8]

In this atmosphere of warm personal feelings and cooperation among its leaders, Fiji's first general election was held in 1972 (Figure 9).[9] At the London constitutional conference, it had been agreed to go into independence without an election to avoid disturbing the harmony of the preceding period. The Alliance, experienced, united, and led by a hugely popular Mara, presented itself to the voters as the only party fit to lead the country. It talked of peace and prosperity and responsible leadership. The NFP, reverting to its earlier populist rhetoric of the late 1960s, talked of social welfare, free and compulsory education, and balanced economic development.

Although the outcome of an Alliance victory was a foregone conclusion —it won 33 seats to the NFP's 19—the extent of racial polarization at the polls was startling. Most Fijians, 82.6 percent, voted for the Alliance Party, rallying to the call for ethnic solidarity and political unity under chiefly leadership. Predictably, the majority of the Indo-Fijians, 74.2 percent, voted for the NFP. The General Electors threw their support (79.2 percent of their communal votes) behind the ruling Alliance. Fewer Fijians

Coalition: Co-operation, Collusion, or Conflict?

Figure 9. A cartoonist's view of Fiji politics in the 1970s. *(Courtesy* Fiji Nation*)*

voted for the NFP than did Indo-Fijians for the Alliance. Fully 24 percent of Indo-Fijian communal votes were cast for Alliance Indo-Fijian communal candidates, a figure that was not to be repeated. The Alliance had a formidable lineup of Indo-Fijian politicians: Vijay Singh, Navin Maharaj, James Shankar Singh, M. T. Khan, and many others. Their presence in the Alliance camp testified to their faith in Ratu Mara as the best leader for the country and a true champion of multiracialism. By the time the decade ended, most of them would have left the party with varying degrees of bitterness at, as they saw it, being used and discarded by the party leadership. Fijian support for the NFP was dismal: a mere 0.8 percent of the Fijian communal votes. This trend of ethnic polarization at the polls, and of fragmentation of ethnic communal votes, would continue throughout the dominion years. It could not be otherwise given the communal structure of the political system.

In the early 1970s, Ratu Mara was at the peak of his career. He had been knighted in 1969, only the second Fijian to be so honored since Ratu Sir Lala Sukuna. His traditional standing in his community was boosted in July 1969 when he was installed as Tui Nayau, the paramount chief of that island and, for all practical purposes, of the entire Lau region. He was only the third person to assume that title, the first being the legendary Roko Nasolo and the second, Ratu Tevita Uluilakeba, Mara's father, in 1948. His moderate stance on many contentious issues enhanced his multiracial image. It was almost an article of faith that Mara was indispensable for a peaceful and multiracial Fiji. Even as late as 1977, the *Fiji Times* editorialized that government without Mara "was almost impossible to visualize," for it was under his leadership that Fiji made "safe and steady passage as a proud and free nation."[10]

At home, Mara enjoyed genuine bipartisan support for his leadership and his policies. On the international scene, he walked tall, both physically (being over six feet tall) and metaphorically as a leader committed to multiracialism and parliamentary democracy. International conferences and visits were frequent and favorably noticed by a wide circle of admirers of all races throughout Fiji. Mara personified Fiji. There were state visits: to India in February 1971, to Australia in June 1972, to Papua New Guinea in May 1974. There was the leadership of international forums (such as the chairmanship of the African-Caribbean-Pacific delegation to Brussels) and regular attendance at heads of government meetings. Foreign accolades were warm and sincere: a doctorate of law from the prestigious University of Delhi (March 1975) and the award of the Grand Master of the Order of the National Lion by the government of Senegal (May 1975); the Walter Dillingham Lecture at the East-West Center in Hawaii; and an address at the Royal Commonwealth Society in London. There would be many other such occasions later, but none of them would evoke the same shared sense of national pride and joy of a young nation as these earlier awards. They would instead be tinged with a vague sense of cynicism and indifference.

What went sour in the latter half of the decade? Both leaders, Koya and Mara, faced internal challenges and charges of a "sell-out" of the interests of their respective communities. Instead of confronting and transcending these, both leaders fell afoul of each other and ended up petulantly retreating to their respective ethnic enclaves. Instead of leading, they both allowed themselves to be led by the ethnic and chauvinistic concerns of their communities, becoming trapped in and consumed by the communal play they had themselves devised.

Siddiq Koya was a Ba-born, Tasmanian-trained Muslim lawyer who had been A. D. Patel's able lieutenant in the early 1960s. Because of the enormous work he did during the Eve Commission hearings, which had thrust him onto the public stage, he had become a kind of folk hero to many cane farmers. Koya was an emotional, ebullient, chest-thumping orator, full of fire and passion, a perfect deputy to the cool, analytical Patel. Koya's misfortune was that he had come of political age in Patel's large shadow; in the eyes of many of the party's strongest supporters, he could not carve a distinctive niche for himself. As Ratu Julian Toganivalu, a leading Federation member, once said: "A. D. Patel was a statesman and a leader. Mr Koya was an actor and a nuisance."[11] Koya's own political miscalculations cost him dearly. His surprisingly close friendship with Mara in the early 1970s did not pay dividends, for in the end he had little to show for his cooperation.[12] At the time of the 1972 elections, the Suva branch of the party issued a stinging attack on his leadership. Soon after the elections, K. C. Ramrakha, the intelligent and energetic, though somewhat impatient, party secretary resigned from all party posts, apparently to test Koya's durability and effectiveness as a leader. The challenge failed, and a chastened Ramrakha returned to the fold within three weeks, but not without publicly indicating the deep rifts in the top echelon of the party hierarchy, something unheard of during the 1960s.[13] Koya's days as the unchallenged leader of the party and of the Indo-Fijian community were problematic, and they were numbered.

Mara fared better within his party. His status as the paramount chief of a powerful area of Fiji gave him a great advantage in his own community, where genealogy, status, and protocol counted for a great deal. His keen understanding of the political mantras of local politics, national and international prestige, and a conspicuous lack of any other credible alternative, both within his party and on the national scene, all helped to bolster his position. However, there were some muffled voices of dissent. Some Fijian extremists said that Mara was at heart really an Indo-Fijian in Fijian clothes because he was seen to be advancing their interests at the expense of the *taukei*. There was some muted criticism of his development policies, which tended to favor his own eastern maritime provinces. More important than this internal disquiet about the tenor of Mara's leadership was the criticism of his adversaries on a number of emotionally charged, unresolved issues. This criticism angered him deeply, hardening his political attitude and pushing him into a seemingly uncompromising ethnic corner. These were unhappy developments for Fiji.

The Street Commission and the Constitution

Because the method of election to parliament agreed to by both the political parties in London was an interim solution that provided only for the first House of Representatives elected after independence, both Mara and Koya, in their joint statement of 30 April 1970, had agreed to appoint a Royal Commission to recommend the most appropriate method for subsequent elections. The new parliament, they said, "would, after considering the Royal Commission Report, provide through legislation for the composition and method of election of a new House of Representatives, and . . . legislation so passed would be regarded as an entrenched part of the Constitution."[14] Following this agreement, a Royal Commission was appointed in 1975, with Professor Harry Street as the chairman and Sir William Hart and Professor Sir Keith Lucas as members. The commission convened in Fiji and held several hearings throughout the country. Little interest was shown in the proceedings, perhaps because, as the *Fiji Times* expressed it, the Royal Commission was "an exercise in futility because, no matter what its recommendations, none of the parliamentary parties has the necessary numbers to create a constitutional change."[15]

In its report, the commission recommended a compromise solution to Fiji's thorny electoral system. It agreed that communal representation should be maintained with the same weight as in the 1970 constitution to guarantee ethnic representation of the major communities of Fiji so that no ethnic group felt deprived of electoral representation. But it also recommended that the remaining twenty-five seats be turned into common electoral roll in five constituencies "with no restriction of race or religion for either voters or candidates." These seats, it suggested, should be elected on the basis of a single transfer vote.

These sensible recommendations took into account the unique ethnic composition of Fiji's society (with all the ethnic communities' attendant fears and prejudices) and the need, on the other hand, to transcend these barriers to create an overarching sense of nationhood. However, the recommendations fell on infertile, even hostile, political ground. Why should this be so when both political parties had agreed at the Thirteenth Plenary Session of the London Conference that the findings of the Royal Commission would, in Ratu Mara's words, "be taken into consideration and then become part of the constitution otherwise its recommendations could be subject to the whim and fancies of any Parliament"?[16]

The simple reason is politics. The 1970 constitution had served the Alliance well. Its electoral provisions had worked to its advantage and so, promises notwithstanding, the party saw no pressing need for change. In their public presentations, the Alliance leaders advanced a number of reasons: extreme communalism would be generated if any of the major groups sensed erosion of their representation in parliament; there was a need to consolidate the status quo after dramatic constitutional developments of the previous decade; more time was needed to see how the 1970 arrangement might work. In Vijay Singh's words, "Once we start tinkering with parts of the constitution and agreed to some changes, we would open the floodgates for other people who wanted to change other parts. I think it is in the interest of all the people of this country that the constitution should remain intact, in full, as is."[17]

This fear of the floodgates opening was disingenuous. The constitution could not be changed at the whim of any political party because all amendments to the constitution required the support of three-quarters of the members of both houses of parliament, with the Great Council of Chiefs having the power of veto over any legislation that even remotely touched on Fijian interests and sensibilities. Moreover, the Royal Commission was not proposing to tinker with the integrity of the constitution as a whole, but with only one part of it—the method of election—that had deliberately been left unresolved at the constitutional negotiations.

Ahmed Ali, then an Alliance Party functionary, was candid. "For Fijians the meaning is clear," he said. "The Fijian people and their leaders are not likely to tolerate a political system which might pave the way for political control of Fijians by non-Fijians." He made explicit the ominous comparison with Malaysia. "Like the Malays, the Fijians feel that their security lies in Fiji being in Fijian hands politically. Like the Malays, they are prepared to share political power but not to relinquish it to others."[18] In short, the Alliance's mind was made up. If the commission endorsed its position, the recommendations would be welcomed; if it did not, they would be shelved, which is what finally happened. Ratu Mara was adamant: "If we had common roll we would have bloodshed. I stand opposed to it now until I have finished my political life."[19] This was quite a remarkable about-face from the position Mara had adopted in the mid-1960s when he had publicly stated that a common roll was a long-term goal of his own party.

The NFP had been cleverly outmaneuvered. It tried to remind the Alliance of the "gentleman's agreement" on the implementation of the recommendations of the Royal Commission. It had taken that agreement at face value, believing that the Alliance would honor its commitment. The Alliance, on the other hand, had made the promise as an expedient tactical move to extract concessions on important issues never really intending to abide by its words. Koya expressed surprise at the Alliance's intransigence. He told an NFP convention at Rakiraki in December 1975 how his suggestion that the two parties extend a combined welcome to the electoral commissioners had been "flatly rejected" by the Alliance. Now with the Alliance's attitude to the report of the Royal Commission, his "cup of disillusionment" was full.[20] Party Secretary Ramrakha accused the Alliance of "deceit" and worse, but these were merely words floating in the wind.

Being outmaneuvered by the Alliance was one part of the problem. The other was that the rest of the NFP leadership, for all its fulminations, was not as intellectually or politically committed to the concept of a common roll as A. D. Patel had been. Instead of confronting the Alliance, or making the Royal Commission recommendations a national political issue, the NFP leaders, in the throes of bitter internal bickering, were too often busy in the courts. For them, the ideology of a common roll had lost the political urgency it once had. Indeed, soon after returning from the London conference, Koya defended not pushing the issue at the negotiating table because, he said, Indo-Fijians had waited for a common roll since 1929, and they could wait for some time longer.[21]

While Koya may have had a nominal commitment to the idea, some in his party accepted the Alliance view about the need for guaranteed and equal representation in the parliament for all ethnic groups. In the interests of the Indo-Fijian community itself, they suggested, the old system should be maintained. The Indo-Fijian birthrate had been declining; emigration was slowly reducing the total Indo-Fijian population, and it was a distinct possibility that in the next decade or so, the Indo-Fijian population could become a minority in Fiji. When that happened, the thinking went, the existing formulas would serve the needs of the community best. This argument went against the basic philosophy of a common roll as it had been advocated in earlier decades. It was harmful to the larger interests of the Indo-Fijian community, which rested in political integration rather than ethnic separateness, in joining hands across ethnic boundaries rather than remaining locked in ethnic compartments. The Indo-Fijian leaders had succumbed to the political considerations of the moment, with only myopic visions of the long-term interests of their own people and the nation at large. For this, they and their people would pay a terrible price a decade later.

With the shelving of the Street Commission recommendations, the last opportunity was lost for devising an electoral system that went beyond the politics and ideology of communalism to create a more politically integrated nation. More immediately, the Alliance's refusal to consider the recommendations placed a deeper and steadily growing wedge between the two leaders, Koya and Mara, and the two parties. Political survival took precedence over everything else. A *Fiji Times* editorial noted that "there seems to be an unfortunate emphasis on individual and sectional aspirations with scant thought of the effect on the nation, except in negatively avoiding actual conflict with the national interest."[22] The concept of multiracialism "has now become just words, or perhaps words written on paper. Just words on paper, words spoken in the air," lamented a deeply embittered Koya. "It is unfortunate that all of us now seem to think in terms of communities, and we blame the system not the person. It is the system I am blaming, that we have become prisoners of the system, and very soon the system will eat us all."[23] Ironically, his and his party's lack of tenacity had contributed to the unfortunate state of affairs.

The Issue of Land Yet Again

Another issue that polarized emotions and deepened fears among both Indo-Fijians and Fijians in the mid-1970s was the perennial question of land tenure. From the late 1940s through the early 1960s, the main issue had been the problems and politics of the reserve policy, which had been an important source of tension and friction between the two communities. The reserve policy had been implemented under Ratu Sukuna's leadership to demarcate and place in exclusively Fijian hands sufficient lands for the future use of that community. By the late 1960s, many of the reserves had been demarcated, and the main issue became security of land tenure.

In 1966 the Agricultural Landlord and Tenant Ordinance (ALTO) was introduced, following the recommendation of the Burns Commission, which attempted to devise an arrangement that would "give tenants a greater degree of security of occupation of land than had previously existed" in the hope that secure leases would remove one of the main impediments to agricultural development in the country.[24] The committee that drafted the legislation recommended that contracts taken out prior to the introduction of ALTO be extended automatically at the option of tenants except where land had already fallen into Fijian reserves or where the lessee had not shown good husbandry. All existing leases should be extended by thirty years and a fair rent board created to ensure fairness in rental matters. These recommendations remained in limbo, criticized by the Provincial Councils for favoring the tenants and by the tenants for not doing enough to give them greater security. Consequently, another committee under the chair of Ian Thompson was set up in 1969 and tabled its report in 1975.

Among other things, the ALTO committee recommended a minimum of twenty-year leases with a further automatic extension of ten years.[25] This recommendation left some Indo-Fijian tenants dissatisfied, although most agreed that these were the best terms they could hope to obtain in the circumstances. Some amendments to the report caused greater controversy, including the provision regarding share cropping. The Indo-Fijian tenants feared exploitation at the hands of their Fijian landlords. Another contentious issue was the assessment of the unimproved capital value of land at the current market price every five years.[26] Koya and his faction objected to this method on the grounds that Fijians were the principal landowners and could create artificially high land values by refusing to open up new areas, thus raising the rate of assessment. Given his recent encounters with the Alliance on the constitution, Koya was particularly adamant that this proposal be deleted.

That was not to be. The Alliance contended that to make further concessions would invite a backlash from the Fijian extremists at the next election. Moreover, land was an important political asset, which, if properly managed, could be used to extract political support from the Indo-Fijian community. As if to emphasize the point, threats were made that blood would flow if Indo-Fijians continued pressing for more secure tenure. Eight of Koya's own parliamentarians, seizing on the proposals as the best they could get, crossed the floor and voted with the Alliance to pass the bill. This paved the way for bitter internal fighting in the NFP. Koya was an alienated and defeated man, his grip on party discipline shown to be weak. He plunged further into communalism to reclaim his popularity in the Indo-Fijian community. The NFP became a party deeply divided, its public esteem lower than at any other time since its founding. Its difficulties lulled the Alliance into complacency about its own chances in the elections just two years away, with important consequences.

Land again surfaced as a major issue in 1979, this time sowing the seeds of a rift between Ratu Mara and Koya's successor as leader of the opposition, Jai Ram Reddy. The issue in 1979 was the imminent implementation of the Alliance government's policy of reserving large areas of Crown land, including Provisional Crown Schedule A land covering 62,240 acres, at least 192 existing leases, and some five government projects.[27] The decision to reserve this land had been made by the Mara cabinet in 1975, but it had never been announced publicly or raised in parliament, for understandable political reasons. Its quiet implementation caused great anxiety in the Indo-Fijian tenant community. After an unsatisfactory private correspondence with Mara, Reddy raised the issue at the annual convention of his party at Ba in 1980. Why, he asked, was the need to reserve Crown land never publicly explained? He argued:

> Given Fijian strength in this area—and Indian vulnerability—is it necessary to take over what little Crown land there is and convert it into Native land? You may have the power to do it, but the power to do what is right and good is also the power to do what is wrong. I would have thought that a reasonable government would preserve as much Crown land as possible consistent with the principles of fairness to all in order to settle future evictees from Native lands now waiting to be resettled.[28]

Reddy argued further that if some *mataqali* needed more land, could not excess land in the possession of other *mataqali* be allocated to them? Or was this a prelude to the conversion of all Crown land into native reserves? He suggested that the reservation of Crown land was perhaps intended to compound the vulnerability of the Indo-Fijian tenant community: "The Indians need no reminding that they are a tenant community. This is an area in which they are already weak and it seems to me that this policy is designed to make them weaker still."

Ratu Mara, as he was wont to with any criticism of his policies, answered with an emotional response. Reddy's plea was a thinly disguised attempt to keep land in Indo-Fijian hands, he argued. Indo-Fijians were never satisfied and did not appreciate the generous concessions Fijians had made over the years:

> All the best Fijian land today is under lease and the majority of the tenants on the best lands are Indians. Most of the most valuable properties in urban

areas are now acquired by the Indian people. Their ownership, like the tentacles of an octopus, has embraced retail, commerce, industry and transport. The Fijians in the name of equity have not asked for an equitable share in these. They abide by the constitutional rights and protection given to property. Yet we are told by the Leader of Opposition that if any Indian tenancy is terminated in accordance with the law, they must in the name of equity be given perpetual leases on Crown land. If his contention is to be accepted, then all Indian tenancies—which cover much of the good land in Fiji—must be held by them in perpetuity; all the most valuable properties in urban areas must be their preserve and, of course, commerce, industry, transport and the professions must be completely controlled by them. And this, I presume, is the principle of equity which the Leader of Opposition advocated. And will such equity preserve the peace and prosperity of Fiji for the future of those who have properties?[29]

We now know the answer to that question. Both leaders had raised concerns vital to their respective communities. Both viewed questions of equity and fairness through communal prisms, though poor Indo-Fijian tenants facing eviction were scarcely in the same category as their well-to-do urban, commercial counterparts. Mara, like most Fijians, saw the Indo-Fijian community as a homogeneous, propertied group with united interests and aspirations. Once again, unfortunately, constructive dialogue over an important national issue had been consumed by the fire of politics, fanned by now deep personal antagonism between the two leaders. This angry exchange could not have come at a worse time, poisoning the prospect for resolving a number of other issues.

The Politics of Balance

Several issues divided the two communities even further in the 1970s and 1980s and were directly related to the way in which resources were allocated between them. Both political parties agreed that there were marked gaps between Fijian and Indo-Fijian communities in their levels of economic and educational performance, gaps that needed to be bridged through legislative means. They also agreed on the principle of balance in the allocation of public resources to meet these needs. Yet the process and the politics of this policy laid the groundwork for further conflict and political confrontation.

Education was one arena in which the principle of parity had been applied early on. The historical record told an unambiguous story: Indo-Fijians were more successful at all levels of the schooling process than Fijians. More of them passed exams, entered the civil service, and swelled the ranks of the professions: medicine, law, management. Both cultural values and political imperatives spurred their drive for excellence. Educational achievement and intellectual pursuits are values culturally cherished in Indian culture—just as communal endeavor is in many Pacific Island cultures. For a community emerging from a history of political and economic servitude and indifference of the colonial government to its basic social and economic needs, schooling offered an important avenue of upward mobility. Private schools, often with little funding and few trained teachers, sprung up with little except "the keenness of the Indian parents and their willingness to sacrifice for their children."[30]

The Fijian experience in education in the twentieth century was less successful, despite government support and the endeavor of the missions from the early years of colonization. It was not that Fijians lacked initiative and ability. The Viti Cauravou in the late 1920s and early 1930s had demanded improved academic education for Fijian boys and girls. The high chiefs, however, in particular, Ratu Sukuna, had advocated vocational and technical education over academic education, believing that the most appropriate calling for Fijian people was the pursuit of practical work, such as agriculture and good animal husbandry. While the Indo-Fijians and Europeans pursued Western education and moved ahead in the professions, Fijians were led on a different path, back to their rural, communal surroundings. Decades of neglect and discouragement of academic education in the old Fijian administration under Ratu Sukuna's guidance came to haunt the Fijian people and their leaders as Fiji approached independence.

In 1969 a Fiji Education Commission was appointed to examine the problem of Fijian education and chart the course of future education in the colony.[31] The commission confirmed what was already generally well known: the geographical scatter of Fijian villages with schools often too small for effective staffing and teaching, the considerable physical isolation of the Fijian teacher from centers of intellectual stimulus, the shortage of academically qualified Fijian primary school teachers, and the rural poverty that made maintaining scholastic standards difficult. The social distractions of communal life in the *koro* and intangible but important cultural and psychological factors added to the educational plight of the Fijian people. These structural and social difficulties, not intellectual inferiority, were at the root of the problem. Colonial rule and policies of enforced isolation had saddled the Fijian people with a severe handicap that required urgent attention.

To bridge the widening gap, the commission recommended that 50 percent of Fiji government university scholarship funds be reserved for Fijians on a "parallel-block" basis, with other ethnic groups competing for their own allotted quota of scholarship funds. In the not unlikely event of the Fijian quota being unfilled, the unallocated balance could be devoted to other specifically Fijian educational needs, such as repeats for university students. These provisions were to extend for a period of nine years, with a preliminary review at the end of six years.

The recommended review did not take place in 1976. By then the situation was complicated by the increasing competition for places in the pre-degree Foundation Programme at the University of the South Pacific. Education became an issue in the 1977 elections. The government awarded scholarships to Fijian students with university entrance pass marks of 216, whereas Indo-Fijian students needed 261 marks to win scholarships. Much political mileage could be made out of this glaring inequity, and was. Koya took the lead. The policy of discrimination, he said, "is bound to produce recriminations, frustrations, bitterness, the destruction of the image of the university and indeed the government of the day in the eyes of the world." That was going too far, especially as the NFP had tacitly agreed to the principle of positive discrimination in favor of the Fijians. Ratu Mara reminded the Indo-Fijians of the many concessions Fijian people had made, such as on land, and stressed the need to give Fijian children time to "catch up." The Alliance government's position was difficult though understandable. As Table 4 clearly shows, Fijians were still lagging behind Indo-Fijians, both in absolute numbers attending schools and in their pass rates in all major external examinations.

The educational problem was not a simple one. To start with, there were internal urban-rural dichotomies in both communities that influenced educational performance, a fact that a communal perspective was quite incapable of recognizing; some Fijian provinces, such as Lau, received proportionately more scholarship funds than others, such as Ba, which had the largest population.[32] The problem of Fijian education was not simply a "Fijian" one but a "national" concern, as many Fijian educators would later argue, but it was not tackled in that fashion. Indo-Fijian parents who could acknowledge the principle of balance in the abstract found it hard to accept that Indo-Fijian children with high marks were denied a scholarship while Fijian students with lower marks received government funding. While the Indo-Fijians complained, the Alliance, under Education Minister Ahmed Ali, moved ahead with great enthusiasm to upgrade facilities in Fijian schools in the early 1980s, providing them with better trained teachers and, in the case of Fijian Foundation students at the University of the South Pacific, with additional facilities for supervised tutoring in the congenial surroundings of the disestablished Nasinu Teachers' Training College six miles out of Suva. In 1985 the Fijian Affairs Board set up a separate fund of $3 million, outside the normal parallel-block awards, exclusively for the training of Fijian scholars and in-service trainees.

The Alliance government's determined efforts to achieve parity between Fijians and Indo-Fijians in the public sector also brought controversy. The claim that Fijians were severely underrepresented in the civil service in the years following independence was exaggerated, as Table 5 shows, but the Alliance used it anyway to justify its pro-Fijian policy. In absolute num-

Table 4. Performance in Major Standardized Examinations by Main Ethnic Groups, 1970–1983

	Fijians		Indo-Fijians	
	Sat (No.)	Passed (%)	Sat (No.)	Passed (%)
Secondary School Entrance				
1970	4181	44.4	4671	69.7
1971	4572	51.6	5386	65.8
1972	5150	46.7	6485	61.3
1973	4323	44.7	6172	62.3
1974	4067	42.1	5724	66.8
1975	4121	46.5	4772	68.4
1976	3786	69.9	4563	69.7
1977	3551	55.6	4776	71.6
1978	3433	62.5	4427	76.4
1979	3391	70.3	4131	82.5
1980	3445	69.6	3856	82.0
1981	3173	73.0	3734	82.4
1982	3350	73.9	3926	84.7
1983	3375	77.5	4028	83.2
Fiji Junior Certificate				
1970	1698	52.4	3268	55.2
1971	1942	54.3	3598	60.6
1972	2258	51.9	4152	51.1
1973	2938	47.8	5037	48.6
1974	3270	48.4	5600	50.6
1975	3365	50.8	5631	51.8
1976	3550	48.7	6213	48.6
1977	4033	50.6	6760	48.2
1978	4460	50.5	6313	50.3
1979	4246	50.5	6436	53.5
1980	4273	54.0	6100	53.5
1981	4085	50.0	5921	56.7
1982	4242	53.0	5782	57.1
1983	4107	54.6	5585	61.3
New Zealand School Certificate				
1970	531	39.2	1670	29.2
1971	797	31.4	2114	29.6
1972	904	27.1	2197	33.7
1973	1081	31.3	2705	32.6
1974	1442	17.1	2940	24.4
1975	1912	18.7	3714	25.8
1976	2156	17.9	4159	26.2
1977	2477	16.9	4609	25.1
1978	2741	20.9	4589	32.8
1979	2835	22.6	4679	38.4

	Fijians		Indo-Fijians	
	Sat (No.)	Passed (%)	Sat (No.)	Passed (%)
1980	3018	28.9	4287	38.2
1981	3050	28.9	4131	43.6
1982	2961	30.9	4066	45.0
1983	2963	30.0	3954	49.5
New Zealand University Entrance				
1970	302	22.3	501	33.3
1971	224	24.6	585	24.9
1972	252	25.0	684	32.9
1973	202	28.7	709	32.7
1974	240	27.9	807	30.9
1975	293	25.9	912	32.8
1976	318	30.2	1107	29.1
1977	478	22.4	1405	29.3
1978	576	29.5	1710	37.8
1979	804	22.7	2036	33.4
1980	922	20.0	2305	33.4
1981	1000	21.9	2278	36.2
1982	1117	23.1	2512	33.3
1983	1300	25.7	2581	36.8

SOURCE: Ministry of Education annual reports for 1970 to 1983. In Fiji Employment and Development Mission 1984, 339.

bers as well as in percentage terms, there were more Fijians in the civil service than Indo-Fijians. Another widely held view was that there were more Fijians than other ethnic groups in the lower rungs of the civil service bureaucracy. This was then used to justify the award of more in-service training opportunities and promotions for the *taukei*. Again, however, Fijians were not so underrepresented in the upper echelons of the public sector. In 1979, to take just one typical example from the 1970s, of all the civil servants earning between $10,000 and $16,000 and over (senior positions), Fijians numbered 151 (32 percent), Indo-Fijians 169 (35.9 percent), Europeans 111 (23.6 percent), and others 40 (8.5 percent).[33]

One cause of the perception of Fijian disparity in the civil service may have been the concentration of senior Fijian officials in certain key ministries that had long been their preserve—Fijian Affairs, Home Affairs, the cabinet, Forests and Fisheries, and the like—whereas Indo-Fijians and others were more evenly spread across the departments. At the decision-making pinnacle of the civil service—the level of permanent secretary—the Fijian presence was strong and dominant. Throughout the dominion years, Fijian permanent secretaries far outnumbered their Indo-Fijian

Table 5. Racial Composition of the Fiji Civil Service

Group	1975 No.	%	1976 No.	%	1979 No.	%	1980 No.	%
European	365	2.9	445	3.3	241	1.5	202	1.3
Fijian	6,421	50.4	6,587	48.6	7,503	47.9	7,511	47.5
Indo-Fijian	5,421	42.6	5,936	43.8	7,047	44.9	7,268	46.0
Other	528	4.1	587	4.3	887	5.7	836	5.2
Total	12,735		13,555		15,678		15,817	

SOURCE: Fiji Public Service Commission reports, 1976–1981.

counterparts; rarely were there more than three or four Indo-Fijian permanent secretaries out of a dozen or so in the civil service.[34]

This trend of rapid Fijian movement up the civil service ladder naturally caused concern to the NFP and attracted predictable criticism. Jai Ram Reddy brought it up in his party's Ba convention in 1980: "Fiji is implementing a policy designed to ensure that all strategic levels of government are staffed by loyal personnel—which in effect means that Fijians are placed in positions of command in order to deliberately create an out group, namely the Indians."[35] Irene Jai Narayan, deputy NFP leader, urged in parliament in June 1980 that in addition to overall racial balance in the civil service, there should be parity at all levels of the bureaucracy as well, but the ensuing debate led nowhere.

Ratu Penaia Ganilau, acting prime minister, argued that the principle of parity applied only at the level of entry and that promotions and other opportunities for advancement through the different ranks of the civil service depended on merit, a claim that, on the available evidence, was not altogether valid.[36] To the charge that many qualified Indo-Fijians had been bypassed in promotions, the Public Service Commission replied with the intriguing assertion that it did not "necessarily follow that a candidate with higher academic achievements on entry to the service will prove to be more efficient at work and receive rapid advancement than one with lower qualification."[37] Be that as it may, the reality was that many Indo-Fijian civil service employees saw themselves as victims of overt racial discrimination under the Mara administration.

The aid and development strategies of the Alliance government, too, brought their share of controversy. Throughout the 1970s and more openly in the 1980s, the Alliance government made strenuous efforts to provide assistance and resources to the Fijian people to enable them to enter and successfully compete in the world of commerce. The Fiji Development Bank, established in 1967, assisted Fijians in a range of economic activities. It provided soft loans to Fijians through the Commercial and Industrial Loans and the Joint Venture Loans schemes and offered fiscal incentives and management-training programs. In February 1974, the Project Evaluation Unit was created in the Ministry of Fijian Affairs to "assist Fijians both individually and in groups to understand, cope and operate within the modern business world."[38] The name of the unit was changed in June 1975 to the Fijian Business Opportunity and Management Advisory Services (BOMAS). This organization and others, such as the Rural Area Appropriate Technology Unit (RAATU), provided financial support, expert advice, and training programs for Fijians wanting to enter the world of business.

From May 1975 to December 1984, the total monetary value of loans given to Fijians through BOMAS recommendations, without parliamentary debates, it might be noted, amounted to $6,721,553,[39] a not insignificant figure for a small country like Fiji. Yet, for all these various forms of assistance, the dream of Fijian success remained unrealized: there were more Fijians than Indo-Fijians in arrears—in 1985, of all arrears in industrial and agricultural loans, 1,921, or 61 percent, were Fijian as compared with 21.6 percent for Indo-Fijians. More Fijians than Indo-Fijians experienced outright failures, and more loans made to them had to be written off.[40] Mismanagement, even corruption and outright plunder, a communal culture incompatible with the commercial ethic, and simply, incompetent advice were all responsible for the failures. However, these factors remained largely unexamined and unrectified.

Aid money, too, went in disproportionately large sums to Fijian enterprises, partly because rural development programs came under the ambit of the Ministry of Fijian Affairs, which naturally concentrated its efforts on improving conditions in Fijian areas. Foreign aid was used to accomplish projects in selected provinces and districts. A substantial portion of the European Economic Community aid money in the 1970s was focused in this way.[41] Between 1976 and 1980, Fiji received total financial aid of $8,774,000, of which $900,000 went to the Native Lands Trust Corporation for land development on Viti Levu and Vanua Levu; $700,000 to the Fiji Development Bank (special loan); $750,000 for the construction of airstrips on Cicia, Moala, and Kadavu, $1,474,000 for the construction of jetties on Koro, Moala, Kadavu, and Saqani; and $2,850,000 for the construction of a road at Natewa Bay. All these areas are in the Tovata Confederacy, home of the reigning Fijian elite. The major agricultural development project of the 1970s, the pine plantations in western Viti Levu and elsewhere, were primarily Fijian-oriented, as were Australian-funded cattle projects in western Viti Levu.

None of this is surprising. The government could justify its spending pattern on the grounds of need and on the necessity for diversifying its agricultural base. The politics of patronage, too, is well known, and it is hardly surprising that a Fijian-dominated government was using its power to benefit its primary constituency. The government's analysis of the problems facing Fiji was deeply flawed, as its own privately commissioned reports powerfully pointed out. One major report, prepared by Stan Stavenuiter for the government's Central Planning Office, concluded that disparities within the major ethnic groups should receive more attention than policies that continually emphasized interethnic discrepancies:

> Within the Indo-Fijian community there are wealthy cane farmers as well as land-poor smallholders; Indo-Fijians have been successful in building up a substantial locally owned commercial sector as well as some manufacturing industry; they are overrepresented in the professions; but they are also over-represented among urban and peri-urban households applying and qualifying for social welfare assistance. And within the Fijian ethnic group as a whole, one finds numerous well-placed urban salary-earners; communities that live well from leased out land or profitable farming activities; as well as those who indeed make only a bare living from subsistence fishing and agriculture, who are unsuccessful in finding remunerative urban employment, or who have insufficient, or insufficiently productive, communal land to (re-) turn to. Present government policies aiming at a reduction of inter-ethnic disparities, such as the fact that 50% of Government scholarships for tertiary education are reserved for Fijians, and efforts at increasing Fijian involvement in business activities would certainly seem to have their place; but there would appear to be an equally strong case for giving more active support to the socio-economically disadvantaged of both races. Support for pursuing a higher education, or making credit-facilities available for setting up small businesses, could well be extended for the poorer sections of society, regardless of ethnicity, and the types of affirmative action now undertaken for the Fijian community as a whole might well be somewhat restricted to the truly deserving by making greater use of means tests in the granting of support.[42]

The Stavenuiter Report was shelved, and its recommendations were not implemented.

The government's approach to solving problems of regional disparity was also problematic. To be sure, some areas were better off than others. The urban and periurban areas in the Central Division (southeastern Viti Levu), for example, scored higher on gross household-income charts than the remote, largely subsistence-based islands of the maritime provinces; the government used this to justify more assistance to these rural areas. Within the more prosperous Central and Western divisions, however, lay many areas, such as Serua, Namosi, and many parts of interior Viti Levu, that were equally, if not more, disadvantaged than their maritime counterparts. They had no industries or major exploitable resources, and they received scant government attention. The result of the government's myopic policies was that nearly half of the population felt left out and neglected. Fijian leaders like Ratu Mara never quite understood why the bulk of the Indo-Fijian population had no incentive to join their party. On the contrary, they wanted a change of government that might be more sympathetic to their needs and aspirations. Many Fijians outside the few favored provinces felt the same way, often using the Indo-Fijians as a target to get at the Alliance's eastern chiefly leadership.

Butadroka, Racism, and the Elections

The mounting subsurface tensions came to a head on 9 October 1975 when Sakiasi Butadroka, a Namosi parliamentarian in southeastern Viti Levu and an Alliance assistant minister, proposed the motion "that this House agrees that the time has come when Indians or people of Indian origin in this country be repatriated back to India and their travelling expenses back home and compensation for their property in this country be met by the British Government."[43] Needless to say, the substance and the sentiment behind the motion caused a furor in the Indo-Fijian community. Seconded by an Indo-Fijian politician, K. N. Govind of the Alliance, so that it could be tabled in parliament, the motion became the subject of an unprecedented emotional debate in the House of Representatives. Coming as it did immediately after the expulsion of Indians from Uganda, it acquired a special significance. Many Indo-Fijians wondered if Fiji would become another Uganda.

Butadroka, by turns emotional, comical, and threatening, argued that Fiji was no longer a Fijian country. The *taukei* were a severely disadvantaged group, marginalized in the professions, commerce, and public life, and would disappear into political insignificance unless corrective action was taken immediately. The Indo-Fijian community, he argued, was the principal cause of this Fijian predicament, and it should be removed. India, he said on another occasion, was a very backward country in need of lawyers, doctors, and other skilled people: "So why be selfish? Send them to their own country, let them develop their own country."[44]

The substance of the motion was rejected by all members of the House in more or less degree, but Butadroka was not a bad reader of prevailing Fijian opinion, according to Ratu David Toganivalu, a leader of the Alliance and a man with extensive ties to the local Indo-Fijian business community. (He was jestingly called a Gujaratu by some.) Butadroka, Ratu David said, might be "echoing the soul of the Fijian people" because "all Fijians consciously, but mainly unconsciously, feel at times in terms of what is expressed in the motion. There is no hiding about it: this is how we feel at times; at certain moments in times of anger this is what we say. He is not the first to say it. It has been said before. I have got to say this . . . because if you have got to vomit, vomit properly, right on the floor, and examine why certain members of our community are vomiting."[45] Indeed, some Fijian members of the House, though avoiding Butadroka like a

Butadroka triumphant at the April 1977 election. He is wearing a blood-red bow tie, his "trademark," which he claimed signified that Indian blood would flow if Indians did not accept a status inferior to that of his own people in Fiji. *(Courtesy Fiji Times)*

plague in public, seemed privately pleased by the strong assertion of the principle of Fijian paramountcy.

Mara spoke out against the motion, but did not go far enough for the opposition, which wanted its outright rejection, a reaffirmation of the rights of the Indo-Fijian people, and public denunciation of "any person or organization which interferes with or disrupts the multiracial harmony in Fiji." Swaying with the prevailing wind, Mara offered an amendment "to reaffirm the credit due to the Indians, as well as to the Europeans, Chinese and Pacific Islanders for the role they have played, are playing and will assuredly continue to play in the development of Fiji, and in particular their concern and willingness to support government's policy in helping the Fijian people to improve their economic situation as quickly as possible."[46] This was Mara at his political best—or worst—attempting to please all sides while retaining center stage.

An embattled Koya, his own credibility in the party undermined by close association with Mara, went on the offensive, arguing that the amended motion did not go far enough. "We are not here under license; we are here as of right. Full Stop," he thundered.[47] Mara's posturing deepened Koya's bitterness and frustration. While the week-long debate was in motion, Koya told a party meeting at the Old Town Hall in Suva that there were within the Alliance Party leaders—he had Mara in mind, no doubt—who were trying to accomplish legally what Butadroka was trying to accomplish illegally.[48] Mara rejected the charge of political duplicity and promised to resign if Koya could prove his allegations, which Koya promised to do before a Royal Commission, which Mara refused to appoint. The breach between the two leaders was now complete. "I used to take the Leader of the Opposition around with me," Mara said later, "but I am not now going to be associated with someone who more or less says that I am a dishonest and insincere person. I mean if I say I don't like you, you go and say nasty things about me. I would not like you to come up home. I might have a great big stone waiting for you."[49] If there was any victor in this sad episode, it was Butadroka. "The loss of that [opposition's demand for outright rejection of the motion] means the total loss of the Indians of Fiji," exulted Butadroka. "Hooray!"[50]

Formally expelled from the Alliance though warmly encouraged by the support he received from many Fijians throughout the underprivileged sections of the country, Butadroka launched his own political party in 1975, the Fijian Nationalist Party. The platform adopted at its December 1976 convention outlined its underlying goals and principles:

The interests of the Fijians must be paramount at all times.
The Fijians must always hold the positions of governor-general, prime minister, and the ministries of Fijian Affairs and Rural Development, Lands, Education, Agriculture, Home Affairs, Commerce and Industry, and Co-operatives.

More opportunities should be given to Fijians to enter business and commerce.

Common roll should be totally opposed.

The Fijian Administration should be strengthened with government financial backing and support.

A Fijian institute should be established to teach Fijians business.

Indo-Fijians should be repatriated to India after Fiji gained "full" independence.

All illegally sold land should be returned to Fijians.

More government projects should be concentrated in rural areas.[51]

With his trademark red bow tie and a simple, earthy manner of speaking, Butadroka took his message to rural Fijians in southeastern Viti Levu, an area that had been neglected in the various development programs of the Alliance government. Although the Indo-Fijian community was his principal target, Butadroka also took aim at Mara and the general eastern dominance of the Fijian political economy. These provincial issues would come to the fore much more forcefully in the 1980s.

With this deeply unsettled atmosphere of strained race relations, political bad blood among the leaders, and a rising tide of Fijian ethnic militancy, Fiji approached its second postindependence general elections in April 1977. The Alliance entered the campaign well funded and confident —if anything, overconfident and complacent—having purged itself of the ethnic extremism represented by the Fijian Nationalist Party. Moreover, the NFP had recently shown itself deeply divided on policies and personalities, and there was the distinct possibility that the party might self-destruct over the selection of candidates. That disaster had been avoided late in 1976 when Jai Ram Reddy managed to separate the office of parliamentary leader and the president of the party to accommodate the different factions.[52] The Alliance hoped its catchy slogan of "peace, progress and prosperity" on the basis of "share and care" would carry the day. The NFP stuck to its populist rhetoric directed principally at the middle classes and rural dwellers.[53]

The election produced a bombshell. The NFP captured 26 of the 52 seats in the House, and the Alliance 24. The 2 remaining seats, both Fijian communal, went to Butadroka, who narrowly defeated Alliance's Tomasi Vakatora (4,640 votes to 4,044) and to a political newcomer in Nadroga/Navoa, Ratu Osea Gavidi, who polled 3,709 votes to defeat Alliance Minister Peniame Naqasima (2,886). Altogether, the Fijian Nationalist Party pulled 20,819 (24.4 percent) of all the Fijian communal votes away from the Alliance, whose share sank from 83 percent in 1972 to only 67 percent in 1977. Indo-Fijian support for the Alliance also declined from the all-time high of 24 percent to 16 percent in 1977. These factors, together with a low Fijian voter turnout, led directly to the loss of six marginal seats by the Alliance Party. The NFP, which had managed to keep its Indo-Fijian communal votes intact (84.9 percent), was the clear beneficiary of the Nationalists' triumph. These two parties had cynically collaborated informally to cause the downfall of the Alliance by splitting the Fijian vote; the Alliance fell into the trap because of its complacency and arrogance.

No one was more surprised at the outcome than the two major political parties themselves. Publicly punctilious about procedure, Mara tendered his resignation to the governor-general, Ratu Sir George Cakobau, on 4 April, cleared his office, and moved out. Koya, stunned by the dramatic turn of events, promised to convene his parliamentary caucus the next day (at 4:15 PM) to elect a leader who would be the new prime minister. The Alliance, meanwhile, had reelected Mara as party leader. Koya, however, was not as lucky, for with the party's unexpected victory, the papered-over unity began to fracture into an unseemly haggling over important portfolios.

The NFP's slim two-seat majority did not make matters any easier, especially as the winning party had to provide the Speaker of the House as well. Old questions were raised about Koya's suitability to be prime minister. The loyalty of the country's armed forces and the civil service to an NFP government were also raised by newly elected Jai Ram Reddy. Overtures were made to the Alliance to form a coalition government in "the best of faith by a party which had a slight majority."[54] The Alliance rejected them as a desperate attempt by a beleaguered, divided party pleading for a political bailout. As Mara said, "Whether they like it or not, the NFP have won the election."[55] Not until Thursday, 7 April, four days after winning the election, and after coalition talks with the Alliance had failed, was Koya elected leader, and then on the second ballot with the narrowest of votes (14 to 12). When he went to Government House to be sworn in as Fiji's second prime minister, Koya was informed by the governor-general that "acting in his own deliberate judgement," he had just appointed Mara to form a minority government. The governor-general's history-making statement read:

In the recent elections, the people of Fiji did not give a clear mandate to either of the political parties. It therefore became the duty of the Governor General under the Constitution to appoint as Prime Minister the member of the House of Representatives who appeared to him best able to command the support of the majority of the House. The Governor General has not been able to act sooner as it was not until this afternoon that he was informed who had been elected leader of the National Federation Party. The Governor General, after taking all the relevant circumstances into account, has come to the firm conclusion that the person best able to command the support of the majority of the members is the leader of the Alliance Party, Ratu Sir Kamisese Mara. In compliance with the Constitution and acting in his own deliberate judgement, the Governor General has accordingly appointed Ratu Sir

Kamisese Mara as Prime Minister. The Prime Minister is now in the process of forming a government.[56]

This decision became a matter of intense controversy. Strictly speaking, the governor-general was acting within his clearly defined constitutional right, if perhaps contrary to the spirit of a Westminster constitution, which requires the parliament to physically resolve the question and not have the governor-general decide in advance what the outcome of the parliament's vote of confidence should be.[57] Section 73(2) of the constitution provided that "the Governor General, acting in his own deliberate judgement, shall appoint as Prime Minister the Member of the House of Representatives who appears to him best able to command the support of the majority of that House." This raised the obvious question: did some of Koya's own colleagues stab him in the back by secretly informing the governor-general of their unwillingness to support him?

K. C. Ramrakha and Irene Jai Narayan, both known Koya opponents, were fingered early as two possible suspects, but both denied, the former on oath, any dealing behind Koya's back. Said Ramrakha: "The brute and undeniable fact is that when Mr Koya went to the Governor General to become the Prime Minister, the Governor General, and the Governor General alone, refused to make him Prime Minister."[58] The governor-general denied having any contact with the NFP during the period in question.[59] Koya later accused his Hindu colleagues of preventing him from becoming prime minister, telling an Indian journalist in 1987 that "Jai Ram Reddy and his supporters, all NFP members, withheld support because they did not want a Muslim Prime Minister."[60] This accusation is perhaps colored by Koya's deep sense of bitterness at being dislodged from power by Reddy and his supporters in the 1980s. Nonetheless, even after the 1977 debacle, Koya was again elected to the leadership of the party, which required Hindu votes.

At the time, however, Koya alleged that he was not allowed to become prime minister because he was an Indo-Fijian; in other words, it was the Fijians, and especially their high chiefs, who were the main opposition. Now, with the advantage of hindsight, that allegation does not seem as strained as it did in 1977. Perhaps the ruling Fijian elite was not prepared to relinquish power, and the squabble in the NFP leadership became a convenient excuse to continue with the status quo. Sitiveni Rabuka has said that he had contemplated the possibility of a military coup had the Alliance not been put back into power.[61] Mara's own statement accepting the invitation to form a minority government makes allusions to traditional Fijian loyalties that are revealing. He said that he "obeyed the command of His Excellency the Governor General, the highest authority in the land and my paramount chief. I obeyed him in the same manner that thousands of Fijians obeyed their chiefs when they were called to arms—

without question and with the will to sacrifice and serve."[62] He would use a similar rationale when called to serve in the postcoup Rabuka cabinet in May 1987, the only difference this time being that Rabuka was not a high chief but a commoner, albeit an uncommon one.

The minority Alliance government lasted from April to September, when it fell to an NFP-led vote of no confidence. New elections were held in September, and the intervening period was one of much activity. The Alliance pulled out all the stops in its effort to get back its Fijian voters, and it is not difficult to suspect at least an element of social coercion by the Fijian Association in the villages when ensuring the return of the Fijian communal vote in the second 1977 election. Butadroka, having been charged under the Public Order Act for inciting violence and being a threat to public peace, was in jail, thus making the task easier for the Alliance. Having witnessed the dramatic events of April, many Fijians, especially those who had voted for the Fijian Nationalist Party in protest against the Alliance's lethargy, returned to the Alliance fold. In the September elections, the Fijian Nationalist Party's support, measured in terms of communal votes cast, declined to 16,000, or 17 percent of the total Fijian communal vote of 92,400.[63] The Alliance had reclaimed its natural political constituency, except for the Nadroga-Navosa Fijian communal seat, which was retained by Ratu Osea Gavidi, an independent.

Disintegration was the trend in the NFP camp. Divisions only barely hidden before the elections, reinforced and energized by the debacle of April, were now out in the open. Two factions emerged within the ranks of the NFP, one dubbed the Dove faction (Koya) and the other the Flower (Ramrakha-Narayan). Both established rival branches and engaged with unseemly viciousness in frantic efforts to establish themselves as the "real NFP." As it turned out, neither was allotted the party symbol, the mango tree. The ensuing contest was not so much between the NFP and the Alliance as it was between these two factions. The Alliance tacitly lent its support to the Flower faction, with Mara saying he would rather step down than work with the NFP leader (Koya).[64]

Koya's own Lautoka seat attracted the most attention. His rival was Jai Ram Reddy, who, by taking on the leader of the Dove faction, became the de facto leader of the Flower faction. It was a contest of exceptional bitterness and anguish between these two men, both lawyers, both Lautoka-based, once good friends, a contest in which religious, cultural, and personal values, contacts, and relationships were viciously exploited. In the end, Reddy won comfortably. The Flower faction took twelve of the fifteen seats won by the NFP (58.2 percent of the Indo-Fijian communal votes), and the Doves captured the remaining three (41.9 percent). The Alliance cruised to an easy victory, with thirty-six seats and 47 percent of the 196,000 votes cast in the election.

Although these electoral contests ruffled racial feathers, they resolved

The NFP disintegrates. After the April 1977 elections, the embattled NFP leader and future Dove faction leader Siddiq Koya is challenged by the party secretary and a Flower faction leader, K. C. Ramrakha, over the NFP leadership. *(Courtesy Fiji Times)*

few of the underlying social and economic issues facing Fiji. The emphasis on communalism distracted attention from problems that cut across ethnic lines. A decade that had begun with hope and reconciliation, fruitful dialogue, and genuine bipartisanship ended on a sad note of stagnation, ethnic polarization, and bitterness.

The 1980s: New Wine in Old Bottles

One change that held the prospect of better relations between the two parties, now that Mara had publicly indicated his displeasure with Koya's style of leadership, was the ascendancy of Jai Ram Reddy to the post of leader of the opposition. Reddy was a relative newcomer to national politics. A South Indian, New Zealand–trained, Lautoka-based lawyer highly regarded for his legal acumen, he was appointed to the Senate in 1972 by Koya, but had resigned in 1976 because he could not support Koya's position on the ALTO bill. He entered parliament first in April 1977 as an elected Indo-Fijian communal member for Ba-Lautoka constituency, and again in September as the Flower leader. Reddy was a self-proclaimed pragmatic moderate. He was an emotional, aloof, determined man without Koya's flair for backslapping and the cut-and-thrust of political debate. He often described himself as "first among equals" in contrast to his predecessor, who made no secret of enjoying the trappings and display of power.[65]

Reddy's tasks were threefold. First, he had to reunite his party, and, to his credit, he did bring about a remarkable degree of reconciliation within five years. He broadened his base to include rejected departing Alliance stalwarts like Sir Vijay Singh, James Shankar Singh, and M. T. Khan, all former Alliance ministers, who had left their party for a variety of reasons and were looking for a new political base. By the early 1980s, the Flower-Dove factionalism had subsided considerably. Reddy's two other priorities were to restart a working relationship with the Alliance leadership and to generate more Fijian support for his party. As early as 1974, he had told the NFP convention in Nadi that "if the National Federation Party is aspiring to govern, then it must acquire a broadly based support among all the races in Fiji. Unless the party acquires such support it must resign itself to being a permanent opposition."[66]

At first, Mara and Reddy cooperated well. Reddy, Mara said on several occasions, was the kind of man he would like to see in his cabinet. This happy situation was not to last long. Just two years later, both men fell afoul of each other. One issue that divided them was the reservation of Crown land; another was the controversy generated by the talk of a government of national unity. The idea attracted a great deal of attention at the time, yet it was just another proposal for nation building that would fall prey to the politics of communalism.

A Government of National Unity

Vague talk of the desirability of a coalition type of government had been floated in the early years of independence; Mara had toyed with the idea, though with no particular vigor, during the 1969–1970 intraparty constitutional discussions. In 1979, however, he again took the initiative and privately circulated a paper to Jai Ram Reddy on the idea and desirability of a government of national unity. Prepared by Ahmed Ali, then an academic at the University of the South Pacific,[67] the paper dwelt heavily on the problems of government in crisis-prone plural societies in which half the population remained voiceless or at least severely underrepresented in the cabinet. Those neglected would become "more disenchanted with the government and country and with little reason for loyalty to a system which excludes them through no fault of their own apart from their attachment to a political party in which they genuinely believe." The paper rejected the concept of coalition government because such a political arrangement, it said misleadingly, was always a temporary measure designed for times of crisis.[68] A "coalition is characterised by compromise, [where] those coalescing modify their policies to make them acceptable to one another for the sake of clinging to the reins of government." The best solution lay in a government of national unity with a cabinet "which draws upon the best talents in the country having in mind simultaneously adequate representation of the various ethnic groups in Fiji." In such an arrangement, an attempt would be made to ensure "adequate participation by all communities in the decision-making processes to obtain consensus for critical policies thereby nullifying the likelihood of a sense of alienation developing in any one or more ethnic groups through apparent or real exclusion."

The paper was strong on analysis but short on prescription. How was power to be shared, and for how long? Who would get what ministries? "The call to a government of national unity without specifying the underlying principles for sharing of power and the machinery of operations left a yawning gap in the proposals," Reddy commented in his detailed response to the proposal.[69] He took issue with the suggestion that the politics of compromise was undesirable: "In plural societies, stable and good government in the broadest sense must include and reflect the hopes and aspirations of the many components of that society," he said. "To say that we want politics of consensus but no compromise is a contradiction in terms. It is a proposition which is rather difficult to understand." Reddy rejected the underlying but unstated assumption of the proposal that the Fijians were the "have-nots" and the Indo-Fijians the "haves" in Fiji. "Any approach that focuses too much emphasis on race and not to those in need is not likely to attract much sympathy or acceptance," said Reddy. "What we need to do," he continued, "is to develop a creed which will require the privileged in our society, be they Indians, Fijians or Europeans, to help those who are the weakest in our community irrespective of race, colour or religion."

This forthright critique brought a predictable response from the Alliance. They blamed Reddy for rejecting the concept of a government of national unity and later attempted to hold him accountable for the collapse of the proposals.[70] The proposal was never formally presented or discussed. Mara himself said in March 1979 that he had not discussed it with Reddy. "I felt that if I had gone to the Leader of the Opposition without discussing it with my colleagues in the Alliance," he said, "that in itself would start to prejudice their minds."[71] For his part, Reddy was cynical, saying that "the fact that so sensitive an issue as a government of national unity was raised for public discussion without real attempt to discuss the issues directly with the Opposition and thereby virtually forcing the Opposition to respond to the proposal in an open forum and the rapidity with which the idea was rejected leaves me wondering whether the whole exercise was not a public relations gimmick, an exercise in public mediation in order to give the government a facelift."[72]

Political motivations may have impelled the proposals. The Indian Alliance, always the weakest spoke in the Alliance wheel, was in disarray. Its once leading members, such as Sir Vijay Singh and M. T. Khan, both former Alliance ministers, had left the party in questionable circumstances, one of them under a cloud, and were beginning to broach the possibility of joining the NFP. By having the NFP as a junior partner in a government of national unity, the Alliance would once again acquire the image of a multiracial organization. Equally, the unity arrangement would help to quell emerging divisions within Fijian society. Butadroka's triumph in 1977, and his continuing influence in rural southeastern Viti Levu, was a warning from an unpredictable electorate that could not be ignored. And in Nadroga-Navosa, Ratu Osea Gavidi, who had triumphed as an independent candidate in both the elections of 1977, was a force to be reckoned with. He would go on to launch his own political party in the west. However, before they could be subjected to public discussion, the unity proposals collapsed on the eve of another electoral confrontation.

1982: Western Regionalism, Elections, and Aftermath

The 1982 general election was a more evenly contested affair than all the previous elections.[73] The NFP was in better fighting shape than it had been in 1977. Reddy had managed to heal the old Dove-Flower wounds to a remarkable degree and had infused much-needed new blood into its ranks. The discarded old stalwarts of the party headed toward the Alliance, demonstrating that the ideological gulf between the two parties had been reduced considerably. To boost the small pool of Fijian electoral support for his party, which was necessary if the NFP were to capture power, Reddy managed to forge a coalition with a Fijian party, the Western United Front (WUF), launched in July 1981 by Gavidi. This was the first serious attempt at a formal multiracial coalition in Fiji since independence.

The WUF was born out of a smoldering dispute over the management of the pine industry in Fiji. Pine planting began in Fiji in the late 1950s and early 1960s. By 1979 about 28,000 hectares were under pine, especially in western Viti Levu. It was projected that by 1986 the total would be 62,039 hectares.[74] During the previous decade, landowners had received $20 million from contract payment, royalties, and land rent and expected twice that amount by 1990.[75] With a rapid expansion in the pine plantation schemes and the growing complexity of the entire operation, the government established the Fiji Pine Commission, with a considerable amount of bilateral development assistance, to "facilitate and develop an industry based on the growing, harvesting, processing and marketing of pine and other species of trees grown in Fiji."[76] The other major "partners" in the industry were the landowners, assisted by the Fiji Department of Forestry. Close cooperation between the landowners *(mataqali)* and the Fiji Pine Commission was essential for the successful operation of the industry.

To harvest the pine and to develop the overall export industry, the Fiji Pine Commission invited proposals from several companies. Four serious ones were received from British Petroleum (South-West Pacific) Limited, the New Zealand–based M. K. Hunt Foundation, Shell/New Zealand Forest Products, and an American company, United Marketing Corporation. The commission accepted the British Petroleum proposal, which it said was flexible and sound and promised an equitable distribution of profits.[77] The landowners, however, favored the United Marketing Corporation's proposal because, they said, it offered them equal partnership in the logging industry.[78] The commission refused to yield to the landowners' pressure. The government declared the United Marketing Corporation's head, Paul Sandblom, a man with a criminal record of conviction for fraud, a prohibited immigrant. Western Fijians interpreted the government's intervention as another instance of interference in their right to control their resources. The battle lines were drawn, abrading the already cold relations between Gavidi and Mara.

The pine issue also brought into sharper relief long-standing western Fijian resentment at their peripheral treatment in the Mara administration. Westerners drew attention to the paucity of western Fijians in high positions in the civil service, provincial administration, and statutory bodies, a disparity that seemed especially glaring in the light of their overall contribution to the economy. The ebullient Tui Nadi, Ratu Napolioni Dawai, resigned from the Alliance Party, of which he had long been a member, when the government decided to allocate $435,868 to reconstruct and renovate certain historic sites in Bau. That money, Ratu Napolioni said, should have been used to meet the pressing needs of western Fijians —education, water supply, roads, and dormitories for schoolchildren from outer islands.[79] It did not help matters when some members of the Great Council of Chiefs vilified Napolioni as a "silly sub-chief."

Capitalizing on the pine controversy and other expressions of western Fijian discontent, Gavidi launched his WUF on 17 July 1981 in the presence of some six hundred supporters and twenty ranking chiefs from the western division.[80] Among the goals of the party were to

protect and encourage the unity of western Fijians,
protect the interests of landowners and defend their rights to develop their
     resources according to their aspirations,
seek changes in the Ministry for Fijian Affairs and Rural Development to
     improve the lives of western Fijians,
improve educational facilities for western Fijians and provide them with
     opportunities in commercial and industrial enterprises, and
fight for the freedom of association and religious expression of Fijians in
     the west and elect representatives to parliament.

At first, Gavidi and the WUF alone wanted to contest the 1982 elections. Faced with biting denunciation by the Alliance, however,—Mara called the WUF a "disruptive" force that preached "ridiculous political ideologies" for selfish gain[81]—and recognizing the desirability of expanding its base beyond western regional themes, the WUF offered to form a coalition with the Alliance's old opponent, the NFP. Reddy seized on the offer because the WUF promised to deliver a swelling pool of dependable Fijian support without the additional burden and expenditure of having to recruit it. There were parallels here with late 1968, after Isikeli Nadalo and Apisai Tora had joined forces with the NFP. The coalition, launched on 11 January 1982, was described as a "partnership of equals" in which each party "is to maintain its independent identity and objectives."[82]

The NFP-WUF coalition energized an election campaign that revolved around issues of political equality, balanced regional development, and the fair distribution of national income.[83] The election would not be remembered today but for an intriguing episode at the tail end of the campaign. This was the leakage on an Australian television program, "Four Corners," of a privately commissioned economic report by Mahendra Motibhai Patel, Mara's business partner, confidant, and a high Alliance Party functionary. Entitled "Report of Consultants to the Prime Minister of Fiji on the Economic and Political Outlook and Options for Strategy and Political Organization," it was prepared by Australian business consultant Alan Carroll, assisted by Thailand-based academic consultant Jeffery Race, Melbourne market researcher Rosemary Gillespie, and Geoff Allen, director of the Australian Industries Development Association.[84] The Australian people's chief interest in the program lay in the alleged misuse of Australian aid money for political purposes by the Alliance Party, specifically the role of aid-funded Clive Speed, who was accused of helping the Alliance's media campaign.

For the people of Fiji, however, the program's main interest lay in the tactics that the consultants recommended to the Alliance to win the election. To prevent slippage of Fijian communal support, the consultants advised bribery (regarding Fijian Nationalist Party leader Butadroka: "Either buy off or take him out of the running") and accelerations of impending prosecutions (regarding Gavidi: "Since he is going to jail anyway, best to pile all effort on and accelerate prosecutions so he cannot run"). "Combine divide and rule with stroking," the report suggested; "capitalize on the existing splits and weaknesses of the NFP"; obtain "Fijian support by getting chiefs on the ticket"; "get credit for pro-Fijian stance currently without jeopardizing expansion of Indian support"; and let dropouts from the cabinet leave happy or "make sure they understand they will be sorry if they challenge the Alliance (get something on them)".

The effect of the disclosures was sensational, made even more so when an exasperated and visibly angry Mara walked off during a tough interview, and when an evidently uncomfortable Mahendra Patel was con-

fronted with evidence (his own signature) contradicting his denial of any
involvement. The NFP campaign officials distributed hundreds of copies
of the television tape throughout the country. The issues it raised were
refuted not by evidence but by anger. Mara called the tape's introduction,
which identified contemporary Fijian leaders as descendants of chiefs who
"clubbed and ate their way to power," a gross insult to high chiefs personally and to the Fijian people as a whole.[85] Calls went up for ethnic Fijian
solidarity and support of traditional identity. Those who had participated
in the program would "not be forgotten or forgiven," said Ratu Mara,
and he promised to resign if his party did not win at least thirty seats.

The final result was a close victory for the Alliance, which got twenty-
eight seats to the NFP-WUF's twenty-four; Mara remained leader of his
party. The pattern of ethnic voting continued, with nearly 84 percent of
Fijians and Indo-Fijians voting for "their" parties, though in the national
seats, more Fijians voted for the coalition, which was a harbinger of things
to come in 1987. That the NFP had come back from the brink of complete
collapse in 1977 to being so close to capturing power caused great anxiety
to the Alliance. Both Reddy and Gavidi had emerged from the election
campaign with enhanced national reputations. Their victory elicited
expected as well as unexpected responses. In Fijian villages in western Viti
Levu, some landowners threatened to evict Indo-Fijian tenants for "not
fulfilling pledges to vote for the Alliance," and Ratu Kaliova Mataitoga,
the paramount chief of Sabeto, said angrily that as the Indo-Fijian tenants
"are the ones who opposed us, I will have them no more."[86] There were
isolated threats and physical harassments in remote rural areas, too.

Of all the postelection traumas, none was more shocking than Ratu
Mara's allegation in a postelection Sydney interview with his long-time
friend, former *Pacific Islands Monthly* publisher Stuart Inder, that the NFP-
WUF coalition had received $1 million from the Russians through sources
including the Fiji-based Indian High Commission, funds that originated
in Canada, Australia, the Middle-East, and India. Mara alleged that the
retired husband of the Indian high commissioner to Fiji, Mrs. Soonu
Kochar, had played a role in the transaction, and some Fijian candidates
had been paid as much as $10,000 to stand against Alliance candidates.
Why would the Russians aid the NFP? Mara explained: "Russia wants
me out because it believes it has been my influence that has successfully
blocked Russian incursions into the Pacific Islands. With me gone, they
think they can pick off the island states separately and gain a permanent
foothold in the Pacific."[87] (Two years later, in another foreign city, Honolulu, Mara would talk of opening Fiji ports to Soviet vessels in the manner
of Kiribati[88]: such were the processes of political transformation in Fiji.)

These allegations of foreign involvement in Fijian affairs caught both
the opponents and the supporters of Mara by surprise. The NFP
denounced the allegations as "false and baseless." Said Reddy caustically:

"The Prime Minister very much needed to refurbish his image, particularly before the Australian people, and what better tactic than to raise the bogey of Russian help to the NFP to obscure the seriousness of foreign involvement in Fiji's general elections?"[89] A subsequent Royal Commission of Enquiry headed by a retired New Zealand judge, Sir John White, cleared the NFP of any involvement in the sordid affair altogether.[90] The inquiry itself, however, was frustrated by Mara's refusal to divulge critical information, which he allegedly had in his possession, on the grounds of national security. The overwhelming impression in Fiji was, and remains, that Mara had no evidence and that the allegations had been made to discredit a party that had come close to dislodging him from power. Discrediting the NFP with the taint of a Soviet connection could, conceivably, bring dissident Fijians back into the Alliance fold. When the new parliament met in December 1982, Mara once again renewed a call for a government of national unity—with the very party that he had just accused of collaborating with the Russians to unseat him from power! Perhaps, though, he was not serious about the prospect. "I was flying a kite," he said, "and waiting to see who will bring it down."[91] His stature was not enhanced by the role he had played in the whole episode, and among the Indo-Fijians, Mara's reputation reached a very low point, to a degree that he probably did not realize.

The bitterness of some Fijian chiefs at the conduct, outcome, and implications of the general election was given further expression when the Senate met in September. The Great Council of Chiefs' nominee, Senator Ratu Tevita Vakalalabure, came perilously close to speaking in the threatening manner popularized by Sakiasi Butadroka, warning that "blood will flow" if the Indo-Fijians did not "cling" to the Fijians. He would have rallied his people to start fighting, he said, if he had seen the "Four Corners" program before the elections. "Any race that does not bear along with the Fijians can pack up house and go."[92] Another Fijian senator, Inoke Tabua from Lau, called for the deportation of NFP leaders who had supposedly insulted Fijian chiefs during the election, adding that there would have been "trouble" if the Alliance had lost the election.[93] He would be one of the leading organizers of the demonstrations against the Labour coalition in 1987.

The NFP condemned these attacks,[94] but the Alliance remained silent in the face of such threatening remarks from some of its own luminaries. The party's silence, the *Fiji Sun* editorialized, "can only be described as tacit approval,"[95] which it probably was. Much worse was to come when the Great Council of Chiefs met at the historic island of Bau in November 1982. Opened for the first time in the century-old existence of the council by a reigning monarch, Queen Elizabeth II, the meeting was full of cultural and political symbolism. With the events of the previous election fresh in the minds of the gathered Fijians, speaker after speaker rose to great heights of racial rhetoric. The tone was set by Ratu Penaia Ganilau, minister of Fijian Affairs and, as such, the chair of the council. Ganilau was a high chief in the conservative mold. He was upset at the unpredictability of the ballot box and the cut-and-thrust of debate that electoral politics generated. Unable to control himself, he wept at the "criticism" heaped on "chiefs" during the campaign. He was particularly upset at the criticism of chiefs by the *lewenivanua* 'commoners'. He urged Fijian unity under chiefly leadership. "Our culture and our way of listening to each other, as is our custom, is the cornerstone of our Fijian way of life," he said. "The foreigners know that this is the bond that ties us together and if that is broken, they would have their wish to rule."[96] Tears flowed as freely as bowls of *yaqona*. It was an emotional moment of unprecedented intensity.

At the end of the meeting, a number of resolutions were passed. Among them, the council called for the assertion of Fijian paramountcy in Fiji's body politic. At least 75 percent of the seats in parliament should be reserved for Fijians, along with the offices of prime minister and governor-general. In tone and substance, these echoed Butadroka's sentiment of a decade earlier, underlining the point that the substance of Butadroka's ideas, if not necessarily his methods, were widely shared among the chiefs, almost all of whom were members of the Alliance Party.

Perhaps more astounding than the resolutions themselves was the Alliance leadership's response to them. Only a handful of cabinet ministers at the meeting, such as Semesa Sikivou, voted against them. Others remained silent and refrained from voting altogether. Among them was Ratu Mara, the man who was counted on to speak out strongly against the rising tide of racist rhetoric.[97] When he was subsequently asked by the press for a comment, he fell back on an expedient distinction. He was at the meeting not in his capacity as a politician, he said, but as a high chief and "in no way obligated to his political party to say what he did or said in the Council."[98] He observed with obvious irritation that he was not obligated to anybody to defend his stance at the meeting. He did, however, call the motions a "waste of time."[99]

Abstaining at the meeting made good political sense. To survive, he had to take into account the views of Fijian chiefs, his natural constituency. Such was the arithmetic of communal politics. By abstaining, Mara did not alienate the Fijian people and signaled to the Indo-Fijians that it was he and other abstainers who stood between them and the precipice. Be that as it may, his standing as a multiracial leader appeared to be tainted, especially in the Indo-Fijian community. By the 1980s, however, an increasingly aloof and seemingly invincible Mara was no longer overmuch concerned with his image within the country. He was looking beyond the reef to the larger regional and international stage on which to make his mark. The pendulum could not have swung farther from the harmonious atmosphere of 1970 to the bitter racial rhetoric of 1980.

1982–1987: Consolidation and Fragmentation

The racially charged atmosphere generated by the 1982 election pervaded political discourse in Fiji for a long time. Having been close to defeat, the Alliance realized the need for quick and concerted action to regain the upper hand. To achieve this, it embarked on a two-pronged strategy: fragment the opposition and consolidate support among the ethnic Fijians. In the end, however, both these strategies backfired in ways that the party strategists had not anticipated, laying the foundations of the greatest political crisis Fiji would face in the twentieth century.

Jai Ram Reddy, the architect of the NFP-WUF coalition and leader of the NFP retreat from the pit of self-destruction, was an early target. The Alliance had sized him up as an emotional man who could be provoked to commit a strategic blunder in a display of temper. No sooner had the new parliament opened than the Alliance's verbal missiles began to fly in his direction, leading inevitably to heated exchanges with an admittedly partisan Speaker, Tomasi Vakatora, who had been elected unilaterally by the Alliance rather than with the bipartisan support characteristic of the Westminster convention.[100] After one such heated exchange, Reddy walked out of parliament in December 1983 and promised not to return until Vakatora had been removed from the Speaker's chair. For obvious reasons, the Alliance would not allow that to happen, and Reddy eventually resigned from parliament in April 1984.[101] Reddy's refusal, even under unanimous pressure from the party's working committee, to reconsider his "irrevocable decision" led, after a short-lived NFP boycott of parliament, to Koya's return as the opposition leader.

The Alliance was elated at Reddy's departure from parliament, the key thorn in its sensitive side who could not be dismissed or manipulated. Koya, it knew, was a more predictable opponent. This was a pyrrhic victory for the Alliance. Unfettered by parliamentary and party responsibilities, and with his stature in the Indo-Fijian community enhanced by his principled decision not to return to parliament, Reddy spent the next two years quietly consolidating his constituency and building bridges with the Alliance's opponents. He told his colleagues that he had discarded his policy of moderation because it had been "sadly ineffective."[102] The Alliance had won a small victory, but Reddy would orchestrate a larger electoral triumph for his party.

Siddiq Koya's return as the leader of the opposition did not help the Alliance. Piqued at his narrow victory for the post over his archrival, Irene Jai Narayan, and keen to settle old scores and place loyalists in key party positions, Koya was back in his old form as a confrontational leader perennially at the center of controversy, and thriving on it. His performance both inside and outside the House alienated many supporters and began to revive memories of the Flower-Dove factionalism of the 1970s. Times had changed, however, and Koya's old style of factional politics and chest-thumping rhetoric reminiscent of the 1960s sounded incongruent in the 1980s. In December 1985, three NFP parliamentarians resigned from the party altogether (Irene Jai Narayan, Satendra Nandan, and H. M. Lodhia), and others refused shadow portfolios under Koya's leadership. Seven Fijian and general elector members of the NFP-WUF Parliamentary Board threatened to resign unless Koya improved his performance.[103]

The sense of disarray was palpable. Vijendra Kumar, *Fiji Times* editor writing in *Pacific Islands Monthly,* noted: "The continual bickering and infighting in the NFP, and the poor performance of Mr Koya in his leadership role, have disenchanted many party followers. The NFP is in a state of disarray and decadence and unless it cleans its house, it is doomed to die."[104] Robert Keith-Reid, a long-time local political commentator, was even more blunt in placing the blame on Koya's doorstep: "In the ten months since he took over from Mr Reddy, Mr Koya has arrived at a point at which all the work of reconstruction achieved by the NFP since the shambles of 1977 has been undone. Half way through the life of the present parliament, the Opposition is a 'shattered force'."[105] Disillusioned with such public display of ineptitude and incompetence—and public ridicule for a political party that had once been in the vanguard of Fiji politics —long-time party faithfuls began looking for other alternatives. The Alliance Party was not counted among them.

The second Alliance strategy for consolidating its power was to shore up its position in Fijian society, and this it did in a concerted fashion. An attempt was made once again to gather under the Alliance umbrella the Fijian communal flock that had gone astray. Ratu Mara himself made a highly significant, bridge-building trip to western Viti Levu in February 1986. In one critical meeting at the home of Geoffrey Reid, managing director of the Emperor Gold Mining Company at Vatukoula, he met Tui Ba from Nailaga, Tui Ba from Sorokaba, Tui Navitilevu from Rakiraki, Tui Tavua, Tui Magadro, and Tui Yakete from the highlands to discuss ways of consolidating Fijian support.[106] In July 1986, some of the founding members of the WUF, by then defunct, were beginning to rejoin the Alliance. One such delegation was led by Tui Nacolo, Ratu Isei Vosailagi.[107] From the other side of the political spectrum, a concerted effort was made to lure back members of the Fijian Nationalist Party, with successful results. The dock workers' leader Taniela "Big Dan" Veitata was enticed with the promise of a blue-ribbon Fijian communal seat, along with lesser luminaries like the former successful Fijian Nationalist Party strategist Alivereti Suinika.[108]

At the same time, efforts were made to reinforce the traditional chiefly order in Fijian villages. To achieve this, the Alliance commissioned (in 1984) and then implemented a special report that recommended the reintroduction of aspects of the old Fijian administration system discarded in 1966, including official recognition of, and remuneration for, the *tūraga ni koro* 'village head', additional funds to the *tikina* 'provincial' councils, incorporation of the Fijian legal system at provincial and district levels into the Western judicial system, and the gradual attempt to make the Fijian provincial administrative system the sole basis of local government administration in the country.[109]

Such efforts to turn the clock back met with little success because the pattern of life, even in the remotest villages, had altered considerably over decades of rapid social and economic change. The adoption of imported tools and equipment increased individual productivity and lessened the need for communal efforts of earlier times. The monetization of the village economy emphasized the primacy of the nuclear family over the communal group. The increasing importance of cash crops—banana, ginger, sugar cane—and growing links to urban centers facilitated by improved communication emphasized the need for individual initiative and enterprise against traditional ways of doing things. Changes in land-use patterns and the tendency toward intra-*mataqali* leasing of land also promised new directions. R. G. Ward remarked perceptively that "the combined introduction of new skills, new technology and money have weakened the functional cement which binds the Fijian village society. This does not mean that the structure has collapsed, or will do so in the near future. It does mean the risk of disintegration exists if other factors shake the edifice."[110] Nevertheless, efforts to reimpose traditional structures and institutions on a rapidly changing society continued.

Together with the move toward restrengthening traditional social structures, the government made attempts to channel more public resources toward Fijian society, particularly in the direction of the eastern maritime provinces. None of the government's efforts was more marked by controversy than its pro-Fijian educational policies. Again, the main beneficiaries were the favored provinces of eastern Fiji. The leader of the government's effort here was Ahmed Ali, minister of education, the author of the ill-conceived government-of-national-unity proposals. Ali was a newcomer to national politics, elected to parliament from the almost exclusively Fijian Lau-Cakaudrove Fijian national seat as Ratu Mara's running mate. Eager to seize the agenda and establish credibility with his political constituency, Ali embarked on a series of measures. Among other things, he moved away from the past practice of "automatic absorption" of newly graduated (mostly Indo-Fijian) teachers into the teaching profession, to the Volunteer Service Scheme, under which the government agreed to pay only a part of the newly hired teachers' salaries—F$3,000—and the (mainly Indo-Fijian) committee-run schools in rural areas were expected to meet other costs such as housing.[111]

The government wanted to have it both ways: although it would not give full employment to the graduates, it reserved the right to call on the services of those it had trained.[112] This arrangement could continue for up to two years before permanent positions became available. The graduates accused the government of reneging on its promise of employment and dramatized their anger by staging hunger strikes in Suva. Both the Fiji Teachers' Union (Indo-Fijian) and the Fijian Teachers' Association (Fijian) accused the minister of acting in a high-handed manner, without any consultation with them. His actions, they said, had "deliberately and consciously created an atmosphere of instability among teachers by publicly threatening them with redundancies, termination of services and labelling them lazy."[113]

Similar protests met the government's other education initiatives such as efforts to open up Suva's premier elementary schools, such as Vieuto and Samabula, to children from middle class Fijian families. The political calculations that underlay this policy were evident, but Ali argued that his main purpose was to break up Fiji's communally oriented, largely monoracial school system. Many teachers thought this move premature, arguing that schoolchildren should be well grounded in their own cultural and social traditions before being hurled into the larger culturally complex world of multiracial Fiji. Children were being asked to cross barriers and set an example of multiracialism that adults had not been able to achieve for more than a century. The strongest opposition came from the Fijian Teachers Association, which complained to Mara that the policy of integration "was not in the interest of developing Fijian education, the preservation of Fijian culture and language and developing Fijian cultural values."[114]

It was not the idea so much as the brazenly dictatorial manner in which these decisions had been made and implemented which alienated the teachers. Fijian educator Tupeni Baba, then at the University of the South Pacific, wrote that "at no time in [our] history have we experienced as much politicization of education as we are experiencing now and if this is allowed to continue, it will undermine the development of professionalism of teachers, educators, educational administrators and will lay open the schools to political abuse."[115] The depth of the teachers' resentment against the Ministry of Education was so great that it enabled the two racially based teachers' organizations to submerge their internal differences and cooperate in opposition to the ministry's actions. Realizing the serious damage that Ali had done, Mara relegated him to the junior Ministry of Information, but the legacy of bitterness and frustration lingered long after he had left, planting the seeds of further political action.

A similar confrontational and unilateral approach was adopted by the government in its handling of the economic crisis facing the country. In the late 1970s and early 1980s, the annual growth rate of the Fijian economy fluctuated widely, registering a 9.6 percent real growth in the gross domestic product in 1979 and negative growth in 1981, the average for the period 1979–1981 being 1.9 percent per year.[116] This was in marked contrast to the situation in the early 1970s (1971–1977), when Fiji's annual gross domestic product recorded a healthy average growth rate of 5 percent.[117] A succession of hurricanes and droughts, causing damage estimated in the millions, devastated the economy. Sugar production declined in 1983 by an alarming 46 percent, accompanied by a sharp drop in the world sugar price (25 percent since 1980). To meet emergencies, funds earmarked for public expenditure (7 percent of the 1985 budget) had to be diverted for relief and rehabilitation work. Compounding matters was a predicted low rate of economic growth and a rising external debt—which had increased at an average rate of 21 percent from F$194 million in 1980 to F$399 million in 1984.[118] Adding to these problems was a burgeoning civil service salary arising in part from the implementation of the Nicol-Hurst report on the reshaping of the pay scale for the seventeen-thousand-member civil service.

The enormity of the problems confronting Fiji was evident enough, but what became an issue was the way in which the government intended to deal with them. It proposed a year's wage freeze beginning in November 1984. This measure, the government argued, would save about F$36 million, which could then be used for job-creating projects in the agricultural sector, especially in such areas as rice farming, cocoa projects, forest replanting, and fishery-related construction projects. More money could be given to such organizations as the Fiji Electricity Authority, the Fiji Development Bank, the Housing Authority, and the National Marketing Authority, all of which had plans in hand for job-creating projects. The savings from the wage freeze would encourage businesses to expand and invest. Exports from Fiji would be boosted and Fiji's foreign reserves kept at a healthy level.[119]

In making this decision, the government bypassed the Tripartite Forum. This body, composed of the Fiji Trades Union Congress, Fiji Employers' Consultative Association, and representatives of the government, had been formed in 1976 to reach "a common understanding [of issues] which affect the national interest such as industrial relations, job creation, greater flow of investment and general social and economic development of the country." Coming immediately after the controversy generated by the Ministry of Education, this unilateral decision was widely perceived as an attempt to weaken the trade union movement in Fiji. The government complained that its arguments favoring a wage freeze "seemed to fall on deaf ears," and it could not abdicate or ignore its responsibilities "just because a policy may not be popular."[120]

Many trade union leaders suspected that the wage freeze was an act of collusion between the political and the business elite to keep wages down. They called the freeze unfair because the cuts would affect the lives and welfare of the lowest income families. As Wadan Narsey, an economics lecturer at the University of the South Pacific, pointed out, "The net effect is that the wages and salaries freeze means a transfer of employees' savings to the employers, regardless of whether the employers will invest the extra savings." Narsey questioned the logic of asking people to sacrifice their meager income to improve the balance of payments: "One must not kill the patient to cure the disease."[121] And he questioned the government's unquestioning acceptance of the International Monetary Fund's assertion —which was used, in part, to justify the wage freeze in the first place—that the Fiji salaries were too high by 15 percent. Too high compared with what? he asked, especially since an extremely diverse group of workers was included, ranging from well-paid top civil servants to garment factory workers living a wretched existence.

A number of other decisions conveyed the distinct sense that the Alliance had become a party grown too accustomed to power. Important policy decisions, such as revoking the antinuclear policy and committing troops to the United Nations peacekeeping forces in the Middle East, were taken by the cabinet without parliamentary discussion or debate. Once-regular prime ministerial press conferences became a rare event. Whispers of corruption became louder, and reached as high as Mara himself, something that would have been unthinkable in the 1970s. His family-owned property, Marella House, had been rented to the Education Department for F$124,051, higher than the F$97,000 recommended by the government valuer. Mara's business empire, which reached into agriculture, commerce, and tourism, came in for scrutiny.[122] What had happened to the Hurricane Relief Funds directly under the prime minister's control? Were immigration and naturalization rules bypassed for certain favored people? How was it that certain prominent and well-connected people were given the opportunity to purchase choice Crown lands in the heart of Suva? The list continues. As local journalist Keith-Reid noted in 1985, the Alliance "shows all the bad old signs of sliding—if it hasn't already slid—back into that dangerous state of arrogant complacency."[123]

Unfortunately for the Alliance, this slide came at a time when the Fiji trade union movement, already antagonized by the government's various unilaterally imposed policies, was coming into its own. In the early 1980s, some forty-six trade unions were registered in Fiji with 42,000 unionized employees. The total Fiji labor force had increased from 176,322 in 1976 to 237,550 in 1986, an annual increase of 3.1 percent.[124] The Fiji Trades Union Congress threatened a national strike to protest the imposition of the wage freeze. In response, Mara threatened to declare a state of national emergency and to deploy troops to run the essential services. The possibility of violent confrontation led to rising talk about forming a labor party. Former pro-Alliance trade union leader James Raman commented bitterly on the "display of non-accommodating and non-compromising attitude by the Government right from the Prime Minister down." They were behaving in a "brute and unmitigated manner to suppress the unions," he said. Addressing the biennial conference of the Fiji Trades Union Congress, Raman suggested that "the trade union movement must find a means of cushioning itself from the onslaught if it is to save itself from the mounting attack which would lead to eventual destruction of everything that the trade unions have built through several years of sacrifice."[125] He urged his listeners to think seriously about forming a party of their own, a labor party that would protect their interests.

The Dragon
Father Tom Rouse

Fiji is a waiting land
   (not the normal waits of a traveller)
Its people wait
For a time yet to come
When the pieces and parts
Of the past meet with
   the present.

Fiji farmers wait for
   the rain
   a better price
   the cane train

Workers wait for
   their raises
   strikes to end
   sometimes for
   work itself

Civil servants wait for
   retirement,
   begun on the job
   long before its time.

Children can't wait
   for a time
When learning has use
Teenagers can't sit
   forever,
   forever young
Waiting for something
   that never happens.

Midst the gentle hills
Of a land at peace
A dragon stirs.

Fiji Labour Party, Coalition, and Campaign

Three months later, in March 1985, the powerful Fiji Public Servants' Association chose that path.[126] Led by its secretary, Mahendra Chaudhary, it amended its constitution by 2,914 votes to 326 to enable it to "associate itself with any organization in pursuit of workers' rights." The Fiji Labour Party (FLP) was formally launched on 6 July 1985. Its inaugural president was a fifty-year old retired community health specialist, Dr. Timoci Uluivuda Bavadra, and its general secretary a former high school principal, Krishna Datt. Born at Viseisei near the western sugar town of Lautoka and educated at the elite Queen Victoria School, Bavadra became a career civil servant, though he had also briefly worked in the Solomons. He was also the president of the Fiji Public Servants' Association. Datt, a New Zealand-trained high school teacher and principal, was the president of the Fiji Teachers' Union.

Calling itself "democratic socialist" in orientation, the FLP advocated promoting social justice, balanced economic development, and regional equalities in Fiji; reforming such institutions as the Native Land Trust Board in consultation with the landowners and others; encouraging public ownership of selected ventures such as the bus industry; nationalizing the gold mine industry; and improving the strained structure of industrial relations.[127] In short, the FLP proposed new visions and new directions to take Fiji away from the policies of communalism and ethnic separatism that had become a way of life under the Alliance.

The timing of the launching could not have been better. In the mid-1960s, a "democratic socialist" Fiji Labour Party had been launched, but it had died a quiet, unnoticed death. Now the situation had changed. The NFP was in disarray, and many of its once ardent supporters, disillusioned by years of divisiveness among its top leaders, were looking for other alternatives. The FLP provided one. It also provided a somewhat reluctant welcome to some of the incumbent NFP parliamentarians. Among those who made the switch were Satendra Nandan and members of the anti-Koya NFP Youth Wing. Others who showed interest were rejected as opportunists jumping a sinking NFP ship, as in the case of Irene Jai Narayan, who soon made an even bigger leap into the lap of her once bitter opponent, the Alliance Party, and later, even more incredibly, into the arms of procoup supporters. The FLP was likewise an attractive alternative for many urban working class Fijians, disenchanted with the Alliance leadership and policies, and caught in the grips of difficult economic circumstances caused by increasing inflation and unemployment. For them, the FLP's policies held the promise of a way to a better world.

The Alliance initially dismissed the new party, and, as if to emphasize its point, withdrew its long-standing recognition of the Fiji Trades Union Congress as sole representative of the trade unions in Fiji. By doing this, however, the Alliance played into the hands of the FLP and helped to strengthen its appeal. The FLP won the Suva City Council elections in 1986, winning eight of the twenty seats and 39 percent of the votes, and came close to capturing the Ba Indian National seat left vacant by Sir Vijay Singh's resignation to head the newly formed Sugar Cane Growers' Council.

Heady with success, the FLP leadership was at first reluctant to consider contesting the forthcoming 1987 general elections in coalition with other parties. The Alliance was obviously out, and so also in the beginning was the NFP, which the FLP manifesto had castigated as a party "that represents the interests of a handful of businessmen and lawyers, often at the expense of those they claim to represent."[128] The younger, more ideologically minded supporters of the party argued that the FLP should remain true to its founding principles and not taint itself by joining forces with parties with dissimilar philosophies, but the Labour strategists were realists. They knew that without a coalition, they would not be able to dislodge the Alliance.[129] This had been one powerful lesson of the Ba by-election, where, in a three-way contest, the Alliance had defeated both Federation and Labour. In that contest, the FLP had won 36.4 percent of the votes to the Alliance's 37.5 percent and the NFP's 23.3 percent. The Labour leaders realized that as an essentially urban-based party, they would need to expand their base to rural areas to have any chance of significant success at the national level. The NFP could provide that crucial link.

The NFP, too, knew that contesting the election alone would be suicidal. The party had lost its vitality. Its younger, better educated parliamentarians had either joined the FLP or were yearning for a welcome there. Many of the NFP's rank and file had already thrown their weight behind the FLP. The results of the by-election warned the leaders that going it alone would result in a humiliating defeat. As a consequence of this thinking, the FLP softened its anti-NFP tirade. Said a suddenly pragmatic Bavadra: "When we looked at the aims and objectives of the Labour Party and the NFP, there wasn't much difference. While we basically represented the workers, the NFP no doubt represented the farmers. There was one aim and that was the betterment of labour conditions and wages."[130] Negotiations between the two parties began, with Reddy representing the NFP and Bavadra, Tupeni Baba, and Chaudhary representing the FLP.[131] After several months of intense, confidential discussions, a coalition agreement was concluded.

The terms of the arrangement were never made public, nor was a public explanation given for establishing the Coalition, something that angered die-hard followers in both camps.[132] However, several things soon became clear. One was a seat-sharing formula according to which the NFP agreed to give the FLP six of its twelve blue-ribbon communal seats as well as half of the winnable Indo-Fijian and Fijian national seats. This formula enabled the FLP to project itself into the hitherto inaccessible rural areas, and the NFP was spared the almost certain humiliation of losing its traditional ironclad grip on the communal seats to the FLP's Indo-Fijian candidates. Another notable feature was the acceptance by the predominantly Indo-Fijian-based NFP of an ethnic Fijian, from another party, as the leader of the Coalition. This was both a tacit acknowledgment of weakness by the NFP and a concession to the nonethnic philosophy of the Coalition. It also represented a significant shift in Indo-Fijian public opinion, which only a decade earlier had rejected a Fijian leader for the party (Ratu Julian Toganivalu).[133] The reality of communal politics in Fiji was that an Indo-Fijian prime minister would not be acceptable to the majority of Fijians; for the NFP to achieve any measure of political power, a coalition with another party with a Fijian leader and a political philosophy broadly compatible with its own was the only route to more equitable power sharing at the national level.[134] The third outcome of the coalition arrangement was the formulation of a compromise manifesto that whittled down some of the FLP's radical-sounding economic policies, such as encouraging worker participation in the management of industry and the nationalization of selected industries. Finally, both parties agreed to present a combined fresh slate of candidates. A start was made by endorsing only five of the twenty-two incumbent opposition parliamentarians.

The Labour Coalition was not the only coalition to contest the 1987 elections. Another consisted of a faction of the NFP that was aligned with the WUF, the NFP's 1982 election partner. This coalition was the handiwork of Shardha Nand, deposed secretary of the NFP, and other politicians discarded by the Labour Coalition's candidate selection committee, including Siddiq Koya. These Indo-Fijian politicians presented themselves as the only true champions of their community's interests, which, they said, had been jeopardized by having a Fijian (Bavadra) as the leader of the Coalition. The WUF was a reluctant partner in the Coalition. Gavidi was busy battling his irate creditors in court rather than fighting political opponents in the election. Since 1982 the party had become a spent force. The policies for harvesting pine, the dispute about which had led to the formation of the party, was now a nonissue, and many of its western Fijian members had been enticed back into the Alliance fold. The WUF had lost credibility with many NFP leaders because of its withdrawal from the royal commission investigating Mara's allegations about the original NFP-WUF coalition receiving Russian money to defeat the Alliance in the 1982 elections.[135] The NFP-WUF's campaign began promisingly, but its prospects vanished when Koya and others withdrew, ostensibly to avoid being tainted with the spoiler's role. Those who did not suffered badly at the polls.

Of all the political parties, the Fijian Nationalist Party (FNP) had the lowest profile in the 1987 campaign. It maintained its anti–Indo-Fijian stance while advocating a platform designed to promote Fijian interests.[136] The party proposed the "thinning out" of Indo-Fijians through an active policy of encouraging migration, to be funded by the British government, which had introduced Indians into Fiji in the first place. The FNP made an issue of the paucity of Fijians in commercial and industrial sectors, which it saw as a direct result of a conspiracy by European and Indo-Fijian members of the business community. It demanded an exclusively indigenous Fijian parliament through revision of the 1970 constitution and absolute Fijian control of the political process to promote Fijian social and economic progress. In the end, however, while there was personal support and sympathy for Butadroka, who won 37.9 percent of the Fijian communal votes, an increase of 7.3 percent over the 1982 figures, the FNP failed to recapture its old ground, though its candidates drew sufficient Fijian support in marginal seats to affect the overall outcome.

The 1987 election was, then, principally a contest between the Alliance and the NFP-FLP Coalition. For its part, the Alliance was confident, well-funded, and dismissive about the impact of the Coalition. One typical campaign advertisement ran: "The opposition factions are fragmented and quarrelling among themselves. Their policies are confused and shift constantly as one group or would-be leader gains ascendancy. Principles are proclaimed as fundamental and are then dropped as pressures are applied by vested interests, or for political expediency." The Alliance, on the other hand, presented itself as the very model of stability, "united in purpose, strong and fully accepted leadership, clear and consistent policies, and a political philosophy with values that have been proved by experience."[137] The Coalition's commitment to democratic socialism was portrayed as a real threat to the ownership of Fijian land and to Fijian cultural values generally.[138] The visit of some Coalition trade union leaders to Moscow (though some goverment ministers had been there, too) was presented as proof enough of the Coalition's sinister designs.

In addition to overconfidence, the Alliance made some strategic miscalculations. One of them was giving space to discarded NFP politicians such as Irene Jai Narayan. The former president of the NFP had joined the Alliance more out of opportunism than a genuine change of heart or political ideology. She was candid about her motivations and the reasons for the switch: "Let's face it, whether one likes it or not, the Alliance will remain in power for a long time"[139]; she wanted to be on the winning side. The Alliance severely overestimated her personal appeal. It placed her in a do-or-die Suva national constituency alongside the Fijian national candidate, Ratu David Toganivalu, which was a serious mistake. The Alliance lost both seats. Another miscalculation was the expectation, no doubt encouraged by the victory in the Ba by-elections, that the party would be able, at long last, to win an Indo-Fijian communal seat. This led Mara to concentrate an inordinate amount of time in the western division, much to the frustration of Alliance candidates, such as Toganivalu, in marginal constituencies in southeast Viti Levu.

The Coalition entered the campaign as a distinct underdog. It was new and inexperienced, underfunded, and comparatively disorganized, unable to match the Alliance in the media war. Its candidates ran their largely self-financed campaigns in pocket meetings in their own constituencies. But the Coalition's message was clear. It charged the Mara administration with abuse of power and reminded the electorate of the mounting economic difficulties for low-income families. In his concluding campaign speech, Bavadra said, "Wage and salary earners remember their extreme hardships and insecurities; parents remember the increased bus fares; squatters remember physical removal and neglect; teachers remember Dr Ahmed Ali's reign of terror in the Ministry of Education; students remember the pain of their hunger strike; the *taukei* remember that most of Fijian development money goes to a few provinces."[140] For its part, the Coalition promised a clean and compassionate government. Its election theme, "time for a change," caught the mood of the electorate as the campaign concluded.

Several features were unique to the 1987 campaign. Undoubtedly the most important of these was that for the first time in Fiji's modern political history, the leaders of the main political parties were Fijians, Mara heading the Alliance and Bavadra leading the Coalition. The contrast between the styles and personalities of the two leaders was marked. As usual, Mara remained aloof and confident of victory. The Alliance expected to win at least thirty of the fifty-two seats in parliament. In contrast to Mara, Bavadra was a newcomer to national politics and not known outside the trade union movement. However, as the campaign progressed, his unassuming character, his common touch and openness projected an image of a compassionate man who could be trusted. Wooden at the podium, he was especially effective in small gatherings discussing issues around the *yaqona* bowl. Commenting on Bavadra's "first among equals" approach to leadership, a colleague noted:

> It is a type of leadership which a democracy requires in the modern world, by the command of the people rather than by an accident of birth. It is a leadership which encourages growth in a team, rather than the banyan tree leadership under which everything else dies for lack of leadership. It is the leadership by a man who is known nationally as a leader, not identified with one particular province of a country; by a man chosen by a genuinely multiracial party; a leader who is easily approachable, not held in awe but affection; a leadership which sincerely believes in collective responsibility for collective decision for the collective good."[141]

For the first time in postindependence Fiji, there appeared on the national scene another Fijian leader who provided a credible alternative to Mara.

The Coalition could boast highly educated Fijian professionals in its lineup of candidates: academics, trade unionists, high-ranking civil servants, and even former Alliance senators, rather than simply parading, as the NFP had so often done in the past, discarded and discredited opportunists who could not find a berth in the Alliance. Consequently, racial fears did not play as large a part in 1987 as in previous campaigns.

Specifically Fijian issues, which had never been raised in as public a manner, came to the fore. The role and place of traditional political institutions in the modern political arena were examples. The Alliance, led by high chiefs, saw no problem with those of high traditional rank running for political office. The Coalition Fijians were of a different mind. Fijian chiefs, they said, should not use tradition to influence politics; nor should they expect to be exempted from political criticism by their opponents. Criticism did not mean disrespect for chiefly values, as some of the chiefs were wont to assert. In Bavadra's words:

> The chiefly system is a time-honoured and sacred institution of the *taukei*. It is a system for which we have the deepest respect and which we will defend. But we also believe that a system of modern democracy is one which is quite separate from it. The individual's democratic right to vote in our political system does not mean that he has to vote for a chief. It is an absolutely free choice.[142]

Bavadra and his modern-minded Fijians went further. Culture and tradition, they asserted, were rapidly becoming a means to preserve the privileges of the elite, who themselves did not have to bear its burdens. "By restricting the Fijian people to their communal lifestyle in the face of a rapidly developing cash economy," Bavadra argued, "the average Fijian has become more and more backward. This is particularly invidious when the leaders themselves have amassed huge personal wealth by making use of their traditional political powers."[143] Some Fijian academics, not necessarily sympathetic to the ideals of the Fiji Labour Party, were making a similar point.[144]

Regionalism and regional disparities acquired a sharper edge in the heat of an acrimonious campaign. Bavadra once again questioned the east-west disparity in Fijian society. He was, of course, not the first to do so. The issue had been raised throughout the twentieth century in a variety of ways and for a variety of purposes. Apolosi Nawai, Apisai Tora and Isikeli Nadalo, Osea Gavidi and Ratu Napolioni Dawai had manipulated western Fijians' grievances. Bavadra, too, was tapping into the subterranean reservoir of western dissent against the existing structure of economic and political arrangements in Fijian society for political purposes. He went further, however, explicitly accusing the eastern maritime Fijians of hijacking Fijian resources to consolidate their own provincial bases. Speaking to the first annual convention of the FLP in 1986, Bavadra said:

It is important that we remind ourselves that the government resources
poured into Lakeba are derived from the wealth produced by others in the
country . . . they only serve to increase regional inequality and take resources away from places where they could be of more benefit to the nation.
It is time that we stopped viewing the rest of Fiji as serving the interest of a
few centres in the east. The people of Lakeba are entitled to a share in the
national wealth, but just a share. It is time that we had a government that is
more truly national in outlook.[145]

Such sentiments, long privately felt but rarely expressed publicly, certainly not in the heat of an election campaign, were now being debated
openly by Fijians themselves. What made matters even worse was the public whispering about Mara's political and business activities. Butadroka
had made them an issue long before, but his accusations lacked credibility
because of his own chequered political past. Bavadra, however, was not
Butadroka. He appeared credible when he spoke of the arrogance of
power, corruption, the amassing of huge private fortunes on relatively
meager salaries, the politics of patronage, and the perpetuation of provincial disparities during the years of the Mara administration. This criticism
of their paramount chief understandably angered the people from Lau.
Senator Inoke Tabua warned of trouble if Mara were forced out of office
by the verdict of the ballot box. Mara himself belittled Bavadra and his fellow Coalition members as a "crazy gang of amateurs," "Johnnys come
lately," untrustworthy and unfit for national office. Mara was determined
to stay:

Time will come, the time may not be long in coming, when the leadership of
this fair land must pass into other hands. That is inevitable, but the hour has
not yet struck! When it does, I will willingly lay down my burden and thank
you for the privilege of serving you. Until then, and for as long as the people
of this blessed land need me, I will answer their calls. I will keep the faith.
Fear not, Ratu Mara will stay.[146]

For Mara, the future of Fiji and that of the Alliance Party were inextrica-
bly linked; one could not, and would not be allowed to, exist without the
other. Without his and his party's leadership, Mara said, Fiji would go
down the path of "rack and ruin"; it would become another of those Third
World countries "torn apart by racial strife and drowning in debt, where
basic freedoms are curtailed, universities closed down, the media throttled
and dissenters put into jail and camps."[147]

For one who had observed and studied all five of Fiji's postcolonial elections, the 1987 election was the most engaging. Thanks to the absence of
racial fears and stereotypes that had long clouded political discourse in
Fiji, substantive issues of ideology, issues of development, and contrasting
visions of the future were aired in a more direct manner than ever before.

One vision promised democratic socialism with multiracial cooperation; the other promised to continue Fiji's communal past. One promised reform and rethinking; the other proposed the steady-as-it-goes policy. One promised the possibility of change; the other sought to restrain it. Whether the Coalition's promises were merely election rhetoric to entice the voters to its fold or whether they were sincerely expressed visions for an alternative future for Fiji is a question that will remain unanswered.

The Coalition won the election by twenty-eight seats to the Alliance's twenty-four.[148] Older patterns of ethnic voting still persisted: 78.2 percent of the total of 120,701 Fijian communal votes went to the Alliance (a 7-percent decline over the 1982 figures), and 82.3 percent of the total 122,906 Indo-Fijian communal votes were cast for the Coalition (a 1-percent decline over the 1982 figures). This ethnic pattern of voting was predictable, but the figures belie the emergence of some new trends. Although Indo-Fijian support for the Alliance remained constant around 15 percent, it was not as broadly based across the community as in the past when the party had been able to draw many South Indian and Arya Samaji supporters to its fold. Its main Indo-Fijian supporters now were the business class and a section of the Muslim community. Although the majority of the Fijians still supported the Alliance, it was significant that 21.8 percent voted for other Fijian parties and independents, indicating that the Alliance was no longer regarded as the sole representative voice of the Fijian people. On the other hand, the Coalition was able to make serious inroads into the Fijian constituency, enough to cause the Alliance's defeat in the marginal seats. The swing away from the Alliance was especially pronounced among urban Fijians and the general electors.

The Alliance's problems were compounded by a surprisingly low Fijian voter turnout in those constituencies where it was particularly vulnerable. In Lomaiviti-Muanikau, the Fijian turnout dropped by 23 percent over the 1982 figures, in Rewa-Serua-Namosi by 17 percent, in Kadavu-Tamavua by 16 percent, and in Ra-Samabula by 13.4 percent. Tamavua, Samabula, and Muanikau all were a part of the greater Suva area and within the Suva Fijian national constituency, which was critical to the victory of both parties. Why the low voter turnout? Was it because of the perception among voters that the Alliance was assured of victory? Or was staying away from the polling booth an act of protest by those who could not bring themselves to vote for the Alliance? In any case, from the Alliance's perspective, the rot was beginning to set in; unless immediate steps were taken to stop it, the party was heading for trouble.

The Coalition's stunning victory was announced around midday on Sunday, 12 April. The news was greeted not with jubilation, but with a sense of apprehension. Will 1977 repeat itself, many wondered? Will the Coalition be able to govern? As the people pondered these questions, Ratu Mara conceded defeat later in the afternoon. "The interests of Fiji as a whole must always come first," his statement said. "There can be no room for rancour and bitterness and I would urge that you display goodwill to each other in the interest of our nation. Fiji has recently been described as a symbol of hope for the rest of the world. Long may we remain so."[149] Then he left for Honolulu.

From his Viseisei home near Lautoka, Bavadra reassured the nation that he was "ready and eager" to form a government. The smooth transfer of power led Sir Leonard Usher, the doyen of local journalists, to write: "It had been a long—too long—campaign, and at times some unpleasant elements of bitterness had crept in. These were now set aside. Democracy, clearly, was alive and well in Fiji."[150] Bavadra was sworn in as Fiji's second prime minister on 13 April. At his first news conference soon afterward, he reflected briefly on the momentous events of the previous week. He viewed the "peaceful and honourable change of government" as the reaffirmation of the "deep democratic roots of our society and the profound unity of our people." He saw in his triumph the dawn of a new era, full of potential and opportunity. "Together," he said, "let us write a new chapter, which, God willing, will be one which we and our children will be proud of."[151] Fate and his opponents had other plans.

6 Things Fall Apart: The 1987 Crisis

By 14 May 1987, the long, arduous campaign was over, and for the first time since independence in 1970, Fiji had a new government, formed not by the long-reigning Alliance but by the NFP-Labour Coalition. The verdict of the ballot box had been respected. The new government, for the first time, genuinely reflected the multiracial character of the nation, encouraging the idea that Fiji might live up to its reputation as a beacon of hope in a war-weary world, a developing multiracial nation where the rule of law and parliamentary democracy prevailed. In many parts of Fiji, preparations were under way to celebrate another important event, the 108th anniversary of the arrival of Indian people in the islands.

In Suva the new parliament was in its third day of sitting. Taniela "Big Dan" Veitata, former Fijian Nationalist Party member, self-confessed prophet, and a leading instigator of the anti-Coalition protest marches, was on his feet making his maiden speech. It was meandering and convoluted. The teachings of Jesus Christ and the legacies of Fijian cannibalism, the land question and the virtues of the chiefly system, the accomplishments of Ratu Mara and the politics of Sakiasi Butadroka, the evils of British colonialism and the Tower of Babylon, the Fijian war club and the political philosophy of Mao Zedong, all found their place during the first thirty minutes of his rambling address.[1]

Then, as the bell atop the Government Buildings chimed ten, several hooded soldiers armed with M16 Armalite rifles entered parliament. "Sit down everybody, sit down," said a masked man. "This is a military takeover. We apologise for any inconvenience caused. You are requested to stay cool, stay down and listen to what we are going to tell you." Lieutenant Colonel Sitiveni Rabuka, dressed in civilian clothes and sitting at the back of the chamber, then moved toward the Speaker's chair. "Please stay calm, ladies and gentlemen," he said. "Mr Prime Minister, please lead your team down to the right. Policemen, keep the passage clear. Stay down, remain calm. Mr Prime Minister, Sir, will you lead your team now."[2] Dr Timoci Bavadra looked toward the Speaker, who nodded that the prime minister should comply. It was all over in a matter of four minutes. As the last sentence in *Hansard* poignantly records, the House "adjourned" at 10:04 AM, never again to meet in its pre–14 May form.

The parliament of Fiji two days before the first coup of 14 May 1987. Front row, from left: Mahendra Chaudhary, Finance Minister; Harish Sharma, Deputy Prime Minister; Timoci Bavadra, Prime Minister; Militoni Leweniqila, Speaker of the House; Ratu Mara, Leader of the Opposition; Mosese Qionibaravi, Deputy Leader of the Opposition; and Tomasi Vakatora, Alliance backbencher. *(Courtesy Fiji Ministry of Information)*

The stunned members of the Coalition were hustled down the aisle of the ornate chamber to army trucks waiting at the entrance of the parliament building. Uncomprehending, many of them, including Bavadra, wondered audibly whether the military takeover was, in fact, a precautionary exercise by the army.[3] As they were driven away, one of them opened Erskine May's guide to parliamentary procedures to check the definition of coup; the word was not mentioned. Jai Ram Reddy, the Coalition attorney general, said to his bewildered colleague that the coup was nothing more than the conquest of one community by another.[4] For the Indo-Fijians, the military intervention appeared to mark the beginning of the second *girmit,* a second-class life lived on the goodwill of the indigenous Fijians. For the country as a whole, it put an end to a century-old experiment in multiracialism conceived soon after Fiji was ceded to Great Britain in 1874. The footsteps of the hooded soldiers will reverberate through the corridors of Fijian history for generations to come.

The coup of 14 May was a far-reaching event, a turning point in modern Pacific history.[5] The issues it raised about the rights and privileges of indigenous peoples in societies with substantial immigrant or mixed populations, about the tension between traditional customs and institutions and modern political ideologies, and about the use of military force to overthrow constitutionally elected but ideologically unacceptable governments, to mention only a few, have deep implications not only for the people of Fiji but for many other Pacific Island and Third World societies. Because of this, as well as its unprecedented and dramatic occurrence in a part of the world long thought to be peaceful, the coup thrust Fiji into the unwelcome glare of international notoriety, engendering a vast outpouring of popular and scholarly literature on the motivations and machinations behind the coup.[6]

Coalition Government

The story of the May coup begins with the unexpected and history-making victory of the Labour Coalition. Bavadra took the oath of office on 13 April, and the rest of his ministers followed the next day. Immediately, the new government began taking steps to deliver on some of its election promises. The initial gestures were largely symbolic and reassuring: removal of outpatient fees at all government hospitals; free bus passes for the elderly and ex-service personnel. Work was under way on a bill requiring parliamentarians to declare their assets to avoid conflict of interest. The pernicious Official Secrets Act was to be repealed. In keeping with their election promise to conduct an open government, some ministers released hitherto classified reports that told a sorry tale of corruption, mismanagement, and unilateral decision making in such statutory bodies as the Nadi-based Civil Aviation Authority of Fiji. Ratu Mara's Hurricane Relief Fund was being probed for signs of possible misuse of funds, as was the Marella House affair.

The Coalition leadership went out of its way to compliment the former government's contribution to the development of Fiji since independence. Defeated Prime Minister Mara was under no pressure to move out of his Vieuto home quickly to make room for his successor. In deference to his national stature and traditional status, he was permitted to retain his personal security staff, a privilege not normally allowed leaders of the opposition. The allocation of cabinet portfolios also showed sensitivity to the realities of Fijian politics. Of the fourteen portfolios, seven went to Fijians and seven to Indo-Fijians, and two ministries of state were allocated to a Fijian and a Part-Fijian. Bavadra observed the convention that had developed since independence that certain portfolios were the prerogatives of the Fijian people. The offices of Prime Minister, Home Affairs (army, navy, police, special branch), Fijian Affairs, Primary Industry (agriculture, forests, and fisheries), Lands and Mineral Resources, Labour and Immigration, Education, Youth and Sports, Rural Development and Rehabilitation were all placed in Fijian hands. Indo-Fijian ministers were given ministries that, even in the Alliance government, had nearly always been occupied by non-Fijians: Foreign Affairs, Trade and Industry, Health and Social Services, Finance, Transport and Communication, and Information and Justice. The only exception was the portfolio of deputy prime minister, which under the Alliance was always held by a Fijian but now went to an Indo-Fijian.

The Coalition cabinet was dominated by members of the Fiji Labour Party (FLP). Eleven of the fourteen ministers were from the FLP and only three from the National Federation Party (NFP). Trade unionists occupied the most important positions in government: Prime Minister and Home Affairs (Bavadra), Foreign Affairs (Krishna Datt), Finance (Mahendra Chaudhary), and Labour and Immigration (Joeli Kalou). Bavadra was widely praised for his political sensitivity even by Sakiasi Butadroka, who otherwise opposed the new government.[7] The Coalition cabinet was comparatively young, the average age being forty-five years, and exceptionally well educated, if not as politically experienced as their opponents. All but three of the ministers were university graduates, and three were senior academics at the University of the South Pacific. All except three were newcomers to national politics who had yet to make their maiden speeches.[8] Their ascendancy symbolized a departure from the past pattern of politics in Fiji. Old men wary of change and antagonistic to new ideas had been replaced by a group proclaiming themselves the harbingers of a new era.

Caution, prudence, and an acute understanding of the realities of Fiji's politics were also evident in the policies the new government proposed to follow. Gone were the ideologically oriented radical-sounding policies propounded in the FLP manifesto. On the economic front, the FLP's founding rhetoric about nationalization and foreign investment was discarded. The new government was "firmly of the view that investors are entitled to a fair return. It is fully cognizant of the fact that the private sector has a very important and key role to play in national development effort through its enterprises and investment." It promised to "take steps to remove obstacles, including bureaucratic ones, which restrict private initiative and enterprise." Export-oriented development strategies promoting balanced development were the essence of the government's economic strategy.[9]

On matters relating specifically to Fijian society, an important and sensitive concern of any government in Fiji, the Coalition government's views were clear: its policy rested "fundamentally on its recognition of Fijian rights and interests as enshrined in the Constitution of Fiji." The government was "firmly committed to protecting those rights and interests." Specifically, it agreed to implement changes recommended in the Alliance

government–commissioned report to restructure and revamp Fijian traditional institutions at the village level[10] even though that clashed with the
FLP's general ideological orientation. Special effort was to be made to facilitate greater participation by Fijians in commerce and business enterprise.
The Fijian Institute of Culture and Language would continue to be
funded, and fisheries surveys would continue, as also would the updating
of the Register of Native Births (I Vola ni Kawa Bula).

The Coalition's foreign policy, which attracted considerable attention
overseas, also showed signs of moderation and tactfulness. Bavadra set the
tone soon after his victory when he talked about "a slight turn here, a
stream to cross there," always bearing in mind that the "welfare of our
nation is linked to the inter-dependence of our nations, particularly our
neighbours in the South Pacific and those nations with which we have
historic and democratic links," which included the United States of
America.[11] Joining the Non-Aligned Movement, which some saw as the
most important departure from the policies of the Mara administration,
was "not one of the pressing things on our agenda," Bavadra said. Foreign
Minister Datt told General Vernon Walters, visiting United States ambassador to the United Nations: "We are collecting a series of formulae from
various other countries; we even have sought some assistance from the US
itself as to their own collection of formalities which they might have with
other countries."[12] Datt was referring to the passage of nuclear-armed vessels through Fiji waters. In taking this position, the Coalition was at pains
to emphasize that it was not the radical party its critics were portraying it
to be. Such pragmatism disenchanted many party supporters, but it was
clear that prudent restraint and not radical rhetoric would guide Fiji's foreign relations under the Coalition.

The Rise of *Taukei* Militancy

Restraint in one camp did not eliminate frustration and anger in the other.
Defeated Alliance politicians were bent on making life for the Coalition as
difficult as possible. Soon after the election results were announced, a
group of them met in the Fijian-dominated Suva suburb of Raiwaqa.[13]
Mara's eldest son, Ratu Finau Mara, was there along with other Fijians
from the east: Filipe Bole, former Fiji ambassador to the United States;
Qoroniasi Bale, Alliance attorney general; Taniela Veitata, Alliance backbencher; Inoke Kubuabola; Tomasi Raikivi; Jone Veisamasama; and
many others. Fiji for Fijians went up the cry; the supposedly Indo-Fijian-
dominated government would have to go, and plans to bring this about
were prepared.

In Tavua, on the western side, Bole's brother-in-law, Ratu Ovini
Bokani, Tui Tavua, ordered his men to erect a roadblock on the King's
Highway directly across from the local police station.[14] Placards at the

sixty-strong protest meeting displayed the messages: "We Hate Coalition. We Don't Need It" and "Labour Government Is Lowest in the World." The blockade was removed when the inspector-in-charge offered a *sevusevu* (traditional offering) of *yaqona* to the Tui Tavua. Militant Fijians, not the government, wielded power where it counted the most. Upset that the police force did not deal with the roadblocks as a breach of law and order, Bavadra dispatched the director of public prosecutions to investigate. Because the director happened to be an Indo-Fijian, the distrust increased between the police force, the government, and the militant Fijians.

On 21 April, two thousand Fijians gathered at Viseisei, Bavadra's home village, proclaiming that Fijian rights were in imminent danger. The *tūraga* and the *vanua* were opposed to the Coalition. "I cannot imagine us listening to government leaders who are not chiefs," said Bulou Eta Vosailagi, from the chiefly village of Nakuruvakarua in Nadroga. "I ask the chiefs here, and all of us, to support, to bring back the control of our government to the Fijian chiefs," she said, and received unanimous support.[15] Reading a fiery speech reportedly prepared by the Alliance information machinery, Apisai Tora breached the Public Order Act and was later charged with sedition. The meeting drafted a petition to the governor-general demanding a change of the Fiji constitution so that the *taukei* "must always control the government to safeguard their special status and rights." Abolish democracy if it stands in the way of *taukei* empowerment. It was a "foreign flower" anyway, unsuited to the Fijian social system, argued Adi Finau Tabakaucoro, University of the South Pacific academic-turned-politician. Fiji must be Fijianized, she told a *New York Times* reporter: "How do you compete with a race that has thousands of years of what we call civilization?" she asked with candor. "When the first Indians arrived in Fiji in 1879, my grandparents were just ten years from eating each other. This is not their country. They still speak Hindi. They still eat curry. They are not Christians."[16]

By late April, the Taukei Movement, a loose coalition of anti-Coalition *taukei,* had formed. It became the chief planner and perpetrator of anti-Coalition activities in the country and the sole indigenous Fijian voice to the outside world. The movement sought to portray itself as the voice of a people faced with the same plight as the politically and economically marginalized indigenous people of Hawai'i, New Zealand, Kanaky, and Australia. It was waging a fight for Fijian self-preservation and dignity to ensure that the *taukei* "are not overwhelmed into oblivion in the fields of commerce and business, education and leadership in local government and their culture and tradition not replaced by a totally strange and foreign one imposed on them through a constitution that does not guarantee Fijian security and interests."[17] It was nothing less than a struggle for Fijian cultural and political liberation waged in the face of "a strange and ever present threatening foreign civilization."

The leaders of the movement saw themselves as selfless servants of the greater Fijian cause. No doubt some of them were, individuals who had a long history of opposing the foundations and practice of a multiracial democracy in Fiji. However, the leading protagonists in the anti-Coalition camp were fighting as much for their personal interests as for the principles they professed to believe in. Filipe Bole, for example, reportedly the intellectual theoretician of the movement, had left his well-paying job as director of the Pacific Islands Development Program at the East-West Center in Hawai'i to enter politics, and given his experience as a senior administrator, had expected a senior portfolio in an Alliance government. He was now sitting on the opposition back benches on a meager salary of F$10,000. Viliame Gonelevu had given up his well-paying and powerful position as chair of the Fiji Electricity Commission. Ratu Meli Vesikula had returned to Fiji as a retired sergeant major in the British Army and was looking for a new career and a way out of his reportedly financially troubled business ventures. Apisai Tora and Jona Qio were awaiting trial for sedition and arson, respectively. Jone Veisamasama, a founding vice president of the Fiji Labour Party, was being investigated by the police for corruption in the issuing of taxi licenses. He later died from an apparently self-inflicted gunshot wound. Taniela Veitata was an unsuccessful trade union leader who had been floundering in the political wilderness as a member of the Fijian Nationalist Party until given a Fijian communal seat by the Alliance. All these individuals came from diverse backgrounds, and all stood to lose financially from the change of government. They were all steadfastly committed to the destruction of the Coalition government at almost any cost.

A careful plan of action was drawn up, beginning with a four-thousand-strong protest march in Suva on 24 April to publicize to the world the *taukei*'s opposition to the Coalition government. Placards displayed the messages in no uncertain terms: "Fiji for Fijians," "Kai Idia Go Back," "It Is Time to Fight for Our Rights," "River of No Return for Fijians," "We Shall Not Be Misled by a Puppet," and *"Noqu Kalou, Noqu Vanua,"* 'Our God, Our Land'.[18] The march expended itself peacefully, influenced perhaps by words of caution urged on the marchers by the Vunivalu, Ratu Sir George Cakobau, by Ratu Sir Penaia Ganilau, and by the Reverend Josateki Koroi, president of the powerful Fiji Methodist Church to which the overwhelming majority of the indigenous Fijians belong. Ganilau told the protesters that they "will deny or make it difficult for the new government to show their leadership potential in Fiji, . . . disrupt the progress and achievements that have been made possible during the last 16 years by the former Alliance Government, [and] forever change Fiji's image and relationship at the regional and international level."[19] Of all the major Fijian leaders, and perhaps the one with the greatest amount of influence, Ratu Sir Kamisese Mara remained silent. He was away in the serene surroundings of Honolulu, pleasantly removed from a palpably seething Fiji.

The Coalition government, which had been deeply preoccupied and paralyzed by the marches, breathed a sigh of relief when it looked as if the marches might soon dissolve. They were sadly mistaken. The Taukei Movement had other plans. A few shaky Coalition members were reportedly promised up to F$70,000 if they crossed the floor.[20] That tactic failed. Such treachery from any Coalition parliamentarian at that momentous juncture in Fijian politics would almost certainly have brought terrible retribution. Veitata and his men had plans to unleash violence of such magnitude in Suva that the governor-general would be forced to declare a state of emergency and form an Alliance-dominated, Mara-led caretaker government. Among the plans canvassed for destabilizing the country were blowing up the huge oil tanks at Walu Bay, torching Indo-Fijian houses, and killing a certain number of Indo-Fijians in and around Suva.[21] On the western side, there were plans for burning Indo-Fijian cane fields (at the rate of six per week), releasing Fijian prisoners to wreak havoc on the predominantly Indo-Fijian western towns, destroying property belonging to Coalition leaders, and, generally, creating a massive, and hopefully unmanageable, law-and-order problem for the government. As a part of this plan, *taukei* extremists firebombed Jai Ram Reddy's law office in Lautoka.

The culminating event in the destabilization process would be a military coup. A combat-hardened, Ireland-experienced Vesikula said that a quick, decisive, surgical military strike was preferred to messy and potentially dangerous civilian-led assaults. Betraying the trust of his military superiors and his oath of loyalty, Rabuka, a staff officer of the Royal Fiji Military Forces, joined the antigovernment conspiracy. He was asked to prepare the coup plan. Rabuka has since asserted that he acted alone without wider involvement, thereby taking credit for his actions. This is flatly contradicted by his fellow co-conspirator, Ratu Inoke Kubuabola, who said that the final decision to mount a military coup was "taken in my office at the Bible Society with Rabuka."[22]

The original plan, according to Kubuabola, had been to use a roll-on-roll-off ship at the Suva wharf to transport the detained ministers to the remote and inaccessible island of Makogai, which had once housed a leprosy hospital. That plan was abandoned when the launching of the coup was advanced by a day to Thursday, as the parliament was not meeting on Friday. Other Fijians remember discussing the coup with Rabuka. One of them was Militoni Leweniqila, the Speaker of the House and Rabuka's uncle. Leweniqila later recalled how "he, Rabuka and relatives had discussed what would happen in a coup. . . . I told him," he said, "if you are going to successfully execute a coup, you may have to take some lives for people to believe there is a coup because no one believes a coup is possible in Fiji."[23] It is not known if Leweniqila told the government what was afoot, but it is beyond doubt that Rabuka was not acting on his own.

A handpicked team of Lebanon-experienced officers, under the leadership of Captain Isireli Dugu, began training in the jungle on the outskirts of Suva. They were not told the exact circumstances in which their training would be put to use. All along, the Taukei Movement hoped that the Coalition would crack under pressure, obviating the need for military action. Such hopes proved vain. Instead of crumbling, the Coalition remained in power, relying on the legal and constitutional guarantees to govern, and mounted a surprisingly adroit response to the forces opposing it. When all the other destabilizing efforts failed, Rabuka moved to the front and staged his coup on 14 May, ending not only the life of a month-old Coalition government but an era in Fiji's history.

The Coup and a Week After

Soon after deposing the government at ten o'clock and detaining Coalition parliamentarians at the Queen Elizabeth Barracks in Nabua, five miles out of Suva, Rabuka went to Government House to personally inform the governor-general, Ratu Sir Penaia Ganilau, of his action and to seek his approval for it. Ganilau had already heard what had happened from a live radio broadcast of the parliamentary proceedings. Rabuka pleaded with Ganilau to "please distance yourself to see what it is we as your subjects can do to take over leadership of this land and the Fijian people until such a time as we think that you should be invited to resume leadership in a position which is rightfully yours and was bestowed upon you by our Father and God Almighty."[24] Ganilau was ambivalent. He did not order Rabuka and his men back to barracks immediately, as might have been expected of a man sworn to uphold the constitutional authority of the new government. "Good luck," he is widely reported to have said, perhaps in exasperation at Rabuka's intransigence, "I hope you know what you are doing." "What have you done?" "You mean I have no job?" "Couldn't you have given them time to carry out their policies? Perhaps they would have shown us in a few months time they were incapable of running the country anyway."[25]

A stubborn and determined Rabuka returned to the Government Buildings to hold a press conference announcing the coup to the world. He disclosed the suspension of the constitution and his plans for an interim cabinet to return Fiji to civilian rule. The interim cabinet was announced at one o'clock the next morning. Headed by Rabuka, who was the only military officer on it, the cabinet was composed overwhelmingly of members of the recently defeated Alliance government, including, most surprising of all, Ratu Sir Kamisese Mara. Their quick, almost eager acceptance of positions in the coup cabinet strengthened the suspicion of those who suspected Alliance conspiracy, or at least complicity, in the unfolding crisis.

While forming the interim cabinet had been easy enough, seeking constitutional legitimacy for it was not. Rabuka's attempts received a severe setback because the governor-general vacillated, was uncertain about what to do, and was mindful of international condemnation of the coup and the Queen's order to stick by the deposed government. He was also keeping his options open in case the coup failed. At two o'clock on 14 May, the judiciary, led by Chief Justice Sir Timoci Tuivaga, told Ratu Penaia that the seizure of power was illegal and invalid, that the independence constitution remained unchanged, and that they were ready "to continue to exercise our duties in accordance with the law of Fiji and our oaths of office." These words carried weight with the governor-general.[26] Later in the day, he taped a message to be broadcast on FM96, Fiji's only commercial station, in the early hours of the next morning. Proclaiming himself deeply disturbed (and according to sources close to him he was) by the "unlawful seizure of members of my government," a situation "which must not be allowed to continue," the governor-general declared a state of emergency and assumed executive authority. The constitution had not been overridden, and he urged the soldiers to "return to their lawful allegiance in accordance with the oath of office and their duty of obedience without delay."[27]

Then Ratu Penaia did an astounding, inexplicable about-turn. Returning from Taveuni, where he had gone to attend the funeral of his aunt, Adi Makitalena of Naselesele, he swore in Rabuka as the head of government on Sunday 17 May, just two days after castigating the colonel as an illegal usurper of constitutional authority.[28] The rest of the military-Alliance cabinet would be sworn into office. Perhaps the governor-general had heeded the advice of relatives and fellow chiefs of Cakaudrove, where he was the Tui Cakau–elect, nominal head of the Tovata confederacy, and Rabuka's paramount chief.

Rabuka was not destined to enjoy his newly legitimized status for long. An hour after the colonel had departed from Government House, the chief justice, an indigenous Fijian, secured an audience with the governor-general. He presented him a four-point plan devised by the judges of the Fiji Supreme Court to take Fiji out of its constitutional impasse. The governor-general was advised to dissolve the parliament and call fresh elections as soon as practicable, to proclaim himself the executive authority under Section 72 of the 1970 constitution held to be still in force, to appoint a bipartisan Council of Advisors to help him run the country until the next elections, and to propose a Royal Commission of Enquiry to "inquire into the efficacy and general acceptance of the 1970 constitution and to suggest such modification as may meet the expectations and assuage the fears of the people of Fiji." Ratu Penaia was also advised to exercise his prerogative of mercy and pardon all those "implicated in the illegal seizure of power, [as] no useful purpose will be served by vindictiveness which might hinder the complete restoration of legitimacy."[29]

All this was sanguine advice in the most difficult of circumstances, but defective in strictly constitutional terms. The prerogative of mercy could be invoked, the constitution stipulated, only after the due process of law had been allowed to run its course. (Charges of treason had not been laid against Rabuka and his men in the military.[30]) The reasons for dissolving the parliament were also dubious.[31] To be sure, the constitution vested executive power in the Queen, to be exercised by the governor-general on her behalf, but he could do so only after consulting the prime minister. The declaration of a state of emergency (under Section 72) also could not be used to justify the dissolution of parliament. The prime minister and his ministers were unable to discharge their duties and responsibilities under the constitution. As Professor F. M. Brookfield has argued, "What was necessary (to save the constitution) was not to dismiss them or to proclaim their offices vacant but for the Governor General to secure their restoration and to provide for government in the meantime."[32] Ratu Penaia's intervention had several effects. As one astute observer has stated:

> The cloak of the rule of the governor general protected the regime from the full force of foreign as well as domestic opposition; cut off the Coalition leaders from access to the Queen and certain foreign governments; enabled foreign governments sympathetic to the coup (like the British) to justify their continued support of it; put the entire administration at the service of the new objectives; protected Rabuka and his collaborators from the due process of law; restored to power the instruments of indigenous Fijian hegemony; and enabled the governor general and Rabuka to maintain their traditional relationship of *tūraga* and *bati*.[33]

In effect, the governor-general had joined the revolution.

Frustrated by Ganilau's vacillation and public intransigence, Rabuka and his unsworn interim cabinet played their trump card when they convened (an unconstitutional) meeting of the Great Council of Chiefs in Suva on Tuesday, 19 May. They hoped not only to get the council to endorse the stated aims of the coup in ringing terms—consistent with the Bau meeting of the council in 1982—but also to put pressure on Ganilau to step into line with Rabuka and his men. As Rabuka's paramount chief, Ganilau could browbeat the colonel in a one-on-one meeting, but was expected to be more constrained in a tense meeting facing his fellow high chiefs and relatives openly sympathetic to the stated aims of the coup and supportive of the man who had engineered it. When he first addressed the chiefs, Ganilau was more guarded, mindful of his constitutional role as the Queen's representative and aware of international opinion. The majority of the chiefs were solidly opposed to his stand, some of them (such as Ratu Meli Vesikula) outside the meeting indulging in the unthinkable act of jeering and booing him as he alighted from his car to address the meeting inside the Suva Civic Centre. For them, the issue was not whether the

1970 constitution should be overthrown but whether, in the event of some legal obstacles, they should go the full distance and declare Fiji a republic.

Ganilau was clearly uncomfortable. He returned the next day (Wednesday) to assure the chiefs that there had been a misunderstanding of the "true meaning and implications of the message contained in my address to you," adding that "we are all aiming at the same result, generally, but that we are considering different methods of achieving this." He went further: "Let there be no doubt in anyone's mind, therefore, that as a native Fijian and as one blessed with Fijian chiefly status, the interests of my people, the indigenous Fijians, are those which I hold and shall always hold dear to my heart." He assured the chiefs that he would place "great weight" on their advice and promised that the "views expressed in this meeting on the need not to ignore or undermine the best interests of the native Fijians shall always be paramount in my mind."[34] Ganilau had declared his hand and acquiesced to the wishes of the chiefs. Had he resisted the pressure to endorse the coup, he might have been isolated, his candidature for the title of Tui Cakau placed in jeopardy, and the Fijian polity possibly split. This was the price of loyalty to the Crown, and Ganilau was not prepared to pay it.

The chiefs were relieved. There was unanimous support for the coup. For the time being, at least, the republican route was shelved, but the chiefs wanted a hand in deciding the composition of the proposed Council of Advisors. The military, they resolved, should be asked to reexamine the 1970 constitution "with a view to changing, abolishing or abrogating it in the quickest possible time and to ensure that Fijians were guaranteed the control of government at all times."[35] Rabuka got the support he so desperately needed. He smiled broadly from the balcony of the Suva Civic Centre as the "Royal" Fiji Military Forces band entertained hundreds of Fijian men and women with such tunes as "I Did It My Way," "Bridge Over Troubled Waters," and "Onward Christian Soldiers." With both his clenched fists raised in the air, he said *Sā noda na qāqā,* "victory is ours." He vowed "not to agree to anything that will destroy the aim of the coup."

When the governor-general announced his Council of Advisors, it became apparent just how far he had gone to accommodate the wishes of the coup supporters. He was no longer an impartial arbiter nor an entirely free agent. "Let me say that some people who have approached me have asked for the impossible," he told his radio listeners. "They have asked that the clock be turned back. That I wave a magic wand and pretend what has happened recently in Fiji never happened. There are many who cannot see beyond their feelings of outrage and hurt. There are many who cannot see beyond rigid interpretations of the law. There are many who see only despair ahead of us."[36] It was a not-too-subtle message for the Coalition. As far as Rabuka was concerned, Ganilau said that the composition of the Council of Advisors "has been discussed with and found

Table 6. Governor-General's Council of Advisors

Name	Political Party or Affiliation	Ethnic Group
S. Rabuka	Fiji Military Forces	Fijian
A. Qetaki	Taukei Movement	Fijian
J. Tavaiqia	Alliance	Fijian
L. Nasilivata	Alliance/Taukei Movement	Fijian
J. Veisamasama	Alliance/Taukei Movement	Fijian
V. Gonelevu	Alliance/Taukei Movement	Fijian
A. Kurisiqila	Alliance	Fijian
Filipe Bole	Alliance/Taukei Movement	Fijian
J. Tonganivalu	Alliance	Fijian
J. Cavalevu	Civil Servant	Fijian
Ratu Mara	Alliance	Fijian
D. Mastapha	Independent	Indo-Fijian
Mumtaz Ali	Independent	Indo-Fijian
S. Siwatibau	Independent	Fijian
Harish Sharma	Coalition	Indo-Fijian
Timoci Bavadra	Coalition	Fijian
P. Manueli	Independent	Rotuman

SOURCE: Fiji Ministry of Information.

acceptable to the military regime and its leader."[37] Bavadra was not consulted. He and his deputy refused to serve on the council, as did Daniel Mustapha, former president of the Methodist Church in Fiji. As Table 6 shows, even as a balance of Coalition and Alliance, this arrangement was lopsided.

The announcement of the Council of Advisors at the end of May ended the first phase of the Fiji crisis. After a brief tussle for power, Rabuka and the Taukei Movement had emerged victorious, with the assistance, witting or unwitting, of the governor-general and a fiercely communal-minded Great Council of Chiefs. This resolve to make the coup succeed was impressive, but it meant that the path ahead was far from smooth.

Coalition and Other Reactions

The deposed Coalition parliamentarians were first taken to the Queen Elizabeth Barracks in Nabua from where they were transferred later in the day to the prime minister's residence at Vieuto. For three days, both Fijian and Indo-Fijian parliamentarians were kept together in detention, where they prayed (frequently), reflected on their plight, resolved to maintain solidarity, and attempted to communicate with the outside world for political help.[38] Then, in an apparent effort to strain the multiracial solidarity of the detainees, Indo-Fijian parliamentarians were hauled off to

Borron House—a state guest house that once was the official residence of
Ratu Sukuna. Both these places, thoroughly guarded by soldiers taking
positions behind rolls of barbed wire, became a magnet for the curious, the
concerned, and a frenzy of international media reporters hungry for news.

The Coalition parliamentarians were released at 10:00 PM on Tuesday,
19 May. The news of their release and of a rally the next day to be
addressed by Bavadra attracted a huge crowd at Albert Park (Figure 10).
Nearly one thousand people, mostly Indo-Fijian women, children, and
men, converged on the park. They had come to Suva by the busloads from
all parts of Viti Levu. At the other end of the town, another crowd was
gathering, determined to break the Coalition rally it saw as a provocation
and an insult. A hundred-strong crowd of Fijian hooligans, armed with
stones, sticks, and iron bars plucked from parked Suva City Council

FIJI FREEDOM FIGHTERS

Today you did not receive your daily newspapers. You have been
cutt off from the rest of the world. Nadi and Lautoka have set an
example for you to follow. All the shops and the transport system
has stopped. Its time now for you to act.

Shopkeepers, you are helping the terrorists. All shops must close
its doors today. The only way for our salvation is non co-operation
with the illegal regime.

All buses and taxis must cease operations today. Time has come to
take action. Children of Fiji, you hold the key to the future of
Fiji. Your help is needed today by the government your parents
elected into office who are now captives of the traitors. You must
not attend school when it opens next week. You must not co-operate
with the puppet regime who claim to rule Fiji.

Workers, wake up we must bring this puppet regime to its right size,
on their knees nobody is to turn up for work from Monday.

Anybody not heeding to the suggestions will be helping and condoming
the illegal regime. Our good unnamed Ministers and Members of Parliament
are locked up by machine-gun equipped rebels.

Fiji needs you today as it never did before. Times has come to stand
up and be counted.

We call on all right thingking citzen of Fiji to help overcome this
ACT OF TREASON.

VIVA FIJI

Figure 10. *(From the streets of Suva, 14 May 1987)*

trucks, marched menacingly toward Albert Park, chasing and beating Indo-Fijians on sight. At the edge of the park, diagonally across the street from the Government Buildings, fierce fighting broke out between the two opposing camps. Intervention by the military prevented the violence from getting out of hand, as the rampaging Fijians dispersed, hitting and kicking Indo-Fijian men and sari-clad women fleeing the scene of the riots.[39] About a hundred were seriously injured, requiring treatment at the hospital. The lines were now clearly drawn, and attitudes had hardened rapidly on both sides. Fortunately, this madness of racial violence did not spread beyond Suva.

Bavadra's first statement after release was defiant. He still was the prime minister of Fiji, he claimed, the dissolution of parliament by vice-regal proclamation notwithstanding. Nevertheless, he put his faith in the impartiality and integrity of the governor-general to restore him and his government to power through constitutional means. "I trust him and the Queen to restore peace in the country," said Bavadra. "Surely that is what we all want. We must all stand behind the Governor General. He knows what to do"[40] (Figure 11). As time went by and Ganilau's lack of neutrality became patently clear, Bavadra distanced himself from him and eventually filed a suit challenging the constitutional propriety of the governor-general's decision to dissolve parliament. The world, too, became aware of Ganilau's reluctance to uphold his authority more forcefully, though during the first week, the international community rallied behind him.[41]

Fiji was a cauldron of confusion after the military takeover of 14 May. The two local dailies were closed down for a week for denouncing the coup. Radio Fiji, controlled by the military, broadcast contradictory statements, a situation not helped by the garbled signals coming from Government House. The streets of Suva were unsafe. Shops, schools, and public transport shut down as frightened people sought the shelter of their barricaded homes at night. Many Indo-Fijians thronged the Australian and New Zealand embassies for visas to emigrate. Fiji was placed under a state of emergency, which restricted the movement of people and their right of assembly and any activity judged likely by the security forces to provoke a breach of the peace.[42] This frustrated the Coalition's efforts to conduct political meetings among themselves and throughout the country. Unable to accomplish much locally, Bavadra and his close advisors (Bhupendra Patel and Jai Ram Reddy) traveled to London to seek the Queen's advice and assistance in restoring his government to power. Bavadra was naively optimistic. "She is my Queen; she is the Queen of Fiji," he said. "She is bound to at least listen to me," he said on arriving in London.[43]

The Queen, however, saw herself under no such obligation. Acting on the advice of Ganilau, still her representative in Fiji, and somehow believing in his impartiality and his continued loyalty to the Crown, she refused to meet the deposed prime minister. Bavadra did meet with her private

SUPPORT THE G-G

The Press and the Radio are no longer free. But we express our
respect and appreciation for the inspiring stand of the
Governor-General, Ratu Sir Penaia Ganilau. He has
courageously stated that he is still the rightful Head
of Government and he does not support the military take-over.

He is under arrest and is no longer able to speak to the
Nation. This undignified detention of such a highly-placed
and respected leader is an insult to the tradition of this
land.

We appeal that Ratu Sir Penaia be given a full and free
opportunity to address the nation.

Brothers and sisters, let us be warned, now that freedom has
been curtailed, that this regime will use any tactics to
instill fear amongst us.

Let us not spread rumours that incite violence or convey
fear. We can decide that we will not be governed by fear.
So long as we resolutely stick to NON-VIOLENCE and our
actions are just, we should not hold back.

If we will not act, how can we expect others to do so?
If we take one small step in courage, perhaps we will discover
greater courage. Immediately you could make copies of this
and begin passing them around.

Each one, tell one.

Paint signs and prepare posters saying :' WE SUPPORT G - G '
'LET G-G SPEAK' 'FREE OUR G-G' or 'PEOPLE OF FIJI RESIST
THE MILITARY REGIME'.

MAY GOD BLESS FIJI

Figure 11. Support the governor-general. *(From the streets of Suva, May 1987)*

secretary, Sir William Heseltine, though the content of those meetings is
not known. At the Commonwealth Secretariat, too, the reception was
lukewarm. Sridath Ramphal, Guyanese-born secretary-general, expressed
sympathy but little else, noting that the Commonwealth was powerless to
act. The secretary-general, wrote the respected *Guardian Weekly,* saw Bavadra as "a man who won the last election, but no longer as the legitimate

Prime Minister."[44] The view of the Commonwealth Secretariat was that it was for the regional governments to bring pressure on the military regime in Fiji.

That was hardly likely. A week after the coup, the Melanesian Spearhead group meeting in Rabaul had issued a strongly worded warning against any foreign intervention in Fiji. Their statement read: "We will not hesitate to take appropriate diplomatic action to deal with external threats to Fiji's sovereignty from wherever they might come. Fiji's future, including any change to the Fiji constitution, should be determined by the people and leaders of Fiji."[45] The statement was warmly praised by Fiji's military regime as an expression of indigenous solidarity for their actions. To show admiration for Rabuka, a senior Papua New Guinean Foreign Affairs official named his newborn son after the Fiji coup leader.

Coalition ministers Krishna Datt, Joeli Kalou, and Tupeni Baba encountered a similar hostile attitude when they tried to press their case at the South Pacific Forum in Apia in late May. They pleaded with the regional governments to stand on the side of law and order and constitutional government; they assured them that Fijian land rights were never, and could not have been, in any danger; and they urged that their personal loyalties and friendship with Ratu Mara should not prevent them from condemning the coup. Regional considerations were important, too: "The installation of a military regime in Fiji must be seen as a direct threat to regional solidarity and the democratic institutions that form the basis of regional cooperation between the countries of the South Pacific. We urge you," the ministers implored, to look "objectively at the facts and decide your response in accordance with your conscience and the broader interests of the multiracial communities in Fiji and the South Pacific."[46] They were frustrated. Not allowed to address any of the sessions, they were kept hovering in the corridors and spoke only in private informal conversations. Said Sir Tom Davis, premier of the Cook Islands and the Forum's spokesman: "No real blooded ethnic Fijian could let a bunch of Indians run the country. What would you do? Take that lying down? I'm glad they didn't."[47] He suggested, only half jokingly, that Australia might settle the Indo-Fijians in the barren deserts of central Australia, a sentiment reminiscent of Ragg's and MacMillan's proposals in the 1950s. In the end, and not surprisingly, the Forum passed a weak resolution expressing sorrow at the events in Fiji and asking for understanding and sympathy for its people. If the Fiji governor-general agreed, the Forum resolved, it would send a three-person team on a fact-finding mission to Fiji. Ganilau rejected the idea, and the matter was dropped forthwith.

The Coalition had more success in Australia and New Zealand. In both these countries, there was a popular outcry against a military coup that had deposed a fraternal labor government. Trade unions there imposed trade bans and pressed for sanctions. Both Bob Hawke and David Lange issued rhetorically appropriate condemnations of the coup, the latter more vociferous and forthright than the former. Lange pointed a direct finger at Mara and accused him of treason, but did not persist. There was for a brief moment some sensational speculation about a possible military countercoup, with the assistance of Lebanon-based Fiji troops led by Ratu Epeli Nailitakau, commander of the Fiji Military Forces, who was visiting Australia at the time of the coup. Mercifully, the thought was quashed early. Cooler heads realized that their options were limited. Sensitive about charges of racial arrogance, mindful of the regional governments' tacit support for the coup, and legitimately concerned about the fate of Suva-based regional organizations, there was little that these two governments could usefully do. As New Zealand Foreign Minister Marshall said in August 1987, "Whatever our Western constitutional anxieties might be, we have to be careful [that] what we do does not make us sound white, guilty, patronising, and having a neo-colonialist attitude."[48] In the end, defense and aid ties were put on hold and long-planned official visits to Fiji canceled, but for the most part, a pragmatic approach consonant with conventional diplomacy prevailed.

Seeking a Constitutional Solution

A series of overseas visits raised international consciousness about the situation in Fiji and brought the beleaguered Coalition leaders some breathing space. But the visits also emphasized the obvious fact that the fight for democracy would have to be fought in Fiji itself. As an editorial in the *Melbourne Herald* aptly stated: "In world capitals, the deposed Prime Minister managed to muster some obligatory tut-tutting, but that was about all. His disappointing reception in countries which publicly make so much of their support for democratic institutions has taught him much about realpolitik."[49] India was the only country that took more than just a stand; it lobbied actively, but for the most part unsuccessfully, in several Commonwealth capitals for a stronger stand against the military regime in Fiji.

By June the state of emergency was beginning to be relaxed somewhat, making it possible for a few authorized political meetings to be held throughout the country. At these gatherings, the Coalition leaders tried to boost opposition to the coup and to the determined, military-backed attempts to overthrow the 1970 constitution. The supporters and leaders of the Taukei Movement, on the other hand, took a hardline position at the other end of the political spectrum. Meanwhile, hundreds of people, mostly Indo-Fijians, queued daily for visas to emigrate to Australia, New Zealand, and North America. Shaken businesspeople desperately tried to take as much of their liquid capital as possible out of the country. Meanwhile, cane farmers refused to harvest their crop, concerned that in the financially straitened circumstances, they might not receive any payments at all.

At Government House, the governor-general proposed a complex plan to resolve the constitutional impasse and return the country to parliamentary government.[50] As a first step, it involved the appointment of a sixteen-member Constitution Review Committee made up of four representatives each from the Coalition, the Alliance, and the Great Council of Chiefs, and the governor-general. In the second stage, the committee would hold public hearings on the appropriateness of the 1970 constitution and announce its recommendations on "ways and means of strengthening the political rights of the indigenous Fijians." This would be followed by the formation of a Council of National Reconciliation, which would review the proposed changes to the constitution and prepare a covenant of national reconciliation. If consensus were reached, as the governor-general hoped it would be, then the recommendations of the Constitution Review Committee would pass into law. The pre–14 May House of Representatives would be convened for a sitting to approve the changes, which would then pave the way for a new election under the revised constitution.

Rabuka welcomed the proposals. "I have seen the plans," he said, "and I believe they can achieve the objectives I set out to achieve."[51] The Coalition was opposed. It would be clearly outnumbered on the Constitution Review Committee by groups that supported the coup and changes to the constitution. The governor-general, it noted, had already agreed with the Taukei Movement's assertion that the constitution needed changing, without testing public opinion through a national referendum. If a change were contemplated, the Coalition suggested, it should be under the guidance of an impartial Royal Commission of Enquiry composed of eminent jurists from abroad.[52]

Negative reaction came also from the international media. The conservative newspaper *Australian* called the governor-general's proposals a triumph of "Melanesian chauvinism and exclusivism," fulfilling the objectives of Sitiveni Rabuka "with the added bonus of having been achieved through a vote in parliament, the only institution that is empowered to change the constitution."[53] The *New Zealand Herald* called it "a face saving charade of consultation,"[54] while the United States warned that the "creation of any system in Fiji which did not respect and protect the rights of all Fiji's people, regardless of its label, should not expect support from us."[55]

Despite all its reservations, the Coalition agreed to participate in the Constitution Review Committee. This it did after the terms of reference of the committee were amended to read that "any amendments which will guarantee indigenous Fijian political interest" would be made "with full regard to the interests of other people of Fiji." There was much local and international pressure on the Coalition not to boycott the proceedings and thus be seen as impeding plans to restore Fiji to some form of parliamentary democracy. The discussion could be used to inform the people of the country about the entrenched provisions of the 1970 constitution, and could thus undermine the thrust of the Taukei Movement propaganda.

The Constitution Review Committee began its deliberations in the middle of July, conducting public hearings in four major towns throughout the country. Eight hundred submissions of varying lengths and viewpoints were received.[56] The bulk of these, from individuals and groups supporting the Coalition, urged that pending a national referendum, the 1970 constitution should be retained in its entirety. Most social and religious groups within the Indo-Fijian community—the Sangam, the Arya Samaj, the Sikh Gurudwara Committee, Sanatan Dharm Pritinidhi Sabha, and local village committees—supported this stand. The only exception was the leadership of the Fiji Muslim League, which supported the Taukei Movement, hoping that by doing so, they would at long last be able to obtain separate political representation for Muslims in parliament. The Muslim League's submission deeply split the usually cohesive Muslim community.[57]

Opinion within the Fijian Christian community was divided. The Catholics criticized the coup and reminded the Fijian leaders of the dangers of overprotecting their people. (Ratu Mara is a staunch Catholic.) However the views of the Methodist Church, to which the majority of the Fijians belong, were the ones that really mattered. The church had long been a staunch backbone of the Alliance Party. Now many of its leading members, like Tomasi Raikivi, were leaders of the Taukei Movement; even Rabuka was a lay Methodist preacher. However, the church had many Indo-Fijian members as well. One of its former presidents was the Reverend Daniel Mustapha, who had resigned from the governor-general's Council of Advisors because, as he said, it would have interfered with his performance as a church minister in a multiracial community.

When the internal debates were over, however, the church went along with the views of the coup supporters. Fiji should be declared a Christian state, guided by Christian precepts and ideals; Fijian seats in parliament should be increased from twenty-two to thirty and the existing allocation for Indo-Fijians and general electors (twenty-two and eight respectively) retained; in the Senate, the Great Council of chiefs' nominees should be increased from eight to thirteen, of whom at least three were to represent the three existing Fijian confederacies.[58] This was a great victory for the coup supporters, for the church's stand sent a powerful signal to the bulk of the Fijian community already torn between their political conviction and their Christian beliefs.

Bavadra presented the Coalition's case. His party, he said:

maintains that the present system of political representation is just, fair and equitable. The system has withstood the test of time and has become accepted by the majority of the citizens of this country. It protects the special interests of the indigenous Fijians through special provisions of power of veto by nominees of the Great Council of Chiefs. To devise changes to the existing constitution on the basis of the preponderance of any particular race must in the end be harmful to race relations as it would enhance polarization of our communities along racial lines. It will also disturb the balance of power in the current constitution. This could lead to a loss of confidence in the long term stability of the country which would translate into serious economic results, similar to what has been evidenced since the coup.[59]

He affirmed his party's commitment to genuine multiracialism and power sharing, arguing that it "is illogical to assume that the strengthening of Fijian interests can only be achieved through the curtailment of the political rights of others."

The Taukei Movement could not have disagreed more. The Coalition's victory, it asserted, had breached the "unwritten assumption" that Fijian chiefs will always control the reins of power in the country, an assumption it saw as the ideological basis for multiracial cooperation in independent Fiji. The 1970 constitution had worked to the great disadvantage of the Fijian people, though it did not check the "exuberance and excess of any [other] culture in acquiring a greater proportion of the fruits of development."[60] The fundamental values of democracy, such as liberty, freedom of speech, and equality, they repeated, were foreign to Fijian tradition "and are indeed contrary to Fijian way of life where liberty, which exists only within one's own social rank and equality, is strictly constrained by a fully developed social hierarchy." The Taukei Movement proposed a two-tiered parliament, with an upper house (Bose Vakatūraga) consisting of chiefs, their nominees, and some elected members, and a lower house (Matanivanua) of elected Fijian members. The Bose Vakatūraga would enjoy complete veto power over all legislation. In short, Fiji should be converted into a huge political *koro* under chiefly leadership, where non-Fijians would be seen but not necessarily heard.

In his submission, Bavadra had called the Taukei Movement a "group of vocal minority," but the sentiments expressed by its leaders appeared to be widely shared within the Fijian community, if the responses of the various provincial councils were any guide. These had been convened by Ratu Josua Toganivalu, the governor-general's advisor on Fijian affairs, to test Fijian opinion on constitutional change.[61] Judging by the various resolutions that were passed, the fourteen provincial councils differed from each other only in the extent to which the other ethnic groups were to be excluded from the political process. Without exception, they all agreed to give Fijians a preponderant majority in parliament and emphasized the need for legislation giving Fijian people preferential treatment in the public sector, including the civil service.

Some councils went further than others. Under the influence of Apisai Tora, the Ba Provincial Council, for instance, wanted fifty of the fifty-two seats in parliament to be reserved for Fijians, the remaining two going to

Rotumans. Indo-Fijians were to be completely excluded from participation in national politics. Following the Malaysian example, the council wanted Fijians to be given fixed shares in all business ventures in the country. The Rewa Provincial Council wanted the interpretation of the constitution to be left not in the hands of the Supreme Court but in the hands of a committee appointed by the Great Council of Chiefs. From Lomaiviti came the call to reserve 75 percent of police force and permanent secretary positions for Fijians.

With such pro-Fijian views publicly aired in the provinces, there was very little doubt which way the proceedings of the Great Council of Chiefs would go when it met in Suva in July. The only question that remained in doubt was whether the chiefs would heed the impassioned pleas of the Taukei Movement to declare Fiji a republic as a way out of the constitutional crisis. That issue was debated at great length, but in the end most of the chiefs sided with the views of Mara and Ganilau that the deeply cherished link with the British Crown should not be severed. The link with the Crown not only entailed a lifeline to legitimacy, but also was a symbolic buttress to the system, in particular, land.

After several days of intense debate, the council produced a lengthy submission to the Constitution Review Committee.[62] Fiji should be declared a Christian state, the chiefs said, and the new constitution should have express provisions for affirmative action enabling Fijian people a greater degree of participation in the public sector, in statutory bodies, and even in private companies. The Crown's right of eminent domain should be revoked, and the Fijian people given complete ownership of all underground water; unextracted minerals, including petroleum; geothermal heat and energy; foreshore, including mangrove swamps and lagoons, reefs and sandbanks; fishing rights; river-beds; traditional intellectual property rights; and paleontological and archaeological excavations. The chiefs had been demanding these for some time; the coup provided a golden opportunity to realize them.

Regarding the constitution of the parliament, the chiefs recommended the abolition of the bicameral legislature and its replacement by a single-chamber house of 71 seats. In it, Fijians would have 40 representatives (28 nominated by the Provincial Councils, 8 by the governor-general, and 4 by the prime minister); there would be 22 Indo-Fijians, 8 general electors, and 1 Rotuman nominated by the Council of Rotuma. All Indo-Fijian and general seats were to become completely communal, and the Fijians were to lose the right of direct voting and secret ballot to consensus nomination through the provincial councils. To further entrench Fijian power, the most important offices of state were to be reserved for the *taukei*. The prime minister was always to be an ethnic Fijian, as were the ministers of Fijian Affairs, Agriculture, Home Affairs, Finance, and Industry. The post of commander of the Fiji Military Forces, the commissioner of police, the chair of the Public Service Commission, and the secretary to the cabinet were also to be reserved for Fijians. The governor-general was to be appointed by the Queen on the advice of the Great Council of Chiefs. In short, the chiefs wanted Fiji to become primarily a Fijian state, notwithstanding the fact that more than half the population was non-Fijian. The only difference between the council and the Taukei Movement extremists was that while the latter were forthright in their demands, the former wanted to retain the paraphernalia of parliamentary democracy and give the appearance of reasonableness while striving for the same goals.

In view of the diametrically opposed submissions from the two camps, the Constitution Review Committee was unable to present recommendations that would form the basis of a solution acceptable to all parties. A majority report endorsed by all the Alliance and Great Council of Chiefs' representatives and two of the governor-general's was issued, along with a minority report endorsed by all the Coalition nominees.[63] The majority report accepted many of the most important points in the Great Council of Chiefs' submission. It recommended, for instance, the concept of a single seventy-one-seat House of Representatives, Fijian-dominated along the lines demanded by the chiefs, elected entirely from communal rolls, with its most important offices permanently in the hands of Fijians. The Great Council of Chiefs would retain the power to nominate the governor-general. The Alliance Party's support for constitutional change came as a shock to its non-Fijian supporters, several of whom, particularly in the Indian Alliance, resigned in protest. Certainly, it was at variance with its election promise to maintain a just and fair constitution for all the people of Fiji.

The Coalition, on the other hand, reasserted its view that there was no need to change the 1970 constitution, at least not without first testing national opinion through a referendum. The implementation of the recommended changes, it said, would lead to legalized racial discrimination, further segregation of the two major groups into unproductive communal compartments and general national demoralization. It added:

A fair and democratic constitution should be one that provides for stability and allows for the possibility of change of government. An outright majority of parliamentary seats constitutionally guaranteed to a single race is not only discriminatory but it also means that a party, however corrupt, inefficient or oppressive, can remain perpetually in power through this in-built advantage. This is a most dangerous situation for any country and therefore the most compelling argument against granting extra seats on purely racial lines.[64]

While the Constitution Review Committee conducted its public hearings around the country, another group was at work suggesting to the governor-general a way out of the constitutional crisis. This was the "Back to

Early May" movement, led by a multiracial group of leading nonpolitical public figures and formed a month after the coup.[65] Its aim was not to attempt to restore either the Bavadra or the Mara government, but rather to provide a broadly acceptable breathing space conducive to calm and reasoned dialogue.

The movement proposed a six-point plan to achieve this objective. As an interim measure and to provide a legal framework for discussion, the independence constitution should be retained. The democratically elected but now dissolved parliament should be reconvened to form a government of national unity. A royal commission should be appointed to review the proposed changes to the constitution. After being endorsed by the bipartisan government of national unity, the changes should then be subjected to a national referendum. Meanwhile, the military personnel should be sent back to the barracks and the amnesty that the governor-general had granted to all those involved in the coup should be respected. Finally, the responsibility for law and order should be handed back to the judiciary and the police force instead of being vested in the army. These proposals were presented to the governor-general on 12 August 1987, together with an astounding 107,719 signatures endorsing them, of which 96,973 were from Indo-Fijians, 9,139 from indigenous Fijians, and 1,607 from others.[66] The signatures had been gathered within just four weeks and under the most trying conditions.

What direct impact the Back to Early May movement's proposals had on Ganilau's thinking is difficult to tell, but his subsequent actions clearly reveal the imprint of its ideals. Realizing that the Coalition was not ready anytime soon to accept "the reality of the situation" and acquiesce voluntarily to his Taukei Movement–supported plans, he initiated a series of private meetings between the two political parties early in September. After several initial setbacks, in part caused by clinging to publicly proclaimed uncompromising positions and in part by the general atmosphere of tension and violence in the country, an accord was reached at Deuba to be announced to the nation on 25 September.[67]

The accord provided for a bipartisan caretaker government to be formed to "guide the country to a solution to Fiji's constitutional problems; re-establish Fiji's respect for law and order; and put the economy upon a firm footing." The new council of state chaired by the governor-general would consist of twenty members drawn from the two political parties and sharing power on an equal basis. Of these, six members, three each from the Coalition and the Alliance, would constitute a new Constitution Review Committee to be chaired by an independent expert from overseas. The committee would recommend a permanent constitutional solution acceptable to all the people of Fiji and propose arrangements for an early return to parliamentary democracy, taking fully into account the social, economic, and political aspirations of the indigenous Fijians while bearing in mind the interests of the other communities as well. "Fiji is now set to walk out of the darkness and find its place in the sun again," the *Fiji Times* editorialized on its front page. "Now let us all walk together towards the dawn."[68]

The September Coup and the Birth of the Fiji Republic

With the achievement of the accord at Deuba, events appeared to have come full circle. Soon after the May coup, the justices of the Fiji Supreme Court had broadly suggested the line of action the governor-general was now proposing to implement. What the future of Fiji might have been had he heeded their advice will now remain a mystery. Throughout June, July, and August, attitudes on both sides hardened and public opinion became deeply polarized. To counter the Taukei Movement propaganda, the Coalition launched its Operation Sunrise in the west to educate the Fijian people about their entrenched rights in the 1970 constitution. The judiciary took an activist role in upholding law and order and in reminding the security forces of their proper responsibilities.[69] The Indo-Fijian cane farmers threatened to strike if their demand for assured payment for their crops was not met. And overseas, particularly in Australia and New Zealand, Coalition supporters were active in organizing opposition to the procoup forces in Fiji.[70]

At the other end of the spectrum, the Taukei Movement capitalized on heightened Fijian anxiety and suspicion in this critical period. Its leaders felt that the provisions of the 1970 constitution were biased against the interests of the Fijians. They threatened to "pick up our clubs, the old and the new, and protect our interests and supremacy with all our might."[71] Their anger crystallized around a few issues. One was Bavadra's lawsuit against the governor-general for the apparently unconstitutional dissolution of parliament. The Taukei Movement saw it as a cultural matter. One of its supporters wrote:

> It could be argued that he [Ganilau] may be appearing not as a person but as the holder of the venerable office of G-G [governor-general]. That, most people know. But to diehard Fijians whether he appears in court as G-G or holder of and exerciser of sole "executive authority" is immaterial and secondary to their understanding. To them and, I assume, to the Taukei Movement as well, the appearance of Ratu Sir Penaia will not be taken in the light of his role as the G-G but as Ratu Penaia the paramount chief of "Lalagavesi." That to those well-versed in the intricacies of Fijian socio-political nuances is something that is tantamount to insulting not only the whole vanua of Cakaudrove let alone its ramifications to the Kubuna and Burebasaga Confederacies if the Vunivalu or Roko Tui Dreketi were in a similar position.[72]

Such contrasting perceptions of the situation in Fiji further widened the gap between the two camps. As far as the procoup Fijians were concerned, the governor-general's efforts to resolve the constitutional crisis through compromise and negotiation were completely unacceptable. They would be "forcefully opposed," thundered the Fijian Nationalist Party. "It is taking the Fijian people back to square minus one," said Ratu Meli Vesikula.[73]

To demonstrate their resolve, the Taukei Movement supporters flooded the local dailies with violence-threatening letters. Simultaneously, they reactivated their destabilizing plans intended ultimately to make Fiji ungovernable without their full participation. Early in September, the central business district of Suva became the target of a well-orchestrated campaign of arson and looting. Worse was to follow. On 24 September, a day after the governor-general's address, 114 prisoners "broke out" of the Naboro Prison, and fifty-two of them marched through Suva, escorted by the military and the police, to meet with the governor-general. They expressed their concern at the continuing instability in the country and at the impending court case regarding the dissolution of parliament.[74] After breakfast at the vice-regal lodge, and having made their point, the escapees returned to the prison peacefully, leaving a *Fiji Sun* editorial to ponder whether the Naboro prison breakout was "engineered and later assisted and condoned by elements within the security forces whose principal objective is to ensure that the fragile talks at Deuba fail and anarchy prevails throughout the land."[75] That was, indeed, the case. The prison breakout was intended to be a prelude to other more violent acts, such as killing leading Coalition members, destroying the property of Coalition supporters, and fostering other such activities to plunge the country into chaos and anarchy.

Rabuka watched these tense developments with mounting unease. The uncomfortable truth was that he was riding a tiger he could not dismount at will. His dilemma was compounded by his exclusion from the negotiations that the governor-general had set in motion, apparently at the insistence of the Coalition. With good reason, Rabuka feared marginalization from the national political process on the one hand and repudiation by his militant supporters on the other. He could afford neither. He also feared that a future caretaker government might impose strict controls on the military and restrict "its capacity to stage another coup."[76] It thus came as little surprise to most keen observers when Rabuka executed his second coup at 4:50 PM on 25 September 1987.

The second coup was much more professionally executed and tightly controlled. A curfew was imposed immediately, overseas travel for Fiji citizens banned, communication to the outside world cut off or placed under the control of the military. The newspapers were forced to close down, one of them, the *Fiji Sun,* permanently. Radio Fiji became the mouthpiece of the military.[77] Within hours of the coup, about two hundred people, Coalition parliamentarians and their supporters, judges, journalists, senior civil servants, academics, and others who for some reason had incurred the wrath of the Taukei Movement, were detained for varying lengths of time and with varying degrees of hardship. Rabuka decreed himself head of an interim government. The country was plunged into yet another round of turmoil.

On 28 September, all political detainees, except Bavadra and some other Coalition members, were freed. The next day, Rabuka held his first press conference. Fiji had been declared a de facto republic, he announced, though he still wanted to retain the country's connection with the Commonwealth, and especially with the British Crown. The governor-general had been requested very diplomatically to accept the invitation to head the new government. The judges had been approached to continue in their jobs, though they declined to breach their oath of office. Strong messages of support came from around the country, Rabuka said, especially from the chiefs of Cakaudrove, some of whom were prepared, or so they said, to sacrifice their lives to attain the coup's stated aims.

On 1 October the 1970 constitution was formally revoked. Meanwhile, behind the scenes, intense negotiation was under way to see whether some solution to the constitutional crisis could not be found before Fiji severed its ties to the Crown. At a meeting in Lautoka on 5 October, attended by Ganilau, Mara, and Bavadra, Rabuka made a number of demands, including one to adopt the constitution approved by the Great Council of Chiefs and another to guarantee the military a role in the political affairs of the country. The Coalition refused to meet these "minimum demands."

Frustrated, Rabuka went on the air at midnight on 7 October to read a decree making Fiji a republic. He also announced an eighteen-member Council of Ministers, composed largely of hardline supporters of the Taukei Movement, to help him run the country; three more would be added two days later.[78] Among the ministers was Ratu Filimone Ralogaivau (in charge of Education), who had been the Labour Coalition's minister of state for Fijian Affairs, and Irene Jai Narayan, once the deputy leader of the National Federation Party. Ahmed Ali was made an advisor to the Executive Council. Rabuka told the inaugural gathering of his ministers: "I firmly believe and I am sure that the nation is with me that the declaration of the Republic, the formation of the Council, the selection of its members and the choice of the objectives have the blessing of God."[79]

At the very least, the coup had the blessing of many island governments across the Pacific. King Taufa'ahau Tupou IV of Tonga dispatched Crown Prince Tupoutoa to personally convey his message of support to Rabuka. He made it clear that he would have "acted like Colonel Rabuka, if I had been in his place."[80] From Papua New Guinea, separatist leader Josephine Abaijah sent a rhapsodic telegram: "I support your philosophies, sentiments and aspirations for your country. Your humbleness, sincerity, courage and the dignity which you exercised in achieving your goal touched the hearts of many friends in Papua New Guinea."[81] Other Melanesian leaders offered support, though in a more subdued fashion. However, some leaders, such as Father John Momis and Justice Bernard Narokobi, were critical of developments in Fiji.

From across the Pacific Ocean in Vancouver, where a Commonwealth Heads of Government Meeting was in progress, came a decidedly different message. Referring to the second coup, Sridath Ramphal said: "This is an act of intervention against a political process that was succeeding, not one that was failing."[82] Consequently, at India's urging and over the United Kingdom's objections, Fiji's membership of the Commonwealth was allowed to lapse. At this writing, Fiji is still excluded from membership. Readmission would require unanimous approval of all members. India has indicated that it will continue to oppose Fiji's reentry unless the constitutional crisis is resolved to the satisfaction of all its people.[83]

Such acts of international condemnation outraged members and supporters of the military regime, who retaliated by taking their anger out on local Coalition supporters, both Fijian and Indo-Fijian. The mobility of Indo-Fijians was severely curtailed. Senior civil servants suspected of being anticoup were "questioned," demoted, transferred to lesser jobs, or simply retired. Some of the more exuberant members of the Taukei Movement went further, harassing, torturing, and sexually molesting Coalition supporters in Ba, Labasa, Nausori, and Lautoka in the name of security or to extract information about supposedly seditious activities.[84]

A series of decrees were issued that placed further limits on freedom of speech and conscience. The Sunday Observance Decree banned all recreational and sports activity in order to enforce a strict observance of the Sabbath. The Fundamental Freedoms Decree effectively outlawed any political activity deemed contrary to the views of the regime. Soldiers were vested with the power to "shoot to kill" while "making a lawful arrest or preventing escape, to suppress a riot, or to prevent a criminal offence." The Fiji Service Commission and Public Service (Amendment) Decree stipulated that at least 50 percent of positions at all levels of the civil service be allocated to Fijians and Rotumans, thus necessitating the transfer or, in some cases, enforced resignation of many senior Indo-Fijian civil servants. The Public Service Commission was empowered to dismiss any officer on the grounds of "public interest." The situation was particularly odious because the victims of these discriminatory measures were largely the members of one ethnic group, the Indo-Fijians.

For most ordinary people, the misery caused by social and institutional repression was compounded by a sharp deterioration in the economy. At the time of the May coup, the Fijian economy was in a relatively robust state. Foreign reserves were high at $190 million, inflation was low at 1.8 percent, unemployment was at a containable rate of 7.5 percent, and interest rates were falling. The coups changed all this. Cash flowed out of the country, $13 million in the first week after the coup.[85] The dollar was devalued by 35 percent, and salaries in the public sector were cut by 25 percent. The average real income fell by almost 13 percent and real investment by 42 percent. Tourist arrivals were down by 26 percent on the 1986 level, and the total deficit for 1987 increased from a budgeted $86 million to $109 million.[86] Whatever remnants of investor confidence remained in the country after the May coup were fast vanishing. Fiji faced the very real prospect of bankruptcy by the end of the year.

The September coup caused other problems as well. For many who had supported the May coup, events had gone further than expected. What had begun as little more than an attempt to reinstall an Alliance government under Ratu Mara had taken unexpected and undesirable turns. A normally placid Ganilau was visibly angry at Rabuka for disconnecting his phone, apparently to prevent him from seeking outside advice. Mara was said to be furious at being upstaged. For these chiefs, both knights and both groomed for their later careers by paternalistic colonial officials, severing the deeply cherished and politically valuable links with the British monarchy hurt deeply.

Other reasons, too, contributed to the high chiefs' disquiet. As events unfolded, Fijians saw the military cabinet dominated by middle-ranking chiefs from politically dormant areas (Vesikula from Verata and Ralogaivau from Bua) and educated commoners, and they began to realize that the latest coup may have been a blow against their paramount eastern chiefs. What they heard over the air confirmed their suspicion. Fijian leaders such as those in the military cabinet were like prominent chiefs of precolonial times, self-made men, of achieved and not ascribed status, who had attained power, influence, and prestige through demonstrated ability and political cunning. The institution of paramount chieftainship, they heard, was a Polynesian intrusion of recent coinage. The distinctly Melanesian roots of Fiji were being emphasized. The inclusion of Butadroka in the cabinet lineup, the harshest Fijian critic of the eastern establishment in postindependent Fiji—he had called Mara unseemly names soon after the May coup ("the bastard who sold Fiji," "the bloody Judas Iscariot")[87]—signaled to nervous easterners the incipient ascendancy of "mainlanders" over "islanders." The slippery slide into possible tribal factionalism was threatening.

A frustrated Rabuka was coming to similar conclusions. His military regime, under pressure to deliver the goods to its supporters in quick time, was in disarray and speaking with discordant voices. On the one hand, the regime wanted to resuscitate the economy through foreign investment, and on the other, Lands and Minerals Minister Butadroka was preparing plans to implement his long-held policy to return all fee simple and Crown land to Fijian hands. Not only foreign investors and Indo-Fijians were frightened by this move. It also alarmed many chiefs, who hold title to quite a bit of the country's fee simple land. Obviously, Butadroka had taken the logic of the paramountcy of Fijian interests too close to home for comfort. Some of Rabuka's cabinet colleagues were disenchanted by widespread reports of bureaucratic bungling and internal struggles for power among their colleagues. Some ministers, such as Vesikula, who headed the Ministry of Fijian Affairs, lacked previous administrative experience. The more pragmatic ones wanted both Mara and Ganilau to return and lead the government again, one of them being the mercurial Apisai Tora, who circulated a petition to that effect in western Viti Levu. He recalled:

> My attitude was pragmatic. Ratu Sir Kamisese is an able leader, he is experienced in the ways of government and international politics. It was clear to me that in terms of getting things moving on a steady course, restoring economy, and diplomatic relations and starting aid flowing again, he was the one. He could do the job. There was a message coming through from many overseas Governments—put Ratu Mara back and recognition and aid will flow.[88]

Rabuka yielded, but only after many of his prior conditions were met. These included the insistence that no Coalition members be appointed to the cabinet; that three army officers, including himself, be appointed in the new administration; and that the draft constitution prepared by the military be accepted and any amendments to it be approved by the military's legal advisors.[89] The conditions posed no major problem to Mara and Ganilau. Three military officers and seven members of the now-dissolved military council as well as some of the leading members of the Taukei Movement found their way into the new cabinet.[90]

On 5 December 1987, Rabuka appointed Ganilau as president of the republic. During a solemn ceremony witnessed by representatives and warriors of the three confederacies, Rabuka paid homage to Ganilau's status as a paramount chief, asked for forgiveness for any unintended transgressions of chiefly prerogatives, and disclaimed any ambitions for himself. In his turn, Ganilau thanked the soldiers for protecting the Fijian people and offered his blessing to them. In conclusion, he said, "Firm is our relationship, firm is the cord that binds all Fijians together. May God watch over us in the different roles that we perform. Blessed is Fiji. Let us all shoulder one club for all time. Mana."[91] The next day, Ganilau invited Mara back into his accustomed role as prime minister, which he accepted with "honour and pride."[92] Rabuka said that both he and his two paramount chiefs were agreed on the fundamental requirements for any change in the future. "We differ only in the way to achieve them."[93]

The Causes of the Coup

For most people in Fiji and the outside world, the May coup came as a complete surprise. Even the Coalition politicians walking at gunpoint to

the waiting military trucks parked outside the parliament building wondered aloud whether their kidnapping had been staged by the army as a
precautionary exercise. Not surprisingly, therefore, the question on nearly
everyone's mind was, and to some degree remains: What caused the coup?
What went wrong? Why did things fall apart in a country where parliamentary democracy had worked well for seventeen years after independence? Several conflicting theories were advanced as the events unfolded,
some of which now have much less credibility than they once did.

One prominent early view was that the coup was instigated by the
United States and the Central Intelligence Agency in collaboration with
certain local politicians.[94] The Coalition's victory, the argument went, and
its publicly proclaimed policy to oppose the carriage, testing, storage, and
manufacture of nuclear weapons or the dumping of nuclear waste in the
Pacific threatened US strategic interests in the region. The Coalition's victory came at a particularly inopportune time for the United States: the
ANZUS Alliance was under considerable strain and heading toward rup-
ture; the Soviet Union was fishing for influence in Kiribati, as was Libya
in the troubled republic of Vanuatu; the New Caledonia cauldron was
boiling. Washington made no secret of its deep disappointment at Mara's
defeat. He was its staunchest friend in the region, and with his support the
United States had been able to increase and consolidate its influence.[95]
Not surprisingly, there was "nervousness in Washington as the US government enters the uncertainties of the post-Mara period in the region."[96]

Washington was certainly disappointed with the Coalition's victory, but
was it sufficiently concerned with the change of government in Fiji to assist
in fomenting the coup? The advocates of this view adduce circumstantial
evidence to support their case for American complicity. They allege that
Fiji-based director of the United States Agency for International Development, William Paupe, gave $25,000 to Apisai Tora, a key figure in the
movement to destabilize the Coalition government.[97] They point to the
presence in Fiji two weeks before the May coup of General Vernon Walters, a widely noted harbinger of American-inspired coups throughout the
world.[98] And they note the suspiciously coincidental meeting of the World
Anti-Communist League in Sigatoka at the time of the coup.

In the light of the troubled situation in the region and in view of what we
generally know about the US role in facilitating the overthrow of
unfriendly governments in Latin America and Central America and other
parts of the world, it would be surprising if the United States did not do all
it could to influence events in Fiji to protect its political and strategic interests in the South Pacific. Some funds may well have been passed to the
destabilizers, though many Coalition leaders have pointed privately to
more plausible local sources of financial support. These include a prominent well-connected pro-Alliance businessman and the management of the
Emperor Gold Mines, which had been a particular target of the Coalition
in the campaign.[99]

It is conceivable that the United States knew of the coup plans in advance. But beyond conjecture and speculation, no hard evidence has been unearthed, no smoking gun discovered even by the most ardent theorists of American involvement. There the matter remains. However, the search for external causes, with its odd underpinnings of paranoia and deference, should not be allowed to distort the larger picture. Local actors should not be robbed of the vital role they have played in making their own history. The Coalition's victory had threatened the interests and prospects of a whole array of individuals and institutions within Fiji who had a far more immediate interest in overthrowing the new government. A substantial American role now looks more and more unconvincing, especially in the light of political developments in the country since the coups.

The May coup was caused by a complex combination of local factors, none of which by themselves can be assigned a privileged role in explaining the Fiji crisis. Divergent class interests and regional disparities within Fijian society, the pride and pique of important individuals dislodged from power, ethnic prejudice, and the fear of change in unaccustomed directions—all played their part to varying degrees. To begin with the stated justifications for the coup, Rabuka has always maintained that he staged the first coup because an Indo-Fijian–dominated Coalition government threatened to undermine Fijian land rights, the integrity of Fijian society, and the sovereignty of its people.[100] The Coalition's victory had breached a "solemn pact" at the time of independence that the government of Fiji would always remain in the hands of the Fijian people and their traditional leaders.[101]

There is no record of any solemn pact, and no one has ever produced it, which said that the government of Fiji had always to remain in Fijian hands. The matter was never raised in the confidential constitutional negotiations in Fiji or in London that paved the way for independence in 1970.[102] If this were the case, it would make a mockery of elections and the practice of parliamentary democracy in Fiji since independence. It would also make such Fijian leaders as Mara and Ganilau appear hypocritical. It is true that as independence approached, some Fijians wanted Fiji to be returned to Fijian hands, but that was more a negotiating tactic to extract concessions from the opposition. Said Ratu Mara: "Our people fully endorsed the move towards independence based on the present [1970] constitution which does not stipulate race as a requirement for the post of Prime Minister and other Ministers of government."[103] The claim about a solemn pact must, therefore, be seen as a retrospective justification for the illegal seizure of power.

The claim that the Coalition was Indo-Fijian dominated might appropriately be termed inconsequential in the context of Fiji's electoral system. To be sure, of the 28 Coalition parliamentarians, 19 were Indo-Fijians, 7

Fijians, and 2 general electors. However, within the 52-seat House of Representatives Indo-Fijians had only 22 seats. Within the Coalition, the Fijians wielded the balance of power and held the ministries deemed to be a particular privilege of the Fijian people. During the 1987 general elections, the Alliance Party insinuated that these Coalition Fijians were anti–Indo-Fijian, in sympathy with the Fijian Nationalist Party, whose political platform had long been "Fiji for the Fijians." Dr. Tupeni Baba, for example, was accused of supporting the Nationalists' policy of "thinning Indians from Fiji."[104] If these allegations were true, and the Coalition Fijians were anti–Indo-Fijian racists masquerading in Labour's multiracial garb, then it would follow that they could not have collaborated with their Indo-Fijian counterparts to deprive their own people of their cherished rights and privileges. They could not, in other words, be anti-Fijian and pro-Fijian at the same time.

On the question of the ownership of Fijian land, the Coalition's manifesto was clear: "There will be no change in this recognition nor will the Coalition government attempt to change the existing land laws without the full consultation of the Great Council of Chiefs."[105] The veto power vested in the Great Council of Chiefs' nominees in the Senate ensured that no government, not even the Fijian-dominated Alliance, could introduce any changes without their support. Nor could the Coalition government use the powers of eminent domain to acquire Crown or other property, including land, in an indiscriminate fashion. Section 8(1) of the 1970 constitution prescribed that the acquiring authority had to seek the permission of the Supreme Court, and that would be given only if the court was satisfied that the "taking of possession or acquisition is necessary or expedient in the interest of defense, public safety, public order, public morality, public health, town or country planning or utilization of any property in such a manner as to promote public benefit." The Chief Justice himself was an ethnic Fijian, and only two of the seven Supreme Court justices were Indo-Fijians. Finally, above all these restrictions was the reserve power of the governor-general who, exercising his deliberate judgment, could veto any legislation in the name of law and order.

What the Coalition proposed to do was to demand greater efficiency and accountability in the administration of the Native Land Trust Board (NLTB). The board consisted of the governor-general as president, the minister of Fijian Affairs as chairman, five Fijian members appointed by the Great Council of Chiefs, three Fijians nominated by the Fijian Affairs Board from a list submitted by the provincial councils, and not more than two members of any other ethnic group.[106] Its bloated bureaucracy had become the target of much criticism for inefficiency, mismanagement, and nepotism, especially among Fijian landowners in western Viti Levu. A report published by the government in 1977 had found the NLTB to be in a "state of disarray," accusing it of inordinately long delays in processing leases or dealing with applications, failure to re-assess or collect rents, failure to answer correspondence and also failure to run itself efficiently on the apparently large sums available to it from its "poundage" on rents and license fees, etc; with the resultant present need for financial assistance from Government to stave off bankruptcy.[107]

These problems were brought to public notice for the first time in the surveys of the controversial Carroll Report in 1982, which had found that only 44 percent of Fijian landowners and 30 percent of Indo-Fijian tenants thought the NLTB was doing a good job, while 39 percent of Fijians and 38 percent of Indo-Fijians interviewed thought it was doing a "bad job."[108] In his inaugural speech launching the Fiji Labour Party, Bavadra had said:

> The NLTB must be democratised so that it comes to serve the interests of all Fijians and not just the privileged few and their business associates. In addition, more effort must be made to see to it that those whose land is being used get more for their money out of the NLTB. It is impossible at present to see how the level of administrative charges that are levied are justified on the basis of services performed. If the NLTB is to take the money that it does, then it must do more for those who it is supposed to be serving. It is also important that steps be taken to rationalise the benefits derived from land use in Fiji. The system must be rationalised so that all Fijians, not just a few, benefit more. In addition, a great deal more must be done to enable the people of Fiji to increase the productivity of their land. More services and better infrastructure must be provided. This may be difficult, but ways must be found.[109]

To this end, the Coalition proposed the creation of a National Lands Commission, consisting of government representatives, landowners, and the tenant community, to keep a watchful eye on the administration of the NLTB, adjudicate land disputes, and facilitate better communication between the owners of the land and its users. The structure of the NLTB was to remain intact; only its efficiency was to be improved. To those disapproving of an "Indo-Fijian dominated" government, and to the predominantly eastern Fijian staff working in the NLTB, the Coalition's proposal appeared to be the thin end of the wedge, which could eventually lead to "the slipping away of native land."[110] The Coalition's talk of reform thus reinforced their opposition.

Whether the Coalition could have tampered with the cultural and social institutions of Fijian society is also to be viewed skeptically. Even though the Coalition government was committed to continuing many of the Alliance government's policies concerning Fijian society, all important matters pertaining to the governance of the *taukei* came within the jurisdiction not of the parliament but of the Great Council of Chiefs and its executive secretariat, the Fijian Affairs Board. The law provided that the council be headed by the minister of Fijian Affairs and consist of all Fijian members of the House of Representatives (in 1987, 15 Alliance and 7 Coalition) as well as nominees of the minister (15, of whom 7 had to be chiefs), Fijian members of the Senate, and a stipulated number of representatives nominated by all the fourteen Fijian provincial councils.

The entry of seven Coalition Fijians into this august body of conservative Fijian representatives was hardly likely to cause major tremors. Simple numbers and common sense dictated that the Coalition could not embark on any major, or even minor, reforms without the support of Fijian chiefs in the council. However, there may have been some hidden dangers that could have sent alarm signals to those chiefs from the maritime provinces who had long dominated the affairs of the council. In his capacity as minister for Fijian affairs, Bavadra had the opportunity to nominate a number of his own representatives, both chiefs and commoners, to the council. Given his political ideology and background, it was likely that he would nominate more people outside the Fijian-Alliance establishment and others who were sympathetic to his multiracial philosophy. This might have somewhat altered the balance of power in the council and threatened the power base of the Alliance politicians, eastern chiefs, and other vested interests in the Fijian community. Bavadra's election thus introduced many unknown and unpredictable variables in a forum that had an inherently conservative attitude toward change and innovation.

In the all-important policy-making Fijian Affairs Board, however, Bavadra's hands were even more tightly tied. The board is a corporate body with perpetual succession and charged with the duty of making recommendations and proposals to "advance the social and economic welfare of the Fijian people."[111] It consists of the minister and the permanent secretary of Fijian affairs (always Fijians), eight Fijian members of the House of Representatives to be elected by all Fijian parliamentarians, two nominees of the Great Council of Chiefs who were not members of parliament, and a legal and financial advisor. Board elections took place after each general election, and in 1987, all eight Fijian parliamentarians elected to the board were from the Alliance Party; the only Coalition member on it was the minister of Fijian Affairs, Bavadra himself. As chair, he had the unenviable task of presiding over a board that consisted of his staunch political opponents, some of them of extreme militant persuasion.[112] The Alliance Fijians gave a hint of things to come when they boycotted the opening of the new session of parliament.

The Coalition's victory did not, indeed, could not, endanger Fijian rights, but it held the potential for breaking from past patterns of political thinking and behavior in Fiji. The Fijian establishment, long dominated by chiefs from the maritime provinces, had good reason to be displeased with the Coalition's victory. For the first time in the modern history of Fiji, a paramount chief such as Ratu Sir Lala Sukuna, Ratu Sir George Cako-

bau, or Ratu Sir Kamisese Mara was not at the head of national Fijian
leadership. Instead, a middle-ranking chief from traditionally neglected
western Viti Levu had been elected to the highest office in the land. In a
society where ascribed status, hierarchy, and protocol are accorded great
weight, and where traditional ideology holds that the business of government is the prerogative of chiefs, and chiefs alone, Bavadra's elevation
posed troubling questions. Quite apart from anything else, a successful
performance on his part would discomfort chiefs who already felt themselves under seige from the corrosive effects of modern life and were struggling to reassert their authority over their people. Bavadra's pledge to educate his people to recognize the difference between their traditional and
their political obligations aggravated their fears. His elevation seemed to
send the message that, at long last, after nearly a century of struggle, the
western Fijians were within reach of gaining a measure of the power that
they felt was their due.

Timoci Bavadra and his Fijian colleagues in the Coalition represented,
in many ways, the coming-of-age of a new generation of Fijians. These
were urban-based professionals who had achieved success by dint of their
individual efforts and sacrifices. They were people of achieved status and
essentially middle class values. They still paid dues to the traditional system and kept up their ties with their home villages; but the psychological,
as well as social, distancing from their traditional roots was becoming
increasingly clear and irreversible. For their livelihood as teachers, doctors, civil servants, and skilled workers, they depended on the modern
multiracial community. Their social and material world had widened considerably, beyond the comprehension of their kin who remained close to
the communal culture in the isolated villages. However, although the
importance of class and regional factors in Fijian politics should be recognized, they should not be pushed too far. Many urban, middle class Fijians
still supported the Fijian establishment and were active opponents of the
Coalition government. Prominent western Fijians, such as Tui Vuda,
Ratu Sir Josaia Tavaiqia, and Apisai Tora, were among the leading members of the Taukei Movement even though they privately supported Bavadra's public criticism of eastern dominance in Fijian affairs.[113]

The long-reigning Alliance Party's prospects looked uncertain in the
aftermath of the Coalition's victory. There was a shift away from the Alliance to other parties, though this did not occur on a significant scale. It
was not the numbers so much as the trends they represented that were significant. Most of the Coalition's Fijian support came from urban and
periurban areas with a rapidly increasing Fijian population base. Some
Fijian Coalition politicians privately talked of creating a separate Fijian
communal constituency for Suva, which had 58,135, or 17.6 percent, of
the total Fijian population in 1986.[114] In the old electoral boundaries,
Fijians scattered over several hundred miles of land and sea were grouped

together as a single constituency, with Suva's Muanikau Ward voters lumped together with Fijians from the remote islands of Lomaiviti, and Samabula Fijians voting with Kadavu Islanders scores of miles away. The strategy of having large constituencies straddling both rural and urban areas had worked to the advantage of the Alliance because it preserved communal and traditional loyalties over common class interests, and any redefinition of electoral boundaries, especially in the rapidly expanding and politically unpredictable urban areas, would have threatened the party's prospects.

The Alliance felt threatened by the Coalition in other ways. The Coalition had made the removal of excessive secrecy in the conduct of government an important part of its campaign. Soon after it came to power, it began releasing classified reports of independent investigations, which revealed abuse of power by those in authority, mismanagement of public funds, and dereliction of duty. For defeated Alliance ministers, the loss of status, high salary, free housing, business contacts, overseas travel, and numerous other opportunities that access to power provided was bad enough, especially for those who had few marketable skills outside politics. The prospect of facing embarrassing revelations about bribery and corruption made the situation worse. Not surprisingly, many of them quickly joined the coup cabinet.

Finally, there was the question of the role of the Fiji Military Forces. As an almost exclusively Fijian institution, the army provided a prestigious and noncompetitive career shelter to young Fijian men. To many others, it was a great symbol of power, the ultimate guarantor of Fijian rights, which could be relied on to intervene in the political arena in the event of a political change unacceptable to the Fijian establishment. This gave comfort to many Fijians, but became a source of much anxiety to others. Throughout the 1970s, the NFP had called for a "more open door policy" regarding the admission of Indo-Fijians into the army.[115] The FLP had raised questions about the proper role and function of the army in its founding manifesto:

Something should be done about the Fijian military. Our army is in danger of becoming little more than a band of mercenaries. This is unfortunate, for we have a military heritage that in many ways we can be proud [of]. Again, we must see to it that our military serves our needs and not those of others. In this regard, we must be particularly mindful that we can pay for it ourselves, and especially the pension.[116]

Once in office, however, the Coalition modified its position. It affirmed its support for the military, though it promised to review the military's role in the areas of defense, nation building, internal security, and international peacekeeping. To the dismay of some Coalition supporters, the government pledged to continue the Fijian contribution to the UN peacekeeping forces in the Middle East. One Coalition figure reportedly met informally with officers of the Fiji Military Forces and asked what steps could be taken to admit more non-Fijians to the army.[117] A senior officer said financial constraint was the major problem. He saw no particular difficulty in admitting more soldiers if funds were available. Rabuka, however, remained silent. He had written an essay (as part of his master's thesis at the Indian Defence Services College in Madras) on the socioeconomic role of the army in developing countries. The army was close to his heart; it had been his rite of passage into manhood and power, and he was opposed to the idea of opening it up to Indo-Fijians.[118] Perhaps he thought it prudent to act before it was too late.

All these developments, and the anxieties and confusions that they created, took place in an environment poisoned by fears of racial dispossession and subjugation, the legacy of a century of racial compartmentalization and the politics of communalism. Unfortunately, both Fijian and Indo-Fijian communities had long seen each other through a prism of prejudice, reinforced by contrasting life-styles, cultural attitudes, and historical experiences. Generations of racially oriented politics had pitted the interests of one group against another, despite overarching common interests and problems. They bred suspicion and distrust that ran deep into the Fijian body politic. Many Fijians, at all levels of society, believed their collective identity would endure only under a government dominated by paramount chiefs. The behavior of the Indo-Fijian leaders contributed to the Fijians' fears. Their internecine struggles for power, their factional politics, and their inability to articulate an alternative vision for the nation left a strong, and not altogether unjustified, impression of a bickering and self-seeking Indo-Fijian leadership that could not be trusted with the reins of national power. Their inept performance played into the hands of Fijian militants who believed that whatever the verdict of the ballot box, Fiji had to remain always in Fijian hands.

The Principal Players

Although it is reasonably easy to outline the broad constellation of forces that converged to cause the Fijian crisis, it is less easy to identify the motives of the principal actors in the drama. Yet, without a consideration of these, any analysis of the coups will remain incomplete. The task of assessing motives, always tricky, is made more difficult in this case because none of the major players, except Sitiveni Rabuka, has published anything beyond self-exculpatory accounts. I have sought to place the text of these individuals' public statements alongside the context of their actions to assess the role they played in bringing about the Fiji crisis.

In the Coalition camp, the two main figures were Timoci Bavadra and his attorney general, Jai Ram Reddy. As already noted, Bavadra was a newcomer to national politics, having spent much of his working life in the Fiji public service. On retirement in 1985, he became the founding president of the Fiji Labour Party and on its founding in 1987, the unanimously elected leader of the Coalition. Although unimpressive in his public appearances, Bavadra was an impressive communicator in small gatherings. His common touch and modesty endeared him to his followers and all who came in contact with him. The impression he conveyed to most people was of a simple, honest man with a clean past. He was not seen as someone who was personally ambitious, but one genuinely committed to promoting the welfare of the ordinary people of all races and classes.

These qualities had the opposite impact on his opponents, who saw him as a political novice, susceptible to manipulation by his more experienced Indo-Fijian colleagues and other left-wing Labour advisors. His western Viti Levu and trade union background and his political ideology of democratic socialism had caused suspicion among the more extremist *taukei*. During the 1987 election campaign, the Alliance had spared no effort in attempting to belittle and even ridicule him. One typical Alliance advertisement during the campaign went: "Bavadra has NEVER been in parliament. He has no EXPERIENCE. He has no INFLUENCE. The Great Council of Chiefs does NOT listen to him. The international scene where we sell our sugar and need markets for our exports has NEVER heard of him. He CANNOT get renewals for farmers. He does NOT and dare NOT condemn the Fijian Nationalists."[119] How could this "unqualified unknown," a "Johnny-come-lately" who had not run anything, not even a "bingo party," in Mara's words, be trusted to safeguard the interests of Fijians?

Some of Bavadra's own actions provided ammunition to his critics. By putting the day-to-day running of the critical Ministry of Fijian Affairs in the hands of a minister of state (who did not have automatic access to the cabinet), he increased the apprehension of those Fijians, already distrustful of the Coalition, who watched with suspicion the apparent relegation of a branch of government that had become an integral part of their lives. Was this the harbinger of things to come? many Fijians asked. By appointing, or giving the appearance of considering, some administratively inexperienced loyalists to senior positions in his government, he increased the fears of senior Fijian civil servants who thought their future was threatened by the new government. His failure or refusal to meet with the officers of the Fiji Military Forces to allay their fears, despite several direct and indirect approaches from certain officers of the army as well as outside advisors, sent wrong signals at a critical time.[120] Bavadra's symbolic gesture of seeking the blessing of Ratu Sir George Cakobau, the Vunivalu and the head of the Kubuna confederacy, was seen by many Fijians, rightly or wrongly, as an attempt by the Coalition to manipulate traditional divisions

The principal players. Clockwise, from top left: Ratu Sir Kamisese Mara, Sitiveni Rabuka, Dr. Timoci Bavadra, Jai Ram Reddy, and Ratu Sir Penaia Ganilau. *(Courtesy* Fiji Times *and Fiji Ministry of Information)*

in Fijian society. Bavadra, they said, was committing the same mistake, of politicizing traditional institutions, as he accused the Alliance of committing.

All that said, Bavadra had been in office for only a month, much of it spent in very unsettled circumstances, attempting to allay the fears of the Fijian people and confronting his militant opponents, who were committed to his political demise at any cost. Besides these difficulties, he had to cope with the teething problems that confront all new governments, especially those with no previous experience at the national level. The majority of the Labour parliamentarians, including eleven of the cabinet members, had yet to make their maiden speeches. Nonetheless, Bavadra showed a remarkable capacity for growth. Within a short period, he had risen from trade union leader to respected national figure. Given time, he probably would have made a good prime minister. Bavadra died of spinal cancer in November 1989.

The Coalition figure who engendered the strongest emotion among the anti-Coalition forces was the former NFP leader Jai Ram Reddy. His rise to power and the reasons for his departure from parliamentary politics in 1984 were discussed earlier. He did not fit the mold of a typical Indo-Fijian politician in the tradition of, say, Siddiq Koya, whom many Fijians likened to a catamaran—fast, visible, and easily toppled. Reddy, on the other hand, was more like a submarine—quiet, difficult to fathom, and dangerous.[121] His determination to make a more serious bid for national power than his predecessors, who seemed content with the role of perpetual opposition, added to his image as a dangerous opponent. As the acknowledged architect of the Coalition, he became a particular target of the Alliance strategists during the 1987 campaign, when they tried hard to fan the dying embers of the 1977 Flower-Dove conflicts and the controversy surrounding the Carroll affair of 1982. They hoped to provoke Reddy to make some intemperate or ill-considered remark, such as he had in 1982 when he said that Mara would even open a toilet to shake a few more Indo-Fijian hands. That politically costly remark was publicized by the Alliance as a gross insult to a paramount chief.

At Bavadra's insistence, Reddy accepted the post of attorney general and justice minister in the Coalition government. He had not contested the election but, following the convention established by the Alliance, was appointed to the Senate and from there inducted into the cabinet. Fijians' fears were increased, or so some of them said in letters to the local papers and in placards carried during protest marches ("Reddy Gun—Bavadra Bullet," "Reddy: The Master Mover"). It was not surprising that Reddy was the very first target of the Taukei Movement's arson campaign when his Lautoka law office was firebombed two weeks before the coup. Was Reddy's appointment a political mistake? Would it have made any differ-

ence to the Taukei Movement's coup plans if Reddy had not been in the
Coalition government? The issue for the procoup forces was not the presence of any particular individual in government, however controversial
that person might be. Their main concern was the removal of a government that they themselves did not control. It was not the Indo-Fijian members of government that threatened the interests of sections of Fijian society; the presence of a new generation of non-chiefly educated Fijians
constituted the real problem.

The person sworn to uphold the rule of constitutional government in Fiji
was the governor-general, Ratu Sir Penaia Ganilau. His actions, or inac-
tion, have been the subject of much public debate. Ganilau has not commented publicly on his role during the crisis, but certain things are clear.
The Taukei Movement leaders are on record as saying that they had told
the governor-general that if he did not act to remove the Coalition government from power they would do it themselves.[122] Indeed, Rabuka himself
told Ganilau immediately after the election that "if he did not stage a political coup, I would stage a military coup."[123] Ratu Sir Penaia did not convey this threat to the Coalition, despite his constitutional obligation to.

Soon after the coup took place, the governor-general heeded the advice
of the judiciary and ordered the military back to barracks, proclaiming his
executive authority in the temporary absence of his government. Then his
resolve weakened. On 17 May he swore in Rabuka as head of the interim
government, though he refused to swear in others. Confronted by a near-
mutinous Great Council of Chiefs on Thursday, 21 May, Ganilau showed
his hand. He and the chiefs were on the same side, he told them; they
agreed on the ultimate goal of Fijian paramountcy but differed on the
methods. From then on, Ganilau acted in a manner designed to accomplish the objectives of the coup, and sought the Coalition's acquiescence to
his plans, all within the framework of his constitutional authority. When
the link with the British Crown was severed by Rabuka on 7 October
1987, Ganilau tendered his resignation as governor-general and accepted
the appointment as president of the Republic of Fiji.

Such behavior confounded most observers, local and foreign. In Ganilau's defense, his friends and loyalists argued that in the early stages of the
crisis, he was genuinely committed to upholding his constitutional authority and the decorum of his vice-regal office.[124] He later wavered because he
lacked support, most notably from a man who could have made a decisive
difference, Mara. The way Mara went, Ganilau was told immediately
after the news of the coup reached him, would determine the fate of the crisis. The Alliance leader called Ratu Sir Penaia at about 11:20 AM on
Thursday (14 May) from the Fijian Hotel at Yanuca to confirm the news of
the coup. According to observers at Government House, however, he neither offered nor sought advice about what might be done to prevent further damage to constitutional government in Fiji. A few hours later, Mara

joined the military cabinet without informing him, thereby further restricting the range of the governor-general's actions. It has also been argued that the Taukei Movement activists were in a rampant mood and would not have brooked vice-regal opposition to their goals. Faced with this challenge, Ganilau thought it best to remain in his position to exercise a degree of moderation and calm the turbulent course of events.

The truth of these assertions is difficult to establish, and in the absence of Ganilau's own testimony, it will remain a subject of debate. One interpretation suggests that there was nothing inconsistent or contradictory at all about his actions. He had been an open and honest advocate of the principle of Fijian paramountcy from the 1960s onward, as a reading of his Legislative Council speeches amply reflects. He was a chief who came closest to personifying the Sukuna tradition of responsible authoritarianism, including "sound administration, responsive if conservative chiefly leadership, and an unambiguous lack of compromise towards any proposals deemed likely to weaken Fijian rights and institutions."[125] He was trusted by Fijian people as a staunch guardian of their interests as virtually no other post-Sukuna Fijian leader had been. His widely reported lack of personal ambition in politics was credible.[126] He did not make any special and politically expedient efforts to cultivate a multiracial image; close friends testify to his lack of sympathy for Indo-Fijian interests and aspirations, especially when these impinged on Fijian interests. He had wept at the 1982 Great Council of Chiefs meeting at Bau at the slow disintegration of Fijian society and loss of chiefly leadership. It is a matter of public record that Ganilau and Rabuka were extremely close, as reflected in their common interest in rugby football and the overseas tours they undertook together. Rabuka felt free to discuss his career prospects with him and heeded Ganilau's advice to remain in the army despite Rabuka's growing disenchantment about his prospects there.[127]

Ganilau, then, was first and foremost a Fijian chief proud of his heritage. From the outset, he emotionally supported Rabuka's stated goals for Fijian paramountcy, but felt himself constitutionally constrained in giving them his public approval. He probably did not think a military coup was necessarily the most appropriate means to assert Fijian paramountcy. As time went on, however, his deeper, long-held feelings came to the fore. It is not difficult to understand why, for all his vacillation and inept performance in a moment of great crisis, even certain Coalition politicians felt a degree of sympathy for Ganilau.[128] At least, they said, he remained true to himself and to his convictions.

This cannot be said of the other major player in the Fijian crisis, Ratu Sir Kamisese Mara. He was seen, especially on the international scene, as a leader of a different mettle: father of the nation, multiracialist statesman, staunch champion of parliamentary democracy and the constitutional process. Given this perception, his public behavior during the coups was unsettling to many of his erstwhile admirers. They shook their heads incredulously in bewilderment and begged him to "stand up and show his hand."[129] Instead, the leader they had expected to talk sense to the hot-heads in the army joined the military cabinet within hours of the first coup. How can we explain Ratu Mara's actions and utterances during and immediately after the coups?

First, it is perhaps best to record Mara's own explanations and justifications. Soon after the first coup, when he was asked why he had hastily joined Rabuka's cabinet, Mara replied that his house was on fire, his life's work in danger of being demolished. Thinking nothing of his reputation, or what others might say, he threw his weight behind the coup leaders to prevent his country from plunging into unimaginable disaster.[130] In 1989, he advanced another reason. He feared Australian and New Zealand invasion of his country, he said, and wanted to lend his hand to stabilize the situation at a critical moment. In December 1990, he offered yet another "compelling reason" why he "threw his lot in" with the coup makers. It was out of a sense of racial and cultural solidarity with the indigenous Fijian people that he acted the way he did, he said—"to be where my people are."[131]

Mara also pointed an accusing finger at his political opponents and other critics. Much of the criticism, he asserted, was unfair, the work of his Indo-Fijian detractors, who were bent on destroying his reputation because he stood in the way of their ultimate ambition: to have an Indo-Fijian prime minister of Fiji. If only the Indo-Fijian people had kept faith with him, Fiji would have been spared its worst political crisis in modern times.[132] The Indians had caused political problems in all the countries they had settled, Mara said. "The Indians have not succeeded in living in harmony in Trinidad, in Guyana, in Sri Lanka. So Fiji is not exceptional. The only place they have succeeded very well off India is Mauritius where they completely dominate the population."[133] He also blamed the press for letting him down: "In all these years, I have been a victim of a continuous and prolonged campaign of denigration and personal vilification by a press that lacks balance, professionalism and a sense of responsibility. You people have never given me a fair go."[134] From all this, it would be fair to conclude that it is the image of a selfless man, a Fiji patriot "above the fog in public duty and private thinking,"[135] that Ratu Sir Kamisese Mara would like to leave as his legacy.

The credibility of Mara's assertions is for the reader to judge. Still, it is possible to contest some of his claims. If his house was on fire, argued Justice K. N. Govind, once an Alliance parliamentarian, then the Alliance leader should have joined the fire fighters, not the arsonists. It is very unlikely that Mara knew of Australian and New Zealand plans when he joined Rabuka's cabinet a few hours after the coup, when these governments themselves could not know what was happening in Fiji, much less prepare plans to invade the islands. If social solidarity with the Fijian people was a "compelling reason," his own words, for his joining the coup cabinet, then it undermines his tenderly nurtured reputation as a multiracial leader, not only of a segment of Fijian society but of all Fiji. Blaming Indo-Fijians is an expedient but problematic tactic, for it was the erosion of urban Fijian and general elector support that caused the Alliance's defeat, not the slippage of Indo-Fijian support. The reason for the Indians' apparent capacity for trouble-making throughout the world lies in the historical and political conditions created by colonialism, including the policy of ethnic separation, and not in genetics or race. It also needs to be explained why Indians' support for Mara and his party declined from around 24 percent in 1972 to around 15 percent in the 1980s. As for hostile press coverage, Mara himself was responsible for the dwindling number of prime ministerial press conferences in the 1980s, preferring instead to talk to his favorite foreign journalists, such as Stuart Inder of Sydney.

Nevertheless, no one has produced hard evidence of Mara's personal involvement in the planning and execution of the coups. On the other hand, most people in Fiji and outside are convinced that a person of Ratu Mara's experience, contacts, and stature must have known, if only vaguely, what was afoot, that without his tacit approval and active participation in the events that followed, the coups would almost certainly have failed. If it is not possible to accuse Ratu Mara of committing sins, it is easy to charge him with omission. In other words, what is crucial in assessing his behavior in the Fiji crisis is not what he did but what he did not do.

An alternative interpretation suggests that pique rather than personal sacrifice may have played a very large part in Mara's decisions and behavior. There can be very little doubt that the Alliance leader was deeply upset by his electoral defeat, caused as it was by a "crazy band of amateurs." Mara was intent on continuing his long political innings. "I have not yet finished the job I started and until I can assure that unshakeable foundations have been firmly laid and the cornerstones are set in place, I will not yield to the vaulting ambitions of a power crazy gang of amateurs, none of whom have run anything, not even a bingo party," he told the nation in his final election speech.[136] The people of Fiji rejected his and his party's leadership. This deeply wounded his ego and self-esteem. He was a politician spurned. His whole life had been spent at the center stage of colonial and postcolonial politics. He had nowhere else to go. Returning to Lau to lead his people in his traditional role, as they wanted him to do, was hardly a practical possibility. This predicament probably explains why, after making a terse concession speech, Mara retreated to Honolulu. He refused or was unwilling to publicly disassociate his political colleagues and even his own family members from the protest movements, thus giving early warning of his thinking.[137] Those who had rejected his leadership should face the consequences of their action, whatever those might be.

Mara's quick acceptance of a position on Rabuka's coup cabinet was a critical moment in the early stages of the crisis. Rabuka realized that Mara was his "trump card"—Rabuka's own words—a "must" if the military regime were to succeed. Rabuka had probed Mara's thoughts on the constitution during a now-celebrated game of golf a week before the coup: "We were talking about politics," Rabuka later recalled, "and I asked how can the Constitution be changed? He (Mara) said the Constitution could not now be changed. The only way to change it . . . to use his exact words . . . 'is to throw it out and make a new one, and the likelihood of that is nil'."[138] The choice of words is significant. The words convey the sense not of outright condemnation of a treasonous idea uttered by a third-ranking military officer to the preeminent political figure in the country, but of exasperation at the unlikelihood of attaining the goals Rabuka had in mind. Mara's apparent lack of concern was the final sanction Rabuka required to effect the coup. What is astonishing, if Rabuka is to be believed, is the way in which Mara accepted his invitation, with a simple "I accept." Apparently Mara laid no preconditions for his participation. "I nearly hit the roof as I jumped and cheered," Rabuka recalled later.[139] Well he might, for Mara's presence and public support protected the coup instigators from the full force of international criticism and neutralized the efforts of local anticoup forces. Most important, it isolated the governor-general, undermining his early efforts to preserve the constitutionality of his elected government.

Equally astonishing was Ratu Mara's apparent about-face regarding the 1970 constitution, which he himself had helped to formulate and which had kept him in power for seventeen years. Even as late as the 1987 general elections, Mara's Alliance Party had said that it "will strenuously oppose any suggestion of constitutional change that would weaken or destroy the principle of guaranteed representation of Fiji's major racial groups in the House of Representatives."[140] In an astonishing about-turn, he told the Great Council of Chiefs in May 1988 that the 1970 constitution "can no longer be regarded as an adequate guarantee of their [*taukei*] long term future and as a sufficient basis to ensure the long term peace and harmony of our entire nation." The new constitution, he argued, must show "full recognition of the overriding importance that the indigenous Fijians attach to their communal values of duty and loyalty to the unity and harmony of their community and of obedience to, and respect for, their traditional chiefly authority."[141] A year later, he embraced the ideology of the Taukei Movement even more fully, perhaps revealing an essential nativism hidden in his soul. The Fijian people should make history and not become history in their own land, he told the Lau Provincial Council: "The Fijian people are all too aware of the destiny of the indigenous Aztecs of Mexico, the Incas of Peru, the Mayans of Central America, the Caribs of Trinidad and Tobago, the Inuits of Canada, the Maoris of New Zealand and the Aborigines of Australia, to name a few."[142]

This was an extraordinary statement from an extraordinary man in the twilight of an extraordinary career, lending support to the discomforting, and once unthinkable, thought that the difference between Ratu Mara and the Fijian militants was really one of degree, not one of substance. Precisely what provisions of the 1970 constitution threatened the interests of the Fijian people? How could a culturally vibrant and growing community, nearly half the total population of Fiji, secure in its land and other rights guaranteed by special institutional structures and legislative devices, face the threat of extinction like the Incas of Peru? If that was, indeed, the case, then surely Ratu Mara himself had to shoulder the bulk of the blame, having been at the helm of national Fijian leadership for more than a generation.

Perhaps a leader of Mara's intelligence and experience was not serious in equating the fate of extinct peoples with that of the Fijians. Perhaps he knew that it was not the constitution but the processes of social and economic change, which he himself helped to initiate, that had eroded the foundations of traditional Fijian society under chiefly leadership. In fact, Mara later admitted that it was not the constitution but disunity among the Fijian people that was the main problem. Two weeks after the coup, he said, "I felt the constitution was right."[143] He told an interviewer in 1989 that "I really think that in the previous constitution, if the Fijians were united there won't be any trouble. There was a division then, and if there is going to be division even with a majority, there will be a problem."[144]

In the end, perhaps, it was the combination of chiefly, traditional, and personal power interests that lay at the heart of the matter. Mara could not countenance the threat that the Coalition appeared to represent to the hegemony of the eastern chiefly establishment, nor the prospect of a restructuring of power in Fijian society signaled by the ascendancy of the Fijian middle class and of western Fijians. His political philosophy of communal politics, in which "race is a fact of life," was in danger of being replaced by a nonracial vision. Having spent all his adult life in the public limelight, Mara probably found it difficult to relinquish the center stage. That is only human. In the past, he had negotiated the tough currents of Fijian politics with an astuteness that his opponents both respected and feared. In the 1970s, when the Alliance was on a winning wicket, it was appropriate for him to play the prophet of multiracialism and parliamentary democracy. With the rise of Fijian ethnonationalism and its entrenchment by the coups, it was politically appropriate to project himself as the champion of Fijian demands and interests. By this logic, Mara did little more than keep in step with the communal political trend. After all, in a cynical view, this is what politics is all about. The difference in this case was that the world had come to believe in the sanctity of Mara's multiracial mana. A man who could have done much in defense of principles he proclaimed dear to his heart did little. That is his personal tragedy and the collective tragedy of Fiji.

Sitiveni Rabuka is a much less complex man though in many ways similar to Mara. Like Mara, he saw himself as a man of history, indispensable to the future of his people and his country. Like Mara, he was both authoritarian and autocratic. And like Mara, he adapted his explanations and justifications to suit the needs of the moment. He talked at length about his devotion and loyalty to the chiefs, but showed little hesitation in usurping their authority when they stood in his way—as seen in his response to the Deuba accords. He swore an oath of allegiance to the Queen, yet felt little compunction in committing an act of treason. He talked about the need to return Fiji to civilian rule and political normalcy, but made it abundantly clear that this would be on his terms. The army, he said, would be "the final guarantor of law and order from the time we call a general election to the end of time."[145] He assured Indo-Fijians that they had "nothing to fear" from his rule, but then conceded that he had "looked at the possibility of imposing some form of control on the number of Indians allowed to live in Fiji." He talked of religious tolerance, but warned that he wanted "the Indians to be converted to Christianity." He saw no contradiction between his support for indigenous Melanesian rights and his assiduous courting of military aid from France and Indonesia, among the last of the colonial powers in the Pacific. He talked about encouraging Fijian participation in agricultural enterprises while entertaining the idea of bringing one hundred thousand Chinese workers to Fiji because, in his view, Chinese were not political minded.

In the early stages of events leading to the May coup, Rabuka was very likely a hired gun, a Melanesian *ramo* 'traditional warrior', for various interests that felt threatened by the Coalition's victory. At first, he was genuinely deferential to his paramount chiefs and properly mindful of his place in the Fijian social hierarchy; he saw—and sought to portray himself —as a loyal commoner doing what his chiefs and superiors wanted him to do. Soon after the May coup, however, he became a popular hero to many Fijians who adored him. Many of them felt that he had accomplished in seventeen seconds what the Alliance had not been able to accomplish in seventeen years: removing the threat of Indo-Fijian dominance and entrenching the paramountcy of Fijian interests. As public adulation increased, and he liked the taste of power and privilege that his new *avatar* as the savior of the Fijian people brought him, he underwent a rapid transformation. Instead of quietly fading into the background and taking a back seat, as many hoped he would, he began to demand a prominent niche for himself in the new power structure, convinced that he was indispensable to the Fijian peoples' efforts to redefine themselves in the aftermath of the coups. Increasingly, therefore, he began to see for himself an expanded public role in Fijian politics in the future. In this respect, at least, Rabuka is no different from other Third World colonels who do not easily revert to their traditional military roles once they are out of the barracks. The man who proclaimed his dislike of the hurly-burly of politics began to dream of becoming prime minister, much to the dismay of his chiefly superiors such as Ganilau and Mara.

The year of the coups, 1987, was a watershed in Fiji's modern political history, equal in historical significance to 1874, when Fiji became a British Crown colony; 1879, when the first group of Indian indentured laborers were brought to the islands; and 1970, when Fiji finally obtained its political independence from Great Britain. It was a year that briefly celebrated the triumph of the ballot box and then saw it overturned in the South Pacific's first military coup. It was a year of great hope, tragedy, and confusion for all the people of Fiji. Above all, it was a year that saw the end of an experiment in multiculturalism conceived in hope by Sir Arthur Gordon, unleashing forces that, in the words of Matthew Arnold, poised Fiji precariously to

> Wander between two worlds
> One dead and the other powerless to be born.

7 Broken Waves

Fiji returned to nominally civilian rule on 5 December 1987, when the recently promoted Brigadier General Sitiveni Rabuka dissolved his military cabinet and relinquished formal political power to the newly appointed president, Ratu Sir Penaia Ganilau. Rabuka remained in the cabinet as commander of the military forces and minister of Home Affairs. The interim regime faced a host of tough problems. It struggled to revive an economy severely dislocated by the coups, to maintain a semblance of law and order in the face of increased ethnic tension and social polarization in the country, to devise a constitution to enshrine Fijian supremacy in the political process within an overarching and largely symbolic framework of parliamentary democracy, and to gain international support for its efforts, the ultimate aim of this exercise being to enable Fiji to gain readmission to the Commonwealth. The task proved more difficult than most realized.

Five years after the coups, Fiji is still in a great flux as its people struggle to comprehend a bewildering array of events and processes that have so dramatically altered their lives. It is difficult to write about these developments while the gun, so to speak, is still smoking. What follows is a broad outline of some of the major developments that have taken place in the last few years together with some cautious assessments about the directions these might take.

One obvious result of developments within Fiji since the coups of 1987 has been a weakening of the fragile fabric of ethnic relations between the two major communities, caused in large part by the interim government's determined, pro-Fijian policies. Vacancies in the civil service and the public sector generally, created by the voluntary departure or enforced resignations of Indo-Fijians, have been filled by ethnic Fijians, not necessarily because of merit or seniority but because of their ethnic background and political loyalty to those in power. Plans have been discussed to promote a rapid Fijianization of the bureaucracy. An exclusively Fijian, and so far largely ineffective, Viti Civil Servants' Association was formed late in 1987, with the encouragement of the interim government, to break the power and the multiracial character of the Fiji Public Service Employees' Association. The situation is strongly reminiscent of the emergence of racially based, government-supported unions in the aftermath of the disturbances of 1959.[1] Ever since 1987, the interim regime has taken every opportunity to pass decrees that help to undermine the basis of the trade union movement in Fiji. Only the threat of action by the internatinoal trade union movement has prevented the regime from promulgating further anti-union policies.

The virus of ethnic division and intolerance also infected the broader cultural life in Fiji. Since the coups, the Great Council of Chiefs, supported by the powerful Methodist Church, has sought to make Christianity the state religion of Fiji, even though half its population is non-Christian.[2] The Sunday Observance Decree of 1987 sought to impose a strict observance of the Sabbath.[3] It banned all recreational and sporting activities on Sundays, along with the operation of public transport, commerce and trade, hotels, restaurants, and cinemas. Not surprisingly, the decree, which probably inconvenienced rural and poor Fijians more than other groups, proved very unpopular and was quietly discarded.

The promulgation of the decree, and all that it represented, encouraged the growth of greater intolerance of other faiths among the more militant, fundamentalist Fijian Christians. Among these were members of the Fiji Methodist Youth Fellowship, who went on a rampage in October 1989, burning down and desecrating Hindu, Muslim, and Sikh places of worship in the western sugar city of Lautoka. A few weeks later, a similar incident took place in Nasinu. Such acts of violence, unimaginable in precoup Fiji, shocked the Indo-Fijian community, which responded by organizing a day of mourning and protest throughout the country. It would be hopeful to conclude that these acts of religious vandalism were an aberration, the work of misguided youthful zealots. In the atmosphere of ethnic and religious intolerance engendered by the coups, however, they may unfortunately be a harbinger of things to come, as witnessed by the ransacking or desecration by hooligans of Indian places of worship as late as 1991.

Over the last four years, special efforts have been made to encourage more Fijian participation in commerce. The Fiji Development Bank was asked to accelerate its soft-loans program to potential Fijian entrepreneurs. As a result, the Fiji Development Bank gave an interest-free loan of $20 million to the Fijian Affairs Board to buy shares in profitable industrial and commercial ventures. Individual Fijians also received loans from the bank's Commercial Loans to Fijians Scheme and the Joint Venture Loans Scheme for various projects in tourism, timber, transportation, construction, and mining industries. In 1989 these loans totaled F$6,547 million, which represented an almost 50-percent increase over the amount (F$2,993 million) in 1985.[4] These policies, necessary to bring more Fijians into the cash economy, will continue. They have been accompanied by a grudging acceptance on the part of at least some Fijian leaders "to accept changes if our people are to become part of the mainstream of the economic life of our country."[5] This is stating the obvious, of course, though how the new Fijian "economic man" functions in a society that is trying to revert to its precolonial ways will be worth watching.

The army remains one of the most important institutions of power in the country even though Rabuka is no longer its head, having decided, after much vacillation, to join Mara's interim government in June 1991. His replacement was Ratu Epeli Ganilau (President Ganilau's son and Mara's son-in-law) and not Rabuka's preferred choice, Jioji Konrote, a brigadier general of Rotuman descent. The army also enjoys the support and patronage of the Fijian establishment not only because the army bolsters the power of the establishment, but also, and perhaps more important, because it advocates the complete indigenization of the Fijian bureaucracy, polity, and economy. This was starkly apparent in a submission that Rabuka and his officers made to Ganilau and Mara in September 1989 in which they advocated, among other things, neutralizing the Coalition leadership, abolishing trade unions, controlling the media, appointing a compliant judiciary, giving Fijians control of the national economy by reserving for them 51 percent ownership in all foreign investments, importing Chinese labor to work on cane farms vacated by Indo-Fijian tenant farmers, canceling citizenship for "enemies of state," making Christianity the state religion, requiring that other faiths be "in favour of a new course of action," and, finally, delaying the return of constitutional government for fifteen years.[6] Well trained and highly disciplined, the army is well poised for a prominent role in the affairs of Fiji in the future. In Jim Sanday's assessment:

> In the 1990s, a politicised role for the military appears assured. The military in Fiji will see themselves as protectors of the new Constitution and the values enshrined therein—the inviolability of Fijian political supremacy, the protection of Fijian chiefly interests, including their role in the political economy. As long as there is a government committed to the entrenchment of Fijian political supremacy and Fijian chiefly interests, as well as being able to satisfy the materialist ambitions and personal power interests of the military elite and their militant allies in the bureaucracy, the Taukei Movement and the Methodist church, then the genie of ethnic Fijian nationalism will be mollified and the pretext for another military foray into politics denied. In these circumstances, the military need only remain one remove from politics, operating from behind the scenes as a pressure group.[7]

Sanday was the chief of staff of the Royal Military Forces at the time of the coup and Rabuka's immediate superior officer.

Returning the military forces to their traditional role will be a major challenge for Fijian leaders in the 1990s. Perhaps a more important problem, however, will be strengthening the foundations of the country's economy. The economy was on the verge of collapse in the period immediately following the coup, crippled by a massive outflow of capital, the suspension of the tourist industry, a decline in sugar production caused by hurricanes and droughts and delayed harvesting, and a sharp fall in the foreign-exchange reserves. To deal with these problems, the Reserve Bank devalued the Fijian currency by 35 percent in 1987, imposed strict exchange controls, cut salaries in the civil service, and reduced grants to the public sector. These measures stabilized the situation, but more were needed to revive the shattered economy.

To this end, the government embarked on a number of radical strategies. To start, it deregulated the economy and the labor market to promote efficiency and encourage private-sector investment. Angered by the Australian and New Zealand governments' stance toward the coups, and keen to expand the network of its trading partners, the government sent several high-level trade delegations to Japan, China, Korea, Taiwan, and other Asian countries to seek investment and aid. These efforts met with some success. Several Japanese companies bought up premier hotel and tourist resorts, such as the Regent of Fiji, and invested in the country's fisheries and timber industries. Malaysia secured sole-source rights to supply Fiji's petroleum needs, and its Borneo Finance Group began a joint venture with the government-owned National Bank of Fiji. Pakistan's Habib Bank opened a branch in March 1991.[8] The weakening of Fiji's neocolonial ties to Australia and New Zealand is welcome, but it is not clear whether the country's newfound friends will remain as benevolent as they now seem.

In another effort to boost investment, the interim regime started a tax-free zone scheme in 1988. Under this regime, companies exporting 95 percent of their products and services were given tax concessions (tax holidays for up to thirteen years, no withholding tax on interest, dividend and royalty paid abroad, and freedom to repatriate capital and profit); customs concessions (total waiver of licensing for import of capital goods and other production materials, duty-free import of capital goods and equipment, and exemption from customs duty on importation of raw materials, components, spares, and packaging materials); and other benefits (freedom to import specialist personnel, preferential electricity tariff, and other concessions).[9] At the same time, trade union and industrial action were declared illegal in the tax-free zones.

By mid-1990, some ninety companies were approved to operate in the tax-free zones, of which about a third were local. Over 90 percent of those companies were engaged in garment manufacture, which earned Fiji $100 million in 1990. The tax-free-zone initiative brought much-needed relief to the country's critical foreign-exchange difficulties and provided employment to unskilled workers, but at rates of pay as low as 60 cents per hour. Most of the workers in the garment factories are women from broken homes in desperate situations.[10] The tax-free zone is an ad hoc, band-aid measure that will not provide any long-term solution to Fiji's economic problems, and has not done so anywhere else. As one economist observes:

> The overseas companies are likely to be footloose outfits that are attracted by low wages and have to pay taxes at home if they do not pay in Fiji, while the established local companies are clearly being subsidized by the granting of tax-free status. In either case there is a loss to government revenue. . . . Nobody seems to have calculated the domestic resource cost of earning foreign exchange by providing women and night-shift working men in the zones with a job that transforms an unemployment problem into a poverty problem.[11]

Although postcoup economic problems have been at least partly contained, it remains to be seen whether Fiji will remain "a country with a comparatively favourable natural resource endowment, a sound rural economy (albeit verging on monocrop status), a well-developed entrepreneurial class, good social and physical infrastructure, established structures of public administration, the commercial capital of much of the Pacific Islands group as well as favoured access to international markets and development assistance."[12] It is a very tall order.

A far more critical and potentially explosive problem facing the interim regime and its successors is the renegotiation of the Agricultural Landlords and Tenants Ordinance. This piece of legislation settled the terms and conditions of native leases to Indo-Fijian tenants for thirty years starting from 1966. The leases will begin to expire between 1997 and 2000, and some twenty-one thousand Indo-Fijian cane growers are rightly concerned about what will happen to them then. On what terms will the leases be renewed? Will the rentals be assessed at such a high rate that the growers will be reduced to the level of mere sharecroppers? Will the growers be allowed to participate at all in the lease negotiations? The omens are not good. Some provincial councils are demanding the termination of all leases upon expiry, although Fijians already have sufficient land set aside in reserves for their future needs. Lease rentals have already increased significantly since the coups, in some cases by as much as 500 percent.[13] If a 1991 World Bank report, which recommends renegotiation of land leases at market rates, is adopted, their situation will deteriorate further.[14] Small cane growers, often poor and frequently in debt, without contacts and resources to migrate to other lands, are among the most helpless victims of the coups.

Renewal of leases to Indo-Fijian tenants is only one of the issues, although an important one. Others include reforms in the unwieldy structure of the Native Lands Trust Board and the mechanism for rent distribution among Fijian landowners. "The problems inherent in this system are so acute," Overton and Ward have observed, "that not only are Indian tenants under threat, but also commercial Fijian farmers on their own village land are finding it difficult to secure land rights. . . . A crisis is looming—there must be reform and there must be a more flexible system of land leasing and rent distribution."[15] In the past, the management of the NLTB, which was dominated by Fijians from eastern Fiji, was reluctant to embrace reform, seeing all criticism, however genuine or constructive, as a ploy by outsiders to undermine the basis of Fijian society and to placate land-hungry Indians. If that attitude continues, everyone in Fiji, and not just Indo-Fijian tenants, will suffer.

The anxiety and sense of despair that the land issue raises is not alleviated by the interim regime's determination to impose a constitution on the country that, if successful, will effectively reduce the Indo-Fijian community to the status of a political subclass. The previous chapter showed how the efforts of the Constitution Review Committee in 1987 came to naught when the Coalition rejected the majority recommendation to abrogate the 1970 constitution and to replace it with one that embraced the ideology and platform of the Taukei Movement. Thereupon, the interim cabinet, with the backing of the military, embarked on another exercise to devise a constitution,[16] a draft of which was circulated for public comment in September 1988. A seventeen-member Fiji Constitution Inquiry and Advisory Committee, chaired by retired army commander Colonel Paul Manueli, was appointed on 5 October to

> scrutinise and consider the extent to which the Draft Constitution submitted by Cabinet to the Committee meets the present and future constitutional needs of the people of Fiji, having regard in particular to the failure of the 1970 Constitution to provide adequate and full protection of the rights, interests and concerns of the indigenous Fijian people, and having regard to all the circumstances prevailing in Fiji.[17]

The patently biased terms of reference of the committee and the problematic assumptions that informed them—that the 1970 constitution had failed and that the reality of the prevailing circumstances had to be kept in mind—indicated clearly what was expected of the exercise. (The coup leaders were described by the committee as "members of the security forces who assisted in the change of government in 1987.")

Fundamentally, the cabinet draft, which the committee was charged to examine, differed little in spirit and content from the Great Council of Chiefs' submission to the Constitution Review Committee in 1987. The draft proposed, among other things, to create a Fijian-dominated parliament: to give power to an executive committee of the Great Council of Chiefs to nominate the president, who, in turn, would appoint the prime minister; to place all the most important ministries as well as the chairs of powerful statutory bodies (police, public service, and legal commissions) in ethnic Fijian hands; to install the commander of the military force as a permanent member of the cabinet; to conduct all parliamentary elections on strictly communal franchise; and not least, to "promote and safeguard the interests and aspirations of the Fijian and Rotuman people and in particular to promote and maintain their cultures and traditions and their social, educational and economic well-being" through special government-directed programs of positive discrimination. Predictably, the draft was endorsed by the procoup forces in Fiji.

The Coalition, however, rejected it as "profoundly authoritarian, undemocratic, militaristic, racist, and feudalistic" (Figure 12). Its view was that the draft constitution "would be divisive and sow the seeds of terrible violence. It would retard our social and economic development. It would isolate us from many of our valued neighbours, the Commonwealth and the international community."[18] The new constitution, the Coalition argued, needed to emphasize the respect for trade union rights, individual and religious freedom, and a clear separation of powers between the legislative, judicial, and executive arms of government. Without these safeguards, it said, Fiji would inevitably head toward tyranny and oppression.

In the circumstances, the Coalition's views carried little weight with the Constitution Inquiry and Advisory Committee, which, to no one's sur-

Figure 12. A cartoonist's view of constitutional proposals. *(Courtesy of Ian Sharpe, Canberra Times)*

prise, largely endorsed the terms and the spirit of the draft constitution.[19] Its report became the basis of the new constitution which the interim administration promulgated on 25 July 1990. It is not necessary here to examine the provisions of the new constitution in minute detail; it should suffice to note its most obvious features. To begin, the preamble states, among other things, that the need for the new constitution arose because of "a widespread belief that the 1970 constitution was inadequate to give protection to the interests of indigenous Fijians, their values, traditions, customs, way of life and economic well-being." As a result, "The people of Fiji have expressed the desire to have a new Constitution for the advancement of their beliefs, rights and freedoms and accept that it is desirous that the 1970 constitution be replaced so that the will of the people may be truly set forth and their hopes, aspirations and goals be achieved and thereby enshrined." The evasions and misrepresentations here are too transparent to need comment. They are not statements of truth but justifications for the coup.

The new constitution provides for a bicameral legislature and an executive presidency. The president will be appointed by the Great Council of Chiefs (Bose Vakatūraga) for five years, will serve at the chiefs' pleasure, and will be accountable only to the council. The president will be more than simply a figurehead, enjoying considerable powers in the appointment of public officers, in exercising the prerogative of mercy, and in dealing with emergencies. These powers include the ability to suspend the constitution and civil liberties of individuals to deal with any act that excites "disaffection against the President or the Government" and others that are "prejudicial to the security of Fiji"; exercise personal judgment to appoint a president's council, chaired by the president, to advise the president on matters of national importance. How the presidency will function in practice; what criteria will be used to select the president; and whether the presidency will rotate only among the three existing confederacies of Kubuna, Burebasaga and Tovata, or also include the Yasayasa Vaka Ra (a fourth confederacy proposed by western Fijians; Map 3), are issues that will be watched very closely in the future.

The upper house of parliament, the Senate, appointed by the president, will consist of thirty-four members of whom twenty-four will be Fijians appointed by the Great Council of Chiefs, one Rotuman appointed by the Council of Rotuma, and nine other members appointed by the president alone. In appointing these nine members, the president will be required to "take into consideration the special interests of the minority communities." These would include Europeans, Part-Europeans, Chinese, Pacific Islanders, and others besides the Indo-Fijian community, whose numbers in the Senate would be drastically reduced and rendered effectively voiceless. Besides reviewing bills passed by the lower house, the Senate will have effective veto power over any legislation affecting Fijian rights, cus-

FIJIAN CONFEDERACIES

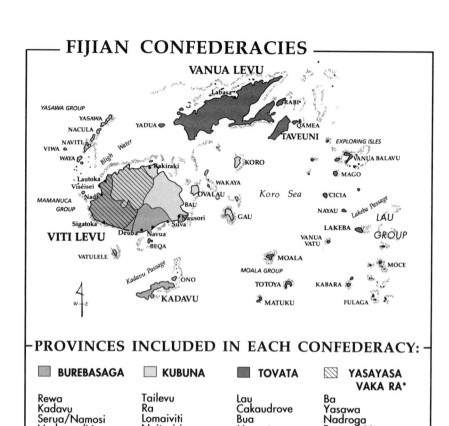

PROVINCES INCLUDED IN EACH CONFEDERACY:

▢ **BUREBASAGA**	▢ **KUBUNA**	■ **TOVATA**	▨ **YASAYASA VAKA RA***
Rewa	Tailevu	Lau	Ba
Kadavu	Ra	Cakaudrove	Yasawa
Serua/Namosi	Lomaiviti	Bua	Nadroga
Nadroga/Navosa	Naitasiri	Macuata	Parts of Navosa
Parts of Ba	Parts of Ba		Parts of Ra
Parts of Yasawa	Parts of Yasawa		Parts of Serua
			Parts of Namosi

* Yasayasa Vaka Ra would be formed out of parts of the original 3 confederacies

3 CONFEDERACIES: ───── 4 CONFEDERACIES:

- BUREBASAGA = 28.6%
- KUBUNA = 49.7%
- TOVATA = 21.7%

- BUREBASAGA = 18.0%
- KUBUNA = 32.8%
- TOVATA = 21.7%
- YASAYASA VAKA RA = 27.5%

Percentage values represent the population of each confederacy as compared to the national total. Data were compiled from the 1986 Census of Fiji.

Map 3.

toms, and customary rights. The consent of at least eighteen of the twenty-four Great Council of Chiefs' nominees would be required for any alteration to the following: the Fijian Affairs Act, the Fijian Development Fund Act, the Native Lands Act, the Native Lands Trust Act, the Rotuma Act, the Rotuma Lands Act, the Banaban Lands Act, and the Banaban Settlement Act. Their consent will also be required for alterations to any provisions of the Agricultural Landlords and Tenants Ordinance. In this respect, the Senate will play a role similar to the one it had under the 1970 constitution.

In the composition of the lower house, the House of Representatives, however, there is an even more marked departure from the provisions of the 1970 constitution. It will consist of seventy members (instead of the previous fifty-two), of whom thirty-seven will be Fijians (48 percent of the population); twenty-seven, Indo-Fijians (46 percent); five, general electors; and one, Rotuman. The principle of parity between Fijians and Indo-Fijians, enshrined in the 1970 constitution, is thus explicitly disregarded in favor of Fijian paramountcy. However, racial discrimination is not the only problematic aspect of the new constitution. It entrenches the principle of communalism in the electoral process to a far greater degree than did the 1970 constitution. Now, all voting will be strictly on racial lines, with Fijians voting only for Fijians, and Indo-Fijian and General Electors voting for their own respective ethnic candidates. National constituencies that provided an opportunity for multiracial voting have been abolished. This is a severe blow to the task of nation building in a racially divided society. Racially based elections provide candidates with no incentives to attend to nonracial issues outside their constituencies. Clearly, the doctrine of "separate and unequal" underpins the foundations of the new order.

Of the 37 Fijian members of the House of Representatives, 32 would be elected from the fourteen Fijian provinces and the remaining 5 from five urban constituencies. The allocation of seats to the different provinces shows a glaring pattern of regional inequality, with drastic underrepresentation of the larger provinces of Viti Levu. To take the most blatant examples, Ba province, with a Fijian population of 55,000 (according to the 1986 census figures), will have only three seats in the parliament, the same number as Lau, with a population of 14,000; and Rewa, with 48,000 Fijians, will have two seats, the same number as Kadavu, with a population of 9,600. Even more glaring than the discrimination against the larger provinces is the discrimination against urban Fijians. According to the 1986 census, 107,780, or 32.7 percent, of all Fijians lived in urban areas. Yet urban Fijians will have only 5 of the 37 Fijian seats in parliament. If the recent trend toward increasing urbanization continues, as is likely, the constitution will marginalize urban Fijians even further. On the other hand, rural Fijians from far-flung provinces will enjoy political representation grossly disproportionate to their population size or contribution to the national economy or virtually any other criteria, except their strong support for the coups. This electoral arrangement is the crowning achievement of the Fijian chiefs in the Great Council of Chiefs, who want to return Fijian society to its rural patterns. In the long run it is likely to be a pyrrhic victory.

The new constitution provides explicit direction to the government to promote positive discrimination in favor of Fijians and Rotumans. It empowers it to direct any government, commission, or statutory authority to reserve scholarships, training privileges, and other special facilities as it may deem reasonable. Similarly, Fijians and Rotumans entering business would also be assisted by requirements stipulating their participation in new ventures. The philosophy of positive discrimination in favor of demonstrably disadvantaged minorities is sound in principle, but the assertion that Fijians and Rotumans alone constitute a disadvantaged group in Fiji is misleading. Income disparities in Fiji run along regional and rural-urban lines rather more than they do along racial lines. Policies that ignore these facts only plant the seeds of further trouble.

The Fijian people may regret other provisions of the constitution in years to come. Fijian customary laws will become part of the laws of Fiji; but in the event of any dispute relating to the interpretation and application of customs, traditions, and usages or disputes concerning landownership or hereditary titles, the Fijians will now be prohibited from seeking recourse in a court of law. The decision of the Native Lands Commission on these matters, the new constitution says, "shall be final and conclusive." This is unfortunate because in recent years, many Fijians had begun to view the court of law as an alternative avenue to adjudicate claims for those dissatisfied with Native Lands Commission rulings. Likewise, the Fijian people, and anyone else for that matter, will be unable to use the office of the ombudsman to investigate complaints against the president or presidential staff, any commission established under the constitution, senior public officials making appointments in the public service and exercising related functions, the director of public prosecutions, the Great Council of Chiefs, the Native Lands Commission, the Native Fisheries Commission, the Native Lands Trust Board, the Rotuma Island Council, and the Banaba Island Council. In short, the most important Fijian-dominated organizations in the country will be beyond public scrutiny and public accountability. Such protection will work to the advantage of selected individuals and organizations, but it is not likely to serve the wider public interest.

Aspects of the constitution that place unrestricted power in the hands of the government or that breach many international conventions are also not likely to serve the wider public interest.[20] Nowhere is this more apparent than in Section 162, which states that all the provisions safeguarding human rights in the constitution shall be declared null and void if an act of parliament

> recites that action has been taken or threatened by any substantial body of persons, whether inside or outside Fiji to cause, or to cause a substantial number of citizens to fear, organized violence against persons or property; to excite disaffection against the president or the Government; to promote feelings of ill-will and hostility between different races or other classes of the population likely to cause violence; to procure the alteration, otherwise than by lawful means, of anything by law established; or which is prejudicial to the security of Fiji.

Once this section is invoked by a simple two-thirds majority of both houses of parliament, the courts will be powerless to intervene and will have to accept the government's determination that such threats actually exist. The government could easily keep this act alive long after the threats have ceased to exist. In Malaysia, from whose constitution this section has been borrowed, such legislation has been in force continuously for thirty years.

When he promulgated the new constitution, President Ratu Sir Penaia Ganilau was optimistic that it would "lay a strong foundation for a Republic with a stable, caring and productive society. . . . We see a new order of hope," he said, "of peace, reconciliation, and progress in which the fundamental rights and freedoms of all citizens are guaranteed. We seek understanding, trust and tolerance." The constitution was not based on "some revolutionary and radical proposition," Ratu Sir Penaia declared; it simply provided "for a continuation, and an enlargement, of an idea which has become an established part of our power-sharing arrangements." He then touched on the reasons for the coup: "The Fijians *had* to preserve their identity, their culture—and, sometimes it seemed, their very existence." Referring to the enhanced role for chiefs in the new constitution, he continued, "The chiefs are a force for moderation, balance and fair play [who have] been mediators and conciliators between the Fijian people and the Indian community [and have] done much to bring Fiji into the modern world and to spur on our economic progress." Addressing himself directly to the Indo-Fijian community, he said that it was never the intention of the Fijian leaders to disenfranchise anyone, for to "have taken such a course would not only have been an affront to accepted principles of human conduct, it would also have been contrary to the cultural values of respect, tolerance, mutual caring and Christian love that the Fijians hold dear." "The time has now come," Ratu Sir Penaia said, "to lay to rest the ghosts of the *girmit* experience, to put aside the sense of grievance of the past. Be positive about Fiji. Have faith in it as a nation with a bright and shining future."[21]

The bulk of the Indo-Fijian community has rejected the new constitution. For them, it does not lay to rest the ghost of the *girmit* experience, but raises the specter of a new one, a life of subservience, lived as a *vūlagi* 'foreigner' on the sufferance of the Fijian people. While the original *girmit* lasted only five years, this one, they feel, is intended as a permanent arrangement. Nonetheless, while rejecting the constitution as racist and iniquitous, Indo-Fijian leaders agreed in July 1991 to contest elections held under it. The first of these were scheduled for early 1992. They rejected as illusory the idea that Fiji will return to parliamentary democracy of the sort that existed before 1987. They argued that by being in parliament they would at least be able to raise issues of concern in the Indo-Fijian community, issues that would otherwise remain unarticulated. "It will be useless for the Indian community to boycott the elections and let irresponsible people become our representatives," said Jai Ram Reddy. "We should take part in the elections and continue protesting against the constitution."[22] For him it was a matter of realistic, practical politics. Reddy's and the NFP's decision to participate ruptured the links between them and the Fiji Labour Party, which decided to boycott the elections.

The postcoup period has been a trying time for most Indo-Fijians, a time of humiliation, suffering, and torment when "everything's gone wrong in terms of their legitimate rights and expectations."[23] So far, their reaction has been one of silent, passive protest, which is understandable given that all the guns are on the other side. As Eugene Genovese has remarked in another context: "If a people, over a protracted period, finds the odds against insurrection not merely long but virtually uncertain, then it will choose not to try. To some extent this reaction represents decreasing self-confidence and increasing fear, but it also represents a conscious effort to develop an alternative strategy for survival."[24] But for how long? Those who see themselves as being permanently excluded from power and reduced to the role of hewers of wood and drawers of water, to be seen but not heard, may decide to take matters into their own hands and confront their oppressors on their own terms. Sadly, this is not as farfetched a scenario as it might appear at first glance. In June 1988, there was a frightening gunrunning affair in which a massive amount of arms and ammunition—AK47 rifles, machine guns, rocket launchers, bayonets, hand grenades, pistols, sufficient to start a small-scale war—were illegally brought into Fiji.[25] Others among the oppressed will bide their time and hope that they, or at least their children, will be able to escape their predicament and emigrate to greener pastures. Already since the coups, some thirty thousand have left for North America, Australia, and New Zealand. Those who cannot may adopt the attitude of a character in a recently published play:

> My country? I have always worked hard—even bring files home and work at
> night. I was doing it all for my country. But my country doesn't give a damn

for me now. So why should I care for my country? As long as my cheque keeps coming in, that's all I'm going to worry about. The country can get stuffed, for all I care![26]

Whether it is a violent struggle, the emigration of the skilled labor force, or resigned indifference, Fiji can ill afford any of these alternatives.

The Coalition initially rejected the new constitution as "immoral and racist," and threatened to boycott elections held under it. "We cannot participate in an election based on a racist system which seeks to entrench the interests of a few indigenous Fijian leaders," said Adi Kuini Vuikaba Bavadra.[27] "It would be immoral. Just because it has been promulgated doesn't give it legitimacy." Adi Kuini was elected leader of the Coalition after Timoci Bavadra's tragic death from spinal cancer in November 1989. In 1990 she resigned from the leadership of the Coalition to marry and settle in Canberra, Australia.

This united stand was short-lived. It vanished—and with it the Coalition itself—when the NFP opted to participate in the elections without the Fijian Labour Party. An attempt by the two parties to merge into a single political entity with a common political agenda failed. Later, because of pressure from the rank and file, the Fiji Labour Party reconsidered its boycott decision. While maintaining their initial stance the leaders agreed to work with other "progressive-minded" Fijian parties to defeat the interim regime at the polls, and allowed its individual members to stand as independents.[28] The supporters of democratic principles in Fiji generally face an uphill struggle. For them,

> there is only the fight to recover what has been lost
> And found and lost again and again: and now under conditions
> That seem unpropitious[29]

The former Coalition leaders do not seem to have their former strength and vigor, always responding to measures initiated by the interim regime rather than proposing and pursuing measures of their own. They seem disheartened by all the violence, political turbulence, social harassments, and economic insecurity they have had to endure. Their disenchantment is all the deeper because many Coalition leaders and advisors have left Fiji, while others have sent their families abroad, detracting from the immediate value of their advice. The interim administration, meanwhile, is adamant that the new constitution is not negotiable and that the aims of the coups will be achieved at any cost. The prolific letter-writing Minister of Information Ratu Inoke Kubuabola has thundered: "We will not shift from our objective of ensuring Fijian political control along with indigenous Fijians having a decisive and determining voice in the economy of Fiji."[30]

In June 1990, the chiefs decided to launch a political party, the *Soqosoqo ni Vakavulewa ni Taukei* or Fijian Political Party, that aims "to promote the unity of the Fijian people and the consolidation of their culture and tradition."[31] They have been encouraged by lukewarm criticism of the new constitution from overseas. India has indicated that it will raise the issue in international forums and oppose Fiji's reentry to the Commonwealth, but both Australia and New Zealand have urged the Coalition to participate in elections held under the new constitution.[32] Most Pacific Islands countries have supported the publicly stated goals of the interim administration all along.

Most of the Fijian people appear to support the new constitution, though in the absence of a referendum, the exact number is difficult to determine. They support increased numbers of Fijians in parliament and those provisions that discriminate in their favor. As Rabuka stated, Fijians of differing political persuasions are "all fighting for the same cause— ensuring political dominance and the protection of indigenous rights. The only difference in our struggle is that we're following different channels to achieve such ends."[33] That may be the case, but beneath the surface unity lurk serious problems that will come to the fore once the threat of Indo-Fijian dominance is removed from the political arena, problems of regional imbalance in economic development and in electoral representation and of reduced participation in politics by urban and commoner Fijians. Signs of discontent and internal squabbles about the distribution of power within Fijian society are already emerging.

Western Fijian leaders, including those who vigorously supported the coups, are concerned not only about the proposed Fijian electoral arrangements but also about other related and potentially more important matters. The enhanced political role of the Great Council of Chiefs in its post-coup reconstituted form has, in Apisai Tora's words, left them feeling "left out of the greater scheme of things with . . . little influence in the power-plays of the so-called eastern chiefs," paving the way for "resentment and machiavellian intrigue" among many western Fijians.[34] In 1989, a twelve-member delegation of western Fijians, led by Tui Vuda, Ratu Sir Josaia Tavaiqia, asked the Constitution Inquiry and Advisory Committee to recommend the creation of a fourth Fijian confederacy, to be called the Yasa-yasa Vaka Ra.[35] The committee deflected the submission on the grounds that it was a matter for the Great Council of Chiefs to decide. The council had rejected the idea in May 1988 because a new confederacy would accentuate chaos and confusion in the Fijian community.[36] The timing of the demand was wrong.

Making matters more urgent for many, but not all, western Fijians is the restructuring of the composition of the Great Council of Chiefs. There is a proposal to reduce the council's size from 154 to 52, removing the automatic membership of all Fijian parliamentarians in the body. The pro-

125. Ganilau speaking on the Fijian Affairs (Amendment) Bill, Legislative Council Debate, 24 May 1966.

126. For Kermode's admission, see Legislative Council Debate, 21 April 1969.

127. See Patel's analysis of the sugar industry in Legislative Council debate, 8 May 1969.

128. Denning to the author, 20 Jan. 1990.

129. Quoted from the verbatim transcript of the arbitration, a copy of which is in my possession.

130. The verbatim transcripts of the arbitration proceedings, valuable for gaining an insight into the workings of the sugar industry, are available in several places, including the CSR and the growers' counsels.

131. *"The Award of the Rt. Hon. Lord Denning in the Fiji Sugar Cane Contract Dispute, 1969."* Supplement to the *Fiji Royal Gazette,* Suva, 1970.

132. Denning to author, 20 Jan. 1990.

133. Ibid., 31.

134. From the "green booklet" produced by the CSR.

135. I should not leave the impression that the CSR had not fought hard to remain in Fiji, for, indeed, it had. It expended a great deal of time and energy in preparing its case for the arbitration, and conversation with some of those involved in the arbitration leaves me with the impression that the CSR might have stayed on had the outcome of the arbitration been more favorable to it.

136. The exact role the government played is unclear, but Karam Ramrakha, a leading NFP figure in the negotiations, is in no doubt that the negotiations were a "result of pressure from Britain." See his comments in the proceedings of the *Fiji Nationhood Seminar* 1975, 56.

137. My understanding of these talks is based on a reading of the confidential transcripts of the proceedings.

138. As Ramrakha would put it later: "There is the criticism that we gave away too much. So we made all these concessions and we hoped that this would assure the Fijians in this country that the Indians were sincere and they were making a genuine attempt to build up a home for everybody and that we had no desire to dominate the Fijian community because we outnumbered them." In *Fiji Nationhood Seminar,* 58.

139. A report in *Vakalelewa ni Pacifika,* 9 May 1969. The Queen's response, received on 18 March 1969, reportedly said that the administration of Fiji did not rest in the hands of the Great Council of Chiefs or the Fijian people alone and that changes appropriate to Fiji were a matter for all the people to decide.

140. Resolution in *Volagauna,* 26 July 1969.

141. See Legislative Council paper 1/1970, which contains Lord Shepherd's report on his visit to Fiji.

142. Quoted in Norton 1990, 33.

143. *Report of the Fiji Constitutional Conference,* Council paper 70/1970, 19.

Chapter 5, The Center Cannot Hold

1. Ratu Sir Kamisese Mara, "Message from the Prime Minister," in *Fiji Independence Souvenir Programme,* 10 (October 1970), 4. See also *Fiji,* vol. 3, nos. 4 and 5 (July 1980), 11.

2. Published in the Labasa Secondary School magazine, *The Labasan 1970,* 3.

3. For an excellent report on some of the fears expressed to a foreign journalist covering the independence celebrations, see John Griffin, "Fiji nears freedom amidst old tensions," in *Honolulu Advertiser,* 9 Feb. 1970.

4. See *Fiji: Patterns of Progress, 1970–1986* (Suva: Government Printer) for more details and statistics.

5. See *Government of Fiji, Bureau of Statistics, Fiji Tourism and Migration Statistics, 1984* for figures. Roughly a third each of Fiji's migrants went to the United States and Australia, a quarter to Canada, 6 percent to New Zealand, and the rest elsewhere. See also Connell 1987.

6. Figures culled from census reports.

7. *Fiji Nation* (June 1970) commented that it "was bouquets to Ratu Sir Kamisese Mara and posies to Mr Koya and cheers for the Government and hurrahs for the loyal opposition."

8. See *Fiji Nation,* May 1971.

9. For an analysis of this election, see Ali 1973*a.*

10. *Fiji Times,* editorial 5 April 1977.

11. Quoted in *Fiji Times,* 22 March 1977.

12. See *Fiji Times,* 4 May 1972.

13. *Fiji Times,* 16 Sept. 1972.

14. *Report of the Royal Commission Appointed for the Purpose of Considering and Making Recommendations as to the Most Appropriate Method of Electing Members to, and Representing the People of Fiji in, the House of Representatives,* Fiji Parliamentary Paper 24/1975.

15. See *Fiji Times,* 8 Aug. 1975.

16. Ibid., 3. See also his remark reported in *Fiji Nation* vol. 1 no. 18 (1970), 7, on the need to be flexible in constitutional dialogue: "No one should think that even when the Constitution is approved and we have resolved all our ideas on representation, that this is the last step and that all is immutable forever."

17. *Fiji Times,* 8 Aug. 1975.

18. See Ali, "Problems of Constitution Making in Fiji," in *Fiji Times,* 3 Sept. 1975.

19. Quoted in *Fiji Times,* 17 May 1976.

20. Meeting briefly reported in *Fiji Times,* 8 Dec. 1975.

21. *Fiji Times,* 13 July 1970.

22. *Fiji Times,* 2 Jan. 1976.

23. Koya speaking in parliament: *Hansard* 25 May 1975, 56.

24. See *Report of the Working Committee Set Up to Review the Agricultural Landlord and Tenants Ordinance,* Legislative Council paper 23/1966.

25. See Parliamentary paper 15/1975.

26. For details, see House of Representatives debate on ALTO early in October 1976; proceedings reported in the press.

27. For more on this, see *Hansard,* 10 Dec. 1980.

28. For this quote and Reddy's response generally, see a transcript of his address to the NFP, a copy of which is in my possession.

29. Mara's response and the quote come from his address to the alliance convention at the Tradewinds Hotel, Suva; a copy is in my possession.

30. Gillion 1977, 119.

31. *Report of the Fiji Education Commission,* Legislative Council paper 1969.

32. For example, between 1984 and 1986, $2,507,560 was disbursed by the Fijian Affairs Board. Lau, with 13,894, or 4.2 percent, of the Fijian population in 1986, received $528,099, or 21 percent, of the total funds. Ba, with a population of 55,296, or 16.8 percent of the Fijian population, received only $156,085, or 6.2 percent of the total. The Tovata Confederacy (Lau, Cakaudrove, and the islands) received 55 percent of all the scholarship money.

33. Public Service Commission *Annual Report,* 30 June 1979, Appendix 2, Table 2.

34. A quick read through the annual reports of the Public Service Commission for the years 1970, 1972, 1980, 1981, 1982, 1985, and 1986 showed that there were 84 permanent secretaries, of whom 41 were Fijians, 24 were Others, and 19 were Indo-Fijians.

35. Quote from his speech, a typescript of which is in my possession.

36. *Pacific Islands Monthly,* June 1980.

37. *Report of the Public Service Commission for the Period 15 March 1974 to 30 June 1975,* Parliamentary paper 28/1975.

38. *Report of the Ministry of Fijian Affairs, 1971–1979,* Parliamentary paper 47/1980, 23.

39. This figure is drawn from BOMAS submission to the Great Council of Chiefs, November 1985, a copy of which is in my possession.

40. See L. Qarase, "Finance for Indigenous enterprises—The Case of Fiji and the Fiji Development Bank," paper presented to the Regional Workshop on Indigenous Business Development organized by Pacific Island Development Program, Apia, Western Samoa, 18–24 May 1986; a copy of the unpublished report is in my possession. On the problem of indigenous Fijian businesses generally, see Hailey 1985.

41. Statistics mentioned here are derived from a monograph prepared by the Australian Government's Legislative Research Service, 81/6159, 29.

42. Stan Stavenuiter, "Income Distribution in Fiji: An Analysis of Its Various Dimensions, with Implication for Future Employment, Basic Needs and Income Policies." Report prepared for Central Planning Office, Government of Fiji, April 1983; a copy is in my possession.

43. See *Hansard,* 9 Oct. 1975, 1104.

44. Sakiasi Butadroka, "Christian Principles and Development Policies," in *Proceedings of the Fiji Nationhood Seminar* (Suva, 1975), 32.

45. *Hansard,* 9 Oct. 1975, 1203–1204.

46. See *Fiji Times,* 10 Oct. 1975, for report and commentary.

47. House of Representatives *Hansard,* 1187.

48. *Fiji Times,* 18 Oct. 1975.

49. Quoted in *Fiji Times,* 6 Feb. 1976.

50. *Hansard,* 1388.

51. *Fiji Times,* 20 Dec. 1976.

52. *Fiji Times,* 10 Jan. 1977. A relieved Koya remarked that for his efforts, Reddy's name "should go down in the history books of Fiji."

53. For an analysis of this election, see Ali 1977.

54. K. C. Ramrakha, *Hansard,* 31 May 1977, 152. Calling the rejection of this

offer by the Alliance "a most tragic event in the history of Fiji," Ramrakha said that "this was possibly one of the greatest errors made by the Rt Honourable the Prime Minister and his party when they rejected this offer of Coalition."

55. Mara's own account of the episode is outlined in his speech in parliament, *Hansard,* 25 May 1977.

56. *Fiji Times,* 9 April 1977.

57. See Murray 1978.

58. See Ramrakha's article in *Fiji Sun* 24 Jan. 1987.

59. *Fiji Times,* 23 April 1977.

60. Saed Naqvi, "Marooned at Home: A Demoralised (Fiji) Indian Community," *India Today,* 30 Nov. 1987, 99.

61. Interview in *Islands Business,* Sept. 1987.

62. See *Fiji Times,* 11 April 1977.

63. For a study of this election, see Premdas, "Elections in Fiji," 1979.

64. *Fiji Times,* 5 Sept. 1977.

65. This assessment is based on my personal observation over a decade.

66. National Federation Party, *Souvenir Programme* (Nadi, 1974).

67. This paper was never published; a copy is in my possession, and the following quotes come from it.

68. It is misleading because the example of the workable coalition between the National Country Party and the Liberal Party in Australia would suggest otherwise.

69. In Reddy's address to the National Federation Party Convention, Ba, 1980.

70. This was done, for example, soon after the coups to justify forming a Fijian government because, it was said, Reddy and his NFP had turned down the proposal for a government of national unity in 1979.

71. Quoted in Reddy's statement to Radio Fiji on 11 Nov. 1980; a copy is in my possession.

72. Ibid.

73. For an analysis of this election, see my "The Fiji General Election of 1982," (Lal 1983a).

74. See Ewen Gregor, Fiji Pine Commission General Manager, "Current Status and Development in the Pine Industry," FPC Information Update, 7 Feb. 1980.

75. See *Fiji Sun,* 1 Nov. 1986.

76. *Fiji Pine Commission Act* No. 5 of 1976.

77. See Leigh Martin, "Political blackmail over the Green Gold," *Islands Business News,* August 1981, 5.

78. *Fiji Times,* 22 May 1982.

79. See *Fiji Times,* 25 Feb. 1982.

80. See *Fiji Sun,* 17 July 1981.

81. In an address to the Fijian Association at Rakiraki. See *Fiji Times,* 18 July 1981.

82. *The Coalition Bulletin,* no. 1 (February 1982).

83. See Lal 1983a.

84. A copy of this never fully published report is in my possession.

85. Taniela Veitata, a militant Fijian nationalist, told the parliament during his maiden speech in 1987 that "it must be realized that our chiefs today are the direct

descendants of our cannibal forbearers who actually rose to power with the proven ability as fighters and administrators. If they survived through the cannibal era, known to be inbuilt with intrigue and savageries, then this is really a hallmark, giving credence to their natural abilities as leaders." See *Hansard,* 14 May 1987, 138.

86. *Fiji Times,* 29 July 1982. For a general account of the aftermath, see Lal 1983*d.*

87. The initial account was published in the Sydney magazine *The Bulletin* and reprinted in the *Fiji Times,* 7 Aug. 1982.

88. *Pacific Islands Monthly,* Aug. 1986.

89. *Fiji Times,* 5 Aug. 1982.

90. *Report of the Royal Commission into the 1982 General Election,* Parliamentary Paper 74/1983.

91. See *Fiji Times,* 9 Dec. 1982.

92. Comment reported in *Fiji Sun,* 16 Sept. 1982.

93. Senate reports in *Fiji Sun* and *Fiji Times,* 16 Sept. 1982.

94. See *Fiji Times,* 27 Sept. 1982.

95. *Fiji Sun,* 17 Sept. 1982.

96. Report in the *Fiji Times,* 3 Nov. 1982.

97. For the NFP's reaction, see *Fiji Times,* 6 Nov. 1982: "It is difficult to understand now why the Prime Minister did not vote against the racist motion in the Great Council of Chiefs meeting."

98. Reported in the *Fiji Sun,* 18 Nov. 1982.

99. *Fiji Sun,* 18 Nov. 1982.

100. For details on the controversy, see *Fiji Times,* 17 Aug. 1982.

101. For details and background, see Vijendra Kumar, "Fiji Opposition in Disarray: What Made Reddy Run," *Pacific Islands Monthly,* June 1984, 22–24.

102. *Fiji Sun,* 6 Nov. 1982.

103. See *Fiji Times,* 21 May 1985, for their joint statement.

104. Vijendra Kumar, "NFP squabbles open way for the Labour Party push," *Pacific Islands Monthly,* October 1985, 52. For a similar assessment, see Asha Lakhan's article in the *Fiji Times,* 17 Aug. 1985.

105. In the *Fiji Times,* 6 April 1985.

106. A brief mention of this meeting is made in the *Fiji Times,* 19 Feb. 1986.

107. *Fiji Times,* 6 July 1986.

108. *Fiji Times,* 19 March 1987.

109. See Cole, Levine, and Matahau 1984.

110. Ward 1987, 36.

111. See Lal 1986*b,* 143–145; and "Teachers Protest: De-Segregating Fiji's Communal Schools," *Pacific Islands Monthly,* January 1985, 53–54.

112. See Ahmed Ali's statement in the *Fiji Times,* 1 March 1985.

113. *Fiji Times,* 2 Oct. 1984.

114. Parts of the petition are excerpted in *Fiji Times,* 3 Nov. 1984.

115. Baba 1985, 30.

116. *The Financial Review Committee Report, 1985,* Parliamentary Paper 54 of 1985, 4.

117. *Report of the Financial Review Committee,* Parliamentary Paper 17 of 1979, 5.

118. Economic statistics related here are derived from the government's state-

ment printed in the *Courier,* no. 92 (July–August 1985) and from its position paper issued at the National Economic Summit in Feb. 1985.

119. National Economic Summit Information Paper, "The Wage Freeze: Summary of Government Position," a copy of which is in my possession. See also other papers prepared at the conference (4–5 February 1985), especially "Fiji's Current Economic Situation and Immediate Future Prospects," "Fiji's Unemployment Problems and Measures to Create Employment," and "Road to Recovery."

120. National Economic Summit Information Paper, 3.

121. See Narsey, 1985.

122. Revealing details of the Mara family fortune and its various commercial ventures are listed in *Fiji Sun,* 2 Aug. 1982.

123. *Fiji Times,* 6 April 1985.

124. For more details, see *Report of the Fiji Employment and Development Mission,* 5. Also for a general account, see Howard 1987.

125. Remarks reported in *Fiji Times,* 10 May 1985.

126. The circumstances leading to the formation of the FLP are discussed in Lal 1986*b*, 134.

127. The FLP manifesto is reproduced in full in Lal, ed. 1986, 148–155. See also Robertson 1985 for internal problems and issues surrounding the launching of the FLP.

128. From the FLP's founding manifesto in Lal, ed. 1986.

129. See, for example, Dr. Timoci Bavadra's comments in *Pacific Islands Monthly* November 1986, 21: "If we contest the same seats, we will be playing right into the Alliance's hands by splitting the vote—especially the Indian vote."

130. Quoted in Robertson and Tamanisau 1988, 38.

131. The first NFP negotiating team was led by Shardha Nand, but he was acting very much on his own, without the approval of the Working Committee, the policy-making body of the NFP. His initiatives were discarded.

132. Koya, Shardha Nand, Vijay Parmanandam, and other former doves launched their own short-lived NFP coalition with the moribund Western United Front.

133. Based on interviews with NFP officials.

134. This was the principal theme of NFP leaders' campaign speeches.

135. See Lal 1983*d.*

136. This is based on the FNP's campaign manifesto; copy in my possession.

137. See advertisements in *Fiji Times* and *Fiji Sun;* and *Alliance Party Election Manifesto 1987,* 2.

138. *Fiji Times,* 11 March 1987.

139. Interview in *Fiji Times,* 8 Nov. 1986.

140. A copy of Bavadra's speech is in my possession.

141. *Fiji Times,* 24 March 1987.

142. Reported in *Fiji Times,* 22 March 1987.

143. See *Fiji Times,* 17 Nov. 1986.

144. See, for example, Ravuvu 1987, 241: "In our present socio-economic and political contexts, our leaders get it both ways, whereas the led get it only one way."

145. Address to the FLP's first annual convention, 17 July 1986; speech printed as pamphlet; copy in my possession.

146. Quote from Mara's concluding election address on Radio Fiji; copy in my possession.

147. Ibid.

148. For a detailed breakdown of the voting figures and for a discussion of the election generally, see Lal 1988*a.*

149. *Fiji Times,* 13 April 1987.

150. Usher 1987, 146. This book was published a week after the elections.

151. *Fiji Times,* 13 April 1987.

Chapter 6, Things Fall Apart

1. See House of Representatives, *Hansard,* 14 May 1987, 135–142.

2. Ibid., 142.

3. Listening to the instructions of the hooded soldiers, Prime Minister Bavadra turned to Education Minister Tupeni Baba and said: "Tupeni, is this for real or is it only an exercise?" See Baba 1988, 4.

4. For this I am indebted to Dr. Satendra Nandan, deposed Coalition minister for Health and Social Welfare.

5. Much of the material in this chapter is also available in Lal 1988*b.* Since this book is not likely to be available to many readers of this study, I have not hesitated to cover the topic in detail.

6. A useful introduction to the literature on the coups and how to find it is Lal and Peacock 1990.

7. See *Fiji Times* editorial of 14 April 1987 and Nemani Delaibatiki's "New Cabinet Designed to Keep Fijians Happy" in *Fiji Sun,* 19 April 1987, and *Fiji Sun,* 25 April 1987.

8. The three old hands were Satendra Nandan, Harish Sharma, and Jai Ram Reddy.

9. The Coalition government's policy statement is published in full in Lal 1988, 158–175.

10. Cole, Levine, and Matahau 1984.

11. *Islands Business,* April 1987.

12. *Fiji Sun,* 2 May 1987.

13. *Fiji Sun,* 20 April 1987.

14. *Fiji Sun,* 21 April 1987.

15. *Fiji Times,* 21 April 1987.

16. Report reprinted in *Honolulu-Star Bulletin,* 5 April 1987.

17. Tomasi Bole, "The Fijian case," in *Fiji Times,* 31 July 1987. See also Inoke Kubuabola's remarks in *Wall Street Journal,* 15 Oct. 1987.

18. This is based on contemporary newspaper accounts and my personal observations at the time.

19. From a copy of his speech in my possession.

20. This was revealed in the trial of Mohammed Kahan, in connection with the gunrunning episode of June 1988, in a London court.

21. "We planned to burn Suva, says Veitata," in *Fiji Sun,* 19 July 1987.

22. *Islands Business,* May 1988, 18.

23. *Islands Business,* May 1988.

24. From a transcript of a ceremony on 5 December 1987, when Ganilau was invited to accept the presidency of the republic.

25. Quotes from Dean and Ritova 1988.

26. The judiciary's advice, dated 16 May, was released to the media; a copy was given to me by Chief Justice Timoci Tuivaga himself.

27. The full text was printed in *Fiji Times,* 15 May 1987.

28. Among those who witnessed the occasion, and had perhaps engineered it, were Sir John Falvey, once an Alliance attorney general, and Isikeli Mataitoga, a Fijian lawyer. See Dean and Ritova 1988, 96.

29. Interview with Chief Justice Tuivaga, late June 1987.

30. See *Fiji Times* editorial, 29 May 1987.

31. See *Fiji Royal Gazette* 114 (38), 19 May 1987.

32. F. M. Brookfield 1988, 253.

33. Ghai 1990, 11. See also Thakur 1990, 55. The *bati* and *turaga* relation between Ganilau and Rabuka is not what it is generally made out to be. Rabuka's social station is that of a fisherman *(gonedau)* to the Vunivalu of Natewa.

34. Speech printed in full in *Fiji Sun,* 23 May 1987.

35. *Fiji Times,* 22 May 1987.

36. Reported in *Fiji Times,* 8 June 1987.

37. *Fiji Sun,* 23 May.

38. I am grateful to Dr. Satendra Nandan, minister of Health and Social Welfare in the Coalition government, for his reminiscences; he plans to publish his memoirs.

39. Reports in *Fiji Sun,* 21 May 1987, and on the Australian television program, "Four Corners." See also Scarr 1988, 85–86.

40. Statement published in *Fiji Times,* 21 May 1987.

41. Among those who backed the governor-general was Mr. John Piper, then Australian ambassador to Fiji.

42. The emergency regulations were published in *Fiji Royal Gazette* 114 (37), 18 May 1987.

43. *Independent,* 8 June 1987.

44. *Guardian Weekly,* 14 June 1987. See also Ramphal, "Our Influence in Fiji is Limited," 134-135. The Commonwealth background is well covered in Kenneth Bain 1989.

45. *Fiji Times,* 22 May 1987.

46. Quote from a three-page Coalition statement dated 28 May 1987; copy in my possession.

47. *New Zealand Listener,* 20 June 1987, quoted in Robertson and Tamanisau 1988, 90.

48. Wellington *Evening Post,* 12 Aug. 1988, quoted in Alley 1990, 50. This article provides a comprehensive and balanced account of the Australian and New Zealand governments' response to the Fiji crisis.

49. 29 June 1987.

50. Ministry of Information press release, June 1987.

51. *Fiji Times,* 13 June 1987.

52. *Fiji Times,* 4 July 1987.

53. Editorial, 15 June 1987.

54. Editorial, 25 June 1987.

55. Statement published in *Fiji Times,* 21 June 1987.

56. I have several dozen of these in my possession. A full set can be found at the National Archives of Fiji; excerpts were published in the two local dailies.

57. See *Fiji Times,* 10 Aug. 1987. The league's submission was reportedly written by Dr. Ahmed Ali.

58. Parts of the Methodist church's submission were printed in *Contact,* 2 Aug. 1987.

59. From a typescript of the Coalition's submission to the Constitutional Review Committee.

60. From the movement's submission; copy in my possession.

61. Reports of the meetings appeared in the two dailies.

62. What follows comes from the 104-page document, a copy of which is in my possession.

63. *Report of the Constitution Review Committee,* Parliamentary Paper 21/1987.

64. Ibid., 77.

65. Among the leaders were Adi Ana Matai McGregor, Mrs. Susan Parkinson, Dr. Rajat Ganeshwar, Mrs. Suliana Siwatibau, Reverend Akuila Yabaki, Reverend Ragho Prasad, Dr. John Garrett, Michael Brook, Ulaiasi Taoi, and Kenneth Zinck.

66. A copy of this submission is in my possession.

67. See *Fiji Sun,* and *Fiji Times,* 23 Sept. 1987.

68. 23 Sept. 1987.

69. See, for example, Justice K. N. Govind's timely statement on the role and responsibility of the judiciary at a time of crisis, published in *Fiji Sun,* 11 Aug. 1987.

70. For this, see particularly the pro-Coalition Fiji Independent News Service's *Fiji Voice,* published in Sydney.

71. See Ratu Meli Vesikula's letter to the *Fiji Sun,* 12 Sept. 1987.

72. Marika Natiri's letter, "What it means to put Ratu Penaia in the dock," in *Fiji Sun,* 15 Sept. 1987.

73. See *Fiji Sun,* 25 Sept. 1987.

74. *Fiji Times,* 24 Sept. 1987. Interestingly, Reverend Tomasi Raikivi, the governor-general's advisor on information, who assumed the role of representative for the 52 escapees, said that the prisoners had actually gone to Government House to report that they were offered money "in efforts to lure them to join a Coalition hit team with the special assignment of dealing with the Coalition demands."

75. 24 Sept. 1987.

76. He made these remarks in an interview with Indian journalist Saeed Naqvi, "Marooned at Home: A Demoralized [Fiji] Indian Community," in *India Today,* 30 Nov. 1987, 100. See also *Islands Business,* October 1987, 16–18.

77. For a blow-by-blow account of events immediately after the September coup, see *Today's Fiji* 1 (1), 18 Dec. 1987.

78. These ministers included Sitiveni Rabuka as head of government, Home Affairs, and Civil Service; Filipe Bole as minister for Foreign Affairs and Civil Aviation; Josua Cavalevu, Finance; Sakiasi Butadroka, Lands and Mineral Resources; Livai Nasilivata, Housing and Urban Affairs; Apenisa Kurisaqila, Health; Irene Jai Narayan, Indian Affairs; Taniela Veitata, Employment and Industrial Relations; Adi Litia Cakobau, Women and Culture; Filimone Ralo-

gaivau, Education; Meli Vesikula, Fijian Affairs; Josaia Tavaiqia, Forests; Viliame Gonelevu, Primary Industries; Lt. Col. Ilaisa Kacisolomone, Youth and Sport; Apisai Tora, Communications, Works and Transport; Inoke Kubuabola, Information; David Pickering, Tourism and Energy; Tomasi Raikivi, Social Welfare; and Jone Veisamasama, Rural Development.

79. *Today's Fiji* 1 (1), 18 Dec. 1987.

80. See Kenneth Bain 1989, 121.

81. Quoted in *Today's Fiji* 1 (1), 16.

82. *Sunday Mail*, 27 Sept. 1987.

83. The text of the Commonwealth communique is in Prime Minister Bob Hawke's speech to the Australian parliament, 5 Nov. 1987.

84. See reports in Kenneth Bain 1989, 210–211, and reports published by the Sydney-based Fiji Independent News Service. The military has denied these allegations. The higher officers were probably not involved. But lists of victims prepared under the auspices of Amnesty International that I have seen and have copies of, complete with names of the individuals victimized, places and dates, convince me beyond a doubt that much abuse of human rights did, in fact, take place.

85. *Dominion* (Wellington), 25 July 1988.

86. The source of these figures and of my understanding of the economic consequences of the coups is Bruce Knapman's excellent article (1990).

87. On the Australian Broadcast Commission's program "Four Corners," 18 May 1987.

88. *Islands Business,* May 1988.

89. *Pacific Islands Monthly,* January 1988, 12.

90. For the sake of historical record, the full cabinet was Mara, prime minister; Josaia Tavaiqia, Forests; Apenisa Kurisaqila, Health; Ishwari Vajpayi, Co-operatives; Tomasi Vakatora, Housing and Urban Development; William Toganivalu, Lands and Minerals; Taniela Veitata, Industrial Relations and Employment; Viliame Gonelevu, Primary Industries; David Pickering, Tourism and Civil Aviation; Irene Jai Narayan, Indian Affairs; Rabuka, Home Affairs; Iliasa Kacisolomone, Youth and Sports; Vatilai Navunisaravi, Fijian Affairs; Apolosi Biuvakaloloma, Rural Development; Sailosi Kepa, attorney general; Berenado Vunibobo, Trade and Commerce; Josefa Kamikamica, Finance; Finau Tabakaucoro, Women and Culture; and Filipe Bole, Education).

91. Quoted from a three-page transcript of the ceremony in my possession.

92. *Fiji Times,* 7 Dec. 1987.

93. Interview in *Today's Fiji,* 18 Dec. 1987, 23.

94. See, among others, Wypijewski 1987, 117–120; and Elena Garcia's two articles: "How CIA Infiltrated the Union Movement," *Direct Action,* 21 Oct. 1987, and "CIA Chiefs behind Fiji coup," ibid., 30 Sept. 1987.

95. Outside Micronesia, Fiji was the largest Pacific Island recipient of American aid, US$10 million between 1985 and 1987. The reportedly CIA-supported Asia-American Free Labour Institute opened an office in Suva in 1984. The person most responsible for the expansion and consolidation of American influence in Fiji was American Ambassador Fred Ecket, who became a close personal friend of Mara's. After the coups, Ecket became a paid consultant to the interim regime to effect a more positive U.S. policy toward Fiji. For details of U.S. interest and possible involvement, see *Wellington Confidential,* no. 36, June 1987.

96. *Washington Pacific Report,* 15 April 1987. This publication is widely regarded as a very reliable guide to official Washington thinking about the Pacific.

97. See *Sydney Morning Herald,* 26 March 1988.

98. For a brief but thoroughly researched biography of Walters, see Ray and Schaap 1986.

99. Geoffrey Reid, general manager of Emperor Gold Mines, was active in bringing about a reconciliation between the Alliance and disaffected western chiefs in 1986. The identity of the local businessman, which cannot be revealed here for obvious reasons, is well known to anyone familiar with the Fijian political scene.

100. The most comprehensive expression of this view is in Dean and Ritova 1988.

101. This view was most forcefully articulated on several occasions by Apisai Tora.

102. I base this contention on a detailed reading of the minutes of confidential meetings that took place in Suva, beginning 12 Aug. 1969. A copy is in my possession.

103. *Fiji Times,* 25 May 1982.

104. The allegations reached such a crescendo that Baba filed a libel suit against one of his accusers, Mrs. Irene Jai Narayan.

105. See Bavadra, "Closing Election Address," extracts from which were published in the media. A full copy is in my possession.

106. For a reliable study of the NLTB, see Nayacakalou 1971.

107. T. L. Davey, *Report on the Native Land Trust Board,* Parliamentary Paper 25/1977.

108. Alan Carroll et al., "Strategic Issues Facing the Fijian Government," (November 1981). A copy of this report, which was confidential and never intended for publication, is in my possession.

109. Quoted from the FLP manifesto in Lal ed. 1986, 150.

110. Ratu Mara's words to the Fijian Association Convention at the Girmit Center in Lautoka. See *Fiji Times* 17 Aug. 1986. See also *Alliance Party Election Manifesto 1987,* 7.

111. The functions of the board are specified in the Fijian Affairs Ordinance under the laws of Fiji. I have already looked at the origins of the board in chapter 3, but see also Lasaqa 1984.

112. The new members were Filipe Bole, Taniela Veitata, Viliame Gonelevu, Apisai Tora (all members of the *Taukei Movement*), Apenisa Kurisiqila, Timoci Vesikula, William Toganivalu, and Mosese Qionibaravi.

113. For more discussion, see Thomas 1990a.

114. This figure from the 1986 census does not include the neighboring town of Lami (12,126 Fijians). The idea of a separate Fijian constituency for Suva was mentioned to me personally by a prominent Fijian Coalition politician.

115. See, for example, Irene Jai Narayan's contribution to the debate in the House of Representatives on 8 Dec. 1977. Former senior Alliance minister, James Shankar Singh, has told me that he personally raised the issue with Ratu Mara on several occasions, to no avail.

116. FLP manifesto in Lal, ed. 1986, 154.

117. It will serve little purpose to reveal the identity of the Coalition leader or the source of my information.

118. See *Islands Business,* September 1987.

119. Advertisement in *Fiji Sun,* 15 March 1987.

120. According to my well-placed source, among those who made the approach were Commander Epeli Nailatikau himself, a prominent local trade unionist, and a leading Fijian intellectual then living overseas.

121. See Gordon Campbell, "Inside Fiji," in *New Zealand Listener,* 6–12 June 1987.

122. This has been asserted by Taniela Veitata on several occasions. For more details, see Karen Mangnall, *Sunday Star,* 15 May 1988.

123. See his interview with Saeed Naqvi, *India Today,* 30 Nov. 1987, 100.

124. This is the assessment of Colonel Jim Sanday, who was briefing the governor-general when Militoni Leweniqila, Speaker of the House, rang around 10:20 AM to inform Government House of the coup.

125. Alley 1973, 64.

126. See *Islands Business,* December 1982 for an interview with Ganilau.

127. See Rabuka's own views on his close relationship with Ganilau in Dean and Ritova 1988.

128. See, for example, Baba 1988, 8.

129. *Fiji Sun* editorial, 6 July 1987.

130. See, for example, *Fiji Times,* 21 May and 24 June 1987.

131. In an interview with Mosese Velia in *Fiji Times,* 10 Dec. 1990.

132. See his interview in *Fiji Times,* 14 May 1990.

133. *Fiji Times,* 15 Aug. 1991.

134. *Pacific Islands Monthly,* June 1990.

135. From Mara's speech published in the *Alliance Messenger,* no. 3, 1986, 3.

136. Quoted from a copy of the speech in my possession.

137. It is a matter of historical record that Ratu Finau Mara was on the steps of the parliament house at 10 o'clock on 14 May, clearing the path for the soldiers to move in. Subsequently, he enlisted in the army with the rank of captain and was in the street in battle fatigues. Adi Lady Lala Mara visited the Queen Elizabeth Barracks in June 1987 and honored Rabuka by placing a garland of *tabua* (whale teeth) around his neck. Deryck Scarr (1988, 134), says that according to some reports, "the army had actually been told to move on 25 September by a very high chief indeed, the head of a confederacy, Ro Lala herself." According to a highly placed, impeccable source, one of Mara's children told a senior officer wavering between his duty to uphold his oath and the pressure to join the coup: *"Mo ni nanumi Ratu ga,"* (whatever your obligations, think of Ratu [Mara] only).

138. Dean and Ritova 1988, 80.

139. Ibid., 78.

140. Alliance Party Election Manifesto, 1987, 5.

141. Speech reported in *Fiji Times,* 5 May 1988.

142. See *Fiji Times,* 11 May 1989.

143. Interview published in *Fiji Times,* 28 May 1987.

144. Interview in *Islands Business,* October 1989. See also his address to the Lau Provincial Council in June 1987 (*Fiji Sun,* 18 June), in which Mara is reported as saying: "I believe that by changing the constitution to allow Fijians leadership will not be fruitful, effective and meaningful if we Fijians cannot shoulder these responsibilities to support our leadership."

145. Unless otherwise stated, all the following quotes come from Dean and Ritova 1988.

Chapter 7, Broken Waves

1. Naidu 1989; Sutherland 1989.

2. See, for example, submissions of the Methodist Church and the Great Council of Chiefs to the Constitution Review committee in 1987 and also the interim regime's draft constitution of September 1988, which, in its preamble, reaffirmed "that the nation is founded upon principles that acknowledge the Deity and the teachings of the Lord Jesus Christ."

3. Fiji Military Government Decree no. 20 published in *Fiji Gazette,* 1 (15), 9 Nov. 1987.

4. For details, see Chandra 1990, 49.

5. Chandra 1990, 52.

6. From a 37-page submission, which, much to the anger of the army, was leaked to the press. A summary appeared in *Fiji Voice,* December 1989.

7. Sanday 1989, 18.

8. See generally Sutherland 1989.

9. See *Islands Business,* March 1988, for more details, and Chandra 1989.

10. See generally Lateef 1990.

11. Bruce Knapman 1990, 81–82; see also Prasad 1989, 41–45. For a more optimistic assessment, see Eleck, Hill, and Tabor 1991; even these authors note that the practice of giving thirteen-year tax holidays to companies "will need to be reversed" (19).

12. Eleck, Hill, and Tabor 1991, 3.

13. See Don Dunstan, Ray Hogan, and Michael Sexton, "Report of the Australian Labor Party to Fiji, 16–22 May 1988," (unpublished), 8–9. Copy in my possession.

14. Report quoted in *Fiji Times,* 20 Oct. 1991.

15. Overton and Ward 1989, 215; quoted in Eleck, Hill, and Tabor 1991, 23.

16. A copy of the draft "Constitution for the Republic of Fiji" (112 pages) is in my possession, and the comments that follow are based on my reading of it.

17. *Report of the Fiji Constitution and Inquiry and Advisory Committee,* August 1989, 3.

18. The National Federation Party and the Fiji Labour Party Coalition's "Submission on the Draft Constitution of Fiji to the Fiji Constitutional and Advisory Committee," 16 Jan. 1989, 2; a copy of this brilliantly argued 48-page document is in my possession.

19. *Report of the Fiji Constitution and Advisory Committee,* August 1989.

20. Here, I am guided by the analysis of Professor Yash Ghai, an internationally acclaimed constitutional lawyer, who helped draft the constitutions of a number of Pacific Island states. See Ghai 1991.

21. Quote from his address to the nation, a copy of which is in my possession thanks to Sandra Tarte.

22. *Fiji Times,* 29 July 1991.

23. Jai Ram Reddy, quoted in *Islands Business Pacific,* January 1991, 26.

24. Eugene Genovese, *From Rebellion to Revolution: Afro-American Slave Revolts in the Making of the Modern World* (Baton Rouge: Louisiana State University Press, 1979), 7.

25. For details, see Scarr 1988, 147–149; and generally Harder 1988.

27. Griffin 1990, 44.

27. *Australian,* 26 July 1990.

28. *Daily Post,* 29 Oct. 1991.

29. T. S. Eliot, "East Coker."

30. *Fiji Times,* 24 April 1989.

31. *Fiji Times,* 26 June 1990.

32. This is based on comments made by Geoffrey Palmer (NZ) and Bob Hawke (Aust) at the South Pacific Forum in Vila, July 1990. Mara said he was "deeply touched" by the understanding showed by these two leaders.

33. *Fiji Times,* 11 Nov. 1991.

34. *Islands Business,* May 1988, 15.

35. *Report of the Constitution Inquiry and Advisory Committee,* 1987, 14–15.

36. For a brief report, see *Fiji Times,* 6 May 1988.

37. Dean and Ritova 1988, 141.

38. Jone Dakuvula's words, quoted in Victor Lal 1990, 238.

39. I am indebted for this comparison to the Coalition's *The Fiji Constitution of 1990,* 70.

40. Ravuvu 1991, 1.

41. Interview in *Bulletin,* 20 Sept. 1988.

42. Belshaw 1964, 288.

43. Nayacakalou 1975, 135. This book is substantially a slight, posthumous revision of the Nayacakalou's doctoral dissertion, which he completed in the 1960s.

44. T. S. Eliot, "Burnt Norton."

Glossary

Adi	A title designating a woman of chiefly rank in Fijian society.
Arya Samaj	A reformist sect of Hinduism founded by Swami Daya-nanda (1823–1884) in 1875; believes in strict adherence to the religion of the Vedas.
bati	Warrior, bodyguard.
buli	Official head of the Fijian Administration at the district level.
Burebasaga	Fijian confederacy consisting, in the main, of the provinces of Rewa, Kadavu, and parts of Nadroga.
colonial secretary	The chief administrative officer of the colony, a rung below the governor.
common roll	Nonracial system of voting on the principle of one person, one vote, one value.
communal roll	Voting based on racially defined mutually exclusive electorates.
Fijian Administration	The bureaucracy that governs the affairs of Fijian society.
Fijian Affairs Board	The executive, policy-formulating branch of the Fijian Administration, and generally of the Great Council of Chiefs.
galala	A Fijian farmer legally exempt from communal obligations.
Ghadr Movement	A revolutionary movement of Asian Indians in North America at the turn of the century, founded to overthrow British rule in India.
girmit	From "agreement" of indenture; generally the Indian indenture experience.
girmitiya	An Indian indentured laborer.

Gujarati	Free migrants from Gujarat in India; dominant group in the Indo-Fijian business community.
i tokatoka	A patrilineal, extended family group smaller than the *mataqali.*
kisan	Farmer, cane grower (in the sense used in this book).
koro	A Fijian village.
Kubuna	Bau-led political confederacy consisting of Tailevu, Naitasiri, and Ra, together with the islands of Lomaiviti.
lala	Goods and services due to a chief from his or her people.
Leader of the opposition	In the Westminster system, leader of nongovernment parties in parliament.
Letters Patent	Royal authority to act on a matter, such as altering the constitutional structure of government.
matanitū	The largest political unit in Fijian society, consisting of several *vanua;* generally the government.
matanivanua	Traditional speaker for the chiefs.
mataqali	Patrilineal descent group and landowning group in Fijian society.
Native (Fijian) Regulations	Rules formulated by the colonial government, on the advice of the Great Council of Chiefs, governing the daily routine of Fijian life.
panchayat	A five-person, village-based conflict-resolving body in Indo-Fijian society.
Ratu	Title denoting male chiefly rank in Fijian society
Roko Tui	Official title of Fijian heads of administrative provinces.
Sanatan Dharam	Literally the eternal religion, orthodox, dominant among Fiji Hindus.
Sangam	Cultural and religious organization of South Indians in Fiji, formed in 1926.
Sangathan Movement	An organization of *Arya Samajis* in Fiji in the 1920s intended to preach their faith and convert Muslims and others to their sect.
Shia Muslims	Minority sect of Islam, which upholds the right of the Prophet's family to lead the Islamic community.

Sunni Muslims	More orthodox followers of Islam, the dominant group in Fiji, which differs with the Shia sect on the question of succession to leadership.
taukei	Owners of the land, original inhabitants of the islands, Fijians.
Taukei Movement	An organization of assorted indigenous Fijians opposed to the Labour Coalition government and behind the coups of 1987; now defunct.
tikina	A government district (Fijian).
Tovata	The third political confederacy, consisting of Cakaudrove, Macuata, and Bua on the island of Vanua Levu, and the islands of the Lau group.
Tui	Title of chiefly office, usually the head of a *vanua* or *matanitū*.
Tūraga ni Koro	Head of the Fijian village under the Fijian Administration; usually of chiefly rank.
vanua	Land in both the physical as well as the psychological sense of attachment to a place; a unit composed of several villages of a *yavusa*.
Vūnivalu	Warlord; title of the chief of the dominant clan of Bau.
yaqona	Fijian word for kava, consumed widely throughout the Pacific.
yavusa	A patrilineal group of several ranked *mataqali* claiming descent from a common founding ancestor.

Bibliography

The bulk of this study is based on unpublished primary sources. I have made particular use of the files of the Colonial Secretary's Office (CSO) housed in the National Archives of Fiji in Suva. These were supplemented by Colonial Office (CO), London, files available in the Colonial Office 83 series. These contain governors' dispatches and Colonial Office minutes and notes. They are available on microfilm in several places; I consulted them at the University of Hawaii's Hamilton Library. Because of the thirty-year rule regarding access to unpublished Fiji government documents, I was able to see CSO and CO files only up to 1959. For the post-1959 period, I made extensive use of both English-language and vernacular newspapers, published government documents, such as the Legislative Council Debates and Papers, and private collections. A careful reading of these sources shows that many important unpublished documents and policy statements were either published in the various papers or read into the official records of parliamentary proceedings. For the most recent period, I have relied on an extensive collection of unpublished material in my possession, and on newspaper clippings, radio and television broadcast transcripts, and other such sources. Needless to say, conversation with people in Fiji and my own observations over nearly a decade have informed my thinking and interpretation of recent events.

What follows is a select list of published and unpublished secondary works cited in the text, along with others I found generally useful.

Ali, Ahmed
   1973a   The Fiji General Election of 1972. *The Journal of Pacific History* 8: 171–180.
   1973b   Fiji and the Franchise, 1900–1937. PhD dissertation, Australian National University, Canberra.
   1976   *Society in Transition: Aspects of Fiji-Indian History, 1879–1939*. Suva: University of the South Pacific.
   1977   The Fiji General Election of 1977. *Journal of Pacific History* 12:189–201.
   1980   *Plantation to Politics: Studies on Fiji Indians*. Suva: University of the South Pacific and Fiji Times and Herald.

Alley, Roderic M.
   1970   Independence for Fiji: Recent Constitutional and Political Developments. *Australian Outlook* 24 (2): 178–187.

1973   *The Development of Political Parties in Fiji.* PhD dissertation, University of
        Wellington, Victoria.
1986   The Emergence of Party Politics in Fiji. In *Politics in Fiji: Studies in Con-
        temporary History,* edited by Brij V. Lal, 28–51. Sydney: Allen & Unwin.
1990   The 1987 Military Coups in Fiji: The Regional Implications. *The Con-
        temporary Pacific* 2:37–58.

Anderson, Grant
1974   *Indo-Fijian Smallfarming: Profiles of a Peasantry.* Auckland: Oxford Univer-
        sity Press.

Andrews, C. F.
1937   *India and the Pacific.* London: Allen & Unwin.

Andrews, C. F., and W. W. Pearson
1916   *Indentured Labour in Fiji: An Independent Enquiry.* Calcutta: Privately
        printed.

Anthony, James M.
1969   The 1968 Fiji By-Elections. *The Journal of Pacific History* 4:132–135.

Baba, Tupeni
1985   Fijian Education in the Context of Modern, Multi-cultural Society. *Fiji
        Teachers Journal* (May): 27–35.
1988   *Developments in Fiji since the Second Coup.* Sydney: Evatt Memorial Foun-
        dation.

Bain, 'Atu
1988   A Protective Labour Policy? An Alternative Interpretation of Early
        Colonial Labour Policy in Fiji. *The Journal of Pacific History* 23:119–136.

Bain, Kenneth
1989   *Treason at Ten: Fiji at the Crossroads.* London: Hodder & Stoughton.

Belshaw, Cyril S.
1964   *Under the Ivi Tree: Society and Economic Growth in Rural Fiji.* London:
        Routledge & Kegan Paul.

Bilimoria, Purusottama
1985   The Arya Samaj in Fiji: A Movement in Hindu Diaspora. *Religion* 15:
        103–129.

Britton, Stephen G.
1980   The Evolution of a Colonial Space Economy: The Case of Fiji. *Journal of
        Tropical Geography* 6:251–274.

Brookfield, F. M.
1988   The Fiji revolution of 1987. *New Zealand Law Journal* (July): 250–256.

Brookfield, H. C.
1988   Fijian Farmers Each on His Own Land: The Triumph of Experience
        over Hope. *The Journal of Pacific History* 23:15–35.

Brown, Emily C.
1975   *Hardayal: Hindu Rationalist and Revolutionary.* Tucson: University of Ari-
        zona Press.

Burns, Sir Alan
1963   *Fiji*. London: Her Majesty's Stationery Office.

Burton, J. W.
1910   *The Fiji of Today*. London: Kelly.

Cameron, J.
1983*a*   The Extent and Structure of Poverty in Fiji and Possible Elements of a
         Government Anti-Poverty Strategy in the 1980s. *Fiji Employment and
         Development Mission Papers*, no. 19.
1983*b*   Historical Background and Current Policy Positions of Trade Unions in
         Fiji. *Fiji Employment and Development Mission Papers*, no. 27.
1987   Fiji: The Political Economy of Recent Events. *Capital and Class* 33:
        29–45.

Campbell, Ian C.
1989   *A History of the Pacific Islands*. St. Lucia: University of Queensland Press.

Cargill, David
1977   *The Diaries and Correspondence of David Cargill, 1832–1843*. Edited by
        Albert J. Schütz. Canberra: Australian National University Press.

Cato, A. C.
1955   Fijians and Fiji Indians: A Culture-Contact Problem in the South
        Pacific. *Oceania* 26:14–34.

Chandra, Rajesh
1979   The Indo-Fijian Population Growth and Stabilization. *Journal of Pacific
        Studies* 5:1–8.
1980*a*   *Maro: Rural Indians of Fiji*. Suva: Institute of Pacific Studies.
1980*b*   Urbanization in Fiji, 1966–1976. *Demography India* 1&2:139–160.
1990   *Tax Free Zone in Fiji*. Report to Pacific Islands Development Program.
        Honolulu: East-West Center.

Chapman, J. K.
1964   *The Career of Arthur Hamilton Gordon: First Lord Stanmore, 1829–1912*.
        Toronto: University of Toronto Press.

Chappelle, Anthony J.
1973   Fijians, Land, and Sir Everard im Thurn. Paper in author's possession.
1975   The Fijian Voice in Fiji's Colonial History. *Journal of Pacific Studies* 1:
        47–62.
1978   Customary Land Tenure in Fiji: Old Truths and Middle-aged Myths.
        Journal of the Polynesian Society 78(2): 71–88.

Chick, J. D.
1972   Fiji: The General Election of 1972. *Pacific Perspective* 1 (2): 54–58.

Cole, Rodney, and Helen Hughes
1988   *The Fiji Economy, May 1987: Problems and Prospects*. Pacific Policy Paper
        no. 4. Canberra: National Centre for Development Studies.

Cole, Rodney V., Stephen I. Levine, and Anare V. Matahau
1984   *The Fijian Provincial Administration: A Review*. Honolulu: East-West Cen-
        ter, Pacific Islands Development Program.

Connell, John
  1987   Population Growth and Emigration: Maintaining a Balance. *Fiji: Future Imperfect?* edited by Michael Taylor, 14–32. Sydney: Allen & Unwin.

Corris, Peter
  1973   *Port, Passage and Plantation: A History of Solomon Island Labour Migration, 1879–1914.* Melbourne: Melbourne University Press.

Coulter, J. W.
  1942   *Fiji: Little India of the Pacific.* Chicago: University of Chicago Press.
  1967   *The Drama of Fiji: A Contemporary History.* Melbourne: Paul Flesch.

Davidson, J. W.
  1966   Constitutional Changes in Fiji. *The Journal of Pacific History* 1:165–182.

Dean, Eddie, and Stan Ritova
  1988   *Rabuka: No Other Way.* Sydney: Doubleday.

Derrick, R. A.
  1950   *A History of Fiji.* Revised edition. Suva: Government Printer.
  1951   *The Fiji Islands: A Geographical Handbook.* Suva: Government Printer.

Durutalo, Simione
  1985a   The Fiji Trade Union Movement at the Cross-Roads: Social and Political Options for the Labour Movement. *Journal of Pacific Studies* 11: 190–209.
  1985b   Internal Colonialism and Unequal Regional Development: The Case of Western Viti Levu. MA thesis, University of the South Pacific, Suva.

Eleck, Andrew, Hal Hill, and Steven R. Tabor
  1991   *Liberalisation and Diversification in a Small Island Economy: Fiji since the 1987 Coups.* Department of Economics Working Paper 91/4. Canberra: Australian National University.

Fiji, Colony of
  1936   *Handbook of Fiji, 1874–1936.* Suva: Government Printer.

Fiji Employment and Development Mission
  1984   *Final Report to the Government of Fiji.* Fiji Parliamentary Paper no. 66. Suva: Government Printer.

Finucane, Morgan I.
  1900   "The Islands and Peoples of Fiji." Lecture delivered 27 November at Royal Colonial Institute, London. Copy in CO 83/71.

Firth, Stewart
  1989   The Contemporary History of Fiji. Review Article. *The Journal of Pacific History* 24:242–246.

Fisk, E. K.
  1970   *The Political Economy of Independent Fiji.* Canberra: Australian National University Press.

France, Peter
  1968   The Founding of an Orthodoxy: Sir Arthur Gordon and the Doctrine of the Fijian Way of Life. *Journal of the Polynesian Society* 77(1): 6–32.

1969   *The Charter of the Land: Custom and Colonization in Fiji.* Melbourne: Oxford University Press.

Garrett, John
1983   *To Live Among the Stars: Christian Origins of Oceania.* Suva: Institute of Pacific Studies.
1990   Uncertain Sequel: The Social and Religious Scene in Fiji Since the Coups. *The Contemporary Pacific* 2:87–111.

Geddes, William R.
1945   Acceleration of Social Change in a Fijian Community. In *Oceania* 16: 1–14.

Ghai, Yash
1987   The Fijian Crisis: The Constitutional Dimension. *Minority Rights Group Report* no. 75, 9–14.
1990   A Coup by Another Name? The Politics of Legality. *The Contemporary Pacific* 2:11–35.
1991   *The Fiji Constitution of 1990: A Fraud on the Nation.* Nadi: Sunrise Press.

Ghai, Yash, and Jill Cottrell
1990   *Heads of State in the Pacific: A Legal and Constitutional Analysis.* Suva: Institute of Pacific Studies.

Gill, Walter
1970   *Turn North-East at the Tombstone.* Adelaide: Rigby.

Gillion, K. L.
1962   *Fiji's Indian Migrants: A History to the End of Indenture in 1920.* Melbourne: Oxford University Press.
1977   *The Fiji Indians: Challenge to European Dominance, 1920–1946.* Canberra: Australian National University Press.

Gordon, Sir Arthur
1897   *Fiji: Records of Private and of Public Life, 1875–1880.* Volume 1. Edinburgh: R. & R. Clark.

Griffin, Arlene, ed.
1990   *With Heart and Nerve and Sinew: Post-Coup Writing from Fiji.* Suva: Rehabilitation Workshop.

Griffin, Vanessa
1988   Women and the Coups in Fiji. *New Zealand Listener,* 14 April.

Gunson, Niel
1978   *Messengers of Grace: Evangelical Missionaries in the South Seas.* Melbourne: Oxford University Press.

Hagan, Stephanie
1987a   The Party System, the Labour Party, and the "Plural Society" Syndrome in Fiji. *Journal of Commonwealth and Comparative Politics* 25: 126–140.
1987b   Race, Politics, and the Coup in Fiji. *Bulletin of Concerned Asian Scholars* 19:2–18.

Hailey, John
 1985 *Indigenous Business in Fiji.* Honolulu: East-West Center, Pacific Islands
    Development Program.
 1988 The Genesis of the Fiji Republic: Its Origins and Implications. *World
    Review* 27(1): 51–66.

Harder, Christopher
 1988 *The Guns of Lautoka (The Defence of Kahan).* Auckland: Sunshine Press.

Heath, Ian
 1974 Towards a Reassessment of Gordon in Fiji. *The Journal of Pacific History*
    9:81–92.

Hooper, Antony, Steve Britton, Ron Crocombe, Judith Huntsman, and Cluny
Macpherson, eds.
 1987 *Class and Culture in the South Pacific.* Suva: Institute of Pacific Studies,
    University of the South Pacific and Centre for Pacific Studies, Univer-
    sity of Auckland.

Howard, Michael C.
 1987 The Trade Union Movement in Fiji. In *Fiji: Future Imperfect?* edited by
    Michael Taylor, 108–121. Sydney: Allen & Unwin.
 1988 *The Impact of the International Mining Industry on Native Peoples.* Sydney:
    Transnational Corporations Project.

Howe, Kerry R.
 1984 *Where the Waves Fall. A New South Sea Islands History from First Settlement to
    Colonial Rule.* Pacific Islands Monograph Series no. 2. Honolulu: Uni-
    versity of Hawaii Press and Center for Pacific Islands Studies.

Howlett, R. A.
 1948 *The History of the Fiji Military Forces, 1939–1945.* London: Crown Agents
    for the Colonies.

Jayawardena, Chandra
 1971 The Disintegration of Caste in Fiji Indian Rural Society. In *Anthropology
    in Oceania,* edited by Chandra Jayawardena and L. R. Hiatt, 89–119.
    Sydney: Angus & Robertson.

Kaplan, Martha
 1987 The Coups in Fiji: Colonial Contradictions and the Post-Colonial
    Crisis. *Critique of Anthropology* 8:93–116.
 1989 *Luve Ni Wai* as the British Saw It: Constructions of Custom and
    Disorder in Colonial Fiji. *Ethnohistory* 36:349–371.
 1990 Meaning, Agency and Colonial History: Navosavakadua and the *Tuka*
    Movement in Fiji. *American Ethnologist* 17:3–11.

Kasper, Wolfgang, Jeff Bennett, and Richard Blandy
 1988 *Fiji: Opportunity from Adversity?* CIS Pacific Papers no. 1. St. Leonard's,
    NSW: Center for Independent Studies.

Kelly, John D.
 1988a Fiji Indians and Political Discourse in Fiji: From the Pacific Romance
    to the Coups. *Journal of Historical Sociology* 1:399–422.

1988*b*   From Holi to Diwali: An Essay on Ritual and History. *Man* 36: 372–391.

1989   Fear of Culture: British Regulation of Indian Marriage in Post-Indenture Fiji. *Ethnohistory* 36:372–391.

Knapman, Bruce
1985   Capitalism's Economic Impact in Colonial Fiji, 1874–1939. *The Journal of Pacific History* 20:66–83.

1987   *Fiji's Economic History, 1874–1939: Studies of Capitalist Colonial Development.* Monograph no. 15. Canberra: Australian National University Centre for Development Studies.

1990   Economy and State in Fiji before and after the Coups. *The Contemporary Pacific* 2:59–86.

Knapman, Claudia
1986   *White Women in Fiji, 1835–1930: Ruin of Empire?* Sydney: Allen & Unwin.

1988   The White Child in Colonial Fiji. *The Journal of Pacific History* 23: 206–213.

Knox-Mawer, June
1965   *A Gift of Islands.* London: Allen Sutton.

Lal, Brij V.
1980   Approaches to the Study of Indian Indentured Emigration with Special Reference to Fiji. *The Journal of Pacific History* 15:52–70.

1982   An Uncertain Journey: The Voyage of the *Leonidas. Journal of Pacific Studies* 8:55–69.

1983*a*   The Fiji General Election of 1982: The Tidal Wave That Never Came. *The Journal of Pacific History* 18:134–157.

1983*b*   *Girmitiyas: The Origins of the Fiji Indians. The Journal of Pacific History.* Canberra.

1983*c*   Indian Indenture Historiography: A Note on Problems, Sources and Methods. *Pacific Studies* 6(2): 33–50.

1983*d*   The 1982 Fiji National Election and Its Aftermath. *USP Sociological Society Newsletter* 5:3–17.

1985*a*   Kunti's Cry: Indentured Women on Fiji Plantations. *Indian Economic and Social History Review* 22:55–71.

1985*b*   Veil of Dishonour: Sexual Jealousy and Suicide on Fiji Plantations. *The Journal of Pacific History* 20:135–155.

1986*a*   Murmurs of Dissent: Non-Resistance on Fiji Plantations. *Hawaiian Journal of History* 20:188–214.

1986*b*   Postscript: The Emergence of the Fiji Labour Party. In Lal, ed. 1986, 139–157.

1986*c*   Politics since Independence, 1970–1982. In Lal, ed. 1986, 74–106.

1988*a*   Before the Storm: An Analysis of the Fiji General Election of 1987. *Pacific Studies* 12(1): 71–96.

1988*b*   *Power and Prejudice: The Making of the Fiji Crisis.* Wellington: New Zealand Institute of International Affairs.

1989*a*   Fiji Indians and the Politics of Exclusion. *Foreign Affairs Reports* 38(7,8): 95–105.

1989*b*   Rabuka's Fiji: A Year On. *Current Affairs Bulletin* 65(8): 4–14.

Lal, Brij V., ed.

1986   *Politics in Fiji: Studies in Contemporary History.* Sydney: Allen & Unwin; Laie: Institute for Polynesian Studies.

1990   *As the Dust Settles: Impact and Implications of the Fiji Crisis.* Special issue of *The Contemporary Pacific: A Journal of Island Affairs* 2:1.

Lal, Brij V., and Karen Peacock

1990   Researching the Fiji Coups. *The Contemporary Pacific.* 2:183–195.

Lal, Victor

1990   *Fiji: Coups in Paradise: Race, Politics and Military Intervention.* London: Zed Books.

Lasaqa, Isireli

1984   *The Fijian People before and after Independence, 1959–1979.* Canberra: Australian National University Press.

Lateef, Shireen

1990   Current and Future Implications of the Coups for Women in Fiji. *The Contemporary Pacific* 2:113–130.

Leckie, Jackie

1987   White Women: Work, Ideology and Empire. *Journal of Pacific Studies* 13: 100–107.

1990   Workers in colonial Fiji. In *Labour in the South Pacific,* edited by Clive Moore, Jackie Leckie and Doug Munro, 47–66. (in press). Townsville, QLD: James Cook University.

Lee, A.

1974   Historical Notes on the City of Suva, with Particular Reference to the Central Business District. Typescript in National Archives of Fiji.

Legge, J. D.

1958   *Britain in Fiji, 1858–1880.* London: Macmillan.

Lewis Jones, W. W.

1957   A Historical Survey of the Development of Education in Fiji. *Transactions of the Fiji Society* 6:109–123.

Lloyd, D. T.

1982   *Land Policy in Fiji.* Department of Land Economy Occasional Paper no. 14. Cambridge: Cambridge University.

Lowndes, A. G., ed.

1956   *South Pacific Enterprise: The Colonial Sugar Refining Company Limited.* Sydney: Angus & Robertson.

MacArthur, Norma

1967   *Island Populations of the Pacific.* Canberra: Australian National University Press.

Macdonald, Barrie
  1982   Self-Determination and Self-government. *Journal of Pacific History*
         17(1&2): 51–61.
  1990   The Literature of the Fiji Coups. Review Article. *The Contemporary
         Pacific* 2:197–207.

MacDougal, R. S.
  1957   *Fijian Administration Finances.* Legislative Council Paper no. 35. Suva:
         Government of Fiji.

Macnaught, Timothy J.
  1977   We Seem No Longer to Be Fijians: Some Perceptions of Social Change
         in Fijian History. *Pacific Studies* 1(1): 15–24.
  1982   *The Fijian Colonial Experience: A Study of the Neotraditional Order under British
         Colonial Rule Prior to World War II.* Pacific Research Monograph Series
         no. 7. Canberra: Australian National University Press.

McNeill, James, and Chimman Lal
  1914   *Report of the Government of India on the Conditions of Indian Immigrants in Four
         British Colonies of Surinam.* Command Paper 7744-5. Simla: Government
         of India.

Mamak, Alexander
  1978   *Colour, Culture and Conflict: A Study of Pluralism in Fiji.* Sydney: Pergamon
         Press.

Maude, H. E.
  1968   *Of Islands and Men: Studies in Pacific History.* Melbourne: Oxford University Press.

Mayer, Adrian C.
  1963   *Indians in Fiji.* London: Oxford University Press.
  1973   *Peasants in the Pacific: A Study of Fiji Indian Rural Society.* 2nd ed. Berkeley:
         University of California Press.

Meller, Norman, and James Anthony
  1968   *Fiji Goes to the Polls: The Crucial Legislative Council Elections of 1963.* Honolulu: East-West Center.

Mishra, Vijay, ed.
  1979   *Rama's Banishment: A Centenary Tribute to the Fiji Indians.* Auckland:
         Heinemann Educational Books.

Morrell, W. P.
  1960   *Britain in the Pacific Islands.* Oxford: Clarendon Press.

Moynagh, Michael
  1978   Land Tenure in Fiji's Sugar Cane Districts. *The Journal of Pacific History*
         13:53–73.
  1981   *Brown or White? A History of the Fiji Sugar Industry, 1873–1973.* Pacific
         Research Monograph Series no. 5. Canberra: Australian National University Press.

Murray, David
  1978   The Governor General in Fiji's Constitutional Crisis. *Politics* 13:
         230–238.

Naidu, Vijay
  1977   The Conflict Model of Pluralism: Some Evidence from Somosomo,
          Taveuni. *Journal of Pacific Studies* 3:55–67.
  1980   *The Violence of Indenture in Fiji.* Suva: University of the South Pacific.
  1986   *The Fiji Labour Party and the By-Election of December 1985.* School of Social
          and Economic Development Working Paper no. 2. Suva: University of
          the South Pacific.
  1989   The Destruction of Multiracial Democracy in Fiji. In *Coup and Crisis:
          Fiji—a Year Later* (2d ed.), edited by Satendra Prasad, 4–12. Carlton,
          VIC: Arena Publications.

Naipaul, V. S.
  1982   *A Bend in the River.* Harmondsworth: Penguin.

Narayan, Jay
  1984   *The Political Economy of Fiji.* Suva: South Pacific Review Press.

Narsey, Wadan
  1979   Monopoly Capital, White Racism and Superprofits in Fiji: A Case
          Study of the CSR. *Journal of Pacific Studies* 5:66–146.
  1985   The Wage Freeze and Development Plan Objectives: Contradictions in
          Fiji Government Policy. *Journal of Pacific Studies* 11:11–44.

Nation, John
  1978   *Customs of Respect: The Traditional Basis of Fijian Communal Politics.* Devel-
          opment Studies Centre Monograph no. 14. Canberra: Australian
          National University Press.
  1982   Fiji: Post-Independence Politics. In *Melanesia: Beyond Diversity,* edited by
          R. J. May and Hank Nelson, 601–622. Canberra: Australian National
          University, Research School of Pacific Studies.

Nayacakalou, R.
  1971   Fiji. In *Land Tenure in the Pacific,* edited by R. G. Crocombe, 206–226.
          Melbourne: Oxford University Press.
  1975   *Leadership in Fiji.* Melbourne: Oxford University Press.
  1978   *Tradition and Change in the Fijian Village.* Suva: Institute of Pacific
          Studies.

Norton, Robert
  1977   *Race and Politics in Fiji.* St. Lucia: University of Queensland Press.
          Revised edition, 1990.
  1981   The Mediation of Ethnic Conflict: Comparative Implications of the Fiji
          Case. *Journal of Commonwealth and Comparative Politics* 19:309–328.
  1984   Ethnicity and Class: A Conceptual Note with Reference to the Politics
          of Post-Colonial Societies. *Ethnic and Racial Studies* 7:426–434.
  1986   Colonial Fiji: Ethnic Divisions and Elite Conciliation. In Lal, ed. 1986,
          52–73.

O'Laughlin, C.
  1956   *The Pattern of the Fiji Economy.* Legislative Council Paper no. 44. Suva:
          Government of Fiji.

Overton, John, ed.
 1988   *Rural Fiji.* Suva: Institute of Pacific Studies.

Overton, John, and R. Gerard Ward
 1989   The Coups in Retrospect: The New Political Geography of Fiji. *Pacific Viewpoint* 30:207–216.

Plange, Nii-K.
 1985   Colonial Capitalism and Class Formation in Fiji: A Retrospective Overview. *Journal of Pacific Studies* 11:91–116.

Prasad, Satendra, ed.
 1989   *Coup and Crisis—Fiji a Year Later.* rev. ed. North Carlton, VIC: Arena Publications.

Premdas, Ralph R.
 1979   Elections in Fiji: Restoration of the Balance in September 1977. *The Journal of Pacific History.* 14:194–207.
 1989   Fiji: The Anatomy of a Revolution. *Pacifica* 1:67–110.

Qalo, Ropate
 1984   *Divided We Stand: Local Government in Fiji.* Suva: Institute of Pacific Studies

Quain, B.
 1948   *Fijian Village.* Chicago: University of Chicago Press.

Rae, Pramod
 1979   Ethnic Factors in Trade Unionism in Fiji, 1942–1975. *Pacific Perspective* 8:32–37.

Rakoto, Aporosa
 1973   Can Custom be Custom Built? Cultural Obstacles to Fijian Commercial Enterprise. *Pacific Perspective* 2 (2): 32–35.

Ralston, Caroline
 1977   *Grass Huts and Warehouses: A Study of Five Pacific Beach Communities of the Nineteenth Century.* Canberra: Australian National University Press; Honolulu: University Press of Hawaii.

Ravuvu, Asesela
 1974   *Fijians at War.* Suva: Institute of Pacific Studies.
 1983   *Vaka Itaukei: The Fijian Way of Life.* Suva: Institute of Pacific Studies.
 1987   *The Fijian Ethos.* Suva: Institute of Pacific Studies.
 1991   *The Façade of Democracy: Fijian Struggles for Political Control, 1830–1987.* Suva: Reader Publishing House.

Ray, Ellen, and William Schaap
 1986   The Modern Mithridates in Vernon Walters: Crypto Diplomat and Terrorist. *Covert Action,* no. 26.

Robertson, Robert T.
 1985   The Formation of the Fiji Labour Party. *New Zealand Monthly Review* (October): 3–7.

Robertson, Robert T., and Akosita Tamanisau
  1988   *Fiji—Shattered Coups.* Sydney: Pluto Press.

Roth, G. K.
  1953   *Fijian Way of Life.* 2d ed. Melbourne: Oxford University Press.

Routledge, David
  1985a   *Matanitu: Struggle for Power in Early Fiji.* Suva: Institute of Pacific
          Studies.
  1985b   Pacific History as Seen from the Pacific Islands. *Pacific Studies* 8(2):
          81–99.

Roy, Theo
  1987   The Fijian Coup: Causes and Consequences. *Pacific Defence Reporter* 14
          (1): 7–9.

Rutherford, Noel
  1984   The 1959 Strike. In *Protest and Dissent in the Colonial Pacific,* edited by
          Peter Hempenstall and Noel Rutherford, 73–86. Suva: Institute of
          Pacific Studies.

Sahlins, Marshall D.
  1962   *Moala: Culture and Nature on a Fijian Island.* Ann Arbor: University of
          Michigan Press.
  1981   The Stranger-King or Dumezil among the Fijians. *The Journal of Pacific
          History* 16:107–132.
  1985   *Islands of History.* Chicago: University of Chicago Press.

Sanday, Jim
  1989   *The Military in Fiji: Historical Development and Future Role.* Strategic and
          Defence Studies Centre Working Paper no. 21. Canberra: Australian
          National University.

Scarr, Deryck
  1973   *The Majesty of Colour. Vol. 1: I, the Very Bayonet.* Canberra: Australian
          National University Press.
  1980a   *The Majesty of Colour. Vol. 2: Viceroy of the Pacific.* Pacific Research Mono-
          graph no. 4. Canberra: Australian National University.
  1980b   *Ratu Sukuna: Soldier, Statesman, Man of Two Worlds.* London: Macmillan
          Education.
  1984   *Fiji: A Short History.* Laie: Institute of Polynesian Studies.
  1988   *Fiji, the Politics of Illusion: The Military Coups in Fiji.* Kensington: Univer-
          sity of New South Wales Press.

Shameem, Shaista
  1987   Gender, Class and Race Dynamics: Indian Women in Sugar Produc-
          tion in Fiji. *Journal of Pacific Studies* 13:10–35.

Shephard, Cecil Y.
  1945   *The Sugar Industry in Fiji.* London: His Majesty's Stationery Office.

Shineberg, Dorothy
  1967   *They Came for Sandalwood: A Study of the Sandalwood Trade in the South-West
          Pacific, 1830–1865.* Melbourne: Melbourne University Press.

Spate, O. H. K.
  1959   *The Fijian People: Economic Problems and Prospects.* Legislative Council Paper no. 13. Suva: Government of Fiji.
  1960   Under Two Laws: The Fijian Dilemma. *Meanjin* 19:166–181. Reprinted in *Let Me Enjoy: Essays Partly Geographical* by O. H. K. Spate, 46–65. London: Methuen.
  1990   Thirty Years Ago: A View of the Fijian Political Scene. Confidential Report to the British Colonial Office. *The Journal of Pacific History* 25: 103–124.
  1991   *On the Margins of History.* Canberra: National Centre for Development Studies, Australian National University.

Subramani, ed.
  1979   *The Indo-Fijian Experience.* St. Lucia: University of Queensland Press.

Sukuna, J. L. V.
  1983   *Fiji: The Three-Legged Stool: Selected Writings of Ratu Sir Lala Sukuna.* Edited by Deryck Scarr. London: Macmillan Education.

Sutherland, William
  1989   The New Political Economy of Fiji. *Pacific Viewpoint* 30(2): 132–141.

Tagupa, William E. H.
  1988   The 1987 Westminster Crisis in Fiji. *Pacific Studies* 12(1): 165–177.

Taylor, Michael, ed.
  1987   *Fiji: Future Imperfect?* Sydney: Allen & Unwin.

Thakur, Ramesh
  1990   Non-Intervention in International Relations: A Case Study. *Political Science* 42:28–61.

Thakur, Ramesh, and Anthony Wood
  1989   Paradise Regained or Paradise Defiled? Fiji under Military Rule. *International Studies* 26:15–44.

Thomas, Nicholas
  1989   Material Culture and Colonial Power: Ethnological Collecting and the Establishment of Colonial Rule in Fiji. *Man* 24:41–56.
  1990*a* Regional Politics, Ethnicity, and Custom in Fiji. *The Contemporary Pacific* 2:131–146.
  1990*b* Sanitation and Seeing: The Creation of State Power in Early Colonial Fiji. *Comparative Studies in Society and History* 32:149–170.

Thomson, Basil
  1908   *The Fijians: A Study of the Decay of Custom.* London: Heinemann.

Thornley, Andrew
  1974   The Methodist Mission and Fiji's Indians, 1879–1920. *New Zealand Journal of History* 8(2): 137–153.
  1977   The Vakamisoneri in Lau, Fiji: Some Comments. *The Journal of Pacific History* 12:107–112.

Tinker, Hugh
  1974a   *A New System of Slavery: The Export of Indian Labour Abroad, 1830–1920.*
           London: Oxford University Press.
  1974b   Odd Man Out: The Loneliness of the Colonial Indian Politician—The
           Career of Manilal Doctor. *The Journal of Imperial and Commonwealth His-
           tory* 2:226–243.

Usher, Sir Leonard
  1987   *Mainly about Fiji: A Collection of Writings, Broadcasts, and Speeches.* Suva:
          Fiji Times.

Van Fossen, Anthony B.
  1987   Two Military Coups in Fiji. *Bulletin of Concerned Asian Scholars* 19(4):
          19–31.

Vasil, Raj
  1972   Communalism and Constitution Making in Fiji. *Pacific Affairs* 45(1).

Von Strokirch, Karin
  1987   Coup d'Etat: The Fijian Response. *Arena* 80:35–41.

Vusoniwailala, Lasirusa
  1985   Communication, Social Identity, and the Rising Cost of Fijian Com-
          munalism. *Pacific Perspective* 12(2): 1–7.

Ward, R. Gerard
  1965   *Land Use and Population in Fiji: A Geographical Study.* London: Her Majes-
          ty's Stationery Office.
  1972   The Pacific Bêche-de-Mer Trade with Special Reference to Fiji. *Man in
          the Pacific Islands: Essays on Geographical Change in the Pacific Islands,* edited
          by R. G. Ward, 91–123. London: Oxford University Press.
  1985   Land, Land Use and Land Availability. In *Land, Cane and Coconuts:
          Papers on the Rural Economy of Fiji,* edited by H. C. Brookfield, F. Ellis,
          and R. G. Ward, 15–64. Department of Human Geography Publica-
          tion no. 17. Canberra: Australian National University.
  1987   Native Fijian Villages: A Questionable Future? In *Fiji: Future Imperfect?*
          edited by Michael Taylor, 33–45. Sydney: Allen & Unwin.

Watters, Ray F.
  1961   Problems of Development in Fiji. *Pacific Viewpoint* 2(2): 155–176.
  1969   *Koro: Economic Development and Social Change in Fiji.* London: Oxford Uni-
          versity Press.

West, Francis
  1960   Problems of Political Advancement in Fiji. *Pacific Affairs* 33(1): 23–37.

Whitehead, Clive
  1975   Education in Fiji, 1939–1973. PhD dissertation, University of Otago,
          Dunedin, New Zealand.
  1986   *Education in Fiji since Independence: a Study of Government Policy.* Wellington:
          New Zealand Council for Educational Research.

Whitelaw, James S.
  1966   People, Land and Government in Suva, Fiji. PhD dissertation, Austra-
          lian National University, Canberra.

Wyatt-Brown, Bertram
  1982   *Southern Honor: Ethics and Behavior in the Old South.* New York: Oxford University Press.

Wypijewski, JoAnn
  1987   The Fiji Coup: Was the US behind It? *Nation,* 15 August.

Young, John
  1984   *Adventurous Young Spirits: Australian Migrant Society in Pre-Cession Fiji.* St. Lucia: University of Queensland Press.
  1988   Race and Sex in Fiji Re-visited. *The Journal of Pacific History* 23: 214–222.

Index

London Missionary Society, 8
Lord Stanmore. *See* Gordon, Sir Arthur
  Hamilton
Lowe, Chief Justice A. G., 167–168
Lucas, Sir Charles, 35
Lucas, Sir Keith, 222
Luckner, Count Felix von, 56
Luve ni Wai, 15

M. K. Hunt Foundation, 246
Ma'afu, 9–10
MacDougal, R. S., 139
MacMillan, A. W., 80, 124, 144–145
McNeill, J. S., 44
McOwan, Islay, 69, 74
Maddocks, Sir Kenneth, 182, 186–187
Madhavan, James, 178
Maharaj, Badri, 38
Maharaj, Navin, 219
Maha Sangh, 128–129, 174
Major, R. M., 188
Malayan War, 149–151
Malviya, Pandit Madan Mohan, 45
Manilal Maganlal Doctor, 41, 46–48, 54
Manueli, Colonel Paul, 321
Mara, L. K., 211
Mara, Ratu Finau, 271
Mara, Ratu Sir Kamisese, 185–186, 190,
  192, 202, 204, 206, 219–221, 273;
  addresses by, 168, 198–199, 215; appoint-
  ments of, 191, 201, 239–240, 296; and
  common roll, 211, 223; and constitution,
  187, 188–189, 198–199, 222–224, 298;
  corruption of, alleged, 247, 256, 264,
  269; and coup, 275, 309–313; and "Four
  Corners" program, 247–248; and Government of National Unity, 243–245; and
  independence, 164, 211, 215; and Indo-
  Fijians, 237, 310; and Jai Ram Reddy,
  243; land policy of, 226–227; and 1959
  strike, 166, 168; as prime minister, 239–
  240, 296; and race relations, 250; relations with S. M. Koya of, 218, 224, 237;
  Russian allegations of, 248–249; and
  western Fijians, 246–247
Marella House, 256, 269
Marks, Sir Henry, 87
Marlborough House, 212–213
Masters and Servants Ordinance, 27, 28,
  67, 82
Mataitini, Ratu Etuate, 119, 141
Mataitini, Ratu Jone, 197
Mataka, Apimeleki Ramatau, 188

Maxwell, G. V., 28, 58
May, Sir Henry, 32–35
Melanesian Spearhead, 283
Mersh, Superintendent, 166
Methodist Church, 286
Mitchell, Sir Philip, 71, 133
Momis, Father John, 294
Morris Hedstrom, 34
Mount Kasi Mines, 62
Mukherji, Dr. Girin, 120
Municipal franchise, 34, 37, 95–97
Municipal Native Workers' Union, 169
Muslims, 78–79, 197, 286
Mustapha, Daniel, 286

Nadalo, Isikeli, 188, 247, 263
Nadi during World War II, 113–117
Nai Lalakai, 194, 196
Nailatikau, Epeli, 284
Na Mata, 21
Nand, Shardha, 260
Nandan, Satendra, 252
Nanovo, Ratu Kiniavuai, 54
Naqasima, Peniasi, 191
Narayan, Irene Jai, 232, 240, 251, 252,
  261, 293
Narokobi, Bernard, 294
Narsey, Wadan, 255–256
Nasinu Teachers' Training College, 159
Natabua Indian School, 86
Nath, Shiu, 176
National Congress of Fiji, 192
National Democratic Party, 203
National Federation Party, 204–205,
  218–219, 229, 238–239, 248–249;
  coalition with Fiji Labour Party, 258–
  260; and common roll, 223–224; factions
  within, 223, 225–227, 241–242, 251–
  252; and independence, 203–204,
  211–212
National Federation Party–Fiji Labour
  Party Coalition, 258–260; 1987 cam-
  paign, 261–266, 269–271, 279–284, 285–
  289, 328–329
National Federation Party–Western United
  Front coalition, 247–248, 260
National Lands Commission, 300
Native Department, 21–22
Native lands: leasing and sale of, 30, 31, 35,
  98–99; ordinances, 30, 70, 102
Native Lands and Fisheries Commission,
  134
Native Lands Commission, 300, 326

About the Author

After teaching Pacific and world history at the University of Hawaii at Manoa for nearly a decade, **Brij V. Lal** now lives in Canberra with his wife, two children, and Rani (the cat), and teaches and researches Pacific Islands history at the Australian National University. He spends his precious leisure hours camping and exploring the Australian bush with family and friends.

Production Notes

Composition and paging were done on the
Quadex Composing System and typesetting
on the Compugraphic 8400 by the design
and production staff of University of
Hawaii Press.

The text typeface is Baskerville and the
display typeface is Compugraphic Palatino.

Offset presswork and binding were done by
The Maple-Vail Book Manufacturing Group.
Text paper is Glatfelter Offset Vellum,
basis 50.